The Eugene B. Adkins Collection

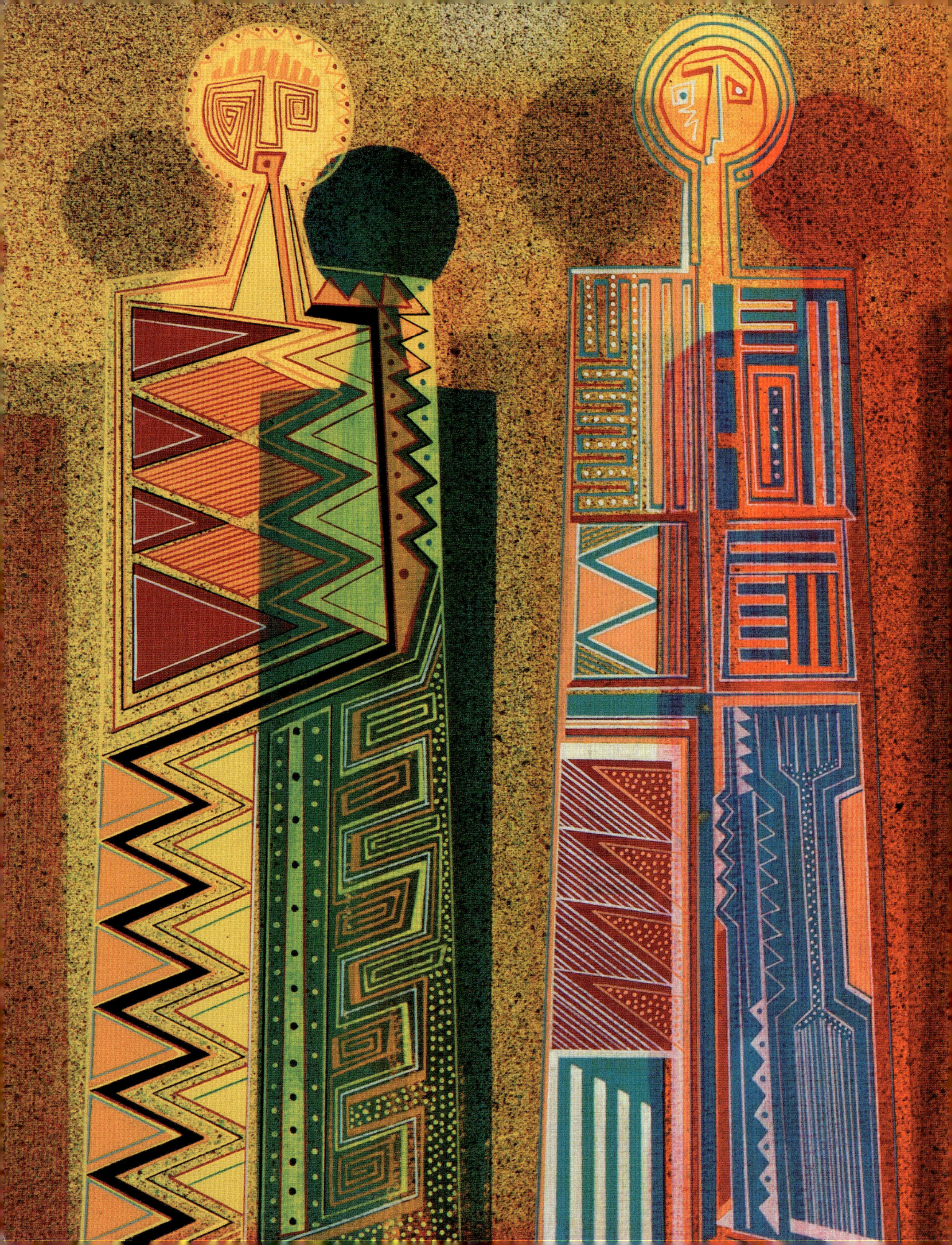

SELECTED WORKS

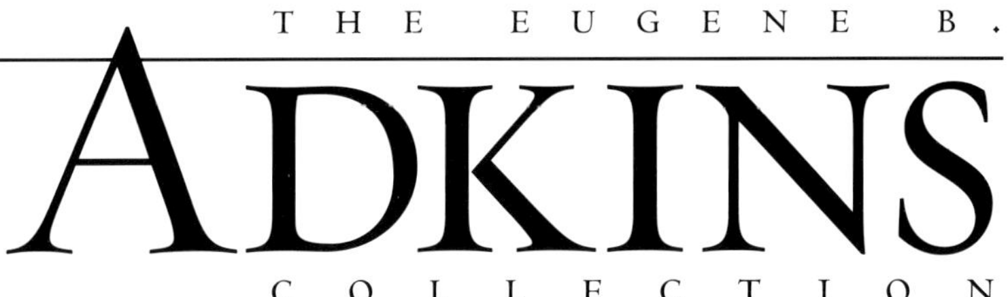

University of Oklahoma Press : Norman

In cooperation with the
Fred Jones Jr. Museum of Art and the
Philbrook Museum of Art

LIBRARY OF CONGRESS CATALOGING-IN-PUBLICATION DATA

The Eugene B. Adkins collection : selected works. — 1st ed.

p. cm.

Catalogue to accompany the opening of an expansion of the Fred Jones Jr. Museum of Art and new facilities to display Adkins works for the Philbrook Museum of Art.

Includes bibliographical references and index.

ISBN 978-0-8061-4100-8 (hardcover : alk. paper) —
ISBN 978-0-8061-4101-5 (pbk. : alk. paper)

1. West (U.S.)—In art—Exhibitions. 2. Art, American—West (U.S.)—Exhibitions. 3. Indian art—West (U.S.)—Exhibitions. 4. Adkins, Eugene B. (Eugene Brady), 1920–2006—Art collections—Exhibitions. I. Fred Jones Jr. Museum of Art. II. Philbrook Museum of Art.

N8214.5.U6E94 2011

709.78'074—dc22

2011001187

P. II: DETAIL OF PLATE 71 (p. 119)
PP. XII–1: DETAIL OF PLATE 44 (p. 79)
PP. 16–17: DETAIL OF PLATE 48 (p. 83)
PP. 96–97: DETAIL OF PLATE 147 (p. 214)

The paper in this book meets the guidelines for permanence and durability of the Committee on Production Guidelines for Book Longevity of the Council on Library Resources, Inc. ∞

1 2 3 4 5 6 7 8 9 10

Contents

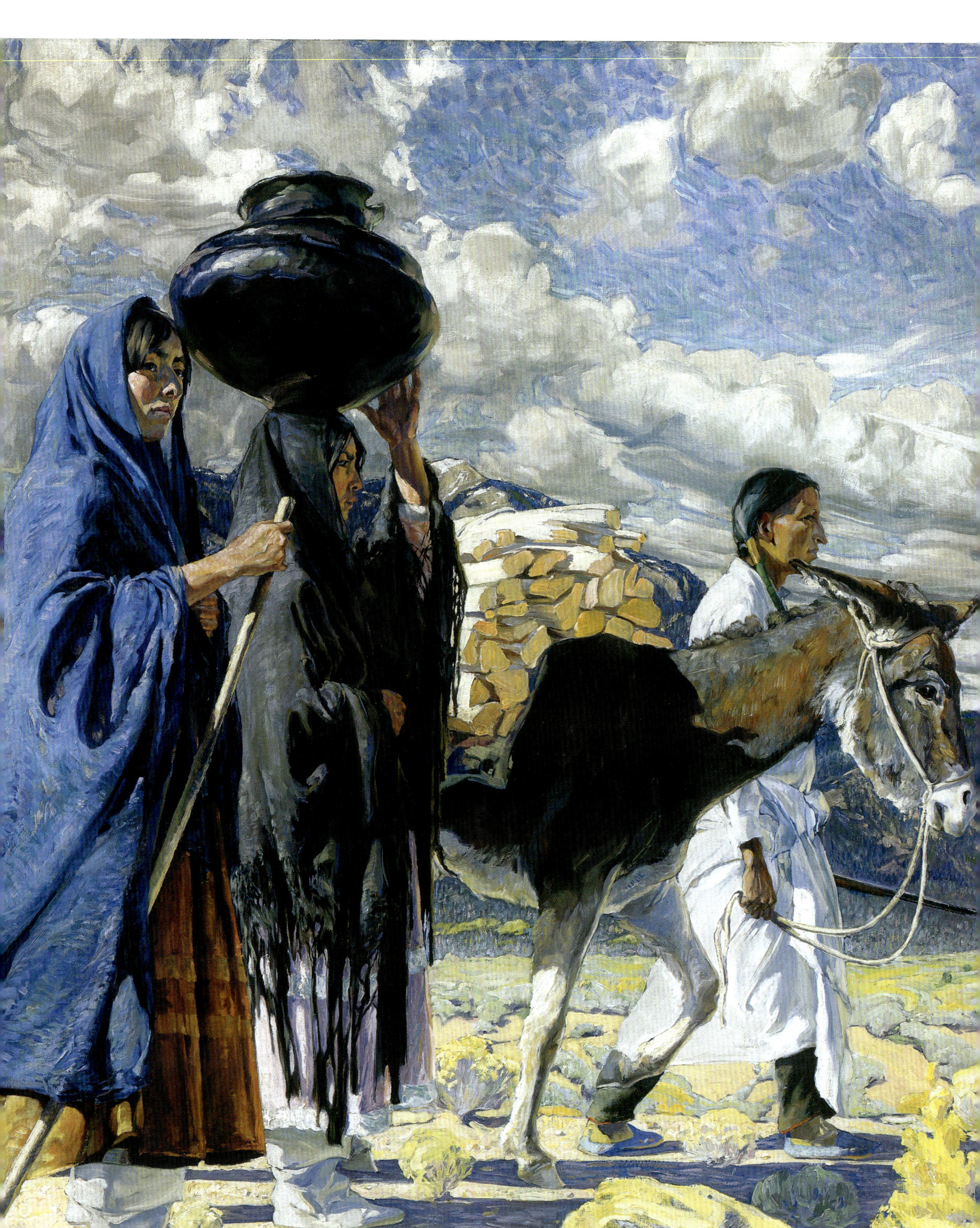

Foreword

David L. Boren

Eugene B. Adkins created one of the premier collections of art of the American Southwest. The University of Oklahoma is pleased to be working with the Eugene B. Adkins Foundation and the Philbrook Museum of Art to encourage research and preservation of this important part of our nation's cultural history. A native Oklahoman, Eugene Brady Adkins had deep roots in Tulsa, where his grandfather, W. Tate Brady, operated the Brady Hotel, one of the city's first. He was a civic leader and an early advocate for the Tulsa Public Schools. Eugene Adkins earned a degree in art history at Dartmouth College and graduate degrees in business at Stanford University. He frequently spent summers in Santa Fe, which kindled the lifelong interest in the American Southwest that fostered his important collection of Native American art and that of the Santa Fe and Taos art colonies. He was a keen judge of artistic merit and had an encyclopedic knowledge of his collection's artists and their cultural roots.

The University of Oklahoma has a rich heritage in studying and supporting the art of the American Southwest, beginning with the arrival of art professor Oscar Jacobson in 1915. Jacobson developed numerous relationships with the art colonies in Santa Fe and Taos and with the Native American artists of the region. This catalogue and the accompanying exhibition of the Eugene B. Adkins Collection continue the university's commitment to this artistic heritage.

As a leader in the academic study of the history and art of Native American cultures and the American West, the University of Oklahoma School of Art and Art History announced in fall 2008 a new Ph.D. program in art history. This unique program, the first of its kind, has two distinct emphases: Native American art history and art of the American West. OU's combined university collections provide rich resources for research as well as publication opportunities for faculty, students, and scholars in this program. The Eugene B. Adkins Collection will allow the university to expand this mission through the creation of traveling exhibitions, sharing this extraordinary art throughout the state as well as nationally and internationally.

DETAIL OF PLATE 46 (p. 81)
Walter Ufer (U.S., 1876–1936)
Going East, 1917

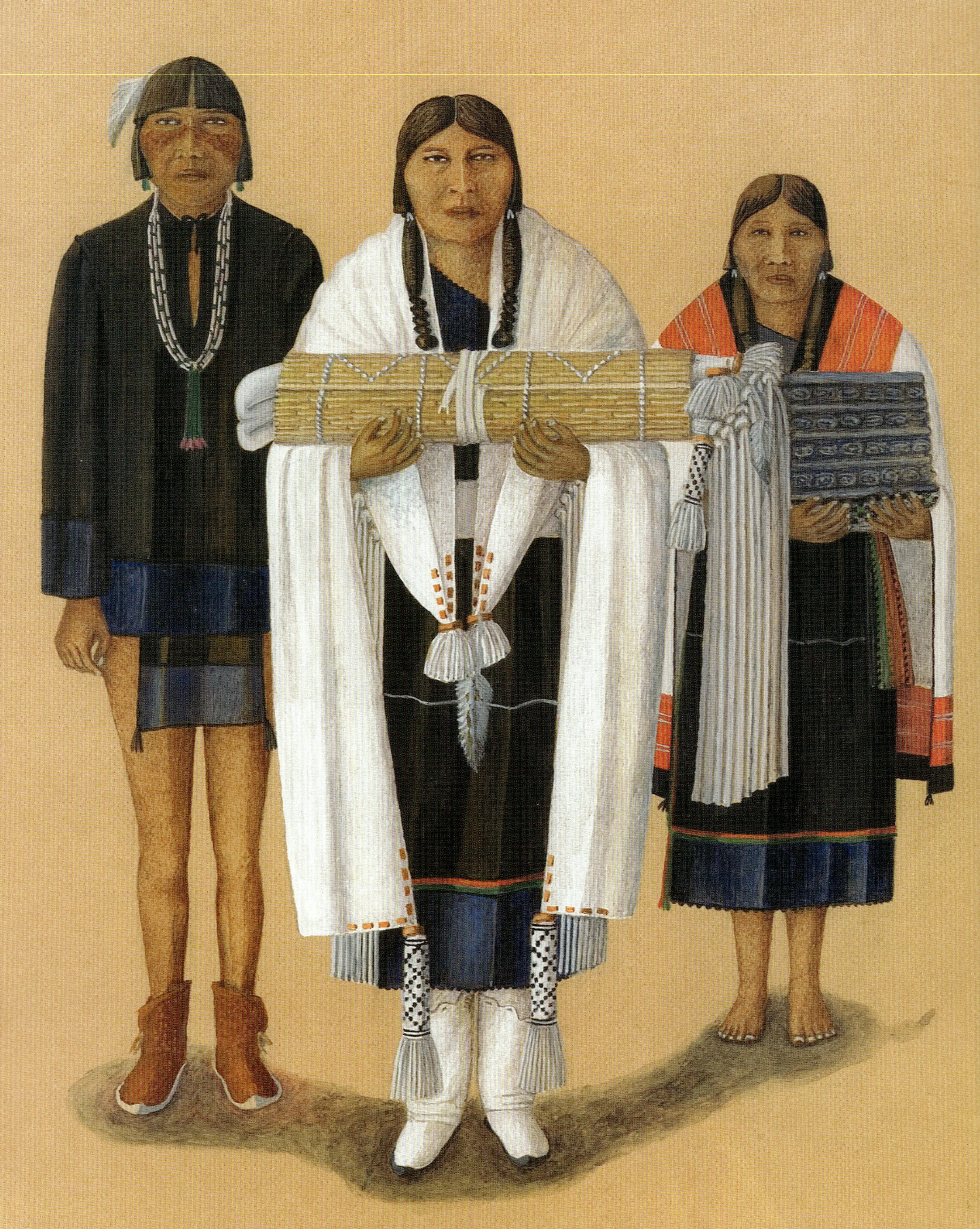

Preface and Acknowledgments

The trustees and professional staff of the Philbrook Museum of Art are extremely grateful to the Eugene B. Adkins Foundation for its willingness to grant stewardship of this remarkable collection to the museum and the University of Oklahoma. The foundation's confidence in this mutual endeavor has provided an extraordinary gift to the people of Oklahoma. It has also inaugurated an exemplary partnership. The museum and the university have embraced collection sharing, discussed collaborative programs, and strategized the development of shared publications and research. This partnership has reached across our state and pulled our institutions closer together.

The Adkins Collection is extensive, of the highest quality, and exceptionally well documented. Philbrook's collection of Native American art is among the museum's strongest suits and one of the best in the nation. Combined, they represent one of the finest surveys of twentieth-century Native American art anywhere. In fact, the singular quality, scope, and stature of these works underscore the potential and purpose of the Eugene B. Adkins Collection and Study Center.

Indeed, the center is dedicated to providing a unique platform of engagement—one that facilitates the intimacy of aesthetic experience while nonetheless supporting the highest level of scholarly research. It will lend momentum to the emerging critical dialogue regarding Native American art and culture while highlighting this vital component of our nation's cultural heritage. This is important work, and Philbrook is proud to place itself at the forefront of these endeavors.

DETAIL OF PLATE 63 (p. 111)
Otis Polelonema (U.S., Hopi, 1902–1981)
The New Bride Woman, n.d.

I must recognize several key Philbrook trustees whose participation was instrumental in supporting our efforts to secure this important collection. Nancy E. Meinig, Board of Trustees chair; Holbrook Lawson; Roxana Lorton; Larry Lee; and Jack Neely each generously gave their time, insight, and direct support to solidify our focus and articulate a direction. In addition, the catalyzing efforts of Jon Stuart, Philbrook trustee and OU regent, warrant special gratitude for providing the invaluable bridge between the museum and the university that ultimately spurred the development of our combined proposal.

Finally, I congratulate the staff of the Fred Jones Jr. Museum of Art and Philbrook for creating this beautiful publication and for establishing a tone of professionalism and respect that will guide this partnership for decades to come.

Randall Suffolk
Director and President
Philbrook Museum of Art

A native of Tulsa, Oklahoma, Eugene B. Adkins spent nearly four decades assembling his extraordinary collection of southwestern art. Although I did not have the honor of knowing Mr. Adkins, through contact with his friends and trustees—especially Ted Riseling—and through familiarity with his magnificent collection and archives, I have come to understand and admire his passion as a collector and his infallible eye for recognizing great works of art.

With the support of President David L. Boren and First Lady Molly Shi Boren, the Board of Visitors of the Fred Jones Jr. Museum of Art at the University of Oklahoma, in particular Regent Jon R. Stuart and his wife, Dee Dee Stuart, have sponsored the construction of a new gallery level to showcase selected works from the Adkins Collection. The Fred Jones Jr. Museum of Art will work in collaboration with the Philbrook Museum of Art in Tulsa to rotate displays and organize traveling exhibitions of the Adkins Collection.

With the support of the Adkins Foundation, the stewardship collaboration between these two Oklahoma institutions will offer Oklahomans the opportunity to understand the genius of Eugene Adkins as a collector and will lead to the promotion—both nationally and internationally—of the state of Oklahoma and its cultural institutions. Visitors to the museums, including students at the University of Oklahoma and all residents of Oklahoma, will now have a unique opportunity to expand their understanding of Western and Native American art.

As director of the Fred Jones Jr. Museum of Art, I have had the pleasure to work with Randall Suffolk, director of the Philbrook Museum of Art in Tulsa, Oklahoma, and Christina E. Burke, curator of Native American Art at the Philbrook. I would like to commend the staffs at both institutions for their great collaborative work and collegiality.

Ghislain d'Humières

Director

Fred Jones Jr. Museum of Art

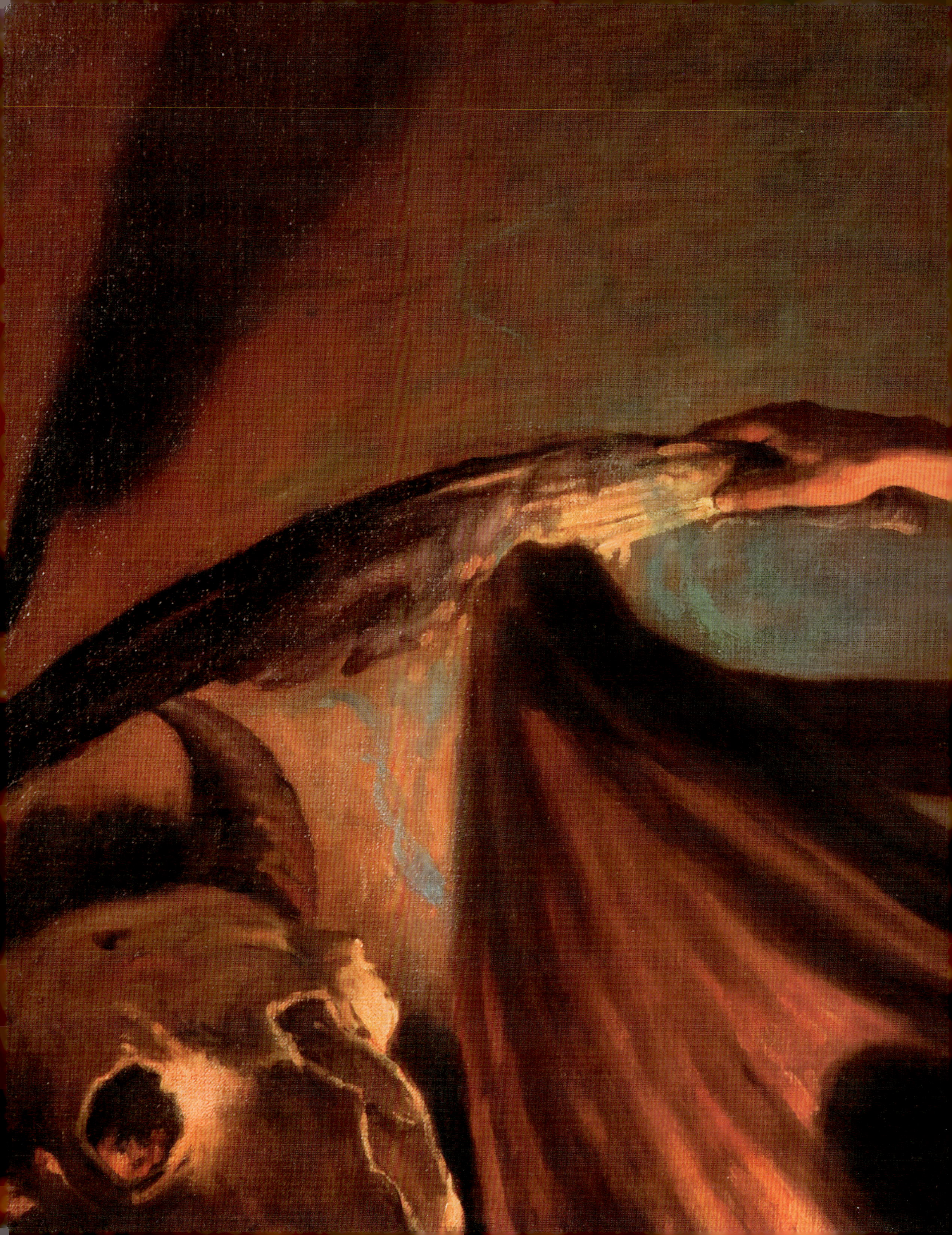

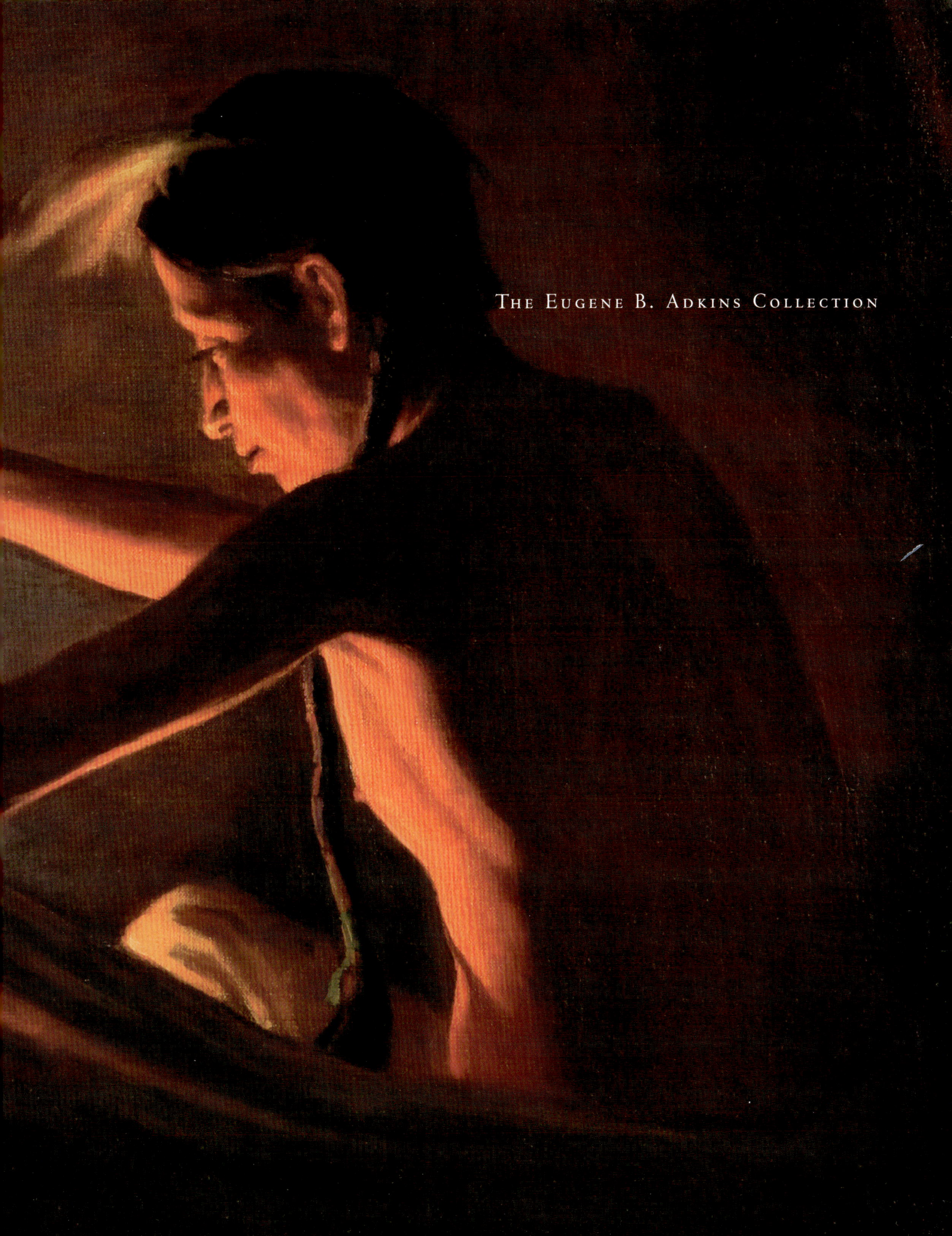
The Eugene B. Adkins Collection

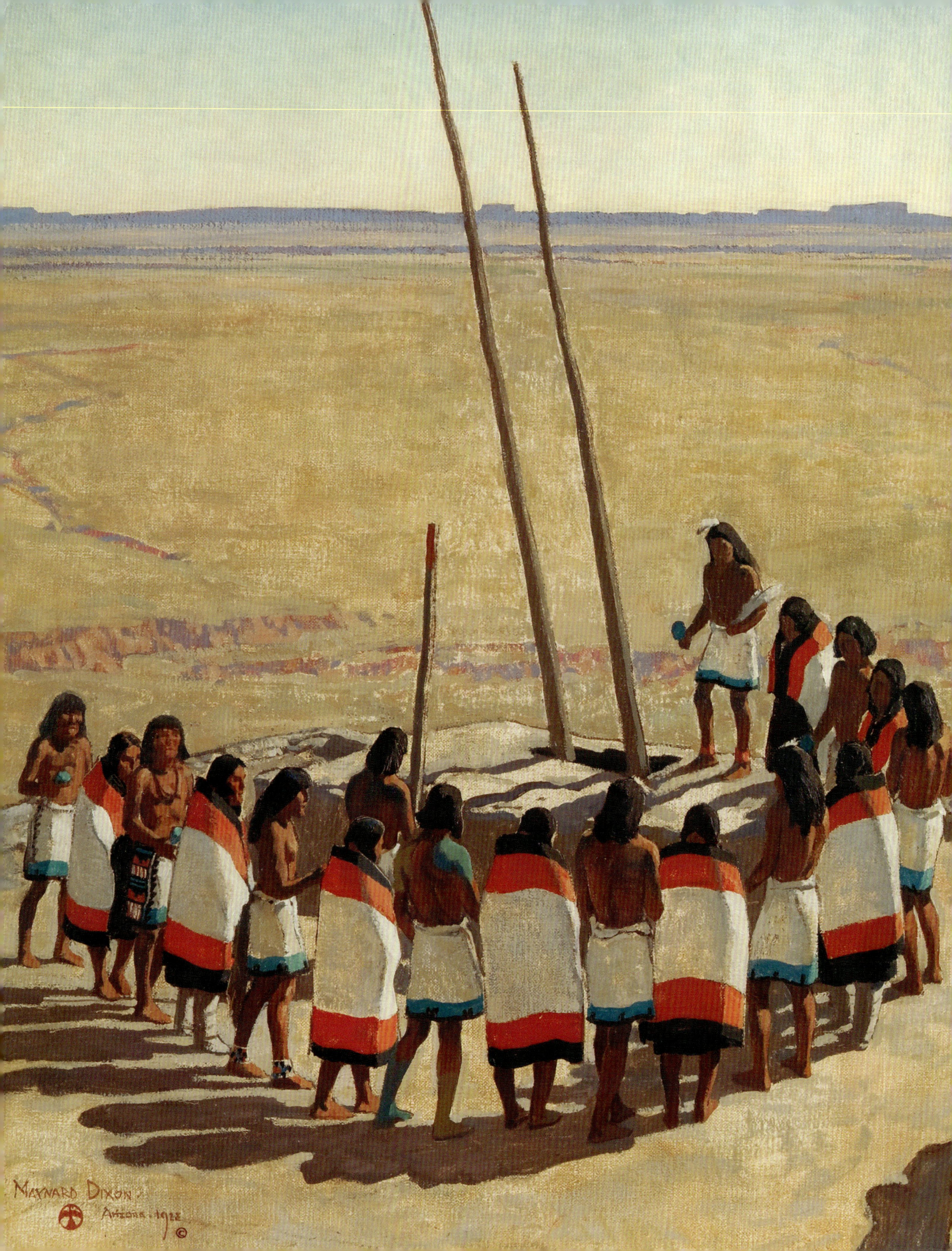
MAYNARD DIXON
Arizona . 1922
©

The Collecting Odyssey of Eugene B. Adkins

B. Byron Price

INTRODUCTION

In 2008, the Fred Jones Jr. Museum of Art at the University of Oklahoma and the Philbrook Museum of Tulsa announced the joint acquisition of one of the largest and most important collections of Native and western American art then in private hands. Gathered by Tulsa native Eugene B. Adkins, with passion and devotion over more than four decades, the wide-ranging assemblage numbers more than 3,300 items and includes jewelry, ceramics, baskets, weavings, photography, and rare books as well as paintings and sculpture. Adkins's holding is remarkable for not only its size and scope but also its quality and depth, containing works by many of the region's most renowned artists and craftsmen.[1]

Eugene Brady Adkins was born in Tulsa on January 5, 1920, the son of Eugene Sloan Adkins, a feed merchant, and Bess Brady Adkins, whose father, W. Tate Brady, was a prominent Tulsa merchant, hotelier, and civic leader. Eugene B. Adkins's paternal grandparents were enrolled members of the Cherokee Nation, and his ancestors included at least one Civil War veteran.[2]

After graduating from Tulsa's Central High School in 1937, Adkins entered Dartmouth College in Hanover, New Hampshire, where he earned a bachelor of arts degree in 1941, majoring in economics and English. He began graduate work in business at Stanford soon thereafter but cut short his academic career in July 1942 to enter the U.S. Naval Reserve training program. Commissioned an ensign two months later, Adkins was assigned to the Atlantic Fleet, where he served on a replenishment oiler and later, on a minesweeper for the duration of the war.[3]

Plate 1
Maynard Dixon (U.S., 1875–1946)
The Circle of Shimaikuli, 1923. Oil on canvas, 39½ × 35½ in.
Philbrook Museum of Art
A2007.0002

He returned to Stanford after the close of hostilities, completed a degree in business, traveled extensively in the United States and Europe, then resumed his education at St. John's College in Annapolis, Maryland, receiving a second BA degree in 1953. After spending several years working in the East, he returned to Tulsa in the 1960s to tend to his family's substantial investments and real estate holdings.[4]

Exactly what triggered Adkins's desire to begin collecting the art and artifacts of the American Southwest shortly thereafter is unclear. He said little about his motivation over the years, though from time to time, he acknowledged that childhood summers spent in New Mexico helped stimulate such interest. In 1971, for example, he told an Arizona newspaper reporter that, as a child, he had always liked the West, especially New Mexico, and after spending time studying and working in the East, he had returned to Oklahoma with a greater appreciation of what his home region had to offer.[5]

Adkins's mother, Bess, who collected antique furniture, porcelain, paintings, and other art objects from European and American dealers, provided an apt model as well. In 1950, mother and son together donated *Chief Yellow Bird*, an oil portrait by New Mexico artist Henry Balink, to the Philbrook Art Center in Tulsa (now known as the Philbrook Museum of Art).[6]

By deciding to collect the art of the American Southwest, Adkins followed in the footsteps of two prominent Oklahomans of the previous generation: Frank Phillips and Thomas Gilcrease. Although oil tycoons, they pursued art with a regional flavor and a connection to Native America. Both men established notable Oklahoma museums to house their collections, but Gilcrease probably had the greater influence on Adkins.[7] "Mr. Gilcrease's taste in collecting was superb," Adkins wrote artist Dorothy Brett in 1964, "as was his sense of history, and his true purpose in creating his collection was to present *aesthetically* a history of the American Indian."[8] As a friend of several board members of the Thomas

Plate 2
Paul Dyck (U.S., 1917–2006)
Carry This Shield of Honor, n.d. Oil on canvas, $47\frac{1}{2} \times 35\frac{5}{8}$ in.
Fred Jones Jr. Museum of Art
A2007.0114

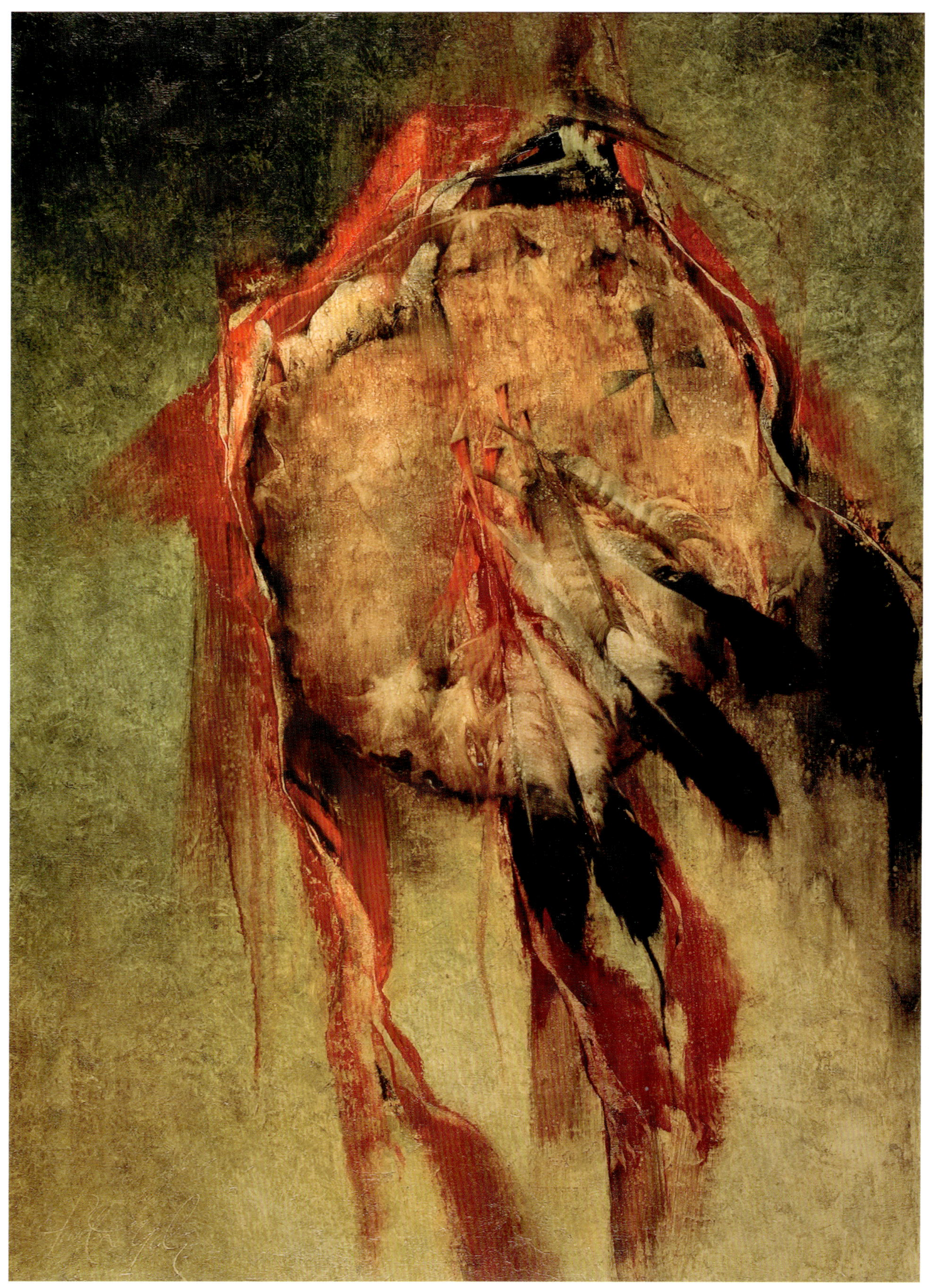

Gilcrease Institute of American History and Art, Adkins was afforded the opportunity to peruse the museum's impressive storage vaults as well as its exhibition galleries. In time, the young connoisseur's collecting impulse and holdings would reflect Gilcrease's overarching interest in Native American culture.[9]

Adkins's developing interest in the art of the American West coincided with a resurgence in the popularity of the genre among the public after World War II. The renaissance was especially strong in the Southwest, which lured a new generation of artists to its mountains and deserts. A host of galleries old and new tapped the enthusiasm and pocketbooks of tourists, who flocked to the burgeoning art scene in such locales as Santa Fe, Taos, and Phoenix. Several new museums with a regional focus opened in the Southwest in the 1950s and 1960s as well, increasing the visibility and credibility of western American and Native American art among collectors.[10]

Gene Adkins made his first large-scale western American art acquisition in 1963 from O'Brien's Art Emporium in Scottsdale, Arizona, buying eight paintings by living artists. His purchases included an Indian portrait by Brownell McGrew (1916–1994); two works by James Reynolds (1926–2010), a future member of the famed Cowboy Artists of America; and five paintings by Mark A. Coomer (1914–2004), an Arizona painter best known for his southwestern streetscapes and genre scenes. Despite Adkins's early attraction to contemporary, non-Native art of the American West, he would collect the genre only sparingly, preferring instead works by contemporary Native American artists and regional masters of the nineteenth and early twentieth centuries, especially members of the well-known Taos Society of Artists.[11]

In Albuquerque, New Mexico, in spring 1964, Adkins met the last remaining member of the Taos Society, Kenneth M. Adams (1897–1966), who had recently retired from the University of New Mexico faculty. A few days later, the Oklahoman purchased a landscape and floral painting by Adams through the Schuyler Art Gallery in Duke City.[12]

Later that summer, Adams joined his fellow New Mexico national academicians at the opening of an exhibition in their honor at the Museum of New Mexico in Santa Fe. Adkins attended the show as well, and in the coming months and years, he added to his fledgling collection works by most of the academy's remaining New Mexico members, Peter Hurd (1904–1984), Randall Davey (1887–1964), Gene Kloss (1903–1996), Doel Reed (1895–1985), Howard Cook (1901–1980), and Theodore Van Soelen (1890–1964).[13]

Adkins began to correspond with some of the group and developed a warm friendship with Virginia Van Soelen, whose husband had died only a month before the Santa Fe show. Not all his dealings with the spouses of deceased artists were as pleasant, however. In October 1963, for example, he had purchased two paintings, *Corn Dance at Santa Domingo* and *Buffalo Dance at Zuni*, by Russian-born artist Leon Gaspard (1882–1964), and on consignment to Jane Hiatt, owner of The Village Gallery in Taos.[14]

Adkins typically bought art on terms, paying for his purchases over months and sometimes years. As was his custom, he had placed a down payment on the Gaspards, with the final amount due the following June. After the artist, who had signed the sale contract, died suddenly on February 21, 1964, his widow, Dora, the executor of his estate, abruptly raised the prices on her late husband's works, including the two paintings Adkins had already bought. The Oklahoma collector promptly sued to acquire the works at the original price, and amid the legal wrangling that followed, the Taos county sheriff took custody of the disputed paintings. Adkins eventually prevailed in his suit and the following year loaned the now notorious works to the Museum of New Mexico for a Gaspard retrospective.[15]

By this time, the neophyte collector had added notable paintings by artists W. R. Leigh (1866–1955) and Thomas Moran (1837–1926) to his collection and had became enamored with the oil *Her Country*, by Santa Fe artist Gerald Cassidy (1879–1934). William M. Balfour, vice chancellor of Student Affairs at the University of Kansas, who owned the canvas, accepted Adkins's financial offer for the work, although not without reservations. He had loaned the painting to the Museum of New Mexico, which was endeavoring to raise the money to purchase it, and which, in the interim, had lent it to the state's chief executive, who had hung it in the living room of the governor's mansion in Santa Fe. Balfour hoped that Adkins would let the work remain in its present location until the governor could replace it, and that the Oklahoma collector would eventually donate it and other works from his collection to the Museum of New Mexico. Although Adkins had the painting delivered immediately, he offered to loan the work to the museum each summer and agreed to entertain the idea of its future donation.[16]

By 1971, Adkins's flourishing painting collection numbered 300 works by such nineteenth-century and early twentieth-century luminaries of American art and illustration as Charles Bird King (1785–1862), Alfred Jacob Miller (1810–1874), Frederic Remington (1861–1909), Charles M. Russell (1864–1926), and Frank Tenney Johnson (1874–1939). The subjects of these works—portraiture, landscapes, wildlife and still life, cowboys and Indians—were wide ranging.[17]

As Adkins and his collection became better known throughout the Southwest, museums began to request works on loan for exhibit. In July 1971, R.D.A. Puckle, associate director of the Phoenix Art Museum, proposed a major exhibition made up entirely of highlights from Adkins's holdings. The collector agreed, and the museum scheduled a November opening to take advantage of Arizona's heavy tourist season and the annual meeting of the museum's influential support group and exhibition sponsor, the Western Art Associates.[18]

Puckle traveled to Tulsa in September to select works for the show, a process that took twelve strenuous hours of give-and-take before the museum and the collector were satisfied with the exhibition roster. Sixty-five works were selected, representing a cross-section of Adkins's painting collection, from Charles Bird King's 1835 portrait of a Potawatomi chief, *Wabaunsee*, and Frank Tenney Johnson's *Apaches at Dusk* to more contemporary works by Peter Hurd and Paul Dyck (1917–2006).[19]

A modest catalogue accompanied the show, as did photographs of the artists, some of them provided by the collector. Although no works by Native artists were included in the exhibit, Adkins's editing of Puckle's brief and laudatory introductory essay, "A Visit with Eugene Adkins," emphasized his fondness for indigenous art and culture and noted his extensive holdings of Indian pottery, jewelry, and weaving.[20]

Western Art from the Eugene B. Adkins Collection opened on November 18, 1971, to uniformly positive reviews in the local press.[21] Marlan Miller, of the *Phoenix Gazette*, praised the exhibition for its "wide range of artists" and "high quality" paintings.[22] The *Scottsdale Daily Progress* thought the show "extremely well rounded" with a "star-studded cast of artists."[23] The latter article, illustrated by the Carl Runguis (1869–1959) painting *Rocky Mountain Goats*, mentioned only three works by name, two of which, *Indian Girl Swinging*, by Alfred Jacob Miller, and *Indian Composition* (c. 1937), by Victor Higgins (1884–1949), featured naked or only partially clothed figures. Perhaps mindful of conservative Arizona museumgoers, the unnamed author of the article hastened to note that the superior "design qualities" of Higgins's large work "outweigh[ed] the impact of the unclothed figure."[24]

The author of the exhibit review in the *Arizona Republic* characterized Adkins as "a modest but wide-eyed Indian art enthusiast who can afford to go after the things he wants." He added, however, that aesthetics motivated Adkins more than investment. "I guess my interest in western art," the collector waxed philosophically to the reporter, "is simply a way of looking at the world. . . . That's why I can't put a price on it."[25]

Fellow collectors and western art enthusiasts were also effusive in their praise of the Phoenix show and of Adkins's collection. Ruth Koerner Oliver, daughter of famed *Saturday Evening Post* illustrator W.H.D. Koerner (1878–1938), no doubt expressed the feelings of many who viewed the display. "Never," she wrote, "have those walls looked so magnificent as they do now with your beauties hanging on them!"[26] The eight works by Nicolai I. Fechin (1881–1955) and five by Leon Gaspard, hung as a group, were especially noteworthy, she believed, and "really wowed the elite of Phoenix. . . . It was a good experience and education for all of us."[27]

Both Russian artists were favorites of Adkins, and within a few years, he had acquired large and important collections by each. In a single 1969 coup, he obtained nine Fechin oils and seven charcoal drawings from art dealers Wolfgang Pogzeba of Denver and Steve Rose of Los Angeles for the sum of $123,750. He bought many other works from Fechin's daughter, Eya Fechin Branham, who had inherited them, and still others that had once belonged to John Burleson, a noted California collector and friend of the artist.[28]

In 1973 Adkins agreed to exhibit forty paintings and drawings, a wood carving, and a bronze, all by the Russian master, at the Museum of Northern Arizona.[29] In the collector's statement Adkins prepared for the show, he explained his attraction to Fechin's work:

> There is an awareness of spiritual reality in all the oils and charcoals by Nicolai Fechin you see here. When I discovered him in 1963, it was love at first sight. He is a great artist, not only because of his underlying superb drawing, his gorgeous color, his brilliant brush strokes, and heavy impasto, but also because there is nothing here that wasn't done with joy and reverence for the perfect truth that lies beneath the surface of the paint and the charcoal. Because of Fechin's greatness and the fascination he holds for me, I have not limited myself to collecting only his works relating to the American Southwest and the American Indian, but have added some done in his pre-revolutionary homeland, Russia, some done during his short stay in New York to which he immigrated in the early 1920s, some from the immediately following ten years or so when he lived in Taos, some later for his travels to Old Mexico and Bali, and finally some from Santa Monica in Southern California where he lived the last years of his life.[30]

Adkins continued to be generous with loans to other Fechin shows, including one mounted by the Phoenix Art Museum in 1976. The Tulsa collector had maintained close ties to the Arizona institution after his 1971 exhibition and four years later donated a 50 × 60 inch oil by Joseph Henry Sharp (1859–1953), titled *Taos Indian Women*, to the museum. Other gifts of art would follow, and Adkins would develop a lifelong friendship with the museum's curator of collections and later director James K. Ballinger.[31]

Sharing his collection through exhibits at prestigious museums throughout the West invariably enhanced the value of Adkins's holdings and his stature as a collector. Although

Plate 3
Nicolai Fechin (U.S., b. Russia, 1881–1955)
Albidia, n.d. Oil on canvas, 30 × 25 in.
Philbrook Museum of Art
A2007.0014

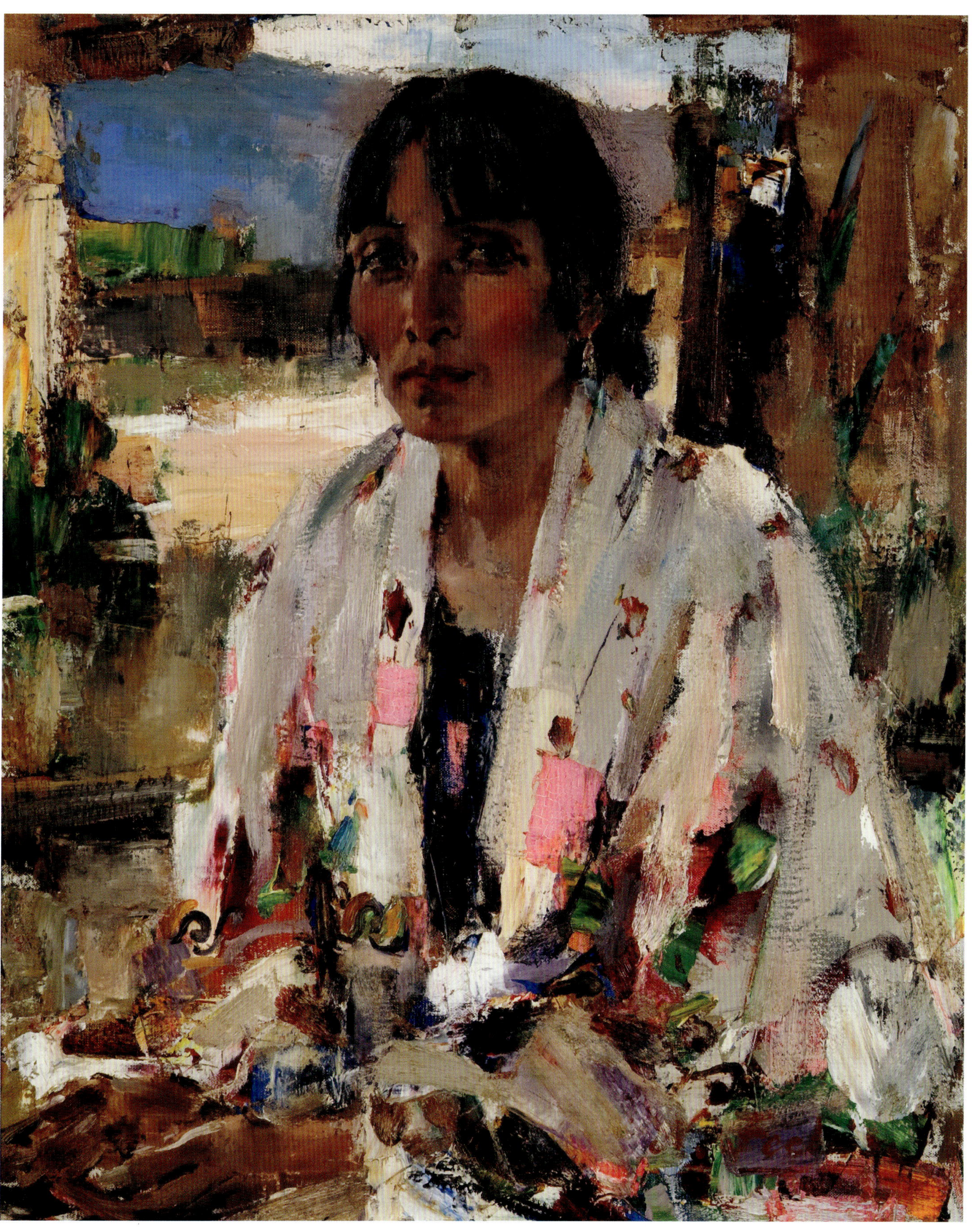

most loan requests involved works created by Euro-American artists, Adkins loaned paintings by Native American artists to important exhibitions on several occasions as well. In 1972, for example, Adkins sent *Indian #19*, a mammoth (72 × 61 in.) oil on canvas by Fritz Scholder (1937–2005), to the Smithsonian Institution's National Collection of Fine Arts, for *Two American Artists: Fritz Scholder and T. C. Cannon*, a traveling exhibition that toured six European capitals.[32]

Besides paintings by indigenous artists, Adkins acquired an impressive and ever-growing collection of American Indian arts and crafts. From baskets to pottery, beadwork to jewelry, weaving to carving, his holdings represented most of the leading artists of the day, including ceramics by Maria Martinez (1881–1980), the internationally acclaimed potter of San Ildefonso Pueblo, jewelry by the equally renowned Hopi silversmith Charles Loloma (1921–1991), and many others. He bought award-winning works with abandon during Indian Market at Santa Fe, the Indian Annual competition at the Philbrook Museum, and other prestigious shows. Stores operated by the Heard Museum in Phoenix and the Wheelwright Museum in Santa Fe yielded other treasures, as did art galleries and reservation trading posts throughout the Southwest. He made many such purchases face to face with the artists themselves but left little documentation of the transactions beyond the host of handwritten notes he scribbled incessantly to remind himself of important people, places, and events.[33]

In the early 1970s, Adkins tried to explain his deep and abiding passion for the art of Native America:

> Collecting has been as natural and healthy a need for me, and therefore as pleasurable a one, as my attending the ceremonials of the Hopis, Navajos, the Zunis and the Pueblo Indians of the Rio Grande. In reality the two pursuits have been intimately related for me, and are two manifestations of the same phenomenon:

> spiritual growth. My witnessing the ceremonials preceded my collecting by many years (my first ceremonial was the Santa Domingo Corn Dance in New Mexico in 1930 as a child; collecting didn't begin until 1963), and the collecting arose spontaneously as a part of a natural flow out of the spiritual nourishment that has come to me after all these years as I was absorbing what went on in the ceremonials.
>
> The awareness that my collecting has always been motivated by such a need came to me suddenly, and not too long ago. Before that realization, I really didn't know why I collected. The awareness of the "why" gave me a feeling of wholeness and peace, and also a keen and deeply satisfying awareness of my close spiritual kinship with those old time people George Catlin described in his "Creed About American Indians."
>
> For me, collecting has meant the getting together of rugs, pottery, jewelry, baskets and textiles, as well as paintings and bronzes, mostly but not exclusively made by or pertaining to the Southwestern Indians, all with great diversity, but related somehow to create a happy and harmonious ambience.[34]

Adkins's enthusiasm for Native American art and culture never waned, and many of the friendships he developed in its pursuit lasted a lifetime. Yet as his tastes in art matured and the focus of his quest narrowed, the Oklahoman's holdings evolved in response. In the 1970s Adkins began to cull his collection of redundant works and art whose subject matter no longer interested him or whose quality no longer measured up. He continually sold or traded works for the rest of his life, acquiring new ones more suited to his developing taste and vision.

Jean Seth's Canyon Road Art Gallery in Santa Fe and O'Brien's Art Emporium in Scottsdale received most of Adkins's early consignments. In 1974 alone, the collector placed a total of nineteen paintings for sale at Canyon Road in two large transactions. As time passed, however, Adkins looked increasingly to New York galleries and auction houses to market his surplus inventory. In the early 1990s, for example, the Oklahoma collector consigned works by such artists as Alfred Jacob Miller, Frederic Remington, Charles M. Russell, and Leon Gaspard to Christie's auction house and Beacon Hill Galleries.[35]

Constant culling notwithstanding, the walls in Adkins's modest condominium were always filled to capacity with art. The collector stacked the surplus frame to frame on the floors of his dwelling, leaving narrow lanes for walking from room to room. In time, ceramics, baskets, kachinas, weavings, and jewelry took over most of the drawers, bookshelves, and cabinets and could also be found under beds, and even in a bathtub. When a party of five representing the Buffalo Bill Historical Center visited Adkins's townhouse in the late 1990s, there was only space enough in the living room for one guest at a time to sit and converse with the host.[36] "Gene Adkins' home," said one friend, "was like a quaint antique shop and he was the skillful and knowledgeable antique dealer. From afar, you did not know where to start looking but the antique dealer knew where every piece was and what spirit dwelled in each. The olla and wedding vases gently rest on the orange velvety couch in his living room, the silver, turquoise, and coral jewelry piled in the china cabinet, the walkways lined with paintings and prints and on and on."[37]

Despite the clutter, Adkins enjoyed showing off his collection to visitors, especially if they were scholars writing books, museum curators seeking loans, gallery owners looking to buy or sell, or fellow collectors eager to compare notes. After one such visit, a museum trustee wrote the collector in 1991: "I am still feeling 'boggled' by your collection—its scope and depth is fascinating and must make museum directors turn green."[38]

Advancing age and a back operation in 1990 slowed the pace of Adkins's collecting activities. Tired of the paperwork, insurance, crating, and other hassles associated with museum loans, he began to turn down most such requests. He continued to relish periodic trips to New Mexico and Arizona, and for a time Adkins contemplated purchasing a condominium in Santa Fe and becoming at least a part-time resident. He loved the city's art scene, its famed opera, and the colorful, fragrant flowers that bloomed in its gardens and along its thoroughfares.[39]

Increasingly introspective and a bit lonely, Adkins filled postcards with accounts of his journeys and the feelings and memories they inspired and mailed them to himself in Tulsa.[40] He regretted some of the changes that had taken place in his old haunts. Arriving in Santa Fe in 1991 after an absence of three years produced "a rush of happy/sad recollections of people now gone, and events of old—all welling up in my consciousness!!"[41] A few days later, heavy traffic spoiled his visit to Taos, prompting a quick return to the state capital and a postcard declaration that "Contemporary Taos is NOT FOR ME."[42]

Adkins's love for the American Southwest, its Native inhabitants, and the art it inspired, however, endured until his death on February 3, 2006. Two years later, the foundation that the collector had established to oversee the disposition of the collection he had amassed with such care named the Fred Jones Jr. Museum of Art at the University of Oklahoma and the Philbrook Museum of Art in Tulsa as its custodians. The two institutions subsequently divided the contents, arranged for their cataloging, agreed to share them with each other and with other museums, and embarked on the construction of new exhibition and storage facilities.[43]

An adjunct to these efforts, this book presents highlights of the Adkins Collection and is divided into sections that, taken together, reflect the collector's overall vision. Several artists, art historians, and curators have been called on to introduce and provide perspective on both the collector and the works he assembled. Although the purpose and format of this volume do not afford the opportunity to explore the complete evolution and full significance of Eugene B. Adkins's connoisseurship, the essays and illustrations presented here do suggest abundant opportunities for scholarly interpretation, museum exhibition, and personal enjoyment. Any collector would be proud to leave such a legacy for future generations.

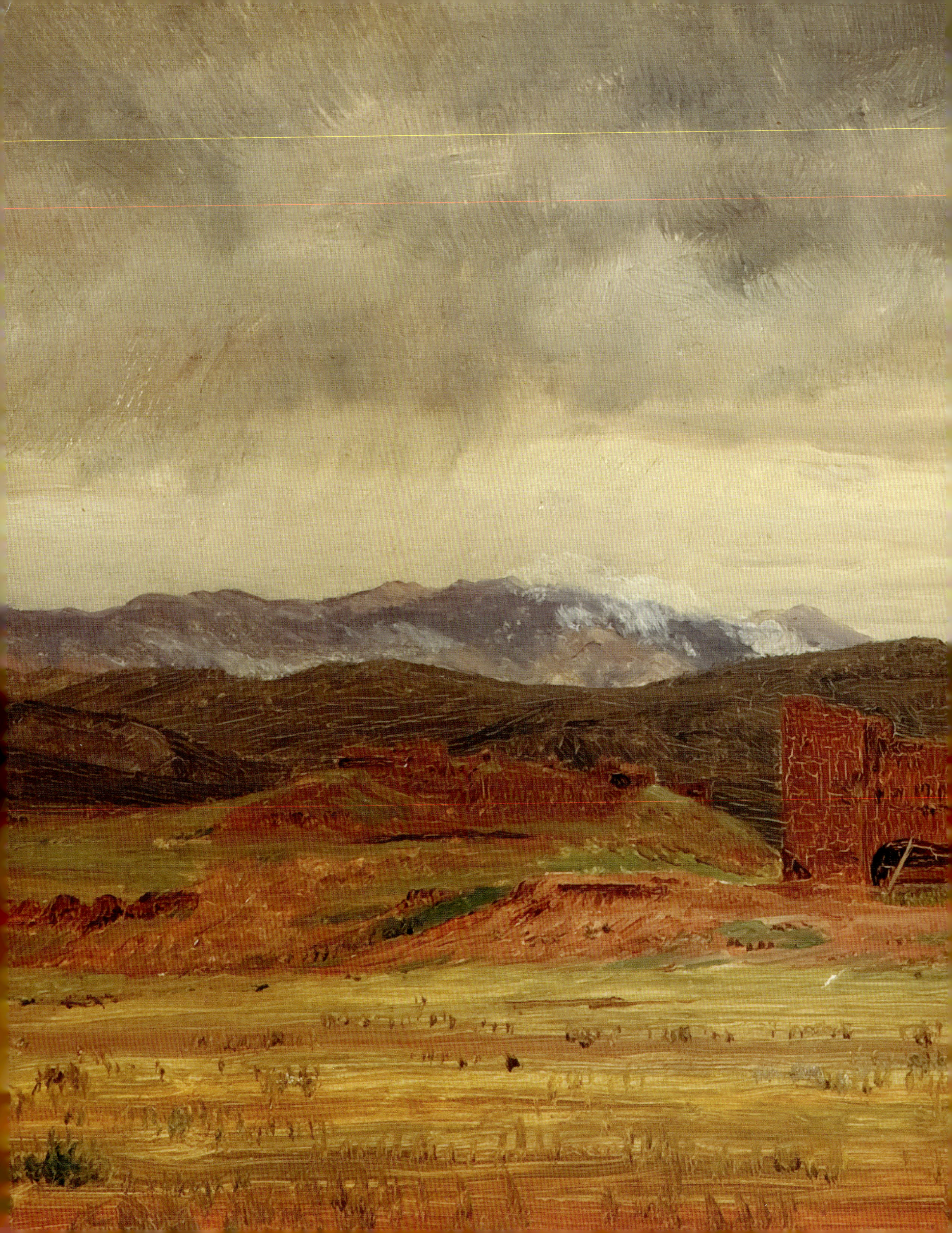

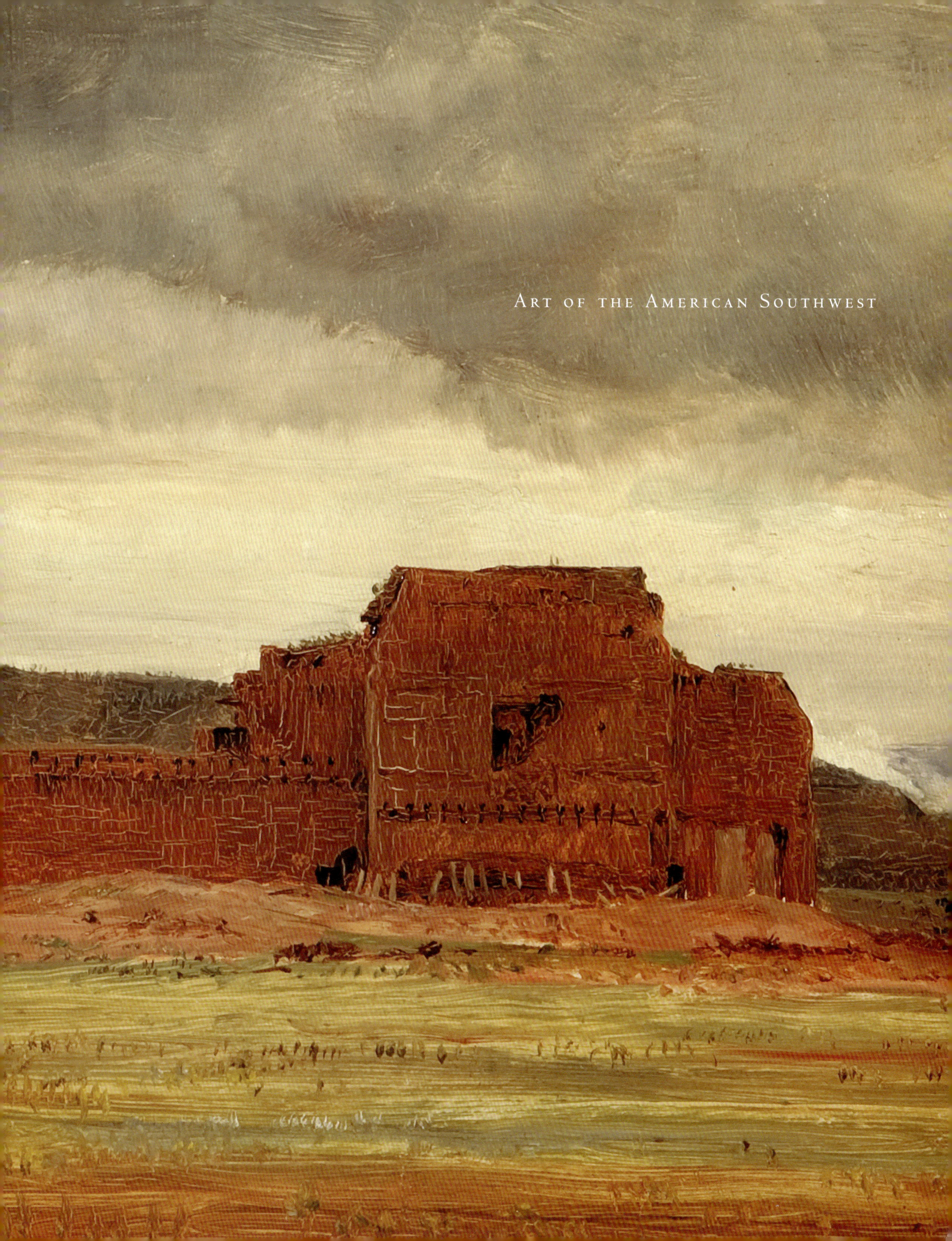

Art of the American Southwest

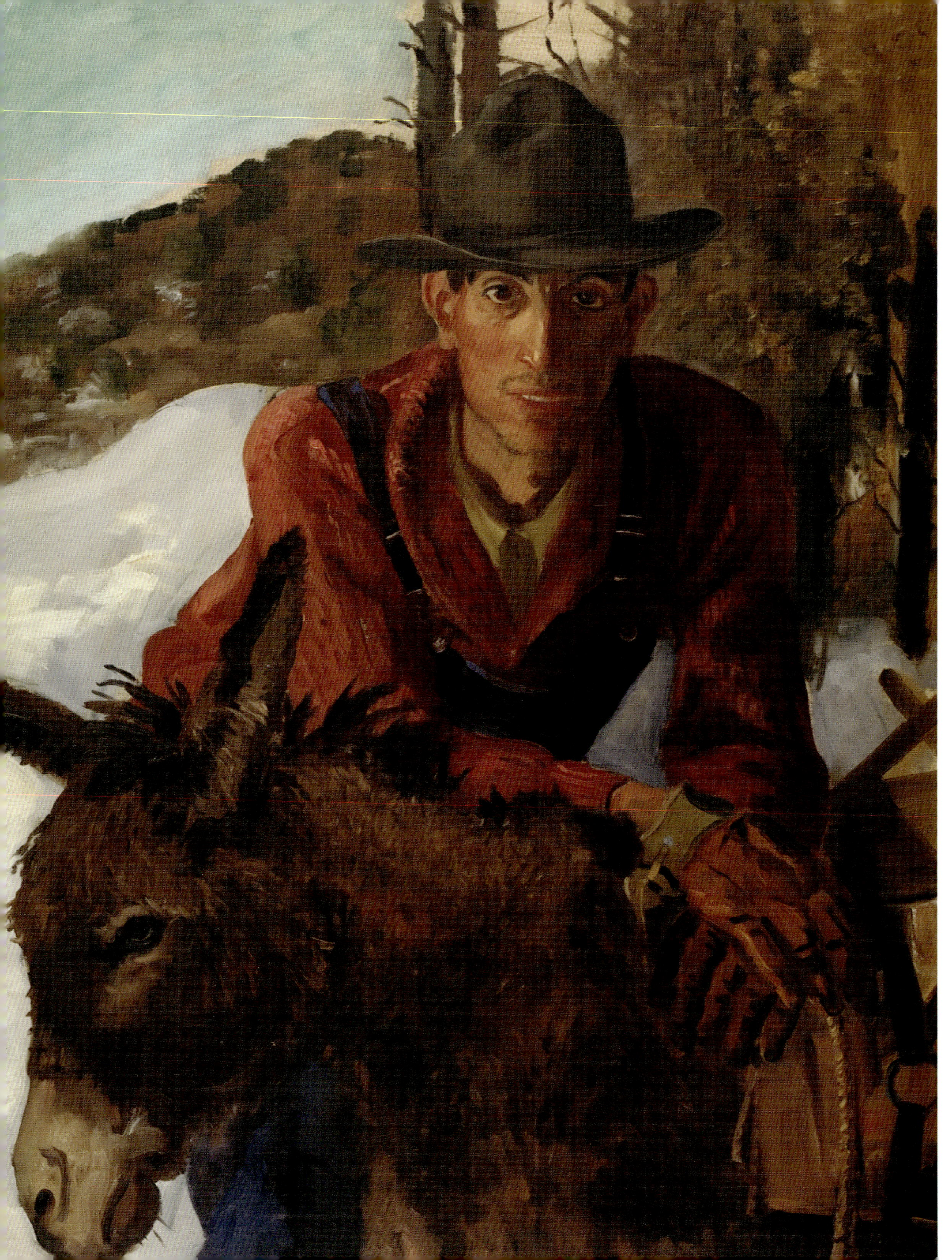

Time and Modernity in the Art of the American Southwest

Mark A. White

CHAPTER ONE

When artist Worthington Whittredge first encountered Pecos Pueblo in 1866, it had been abandoned for nearly twenty years. Whittredge was traveling in the company of General John Pope on his inspection of the Department of the Missouri, which included the Rocky Mountains and New Mexico. On their return route north from Santa Fe to Fort Union, the company likely camped at Pecos, much of which still stood, as Whittredge's *Old Pecos Pueblo Church, New Mexico* (1866, plate 48), indicates.[1] The pueblo, founded a millennium earlier, had been a thriving center of commerce and trade for much of its history.[2] Following Spain's imperial acquisition of the region, Governor Juan de Oñate helped the Franciscans establish a mission there in 1617–18, and Fray Andrés Juárez arrived in 1620–21 to win converts and construct a permanent church; however, recurring outbreaks of disease and Comanche raids forced the dwindling population to abandon the site around 1839 and relocate to Jemez Pueblo.

How much of this history was known to Whittredge is unclear, but the church certainly drew his attention, with its syncretic blend of Puebloan and Hispanic architecture and religion. The ruined church compares in its topography to the Sangre de Cristo Mountains on the horizon, creating a close relationship between the structure and the surrounding landscape. Whittredge suggests a parallel between the inexorable deterioration of the church and the seemingly timeless erosion of the mountains. Pecos Church was returning to the earth from which it came.

This juxtaposition of the timeful and the timeless at Pecos may have left Whittredge with the notion that time progressed differently, and perhaps more slowly, in the Southwest than in the rest of the United States. But by the turn of the century, numerous visitors to the region would recognize the idiosyncrasy of southwestern time; Charles Lummis, in his

Plate 4
Randall Vernon Davey (U.S., 1887–1964)
The Woodchopper (Cruz Gonzales), 1924. Oil on canvas, 40 × 32 in.
Fred Jones Jr. Museum of Art
A2007.0206

notable article "The Land of Poco Tiempo," described New Mexico as "the National Rip Van Winkle—the United States which is *not* the United States. Here is the land of poco tiempo—the home of 'Pretty Soon.' Why hurry with the hurrying world? The 'pretty soon' of New Spain is better than the 'Now! Now!' of the haggard States."[3]

Lummis went on to describe the geography and the Hispanic, Navajo, and Puebloan cultures he found in the Southwest. The lure of the region lay in its dissimilarity to the United States as a whole, whether in the denial of the Protestant work ethic, in the implied resistance to change, or in the syncretism of its culture. Whittredge's painting had engaged issues, probably unwittingly, that would interest Lummis and innumerable artists in the Southwest for decades to come. Artists from Chicago, Los Angeles, New York City, and other metropolitan centers would visit and often settle in the Southwest, seeking in the unfamiliar a respite from the industrial civilization of urban America. For example, images of labor and commerce in the Southwest deliberately avoid mechanization and industrialization in favor of chores closely related to the physical environment. Randall Davey's *The Woodchopper (Cruz Gonzales)* (1924, plate 4) is not only a portrait of the artist's neighbor on Canyon Road in Santa Fe, but also a celebration of manual labor, clearly separate from industrial logging. Davey had come from New York City and, as a protégé of Robert Henri, had ample experience with the plight of the working classes in an urban environment beset by mechanized labor. The seemingly premodern culture of the Southwest promised not only fresh artistic subject matter but also physical and spiritual rejuvenation from the debilitating effects of urban life.[4]

Around the turn of the twentieth century, nothing could have seemed further from urban America than the southwestern desert. Although Americans had once deemed it an inhospitable and unappealing climate, tastes began to change. Impressionism, with its vivid colors, lightened the palettes of American artists, and the desert offered suitable material.

Ethnologist Walter Hough, in seeming anticipation of this change, described the desert near the Hopi mesas with impressionist blues and violets: "Here thousands of square miles stretch in iridescent beauty to the violet horizon or to the velvety blue mountains. . . . The morning and evening reveal new coloring and beauty beyond the power of pen or pencil to depict."[5] John C. Van Dyke, in his influential 1901 book, *The Desert: Further Studies in Natural Appearances,* expressed admiration for the desert's powerful coloration and severe terrain, signaling a new critical appreciation for it as landscape. He found the barren simplicity of southwestern mesas more beautiful than the verdant, Edenic landscapes of the Catskills: "All the glory of the old shall be as nothing to the gold and purple and burning crimson of this new world. . . . The love of Nature is after all an acquired taste. One begins by admiring the Hudson-River landscape and ends by loving the desolation of the Sahara."[6]

Given the enthusiasm of visitors like Hough and Van Dyke, it is little surprise that visiting artists, supportive of the impressionist palette, would find material worthy to paint. Gerald Cassidy combed the lands of the Navajo and Hopi in search of subject matter for two decades. *Road in the Desert* (n.d., plate 28) depicts a lone wagon ambling through the blanched, barren landscape, but it is the monumental sky, diaphanous clouds, and clear light that captured Cassidy's interest in the desert. The painting also conveys the difficulty Cassidy must have overcome in traversing the largely empty country to reach his subject. He had help in this regard from John Lorenzo Hubbell. Hubbell's trading post in Ganado, Arizona, became "a painter's mecca" around the turn of the century, where many artists and writers "discovered the Southwest."[7] Established around 1880, the post had been sanctioned by Navajo leaders, and Hubbell's social standing helped facilitate artists' trips into Navajo and Hopi territory.[8]

Carl Oscar Borg, who had moved in Lummis's circle in Los Angeles, was among the many who received help from Hubbell. Northeastern Arizona entranced Borg, and the close relationships he quickly formed with the Navajo and Hopi led him to believe that in the desert "one is much nearer the creator of it all."[9] His paintings of Navajo horse culture allowed him to combine his interest in the grand skies and sublime desolation of the desert with his corresponding belief in cultural preservation. Borg insisted that Native cultures were threatened with irrevocable change and possible extinction, and he "wanted to try and preserve some of their customs and religious life in a permanent form."[10]

Like Borg, William Robinson Leigh visited the Southwest in hopes of depicting both the desert and Native life, and he, too, received assistance from Hubbell, when he visited Ganado in 1912. The trip introduced him to the Navajo, who became one of his enduring subjects and represented for him a link to the ancient past: "Theirs was such a very primitive life that it carried the imagination back through weird, fantastic lapses of time that stagger credence."[11] The simplicity of Navajo life is expressed in paintings such as *A Navajo Chief* (1916, plate 5), where the subject peers provocatively from the folds of a blanket in the midst of a windswept landscape.

R. Brownell McGrew, an artist working in the post–World War II era, shared Leigh's interest in the antiquity of Navajo life and depicted "neither conflict, mechanization, nor Anglo influence" in his paintings.[12] Traditional Navajo dress, like that worn by the elder in his *Hosteen* (n.d., plate 41), represented resistance to modernization, and for McGrew, as well as for Leigh and Borg, this resistance was an expression of antimodernist desire. Although the Navajo lived within the territorial United States, their values seemed strikingly alien to a largely capitalist, positivist, and Protestant America. Illustrator Will Crawford, who worked for popular American periodicals the *Century* and *Scribner's*, suggested the Navajo's status as outsiders in his *Belly Up to the Bar Boys* (n.d., plate 29). The Navajo stands at the fringe of the composition, and his traditional attire separates him from the community of cowboys and the fashionable greenhorn, advancing on the bar.

Plate 5
William Robinson Leigh (U.S., 1866–1955)
A Navajo Chief, 1916. Watercolor on board, 30 × 22 in.
Fred Jones Jr. Museum of Art
A2007.0030

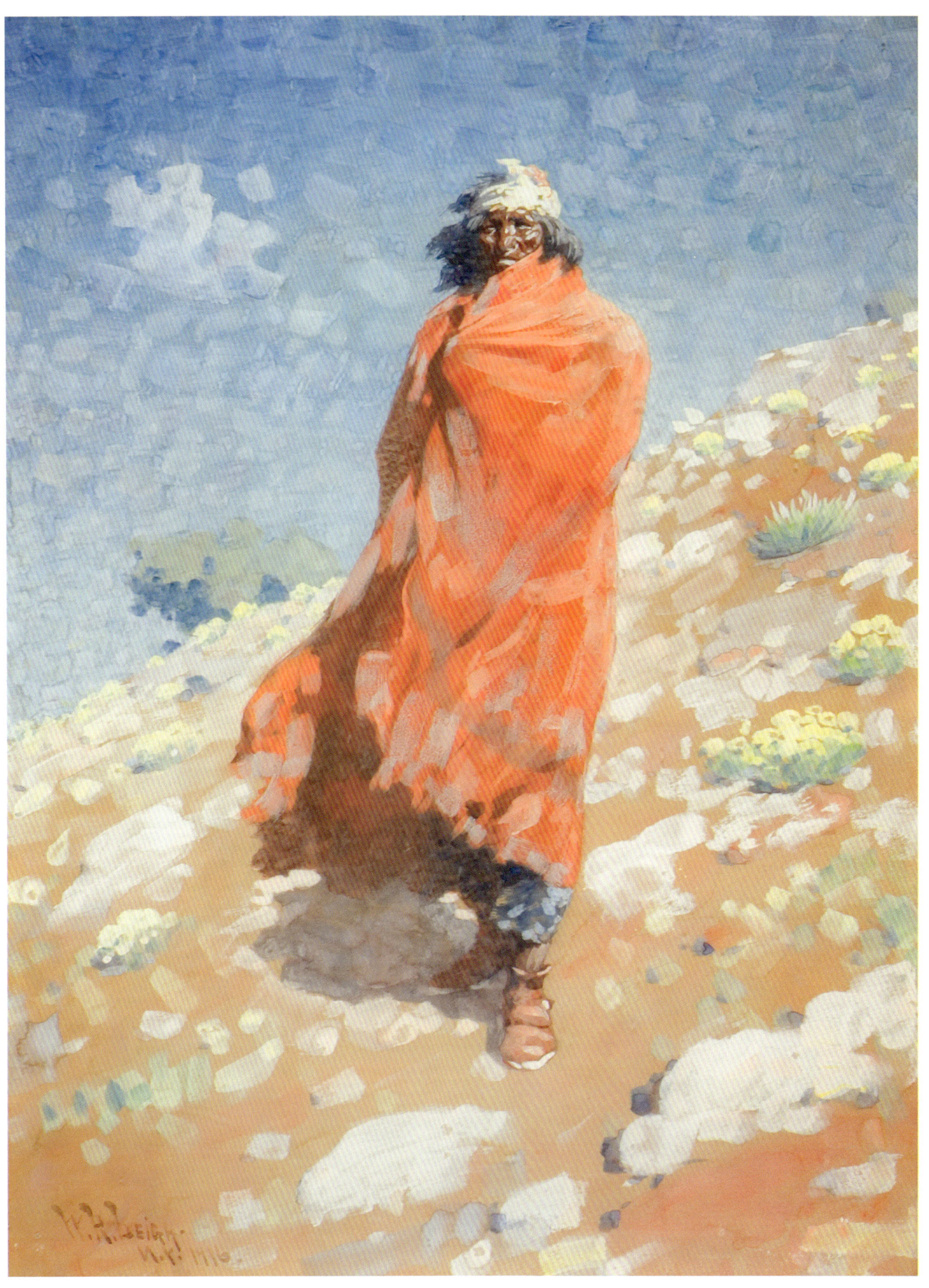

Depictions of the Navajo in their desert lands suggested an analogy between the antiquity of cultural traditions and the eons of geological history. Maynard Dixon's *Land of the White Mesas* (1943, plate 31) sets two Navajo riders and their herd of horses against a monolithic mesa, the erosion of which alludes to a link to the distant past. The previous year, Dixon had described Arizona as "the land of mesas . . . carved and hollowed by the recession of forgotten seas . . . the blind blunt architecture of a pre-human world."[13]

Dixon spent much of his career in Arizona following his visit to Hubbell's trading post in 1902, and like Cassidy, he embraced the desert and its theatrical western skies as subject. *Evening and Afterthought* (1924, plate 30), in which the setting sun tints the cumulus updraft with rose and turquoise, captures the "iridescent beauty" that so entranced Walter Hough. Dixon painted *Evening and Afterthought* following an extended sketching trip on the Hopi Reservation from August to December in 1923. The stay at Walpi exposed Dixon to numerous religious rituals like that in *The Circle of Shimaikuli* (1923, plate 1). Sometimes spelled Shumaikoli or Somaíkoli, the ritual was performed in part or in its entirety by the Ya Ya Society, but it largely fell out of favor in the mid-twentieth century for its magical tricks, which sparked accusations of witchcraft.[14] In Dixon's painting, the men and women encircle the kiva and await the appearance of the Somaíkoli kachina; for the artist, such rituals sparked the imagination and united the ancient past with the present: "These things are for the archaeologist and the painter to understand. From them the scientist recreates the ancient world; the artist creates a new one. . . . The imagination moves free and the past and present are one."[15]

Dixon was not alone in perceiving a glimpse of prehistory in Hopi rituals, as Sharyn R. Udall has argued: "Because of their relative isolation, untainted by sustained Euro-American contact, the Hopi and their ceremonials were widely regarded by scholars and artists as unbroken links to an ancient past."[16] The snake dance attained greatest popularity with lay and scholarly audiences alike, and according to Walter Hough, the 1897 dance drew numerous Hopi, Navajo, and "not less than one hundred white people [who] witnessed the Snake dance at Wolpi [*sic*] in 1897."[17] Cincinnati artist Cornelia Cassady-Davis attended with her husband, Edwin C. Davis, a dealer in southwestern material culture.[18] In her *Hopi Snake Dance* (1897, plate 27), the dancers are caught in midstep with snakes held in their mouths and hands, having rounded the sacred rock. Cassady-Davis, trained at the Cincinnati Art Academy, was concerned not only with the drama of the ritual but with the specifics of dress and dance, giving the painting an air of authenticity.

Later artists, such as William Penhallow Henderson, would be more interested in the dance's spiritual significance. His *Walpi Snake Dance* (c. 1920, plate 37) is based on a pastel drawing of the 1919 snake dance he witnessed with former Chicago mayor Carter Harrison.[19] The abstract forms and vivid coloration of his depiction eschew detail and are meant to communicate a pure spiritual experience. Poet Carl Sandburg claimed that Henderson "was spiritually mortgaged" to Native rituals, and as a result, the artist realized in paint the "fine human and cosmic implications that rise behind and out of the portrayed Indians, mountains, houses, sparse trees."[20] *Walpi Snake Dance* was less a document of a specific dance than a reflection of an archetypal desire for unity with nature.

Henderson was one of a handful of modern artists who had recently arrived in New Mexico. Santa Fe was quickly becoming one of the most important artist colonies in the Southwest, rivaled only by Taos, and the development of art in the region was largely influenced by the diverse artists, archaeologists, ethnographers, and writers who settled there.

Traditional histories of the Santa Fe and Taos art colonies frequently begin with Joseph Henry Sharp. Sharp visited Santa Fe in 1883, but on his return trip to New Mexico in 1893, he spent part of the summer in Taos. He later extolled the virtues of New Mexico to Ernest Blumenschein and Bert Geer Phillips, whom he met in Paris at the Académie Julian in 1895. In 1898, the latter two set out for Mexico from Denver, when a broken wagon wheel forced them to detour to Taos. Phillips settled immediately, while Blumenschein returned to Paris the following year, summering in Taos until permanent relocation in 1919. Other artists

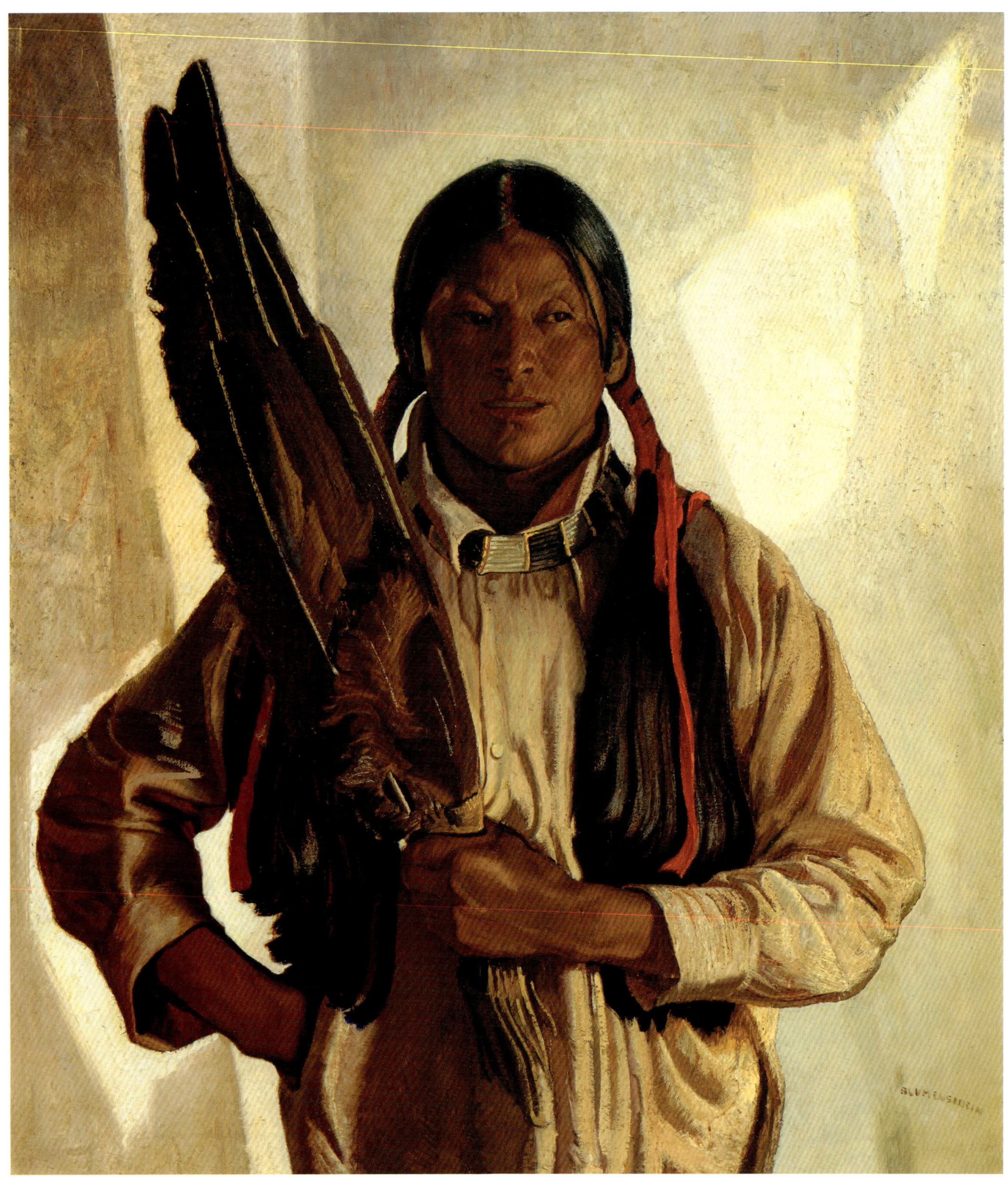

Plate 6
Ernest L. Blumenschein (U.S. 1874–1960)
Eagle Wing Fan, n.d. Oil on canvas, 34 × 30 in.

Philbrook Museum of Art
A2007.0008

soon visited: Oscar E. Berninghaus in 1899; Eanger Irving Couse in 1903; William Herbert Dunton in 1912; and Victor Higgins and Walter Ufer in 1914. These artists, including Sharp, Phillips, and Blumenschein, would form the nucleus of the Taos Society of Artists (TSA) in 1915 and would begin popularizing their image of northern New Mexico throughout the United States, through circuit exhibitions that traveled to major metropolitan areas.

While the majority of the TSA tended toward academic styles of painting drawn from the classicist principles of the old masters, some such as Blumenschein, Higgins, and Ufer would gradually embrace modernist principles. For example, Blumenschein's *Eagle Wing Fan* (n.d., plate 6) demonstrates a clear academic commitment to the figure through the distinct, descriptive contour and careful modeling in light and shadow, yet the artist challenges the volumetric illusion through an abstract pattern of light and shadow that flattens the background. *Eagle Wing Fan*, in this regard, reveals Blumenschein's flirtation with cubism and its challenge to the clear differentiation of figure and space.

The break with academism of some TSA members may be credited to the growing acceptance of European abstraction in the United States and the arrival in Taos of American practitioners of these styles. E. Martin Hennings visited Taos in 1917 and joined the TSA in 1924, bringing with him the influence of Jugendstil, the German variant of art nouveau he had picked up as a student in Munich. More important, the New York socialite Mabel Dodge Sterne arrived in 1916 at the request of her husband, modernist Maurice Sterne. Maurice stayed briefly, but Mabel remained and eventually divorced him for Taos Puebloan Tony Luhan. Sterne had also urged cubist Andrew Dasburg to visit.[21] Dasburg was among the first modernists to summer in Taos, in 1918, and Mabel Dodge Luhan would succeed in luring numerous artists and writers to New Mexico, including D. H. Lawrence in 1924, Nicolai Fechin in 1927, and John Marin and Georgia O'Keeffe in 1929. Luhan's influence in Taos was so recognizable that her death in 1962 seemed the end of an era, and English painter Dorothy Eugenie Brett, who had arrived with D. H. and Frieda Lawrence and then never left, crafted a sentimental eulogy with *Mabel's Funeral* (n.d., plate 7).

Luhan's ability to draw artists to Taos had a Santa Fe corollary in archaeologist Edgar Lee Hewett. His professional interest in southwestern archaeology led him to Santa Fe in 1898, and he supervised the development of the School of American Archaeology (now the School of American Research) and its installation in the historic Palace of the Governors, which was then renovated to fit its new mission as a museum and research institution. More important for the visual arts, Hewett convinced the state legislature to create the Art Gallery of the Museum of New Mexico (later Museum of Fine Arts, or MFA), which opened across the street from the Palace in 1917. Artists had already begun to trickle into Santa Fe by 1917. Californian Carlos Vierra became the first resident in 1904, followed by Gerald Cassidy in 1912, Henderson in 1916, Gustave Baumann in 1918, Randall Davey and Fremont Ellis in 1919, Will Shuster in 1920, and Theodore van Soelen in 1922. Hewett offered all these artists studio space in the Palace of the Governors and exhibition opportunities at the MFA.

Although the artists of the Santa Fe and Taos colonies differed dramatically in their stylistic bent, they were attracted to northern New Mexico as a haven from urban America's clamorous capitalistic drive for modernization, progress, and wealth. Dunton, for instance, valorized Taos as "remote from commercialism and the sordid, restful in its peaceful isolation, quiet along its crooked alleys, in the soft shadows of the adobe walls."[22] He rarely painted the adobe villages that so entranced his contemporaries of the TSA, however, and preferred subjects that suggested the mythical Old West akin to those of his mentor and hero Charles M. Russell (plate 43). His portrait of Bert Phillips's daughter Margo, who married Taos attorney William Beutler, strikes a balance between his admiration for the cowboy and the lingering appeal of the Gibson Girl (plate 32).[23]

But the peaceful isolation of which Dunton spoke drew many of his colleagues to explore the New Mexican landscape. It may have been a quiet stroll in the nearby forests, for instance, that prompted Sharp to collect the aspen branches he used for *A Million Aspen Leaves* (n.d., plate 18). Although the painting's pedigree originates in the floral still lifes popularized

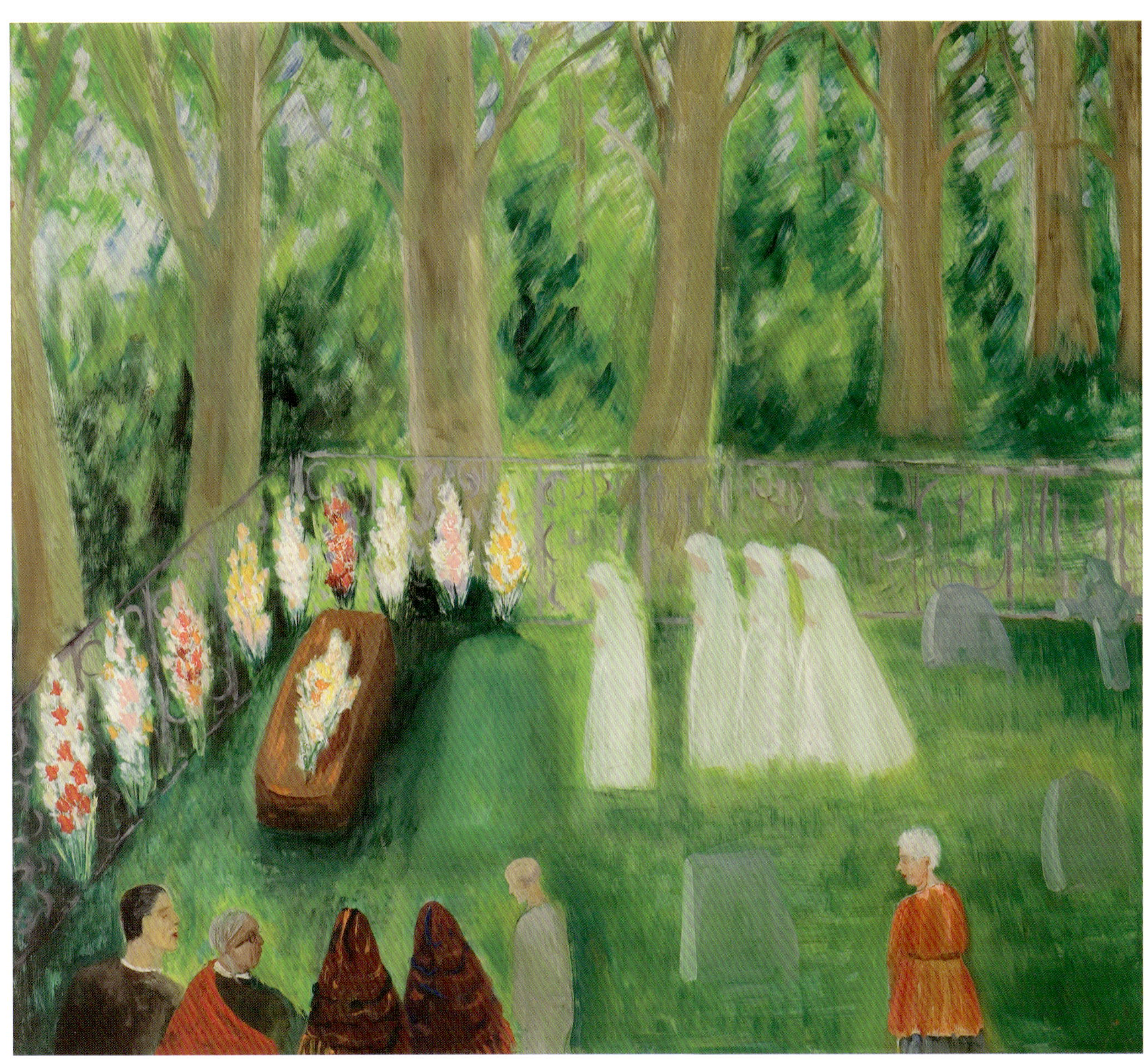

Plate 7
Dorothy Eugenie Brett (U.S., 1883–1976)
Mabel's Funeral, n.d. Oil on board, 24 × 27 in.
Fred Jones Jr. Museum of Art
A2007.0116

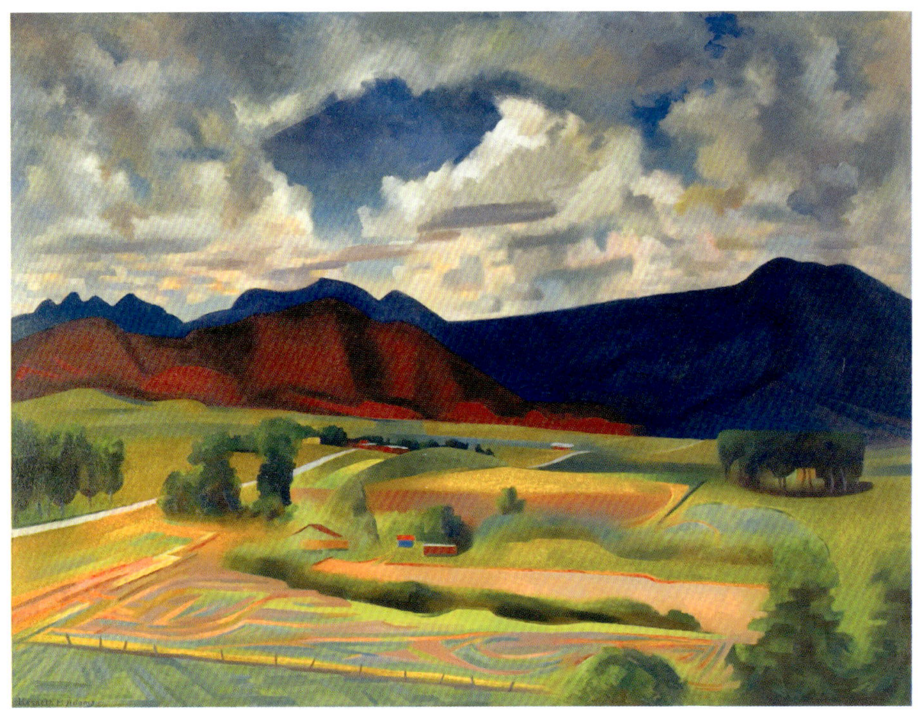

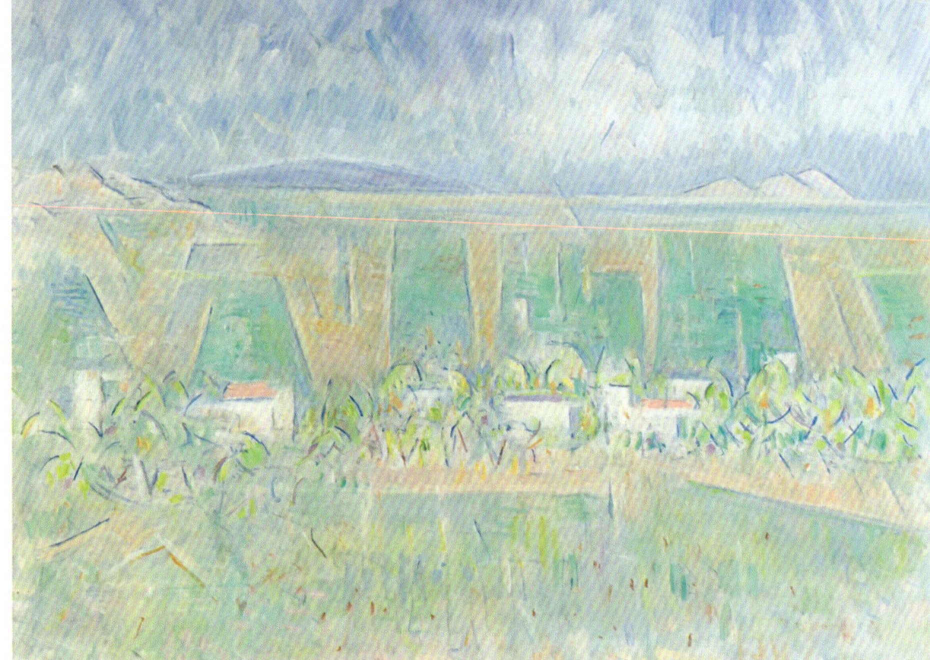

Plate 8 (above)
Kenneth Miller Adams (U.S., 1897–1966)
The Valley, 1952. Oil on canvas, 30 × 40 in.
Fred Jones Jr. Museum of Art
A2007.0063

Plate 9 (right)
Andrew Dasburg (U.S., 1887–1979)
Untitled, 1966. Oil on canvas. 26 × 36 in.
Philbrook Museum of Art
A2007.0118

by East Coast impressionists, Sharp provides a southwestern flavor with the black pot and Navajo chief's blanket.

Quiet repose would also seem to be the theme of Dasburg's 1966 painting of New Mexican agriculture, with its greening fields and isolated settlements, but the repetition of subtle diagonals throughout the composition suggests a landscape in flux (plate 9). Dasburg saw in the northern New Mexican landscape "the vastness of the upheavals of earth that at one time took place, perhaps are going on now. The forces which are in opposition."[24] Kenneth Miller Adams likely viewed his own painting *The Valley* (1952, plate 8) in similar terms, having studied with Dasburg and moved to Taos in 1924 under the latter's encouragement. Adams painted *The Valley* with blocks of vibrant, oscillating color to imply an active earth, continually shaped by telluric currents. Dasburg and Adams applied the principles of cubism, and its depiction of unseen forces, to the New Mexican landscape, and the resulting images were intended to communicate the artists' intuitional communion with nature—a dialogue established more readily at a remove from the relentless noise of American progress.

Dasburg's colleague John Marin was equally interested in the drama of oppositions, and he used the viscous medium of watercolor to suggest what he termed "push and pull forces." He painted Taos Mountain soon after his June 1929 arrival to Mabel's residence, while he was still attempting to come to terms with the unfamiliar terrain, but his choice of subject indicates that Marin was already interested in spiritual centers, given the religious importance of the formation to Taos Pueblo (plate 20).[25]

While the paintings of Dasburg, Adams, and Marin may be subtle in their suggestion of a dynamic earth, Blumenschein confronted directly the powers of tectonic uplift in his *Rio Grande Gorge Near Taos* (1944–1949, plate 24). His original title, *Strength of the Earth*, signals his interest in the physical might of the rock, which is conveyed through defined, angular contours and a rich bronzed coloration. Blumenschein impresses the viewer with the monumentality of the gorge in hopes of creating spiritual uplift, and the jagged cut of the Rio Grande in the background, which imitates a bolt of lightning, evokes the power of the heavens.

Associating spirituality with the southwestern landscape had historical roots for Euro-Americans; in 1719, New Mexican governor Antonio Valverde y Cosío was reminded of the blood of Christ when viewing the ruddy, dawn glow of the northern mountains. The Sangre de Cristo range, as he named it, impressed Carlos Vierra in much the same way when he painted *Sangre de Cristo Dawn* (n.d., plate 47). A lone figure and his dog are immersed in the morning radiance of the range, and Vierra's loose brushwork and vivid coloration indicates his own emotional engagement with a landscape at once glorious and disquietingly reminiscent of the flayed flesh of Christ.

Vierra, of Portuguese descent, was central in the movement to preserve New Mexican cultural patrimony, and "he was always active in protecting old Santa Fe landmarks and grew indignant whenever an old cottonwood was cut down."[26] He also helped conceive what became known as the Spanish Pueblo, or "Spanish-Indian," style of architecture, drawn from influences such as Taos Pueblo and the mission church at Acoma.[27] Vierra and many other colony artists appreciated adobes for their severe rusticity and positioned them as a distinctively American architecture. Fremont Ellis made the plastered wall of an adobe sanctuary his principal subject in *Interior of Church at Santa Cruz* (c. 1940, plate 10). Although Ellis clearly had some interest in the religious folk art of the church, the subtly sculpted wall with its imprecise lines commanded his attention.[28]

The aesthetic possibilities of adobe architecture made it not only a pictorial interest of the colony artists but also a favorite domicile. Adobes harmonized with the desert landscape and offered a kind of visual relaxation, because the plaster "blends with the vivid coloring of the country, while the outstanding lines of the structures are in harmony with those of the surrounding plains and mountains."[29] Victor Higgins sought an image of isolation, peace, and quiet in his winter townscape *Ledoux Street (My House)* (c. 1918, plate 39).[30] Blumenschein also lived in an adobe on Ledoux, and his *Village, Northern New Mexico* (c. 1929, plate 23), sought the tranquility found in Higgins's snow scene as well as a celebration of traditional adobe buildings.[31]

PLATE 10
Fremont Ellis (U.S., 1897–1985)
Interior of Church at Santa Cruz, c. 1940. Oil on canvas board, 45 × 37 in.
Fred Jones Jr. Museum of Art
A2007.0087

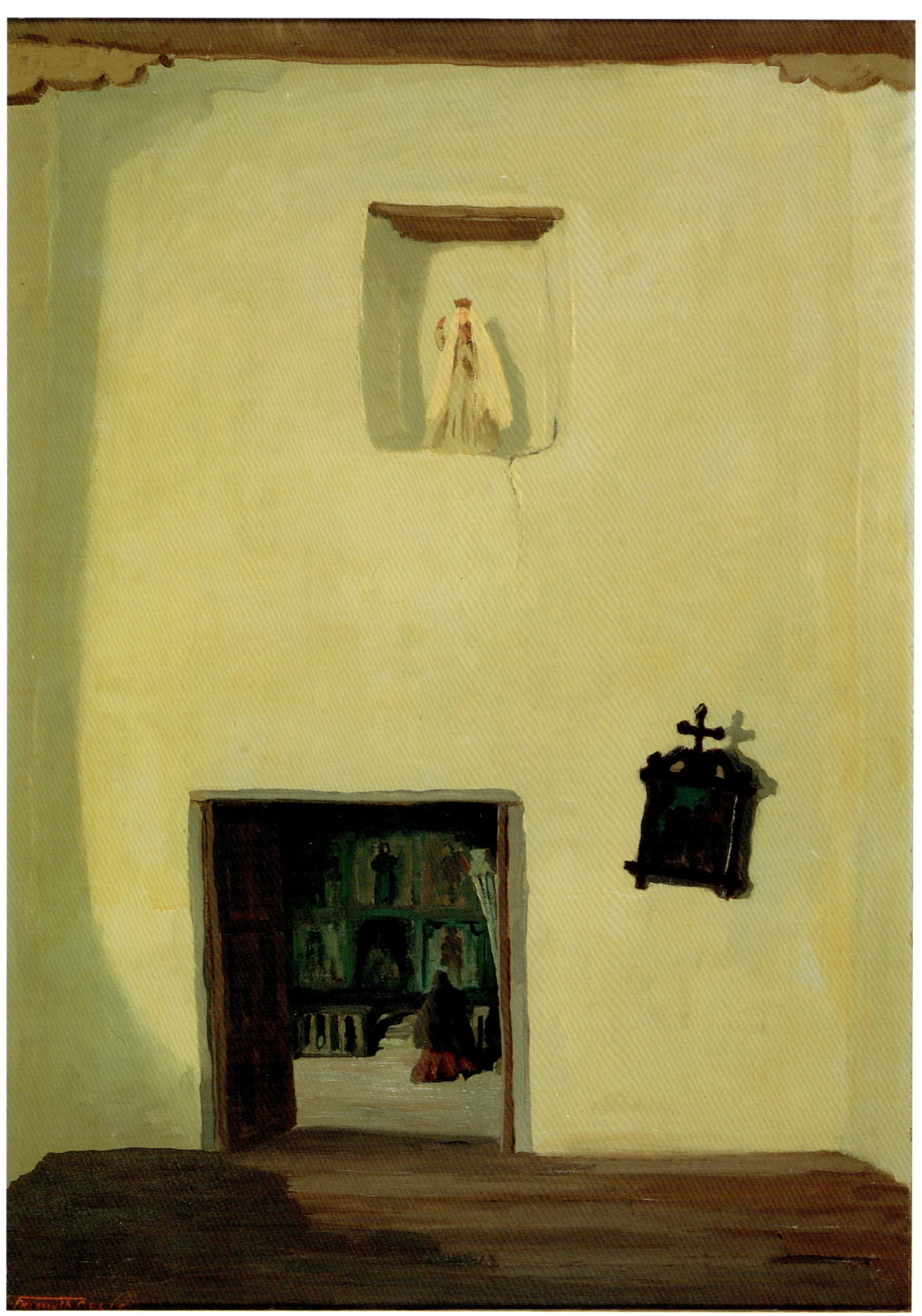

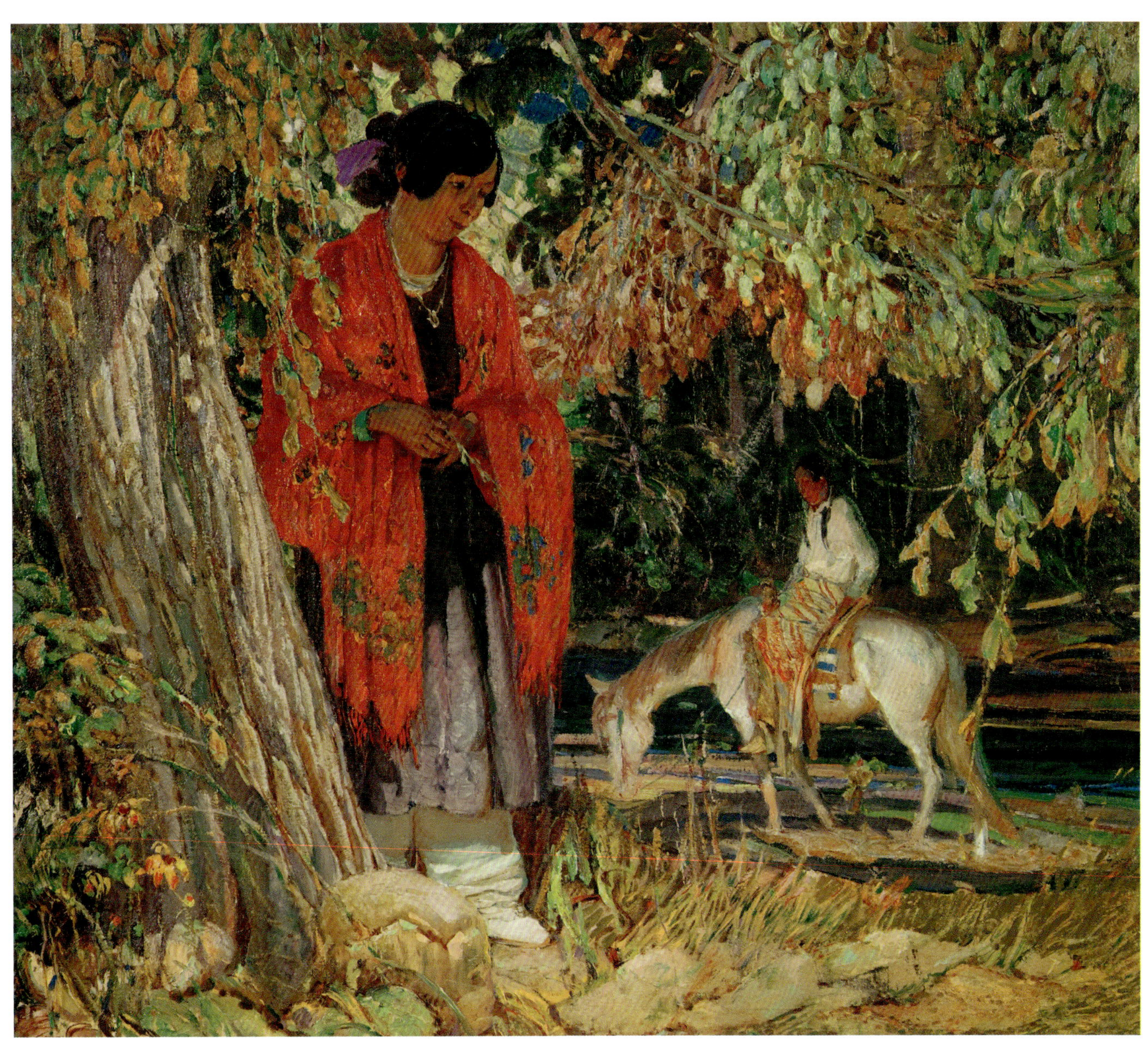

Plate 11
Oscar E. Berninghaus (U.S. 1874–1952)
Taos Idyll, n.d. Oil on canvas, 35 × 40 in.
Philbrook Museum of Art
A2007.0012

It is little wonder that most colony artists were attracted to Taos Pueblo as the epitome of adobe architecture. The pueblo helped inspire much new adobe architecture among preservationists, such as Gustave Baumann, who admired the geometric simplicity of the terraced roofs (see plate 21). James Erwin Boren preferred a more picturesque view of the pueblo set against the mountains (see plate 25), but he and Baumann were undoubtedly united in their fascination over one of the oldest structures in North America, continuously inhabited for a thousand years.

The distinctive architecture of Taos Pueblo drew numerous artists from the colonies, but its inhabitants and their cultural mores proved a more appealing subject. Colony artists under the spell of antimodernism admired the various Pueblo cultures for their dissimilarity to industrial America; as William H. Truettner has argued, the Pueblo relationship to nature and their rich cultural heritage drew the praise of colony artists: "The Indian's innate ability to sense the harmony in nature, to perceive its beauty as a religious phenomenon that pervaded all phases of daily life, to dance and sing in a way that spontaneously evoked a community soul, and to create from an ancient tradition new objects of enduring artistic merit, these became virtues for which his life was celebrated."[32]

The resulting paintings often depicted the Pueblo in an ideal natural setting, free from the pressure of civilization and assimilation. Berninghaus's appropriately titled *Taos Idyll* (n.d., plate 11) situates a Taos couple within a grove, the peace of which is suggested by the autumn foliage and the quiet stream in the background. A serene harmony with the environment is expressed not only by the title, but also by the decorative flora on the woman's shawl and the brilliant fall colors of the man's blanket, both of which compare closely to their surroundings. Nothing in *Taos Idyll* implicitly suggests a spiritual engagement with nature, but the role local geography played in Puebloan religious ceremonies was of unquestionable interest to the artists. In Hennings's *Going to Blue Lake* (n.d., plate 38), a group from Taos Pueblo heads to their sacred lake for an unknown ceremony, and the elaborate brocade of trees, influenced stylistically by Hennings's exposure to Jugendstil, preserves the secrecy of the rite by creating a natural sanctuary.

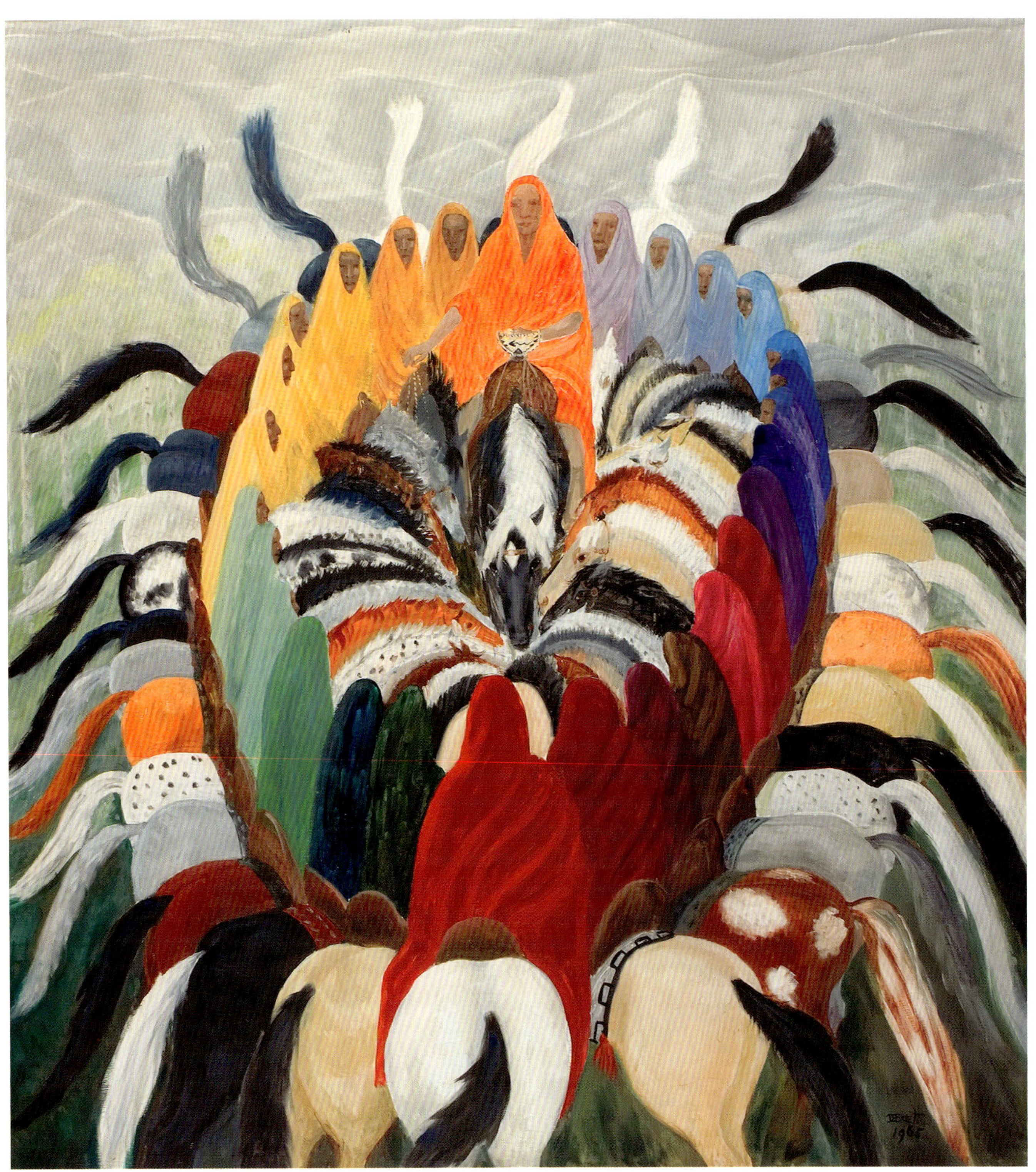

The Puebloan desire to protect the integrity of their religious rituals sometimes prevented artistic depiction. Dorothy Brett's interest in the "inner life of the Indian" and particularly the older, more obscure rituals of Taos Pueblo led her to risk "much in painting the religious ceremonials, those beautiful ritual dances that may not be photographed or drawn."[33] The elders often looked for any violation, although paintings such as *Blessing of the Mares* (1965, plate 12) were usually approved. Brett organized her prismatic depiction of the equine ritual around a uterine ovoid to signify the hope for fertility.

Fertility remains a central concern of Puebloan ceremonies, which are often meant to continue a compact with both the deities and their influence over nature. For example, dances for the deer and buffalo honor the animals that have been hunted over the past year and help to ensure future success. Said dances are open to the public, and the evocative dress and engaging ritual draw artists and tourist alike. Will Shuster likely painted *Eve of the Deer Dance* (1948, plate 45) at nearby Tesuque Pueblo on the night before the public performance, with bonfires illuminating the preamble to the dance. Only a few members of the pueblo are in attendance compared with the larger audience Leon Gaspard witnessed at the Zuni buffalo dance in 1953. Gaspard was equally drawn to the pageantry of the dance, and although he had some concern for the accuracy of details, he heightened his palette considerably, creating an ornamental pattern of blues, pinks, and greens that have their origin in East Asian silks.

Born in Russia, Gaspard had been interested in the nomadic peoples of Asia, and upon his arrival in New Mexico, he believed that Native rituals resembled "the fetes he had seen in remote Mongolia."[34] The colorful pattern he constructed in *Buffalo Dance at Zuni* (1953–1964, plate 35) is reminiscent of the floral silk robes of Mongol bandit Yang San Hungstan and his attendant in the earlier *Falconry in Central Asia* (1936, plate 13). Gaspard visited central Asia in the mid-1930s after his first visit to Mabel's home in Taos in 1918. His interest in the dress and pottery of Taos Pueblo prompted him to travel the old Silk Road.[35]

PLATE 12
Dorothy Eugenie Brett (U.S., 1883–1976)
Blessing of the Mares, 1965. Oil on canvas, 47½ × 44¾ in.
Philbrook Museum of Art
A2007.0124

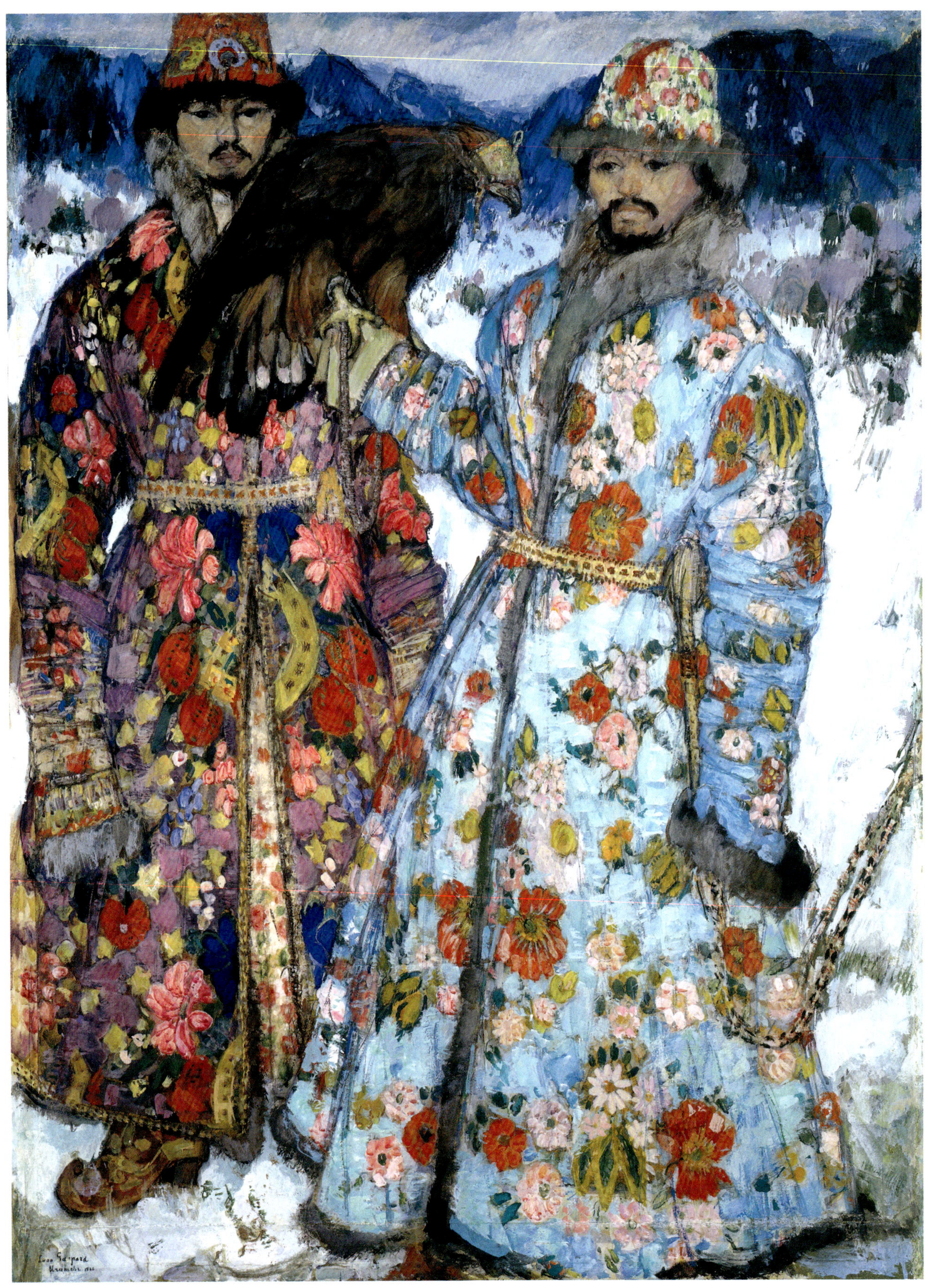

Gaspard's countryman Nicolai Fechin had a similar response to his encounter with the southwestern pueblos. Fechin found the racial diversity of the United States intriguing and sought models of various ethnicities shortly after his arrival in 1923. *Negro Girl with Orange* (c. 1923, plate 33) was the result of his early exposure to those of African descent.[36] His taste for the unfamiliar also prompted his first trip to Taos in 1927, at the invitation of Mabel Dodge Luhan, and he was drawn to the Puebloans, in whom he saw a racial similarity to the Mongols.[37] One of his first models was likely Taos Puebloan Albidia Marcus, who worked as Luhan's maid. Fechin created a formal correspondence between the angular patches of intense color found in Albidia's floral shawl and the surrounding landscape, suggesting a perceived physical and spiritual sympathy with nature (plate 3).

Both Fechin and Gaspard joined their fellow colony artists in an admiration for the Indians' spiritual engagement with nature and seemingly inherent ability to appreciate its beauty. Nature inspired dance, song, and artistic objects that appealed to the modern sensibilities of the colony artists but were inseparably linked to antique traditions. Bert Phillips explored this theme throughout his career in paintings such as *Song to the Moonbow* (n.d., plate 42). The artist had witnessed the lunar rainbow from a cave in which he had camped while on a sketching excursion, yet in his painting, he substituted a Native musician for himself to explore the spiritual potential: "Such a phenomenon produced a religious reaction in the Taos Indians, resulting in prayers that take the form of songs and other ceremonies."[38] Native creativity originates directly from nature, in Phillips's vision, "without the artifice of concert halls, conductors, or composers."[39]

Phillips and his colleagues found Native arts worthy of admiration and emulation and believed that the Pueblo must be protected from assimilation lest those traditions be lost. Sometimes this meant direct political action, and numerous artists and writers in Santa Fe and

PLATE 13
Leon Gaspard (U.S., b. Russia, 1882–1964)
Falconry in Central Asia, 1936. Oil on silk, 57½ × 42½ in.
Fred Jones Jr. Museum of Art
A2007.0001

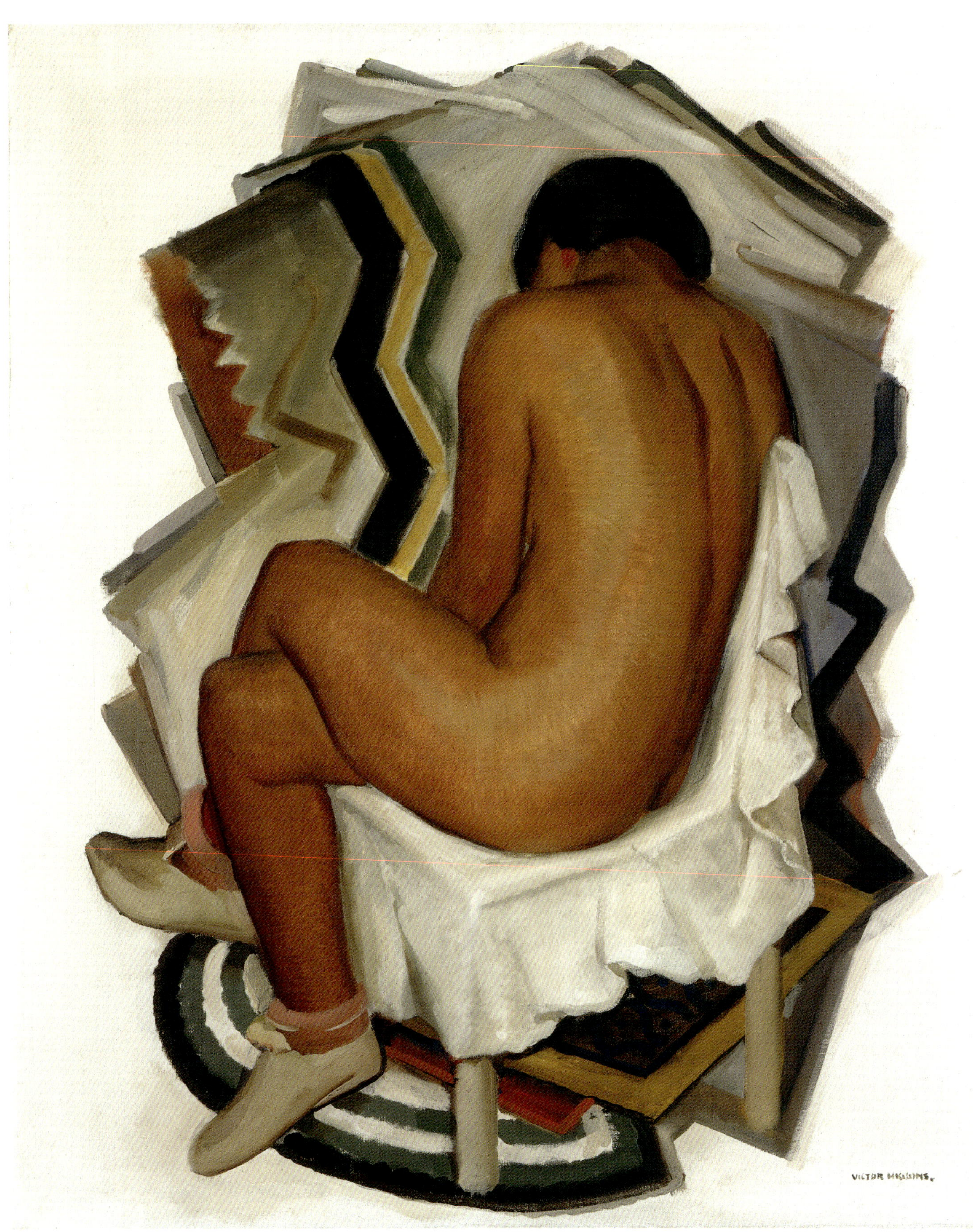
VICTOR HIGGINS.

Taos opposed the 1922 Bursum Bill, which threatened Puebloan land and water rights.[40] But often the artists employed subtler tactics. The persistence of Puebloan traditions testified to a thriving culture that deserved a place alongside that of Western civilization. Sharp's *El Greco* (n.d., plate 44) conjures the mystical imagery of the Renaissance old master to describe a Native shaman performing some rite with an eagle feather fan, pottery, and a bison skull. With a similar intent, Eanger Irving Couse foregrounded and enlarged the pots in his 1916 *Pottery Vendor* (plate 17) to emphasize their importance as fine art and to prove "the nobility of the people who created it."[41] The vendor, Jerry Mirabal of Taos Pueblo, stands stoically behind his wares, as though he is one more aesthetic object among many, but Couse's painting was interpreted in its day as a testament to the strength of the Puebloans, "who are refusing to vanish with the timorous and apathetic haste which tradition has assigned them."[42]

Pottery Vendor posits a physical and perhaps spiritual connection between the creator and his craft out of appreciation for the close relationship between Pueblo art and life. Higgins suggested a similar correlation between his model and the surrounding textiles in *Indian Composition* (c. 1937, plate 14).[43] The nudity of his model was no doubt controversial since Taos Pueblo had strict prohibitions against such posing; however, the unadorned figure likely furthered Higgins's interest in associating creativity with the Native feminine body, as though the patterned, decorative textiles originated directly from the biological pulse or procreative potential of Native women.[44]

Statements on the nobility of Pueblo art and culture offered pictorial support for its preservation and encouragement, but some artists preferred images of daily life, free of the romantic trappings found in paintings such as Sharp's *El Greco* or Phillips's *Song to the Moonbow*. Fellow TSA member Walter Ufer was often lauded for his more realistic treatment of the Pueblo: "He paints the Pueblo Indians at their daily tasks, their religious

Plate 14
Victor Higgins (U.S., 1884–1949)
Indian Composition, c. 1937. Oil on canvas, 38 × 32 in.
Fred Jones Jr. Museum of Art
A2007.0130

ceremonies, recreations and in every natural undertaking that marks their lives."[45] *Going East* (1917, plate 46) depicts a caravan led by Ufer's favorite model, Jim Abbott, heading toward some uncertain location on unknown business. Ufer avoids narrative or commentary, yet he also avoids some of the stark realities of modern life, especially the consequences of assimilation. Theodore van Soelen, by comparison, confronted the issue in *Early Americans* (c. 1963, plate 15). Although his title suggests a depiction of precontact civilization, van Soelen created an image of men waiting idly in front of a dilapidated trading post with a bent, rusted advertisement for Pepsi-Cola, signifying the presence of American commerce. They seem to lack purpose in this new, modern world. Van Soelen shies away from decrying the intrusion of American commerce in the Southwest, but *Early Americans* implies that little good has come from modernization.

As modernization crept into the Southwest around midcentury, it became increasingly difficult for colony artists like van Soelen to ignore the trappings of the urban, commercial, and industrial. This is particularly apparent in Victor Higgins's *New Mexico Landscape Through Auto Window* (plate 40), painted in the mid-1930s from behind the steering wheel of his car.[46] Automobiles were no rarity in the Southwest, except in the work of the colony artists, so Higgins's recognition of the machine and its role in the creation of this painting is strikingly modern, especially when compared with the preindustrial transportation found in LaVerne Nelson Black's *Mexican in Wagon* (n.d., plate 22), painted no more than a decade before Higgins's watercolor. Black, like so many of his fellow colony artists, came from the urbanized East and deliberately sought the archaic in northern New Mexican culture.

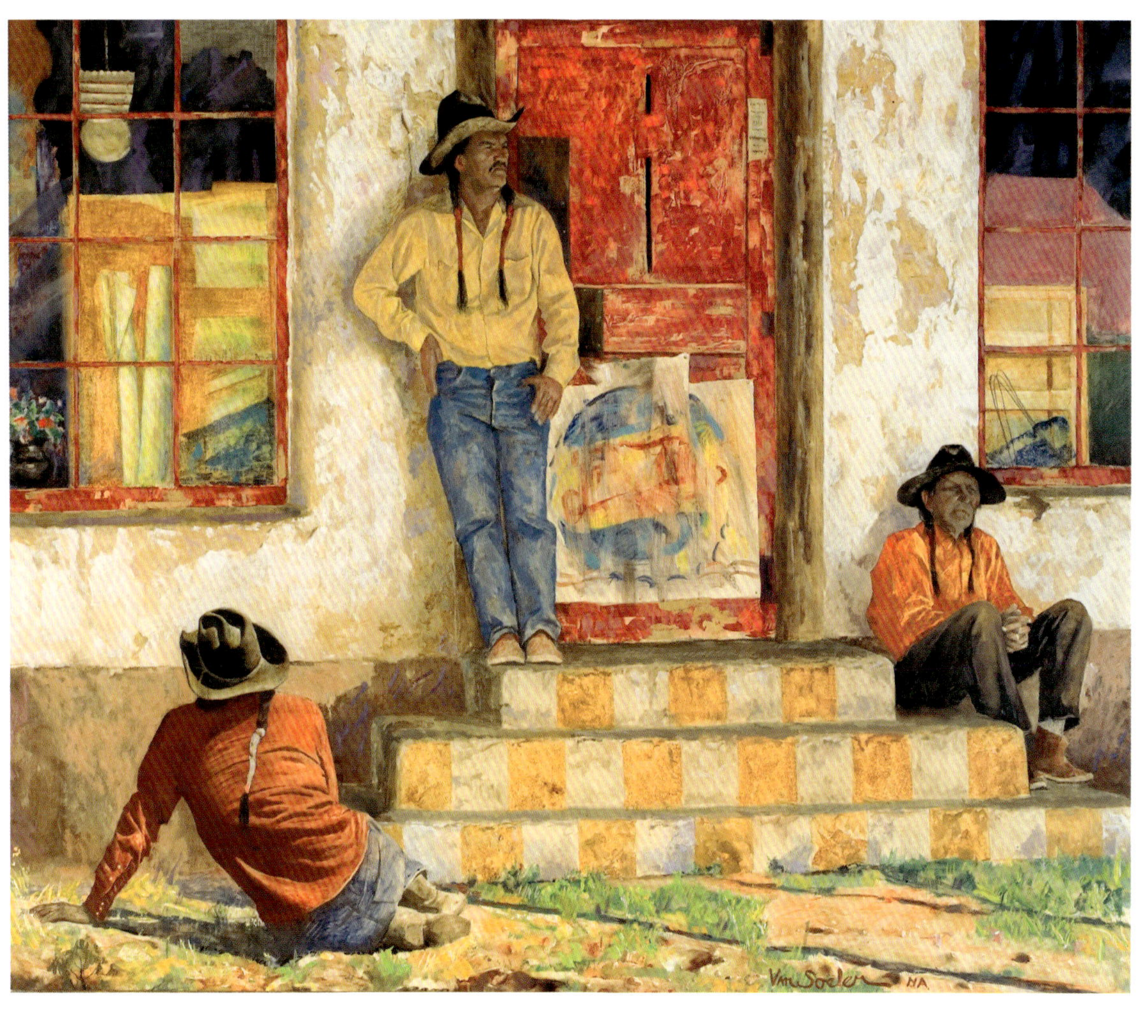

Plate 15
Theodore Van Soelen (U.S., 1890–1964)
Early Americans, c. 1963. Oil over tempera on board, 30 × 36 in.
Fred Jones Jr. Museum of Art
A2007.0029

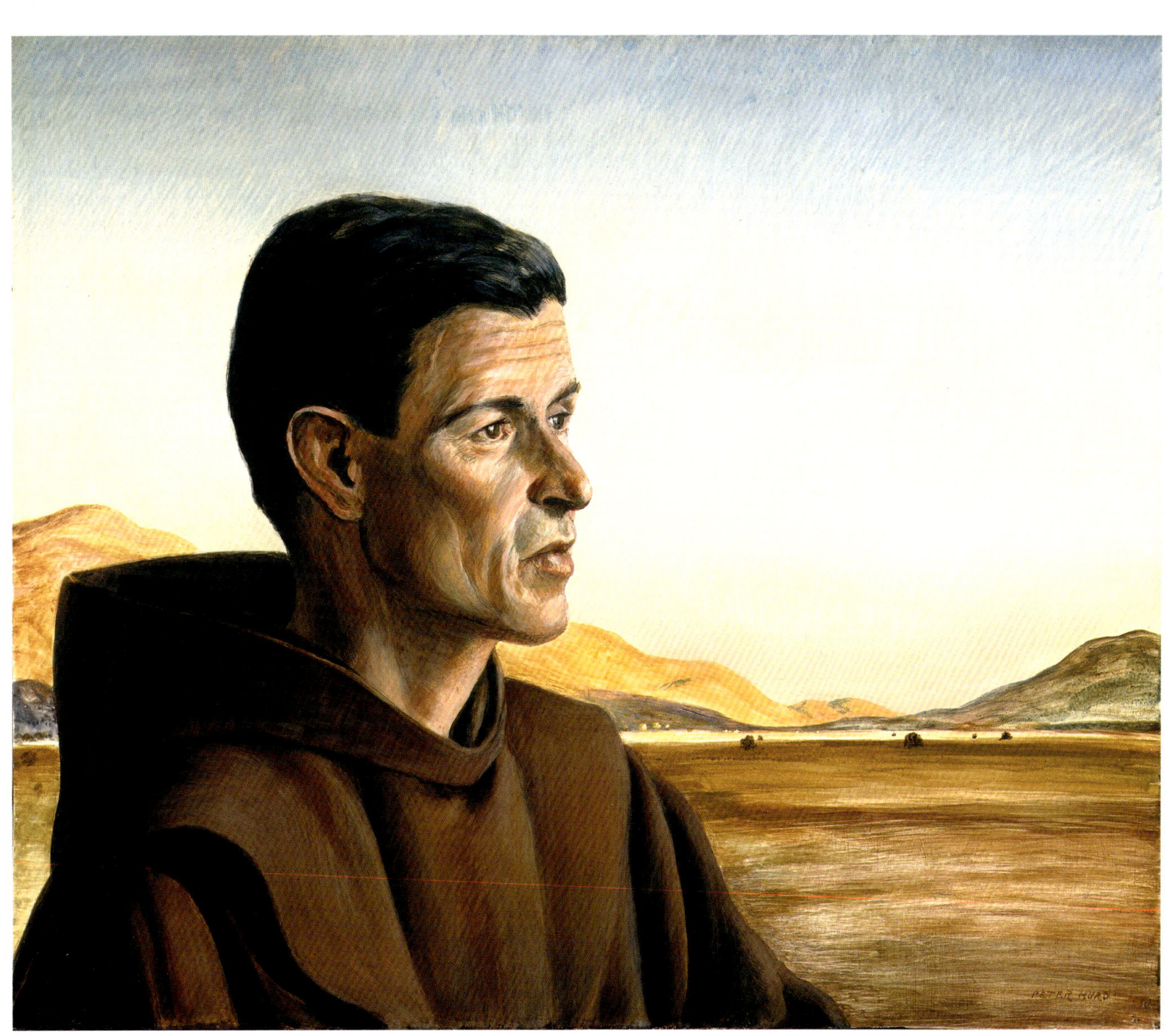

Plate 16
Peter Hurd (U.S., 1904–1984)
Fray Angélico Chávez, 1956. Tempera on board, 20½ × 24¼ in.
Fred Jones Jr. Museum of Art
A2007.0138

The dramatic changes at midcentury must have been particularly apparent to writer Fray Angélico Chávez. Born Manuel Ezequiel, Chávez studied art initially, which earned him the name Angélico, after the Florentine Renaissance painter Fra Angelico. His important accomplishments came as a clergyman and writer, especially in his examination of the colonial past of New Mexico. As the legacy of that history became increasingly remote, Chávez undertook a close study of colonial documents and wrote seminal books on the Spanish history of New Mexico and the Puebloan Revolt of 1680. Chávez's celebrity attracted the attention of New Mexican artist Peter Hurd, a native of Roswell, who had already produced numerous portraits of local ranchers and personalities. Hurd depicts Chávez in his Franciscan habit against the New Mexican desert as if to link him with his past brethren, who introduced Christianity to the region centuries earlier (plate 16).

Chávez's importance as a historian merited his posthumous inclusion in the book *Turn Left at the Sleeping Dog: Scripting the Santa Fe Legend, 1920–1955*, a collection of essays by long-time Santa Fe residents on the city's past and present. Several of the commentators bemoaned the changes that had occurred after World War II. The war had led to the creation of the Manhattan Project and the establishment of Los Alamos, both of which altered the character of New Mexico. Joseph Traugott has argued that "the arrival of the Atomic Age signaled the end of the Southwest's cultural and technological isolation, the seclusion that had powered the tourist economy for sixty years."[47] Industry, commerce, and especially tourism grew increasingly during and after the war years. Developers from outside the state began to change its physical character, according to postwar artist Jerry West, and commercial amenities that had once been rare appeared to add to the appeal "*for* other outsiders."[48] The Southwest as a whole no longer offered the respite from American progress that had attracted the colony artists of the first half of the century. Although Charles Lummis had once declared New Mexico "the United States which is *not* the United States," writer Richard Bradford stated in 2001, as if responding to Lummis, that "New Mexico is now part of the United States."

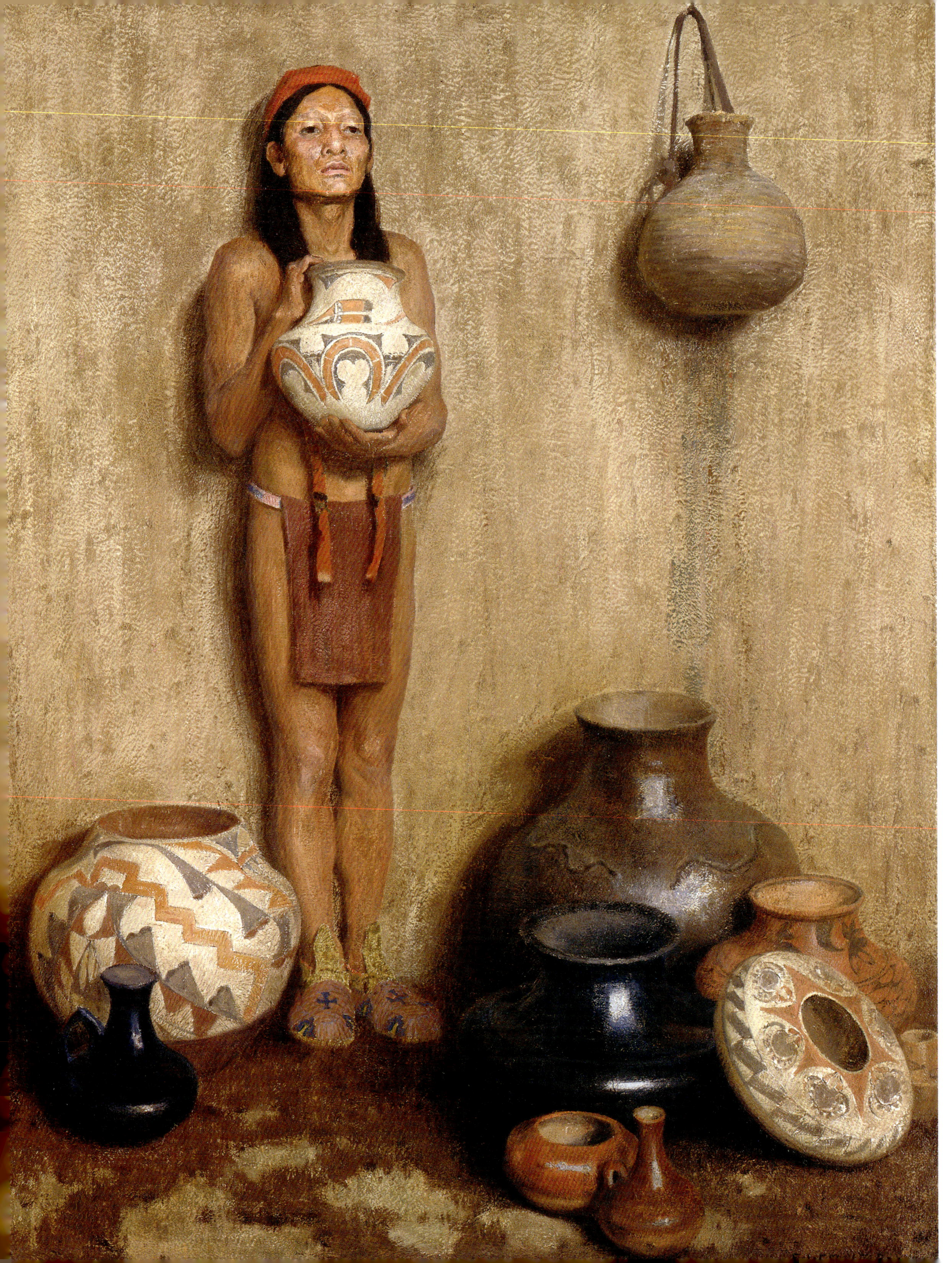

The Character of a Collection

Eugene B. Adkins and the Art of the American West

James Peck

Chapter Two

Eugene Adkins first traveled to the desert Southwest from Oklahoma as a boy. These trips spurred a lifelong love for the American West, a love that ultimately manifested itself through his art collection. About one-quarter of the Adkins Collection falls under the broad rubric "art of the American West," yet it is hard to overstate the importance of western art in the development of Eugene Adkins as a collector. Adkins started collecting art of the American West in the early 1960s, and by the early 1970s, his collecting prowess and astute eye for quality and value earned him a reputation as an expert on western art. In the thirty-plus years that ensued, Adkins amassed one of the most important collections of western art ever assembled, including major works by almost every artist of significance who painted or sculpted the land and the people of the American West.

Adkins's collection was never static; he bought and sold hundreds of paintings during his career as a collector. Today, the Adkins western art collection consists of about seven hundred two-dimensional works of art—watercolors, prints, photographs, acrylic and oil paintings, charcoal, crayon, and pencil drawings—and about seventy (mostly bronze) sculptures. Adkins collected historically famous artists such as Alfred Jacob Miller, Ernest Blumenschein, and Maynard Dixon as well as immensely talented but less well-known artists, both living and historical, such as Henry Balink, Gustave Baumann, and Edward Borein. When considered as a whole, his collection is an impressive survey of both the art of the American West and collecting tastes in the mid- to late twentieth century.

Plate 17
Eanger Irving Couse (U.S., 1866–1936)
Pottery Vendor, 1916. Oil on canvas, 45½ × 34½ in.
Philbrook Museum of Art
A2007.0193

Adkins had a taste for quality, value, and diversity of subjects and artists. To this end, the wide range of artwork he collected included Indian subjects, portraits, landscapes, still lifes, and scenes of western life created by more than 150 different artists. Such diversity of artists and media is unusual among collectors and illustrates Adkins's voracious and all-encompassing passion for western art. Notwithstanding this ecumenical approach, the collection centers on art produced in and about the desert Southwest, particularly Taos and Santa Fe, New Mexico.

Seen from a distance, certain concentrations stand out within the collection. For example, Adkins acquired twenty oils, pastels, and pencil drawings by Leon Gaspard with a single purchase in 1967.[1] The twenty-eight works by another Russian expatriate painting in the American Southwest, Nicolai Fechin, make up four percent of Adkins's western works. Such concentrations of art by two expatriate Russians may strike the contemporary viewer as somewhat odd; however, critics, galleries, museums, and the public held Gaspard and Fechin in high esteem in the 1960s and 1970s. In each of these instances, Adkins's purchases were so large that he was able to influence taste rather than respond to the trends of the day.

Although Adkins pursued all sizes, shapes, and media in his collecting, he had a special place in his heart for the Taos Society of Artists (TSA). The Adkins archive is filled with countless letters, catalogues, and photographs that attest to his pursuit of these old masters of the sagebrush. Many of the more than one hundred framed photographs of artists collected by Adkins over forty years feature TSA members. Over time, he purchased significant works of art by each of the seven principal members: Oscar Berninghaus, Ernest L. Blumenschein, Eanger Irving Couse, W. Herbert Dunton, Bert G. Phillips, Joseph Henry Sharp, and Walter Ufer. Many of these pieces have become icons of the collection, and each tells a different story about Adkins the collector. For example, Adkins purchased *Pottery*

Plate 18
Joseph Henry Sharp (U.S., 1859–1953)
A Million Aspen Leaves, n.d. Oil on canvas, 40 × 48 in.
Fred Jones Jr. Museum of Art
A2007.0013

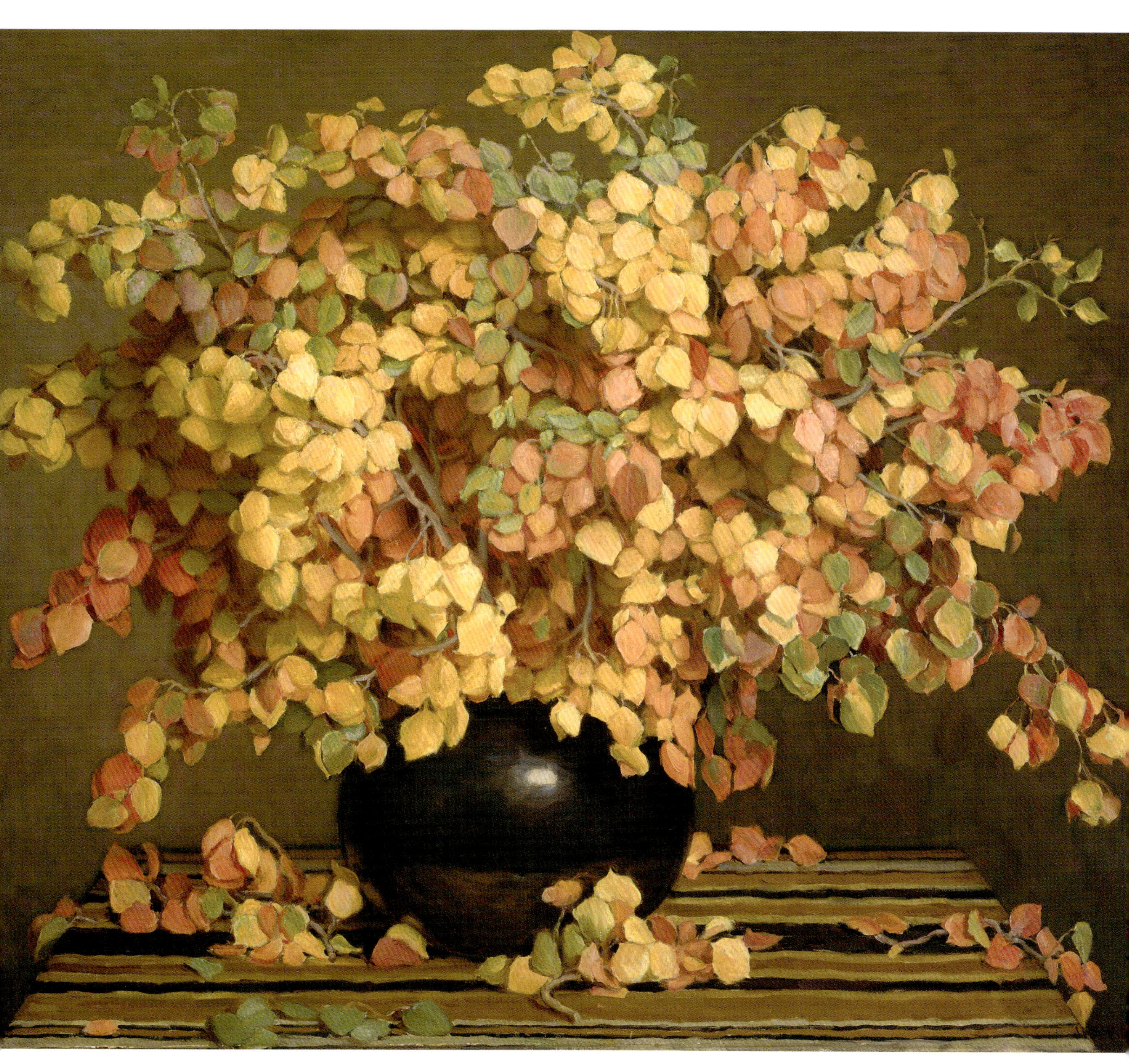

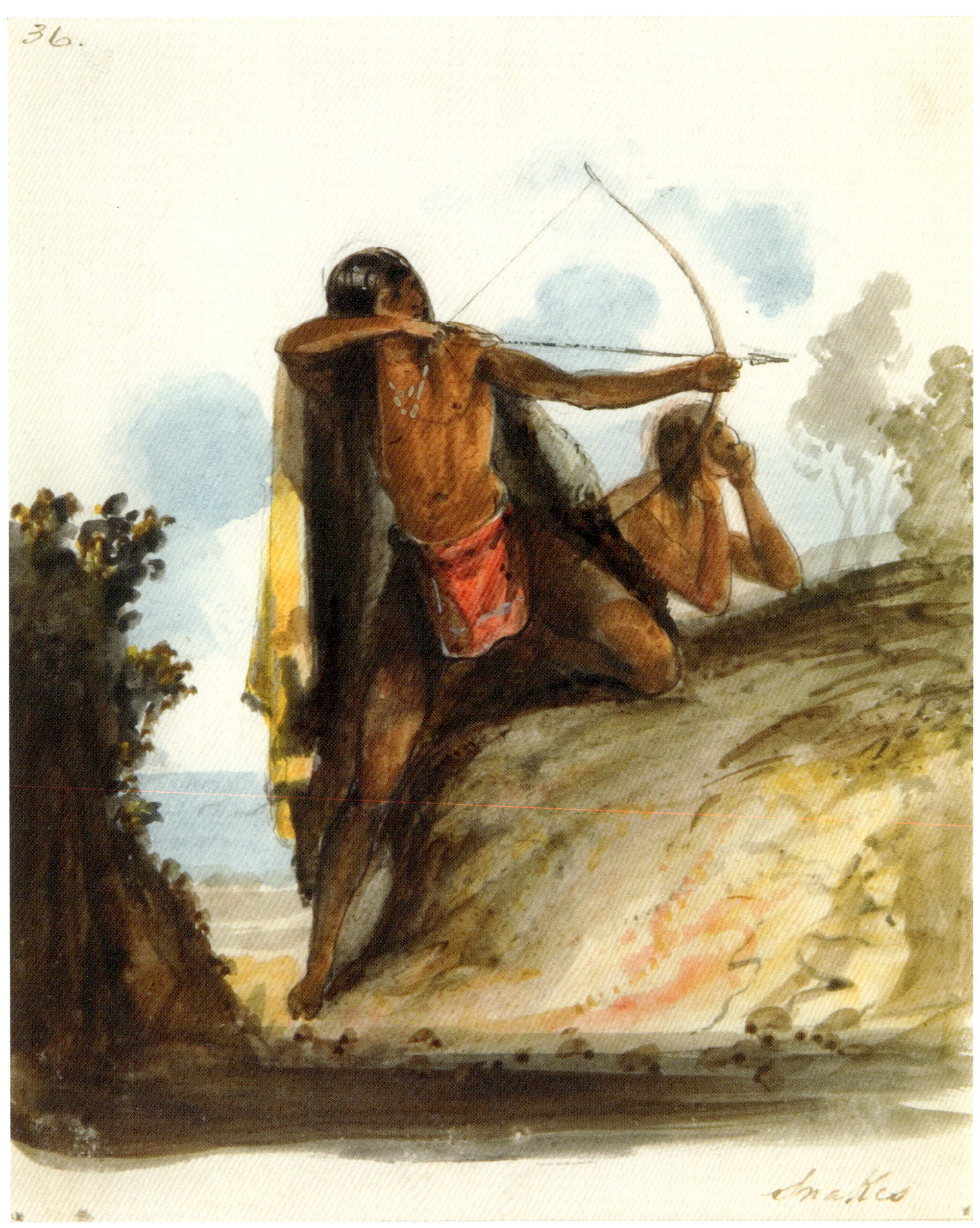
36.
Snakes

Vendor (1916, plate 17), by TSA member Eanger Irving Couse, during his second full season of collecting in 1964. Kibby Couse, the artist's son, initially refused to sell *Pottery Vendor* to Adkins because he felt the price offered by Adkins was too low for such a fine painting. After further negotiations, the two parties came to terms for $25,000, and Kibby sold Adkins two more paintings in the process—another Couse, *Shooting Fish* (c. 1920–1922, later sold), and *A Million Aspen Leaves* (n.d., plate 18), by another TSA member, Joseph Henry Sharp.[2]

Many of the works by TSA members form the core of Adkins's premier paintings collection, a subcategory consisting of the finest paintings by many of the most accomplished artists of the American West. These include the aforementioned *Pottery Vendor* and *A Million Aspen Leaves* as well as *Taos Idyll* (n.d.), by Oscar Berninghaus; *Rio Grande Gorge Near Taos* (1944–1949, plate 24), by Ernest L. Blumenschein; *The Mail Coach*, by W. Herbert Dunton; *Song to the Moonbow* (n.d., plate 42), by Bert G. Phillips; and *Going East* (1917, plate 46), by Walter Ufer. The who's who of iconic names does not end with TSA artists, however. Among the scores of famous names in the collection are first-rate works by Maynard Dixon, famous for his semiabstract Arizona cloudscapes, as well as a suite of fourteen watercolor paintings by Alfred Jacob Miller. The delicate Miller paintings, such as *Snakes* (plate 19), detail the artist's 1837 westward journey to the Wind River Mountains near the present-day Idaho-Wyoming border with his patron, the Scottish nobleman Sir William Drummond Stewart.

Adkins's passion for collecting did not end with galleries; he purchased a significant portion by corresponding directly with several artists. He even approached individual owners directly. For example, Adkins almost certainly purchased Walter Ufer's massive *Going East* (1917), perhaps that artist's single finest work from his best period, directly from a private

Plate 19
Alfred Jacob Miller (U.S., 1810–1874)
Snakes, n.d. Watercolor on paper, 6 × 5 in.
Fred Jones Jr. Museum of Art
A2007.0310

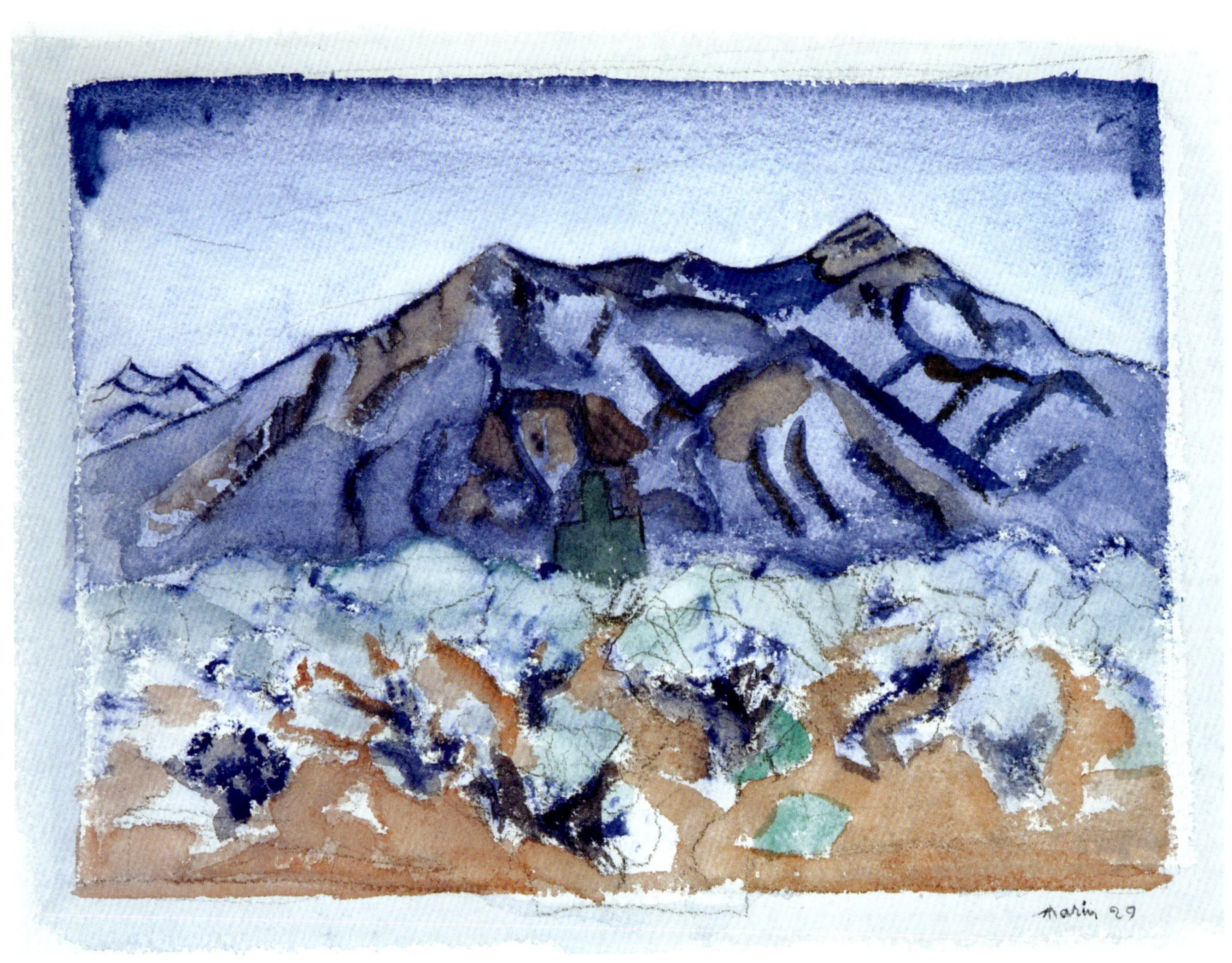

Plate 20
John Marin (U.S., 1870–1953)
Taos, 1929. Watercolor and charcoal on paper, 16 × 20 in.

Fred Jones Jr. Museum of Art
A2007.0145

owner. When Adkins saw the painting in person at a retrospective exhibition in Phoenix in 1970, it was the property of John Connally, the former governor of Texas, forever linked to the John F. Kennedy assassination. Six months after Adkins saw the painting, he owned it. Whether or not he worked through an intermediary, Adkins's passion could become all consuming once he had his heart set on a work of art.

Although most of Adkins's western art collection derives from the realist tradition, he did collect significant modernist works as well. For example, in 1984 Adkins purchased the watercolor *Taos* (1929, plate 20), by John Marin, a modernist painter with connections to Alfred Stieglitz.[3] Marin's abstraction, progressive yet firmly based in the observed world, proved to be a good fit for Adkins, who likewise was progressive in his collecting strategy yet firmly rooted in traditional realism. Other examples of Adkins's keen eye for modernist art include several outstanding oils, pastels, and watercolors by the Santa Fe artist William Penhallow Henderson. Adkins also collected important works by Andrew Dasburg, the leader of the modernists in New Mexico for sixty years, and three stunning, singular oil on glass paintings by Rebecca Salsbury Strand, first wife of noted modernist photographer Paul Strand.

Although photography was not Adkins's collecting focus, he nevertheless amassed over one hundred photographs by three relatively famous photographers and one not-so-famous portrait painter. This collection includes twenty-four photogravures from the *North American Indian* by Edward Curtis, fifty-six gelatin silver prints by Laura Gilpin of the western landscape and Indian subjects, five photographs of the American West by William Clift, and a varied assortment of twenty-nine photographs by John Young-Hunter, a successful British portrait painter who relocated to Taos part time in 1917.

The Adkins sculpture collection is, overall, a relatively small, quiet, and conservative grouping when compared with the two-dimensional art. It consists almost exclusively of domestic-sized bronze casts of familiar western and American Indian subjects by well-established western artists such as Ernest Berke, Joe Neil Beeler, George Carlson, James Earle Fraser, Henry Jackson, Carl Kauba, and Emry Kopta. Of note are seven characteristic pieces by the cowboy artist Charles M. Russell; two small heads by Frederic Remington, *The Sergeant* (1905) and *The Savage* (1905); and five expressionistic examples of sculpture by Nicolai Fechin. Adkins also secured a fine and representative collection of eighteen bronzes by George Carlson, a much-heralded, academically trained artist who has won the Prix de West and numerous gold medals from the National Academy of Western Art.

Today, almost fifty years after Eugene Adkins purchased his first work of western art, we can discern the character of his collection. Studded with masterworks by some of the most sought-after artists of the past two centuries, Adkins nonetheless took the long view when amassing his impressive collection. He was a voracious collector yet was prescient enough to pursue specific works that had eluded him—even, on occasion, buying directly from other collectors. He liked big, colorful, sun-infused paintings by members of the famous TSA, yet he also collected small, delicate charcoal studies and watercolors by lesser-known hands. He preferred paintings and drawings yet made significant purchases in both photography and sculpture. He was a traditionalist who nevertheless eagerly sought out modernist works. In the end, the character of Eugene Adkins's collection reflects the maturation of his boyhood love of the desert Southwest, a love that blossomed into a superb, nearly encyclopedic collection of art from and about the American West.

DETAIL OF PLATE 36 (p. 71)
Leon Gaspard (U.S., b. Russia, 1882–1964)
Taos Pueblo Indian Group, 1918

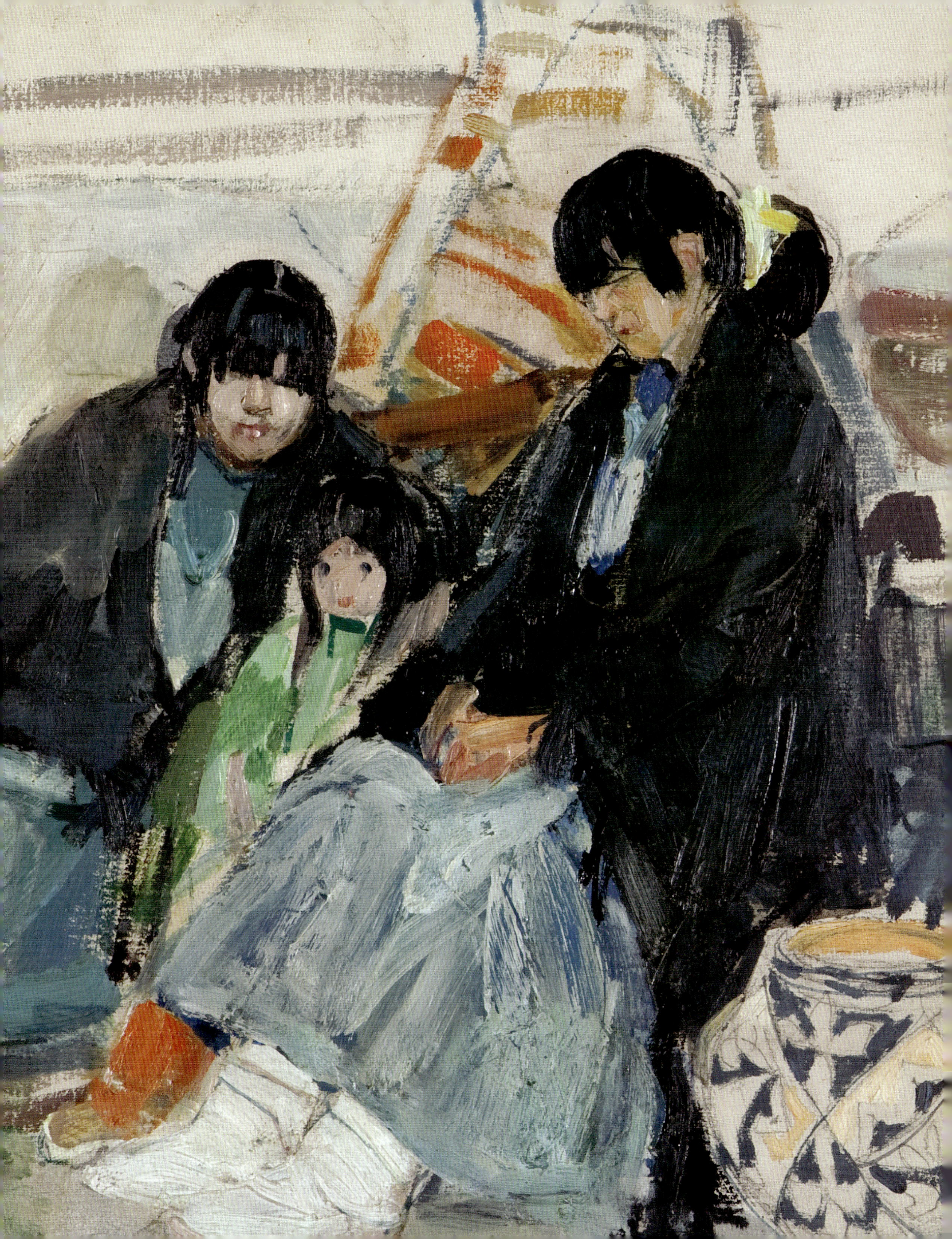

Plates 21–48

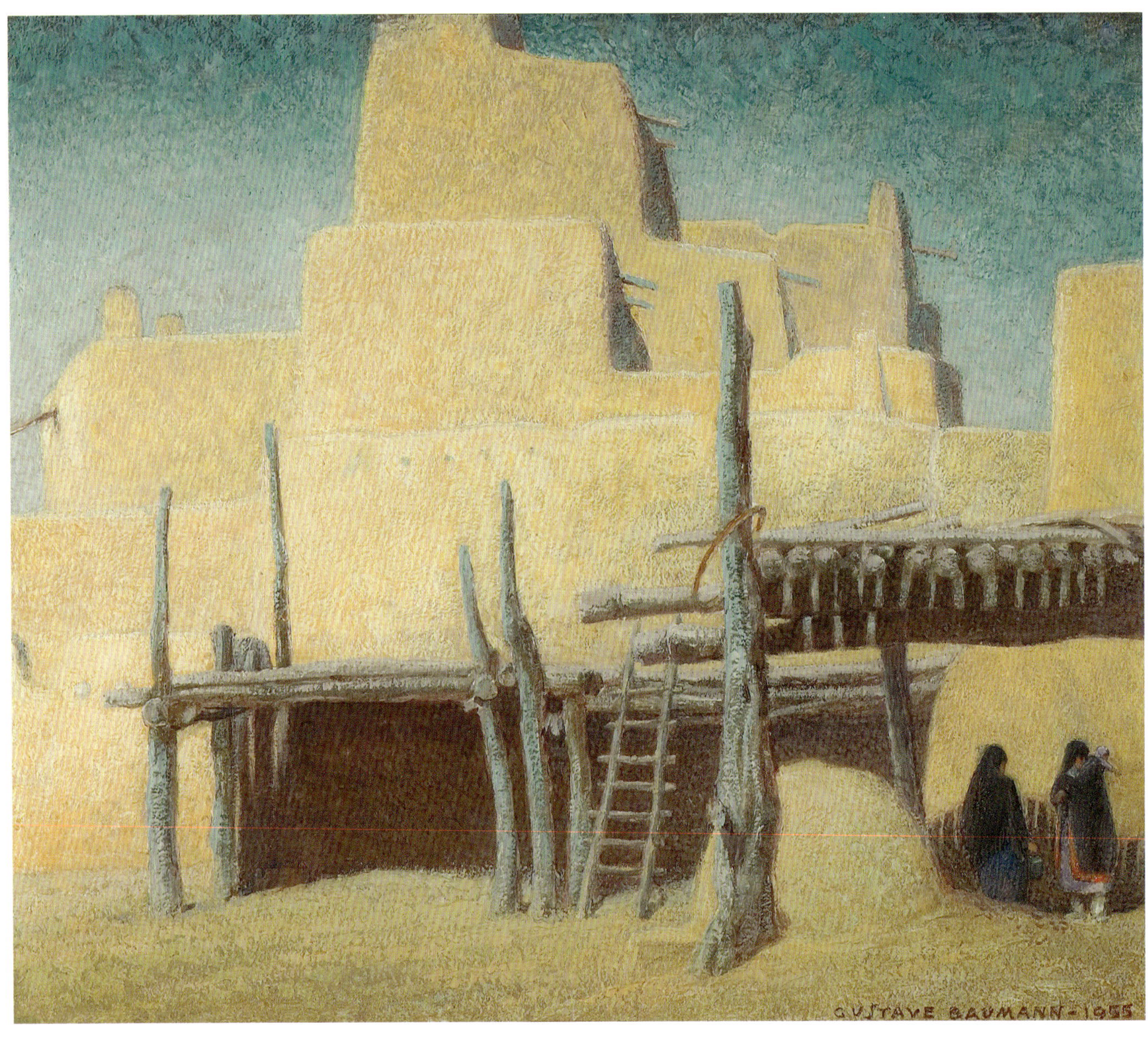

Plate 21
Gustave Baumann (U.S. 1881–1971)
Taos Pueblo, 1955. Oil on board, 21¾ × 25⅜ in.
Courtesy of Ann Baumann
Fred Jones Jr. Museum of Art
A2007.0199

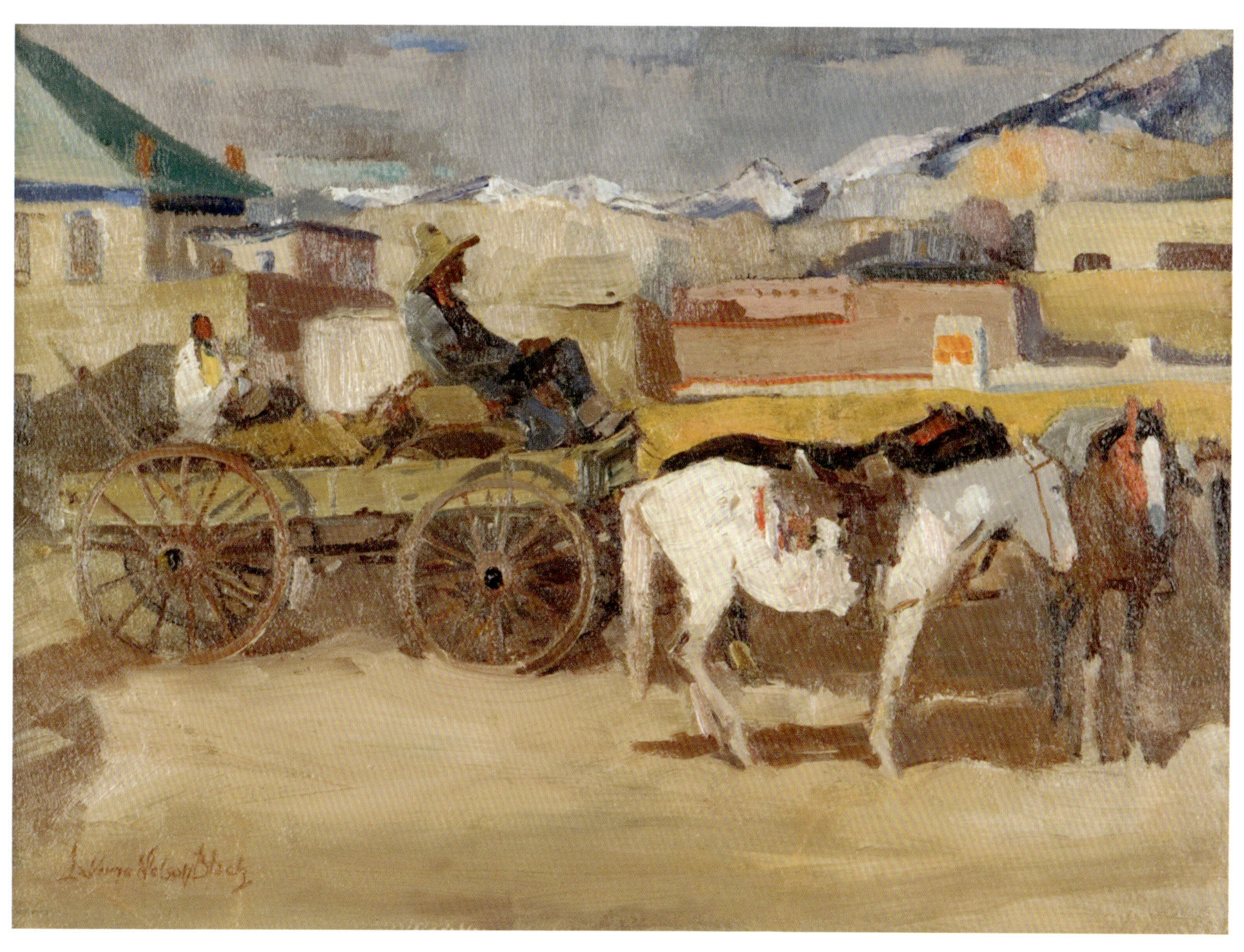

PLATE 22
LaVerne Nelson Black (U.S. 1887–1959)
Mexican in Wagon, n.d. Oil on board, 15 × 21 in.
Fred Jones Jr. Museum of Art
A2007.0160

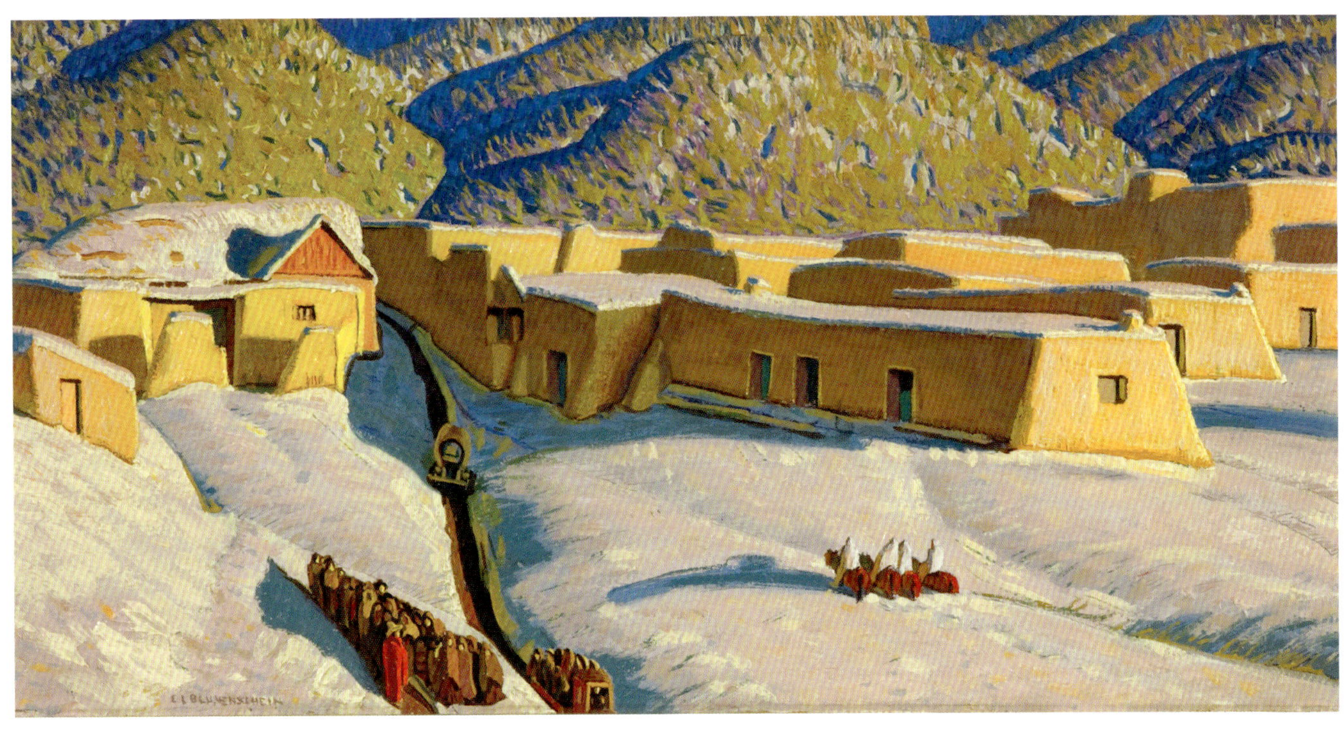

PLATE 23
Ernest L. Blumenschein (U.S. 1874–1960)
Village, Northern New Mexico, c. 1929
Oil on canvas board, 13⅝ × 23 in.
© Courtesy of the Blumenschein Estate
Fred Jones Jr. Museum of Art
A2007.0041

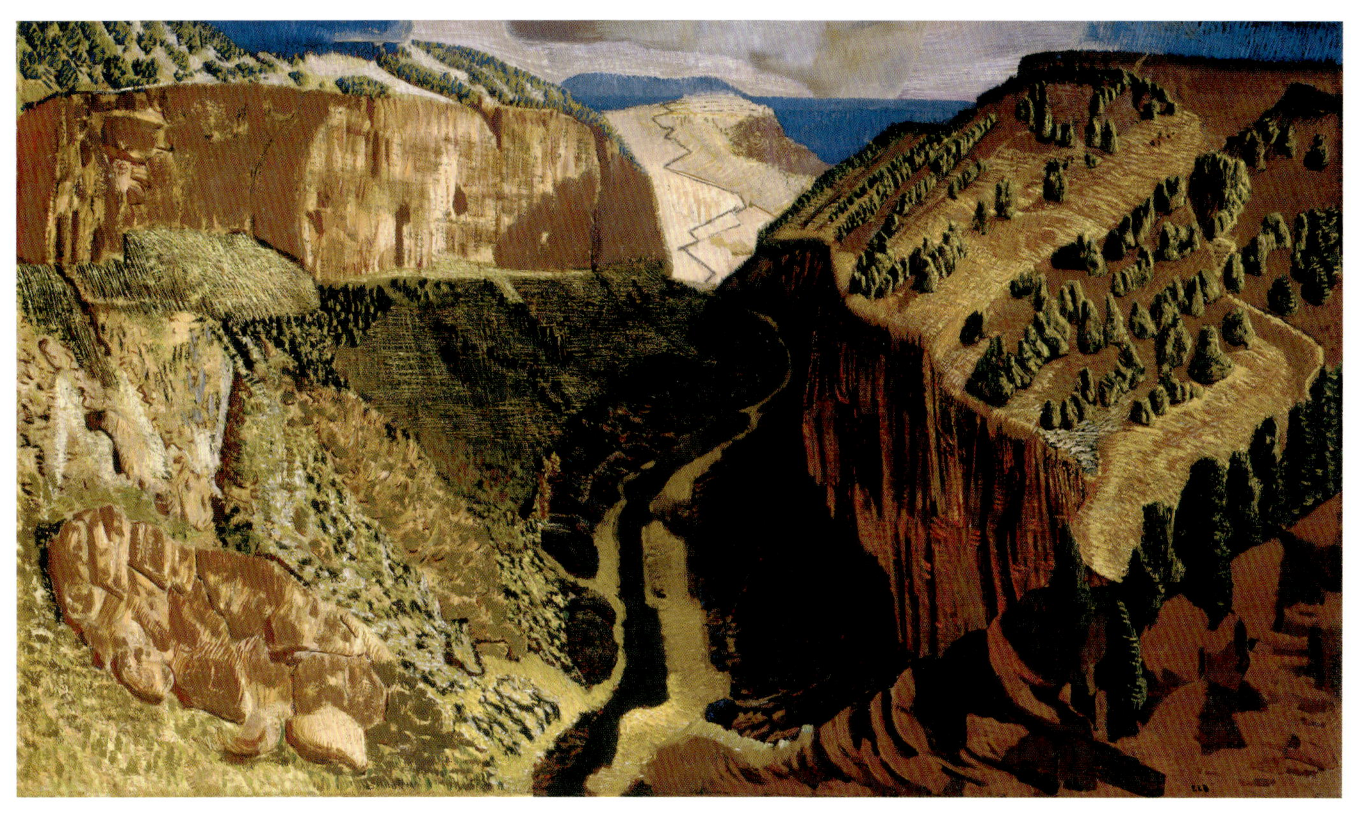

Plate 24
Ernest L. Blumenschein (U.S. 1874–1960)
Rio Grande Gorge Near Taos (Strength of the Earth), 1944–1949
Oil on canvas, 27 × 47 in.
© Courtesy of the Blumenschein Estate
Fred Jones Jr. Museum of Art
A2007.0009

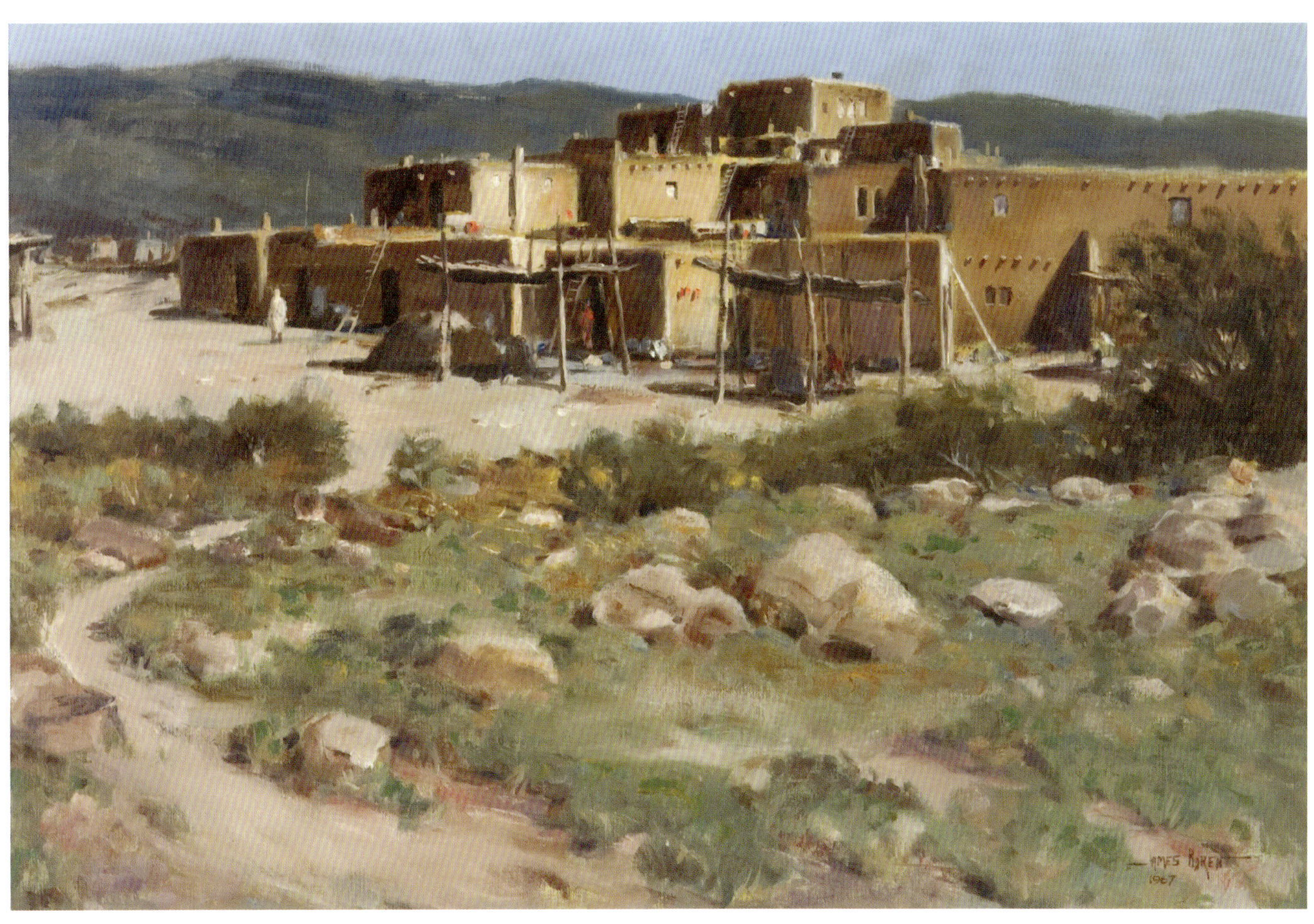

Plate 25
James Erwin Boren (U.S. 1921–1990)
Taos Pueblo, 1967. Oil on canvas, 20 × 30 in.
Fred Jones Jr. Museum of Art
A2007.0209

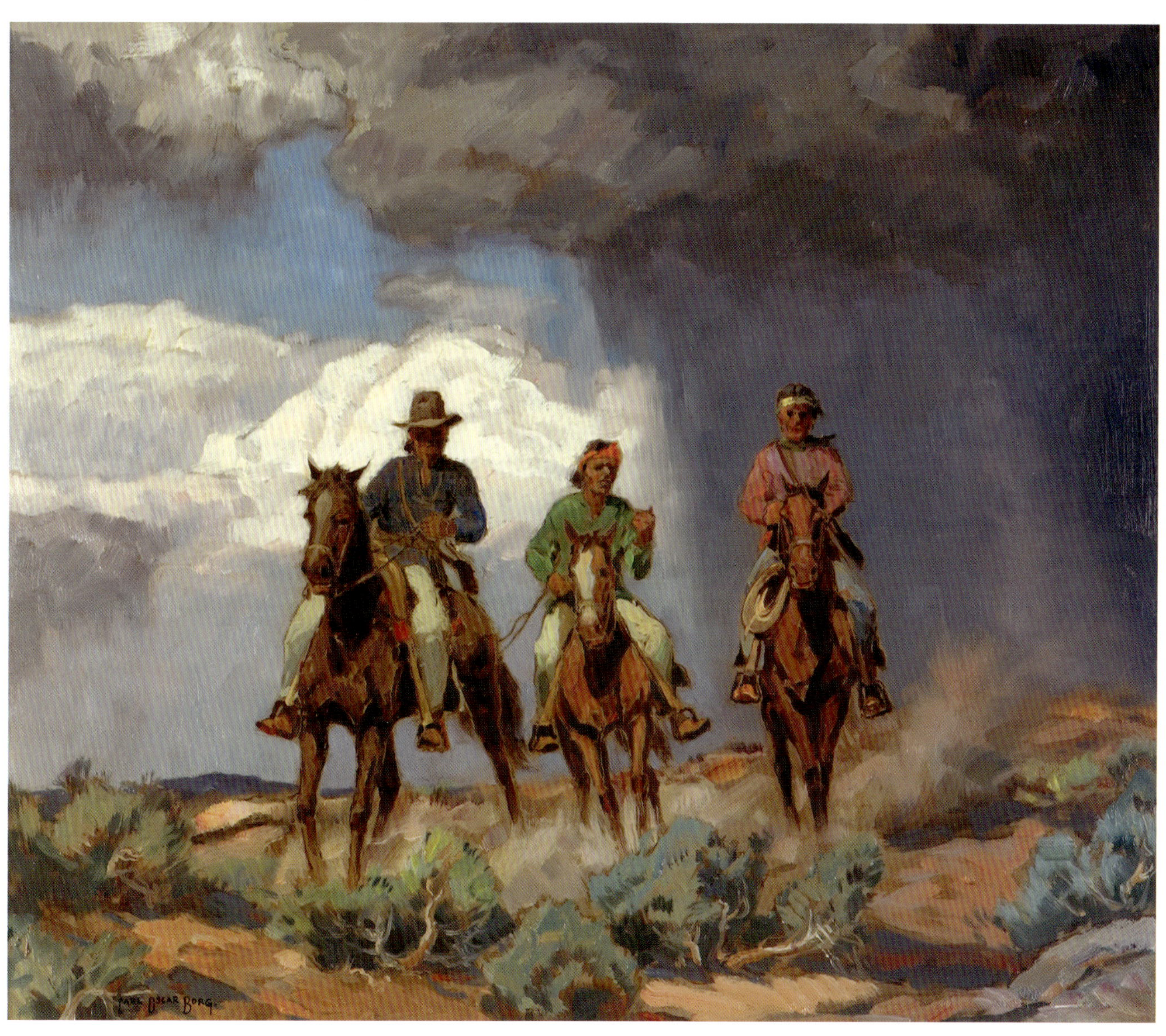

PLATE 26
Carl Oscar Borg (U.S., 1879–1947)
Untitled, n.d. Oil on board, 20 × 24 in.
Fred Jones Jr. Museum of Art
A2007.0113

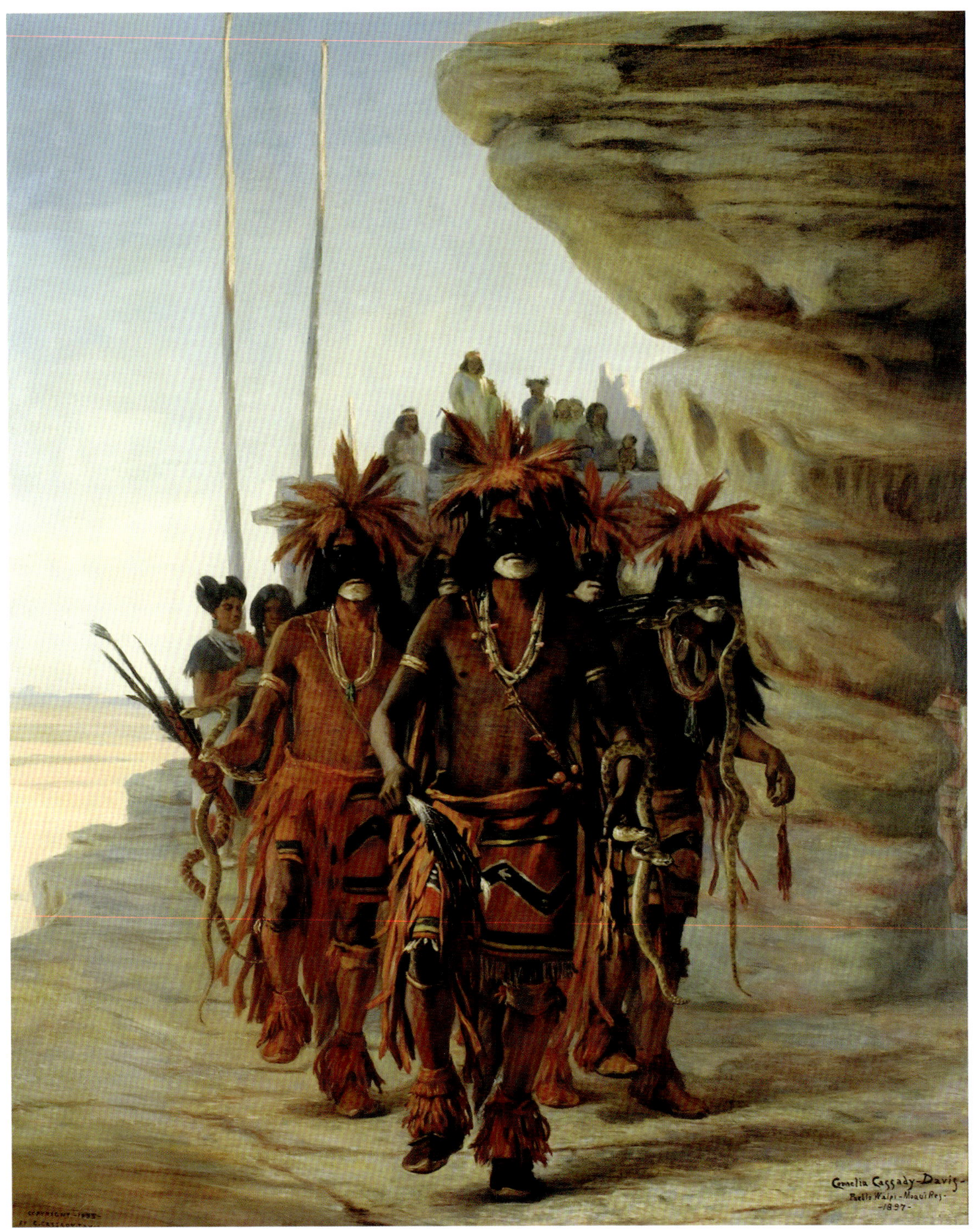

PLATE 27
Cornelia Cassady-Davis (U.S., 1870–1920)
Hopi Snake Dance, 1897. Oil on canvas, 60 × 48 in.
Fred Jones Jr. Museum of Art
A2007.0025

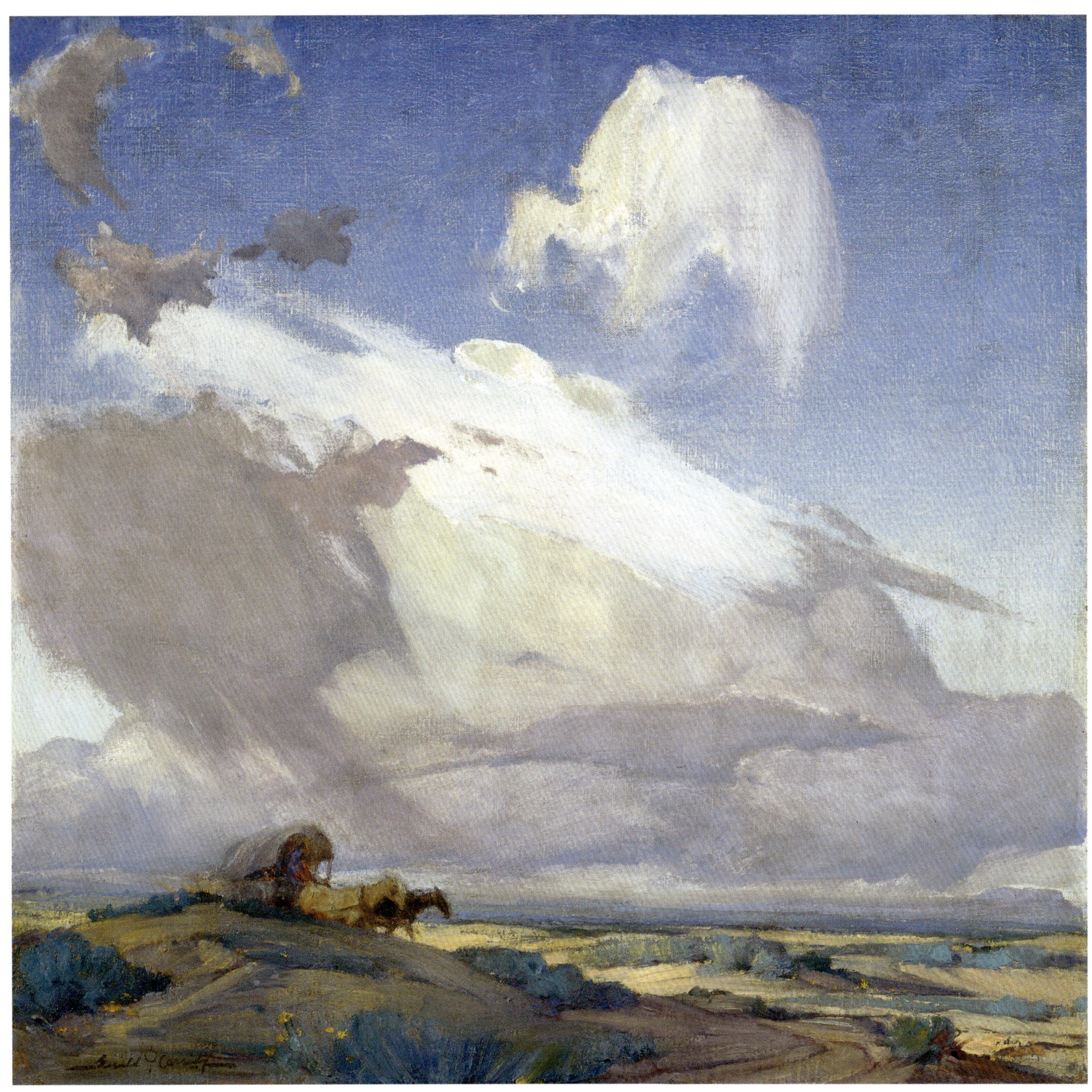

PLATE 28
Gerald Cassidy (U.S., 1879–1934)
Road in the Desert, n.d. Oil on canvas, 28 × 30 in.
Fred Jones Jr. Museum of Art
A2007.0019

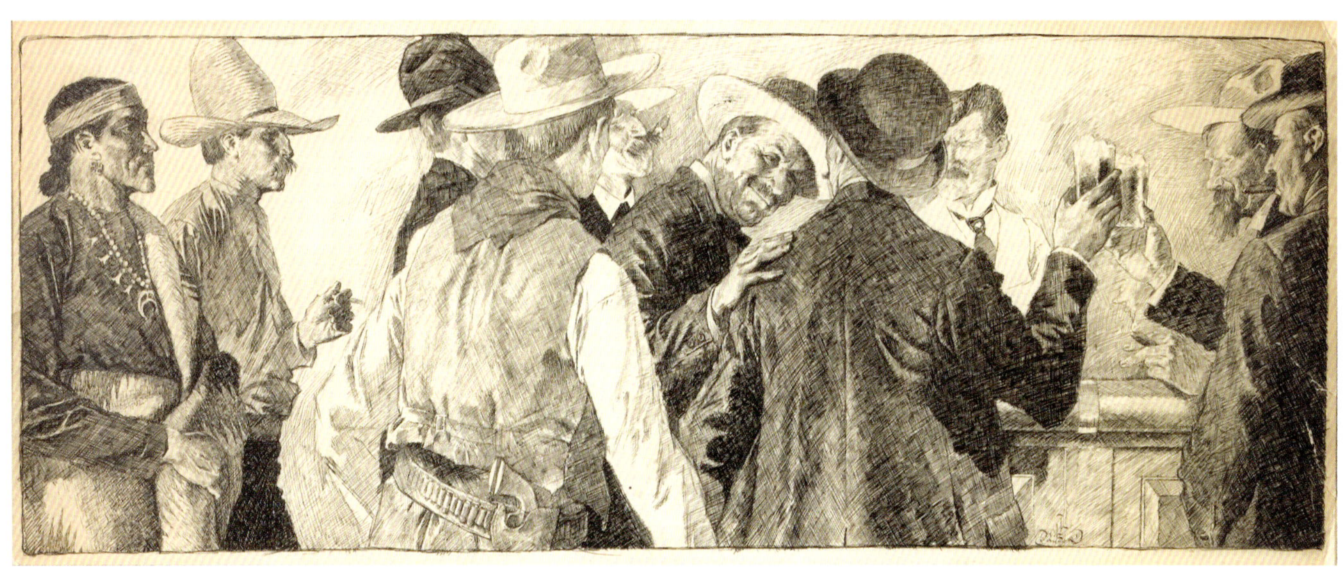

PLATE 29
Will Crawford (U.S., 1869–1944)
Belly Up to the Bar Boys, n.d. Pen and ink on paper, 9 × 22½ in.
Fred Jones Jr. Museum of Art
A2007.0279

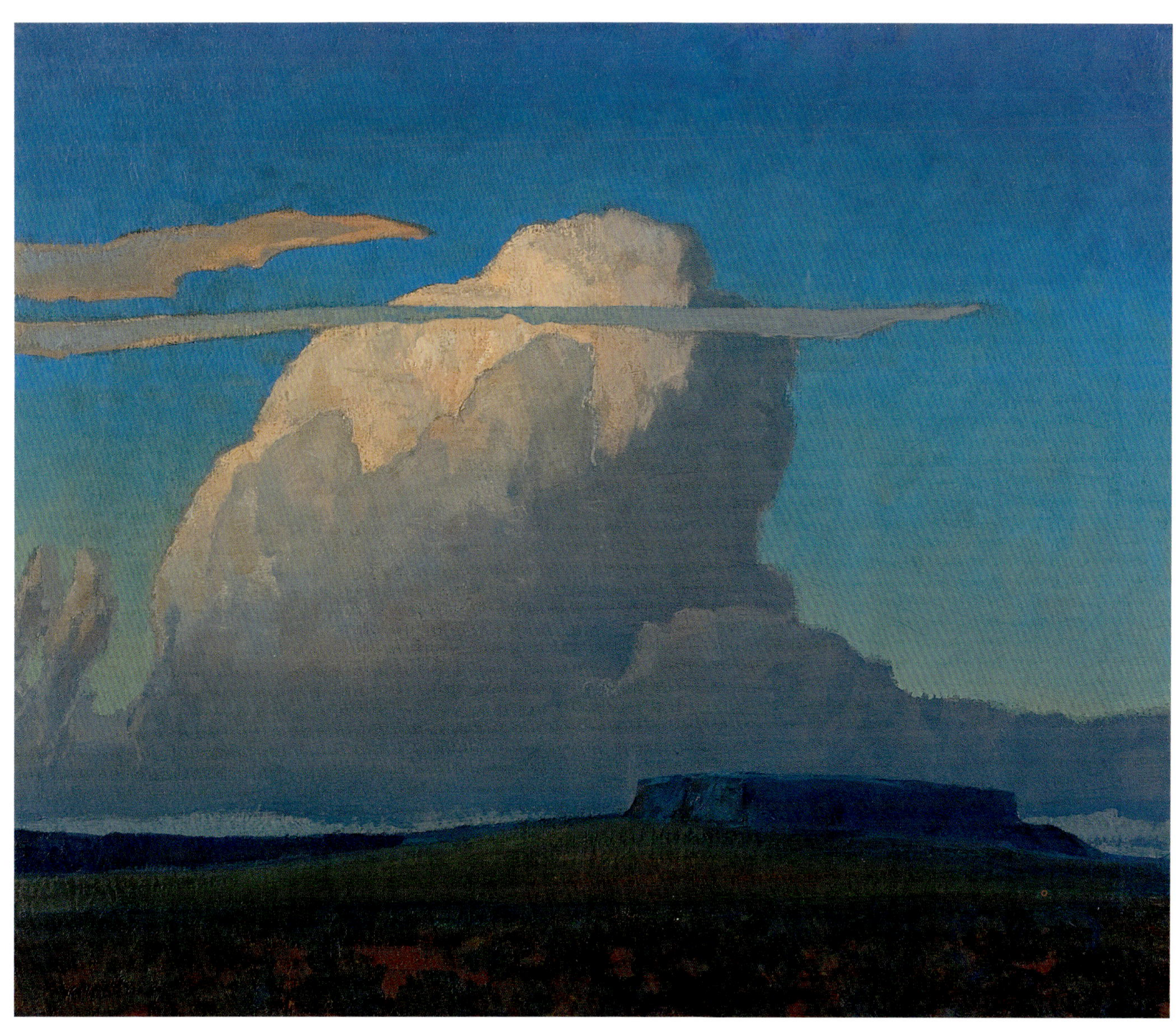

Plate 30
Maynard Dixon (U.S., 1875–1946)
Evening and Afterthought, 1924. Oil on board, 25 × 30 in.
Fred Jones Jr. Museum of Art
A2007.0139

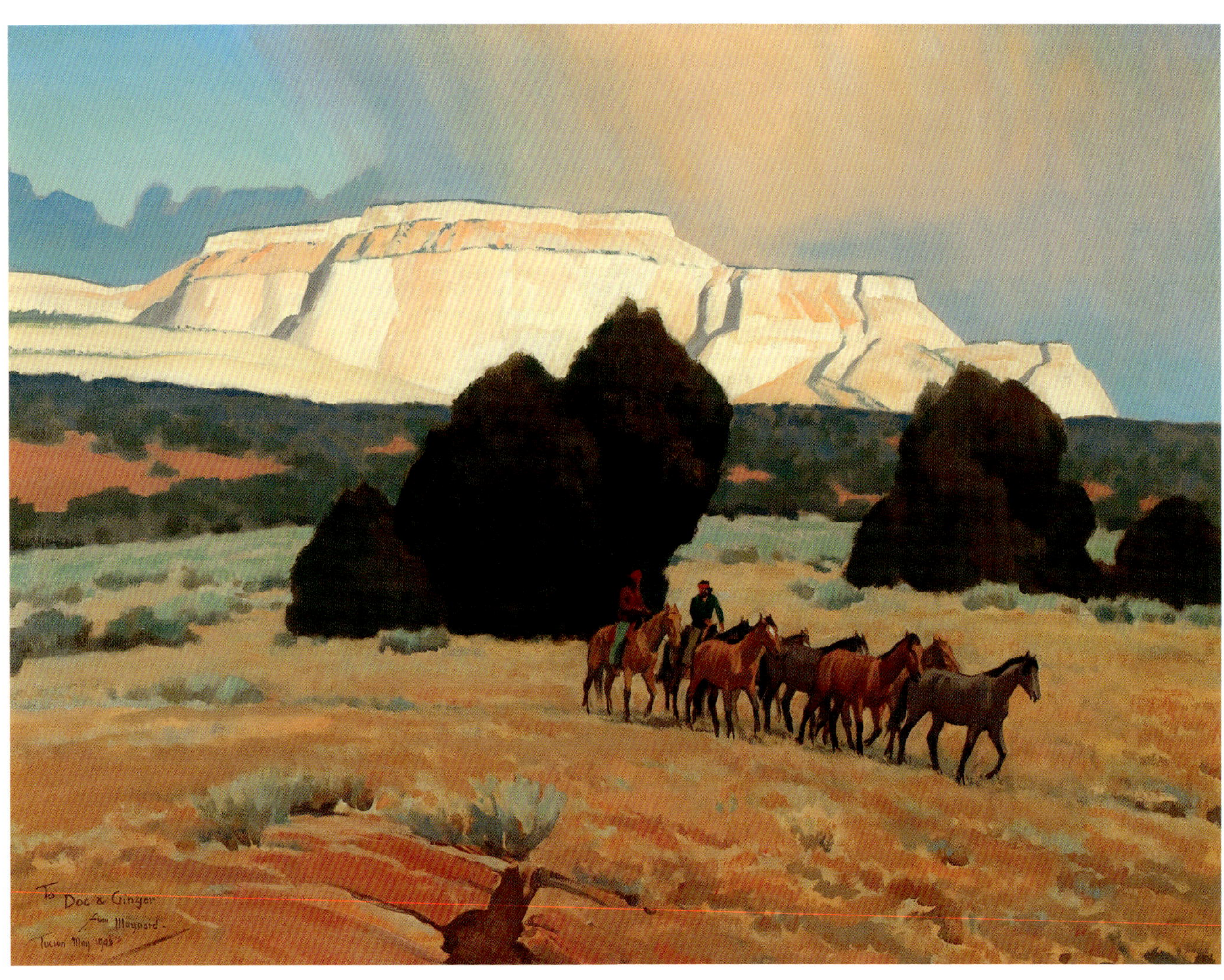

Plate 31 (above)
Maynard Dixon (U.S., 1875–1946)
Land of White Mesas, 1943. Oil on canvas, 30 × 40 in.
Fred Jones Jr. Museum of Art
A2007.0002

Plate 32 (facing page)
W. Herbert Dunton (U.S., 1878–1936)
Margo Phillips Beutler, n.d. Oil on board, 40 × 26 in.
Fred Jones Jr. Museum of Art
A2007.0081

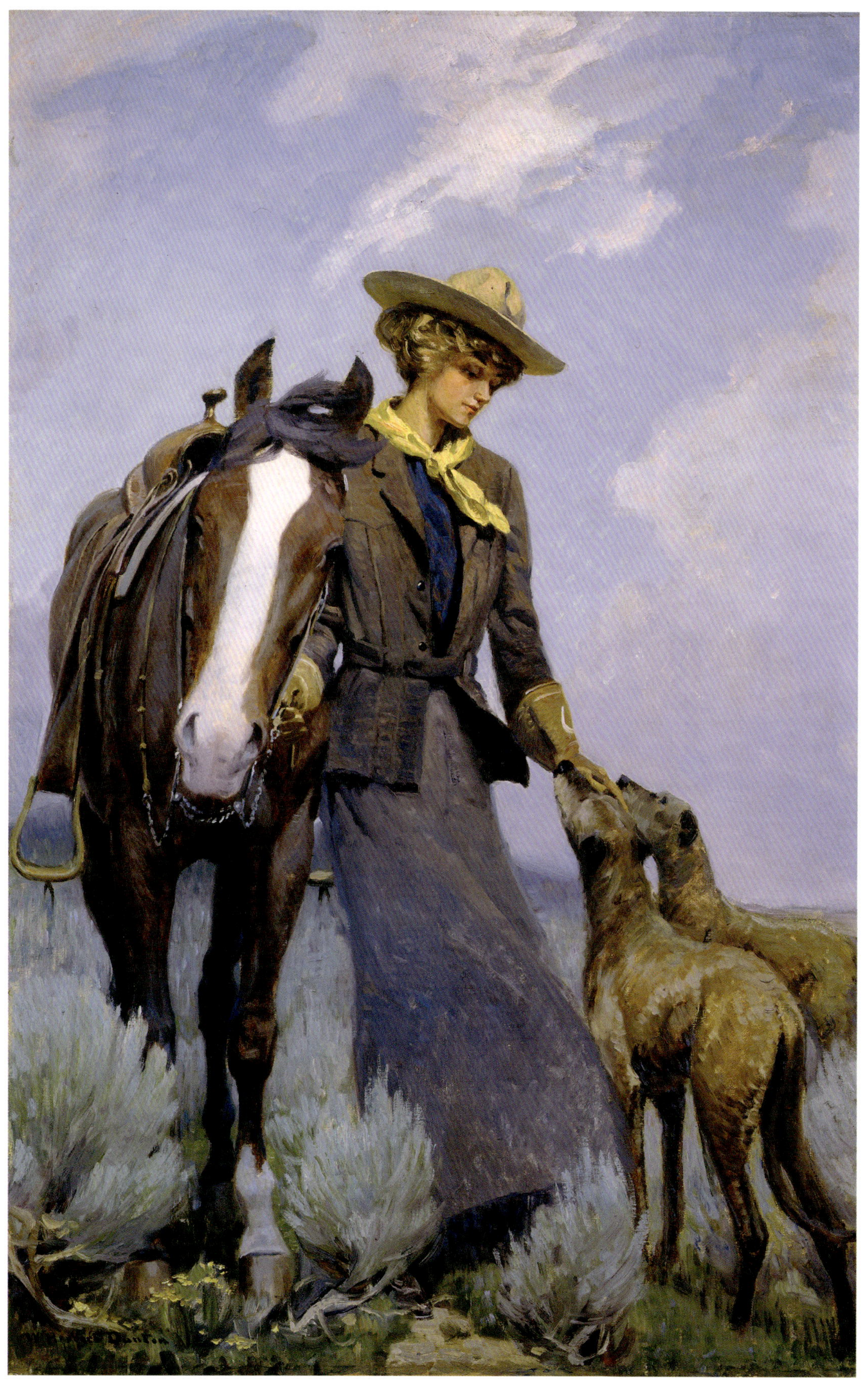

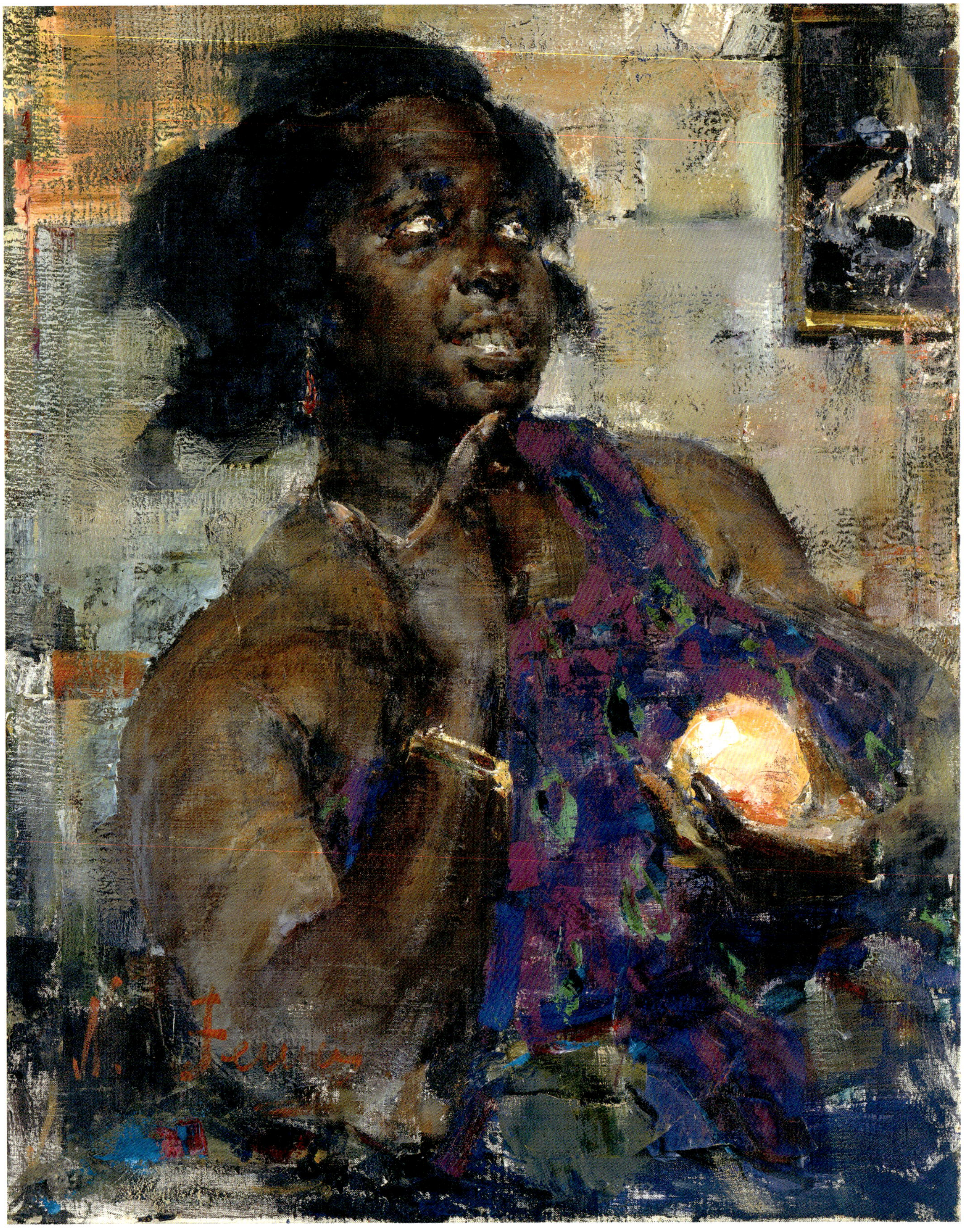

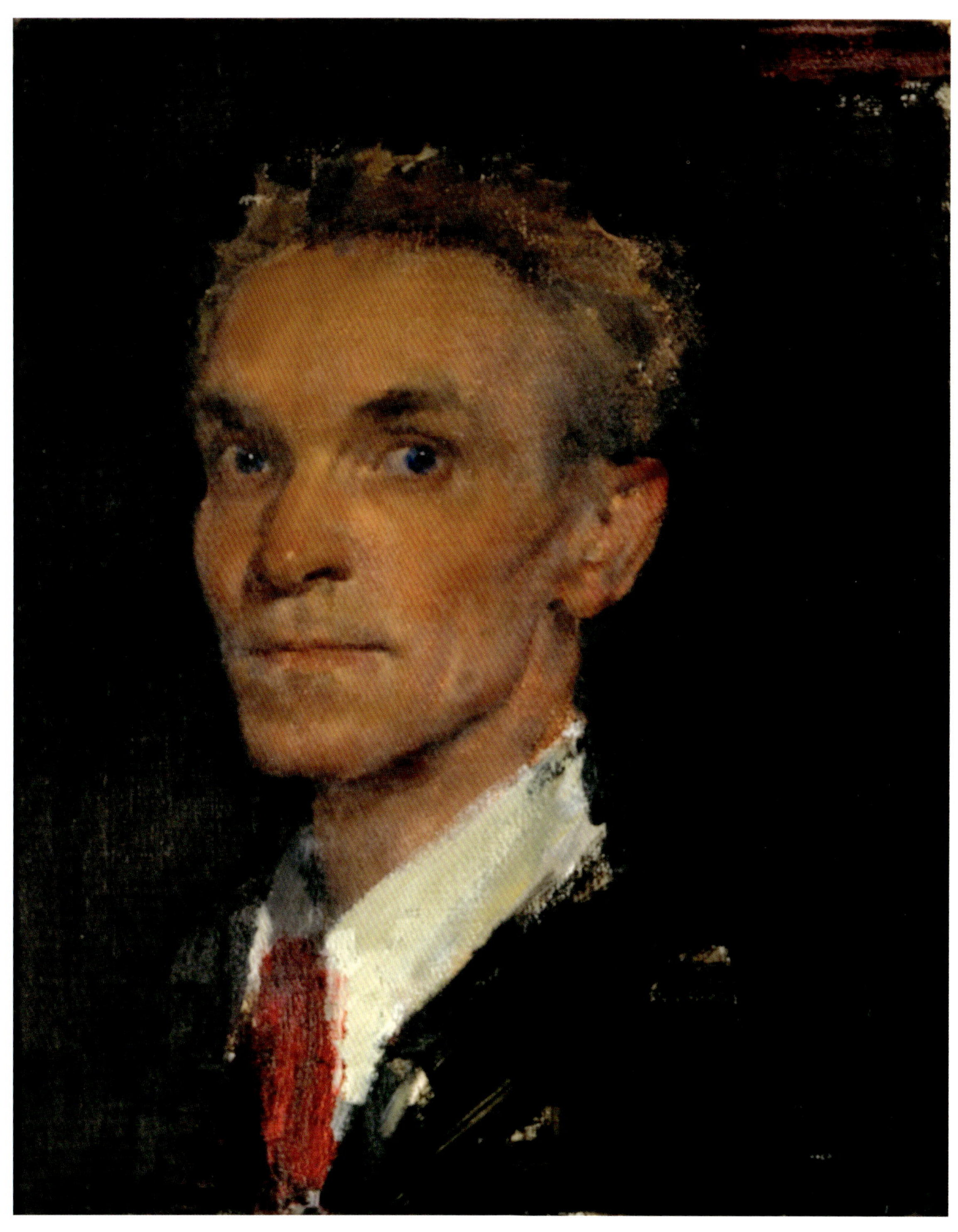

Plate 33 (facing page)
Nicolai Fechin (U.S., b. Russia, 1881–1955)
Negro Girl with Orange, c. 1923. Oil on canvas, 32 × 25 in.
Fred Jones Jr. Museum of Art
A2007.0164

Plate 34 (above)
Nicolai Fechin (U.S., b. Russia, 1881–1955)
Self-Portrait, n.d. Oil on canvas, 20 × 16 in.
Fred Jones Jr. Museum of Art
A2007.0077

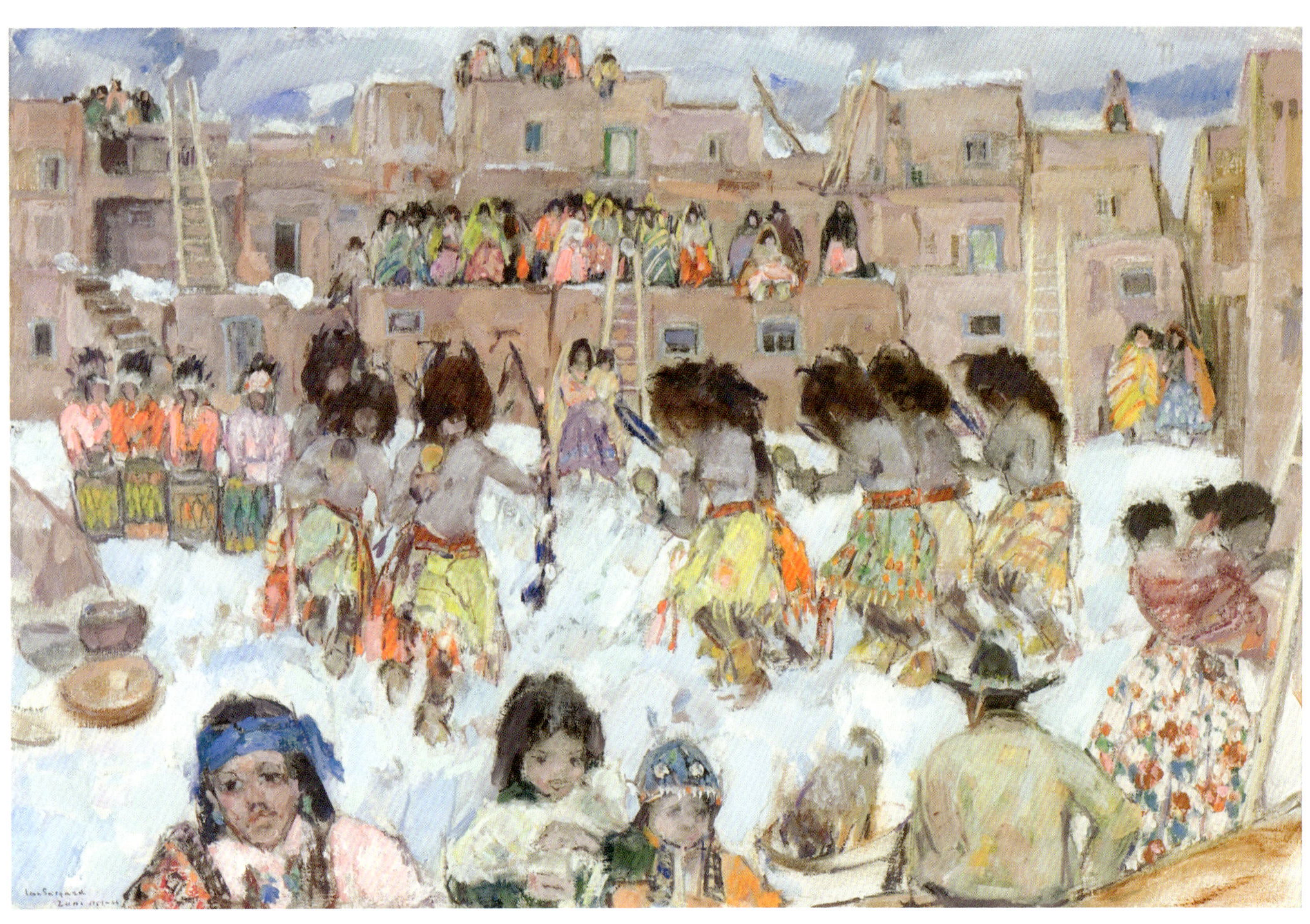

PLATE 35
Leon Gaspard (U.S., b. Russia, 1882–1964)
Buffalo Dance at Zuni, 1953–1964. Oil on canvas, 24 × 36 in.
Philbrook Museum of Art
A2007.0011

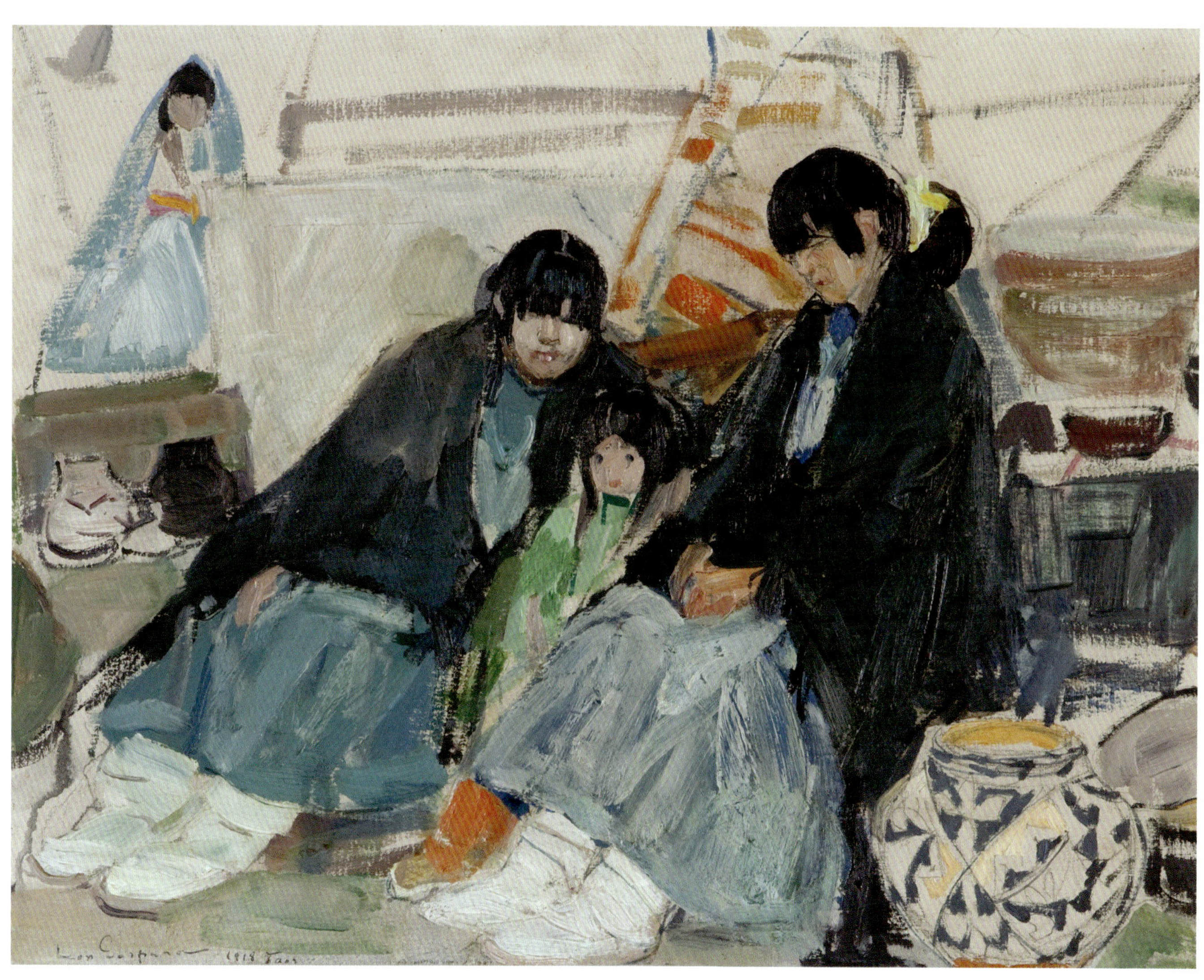

Plate 36
Leon Gaspard (U.S., b. Russia, 1882–1964)
Taos Pueblo Indian Group, 1918. Oil on canvas, 14 × 17 in.
Fred Jones Jr. Museum of Art
A2007.0101

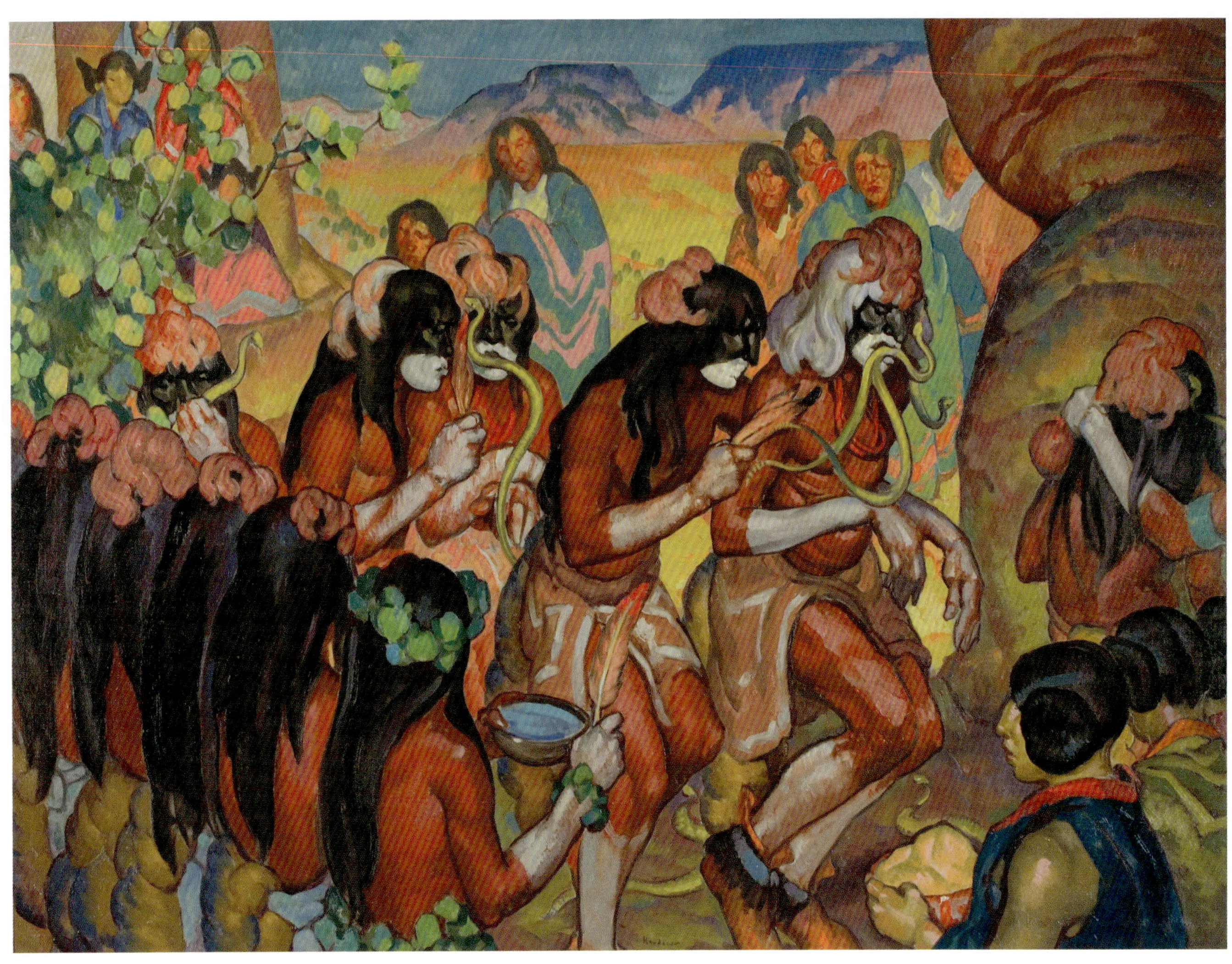

PLATE 37
William Penhallow Henderson (U.S., 1877–1943)
Walpi Snake Dance, c. 1920. Oil on canvas, 42 × 55 in.
Fred Jones Jr. Museum of Art
A2007.0229

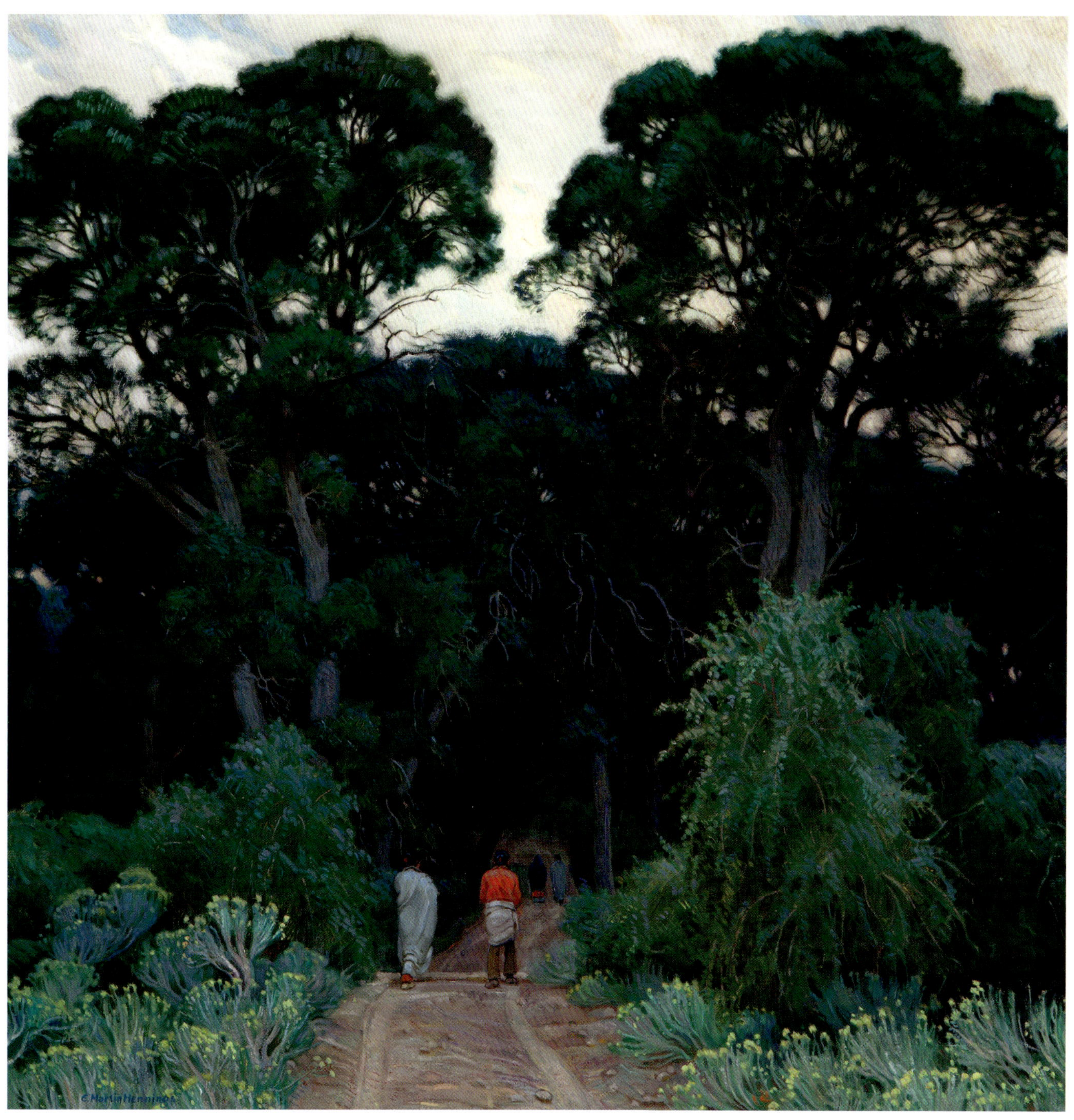

Plate 38
E. Martin Hennings (U.S., 1886–1956)
Going to Blue Lake, n.d. Oil on canvas, $39\frac{1}{2} \times 39\frac{1}{2}$ in.
Philbrook Museum of Art
A2007.0005

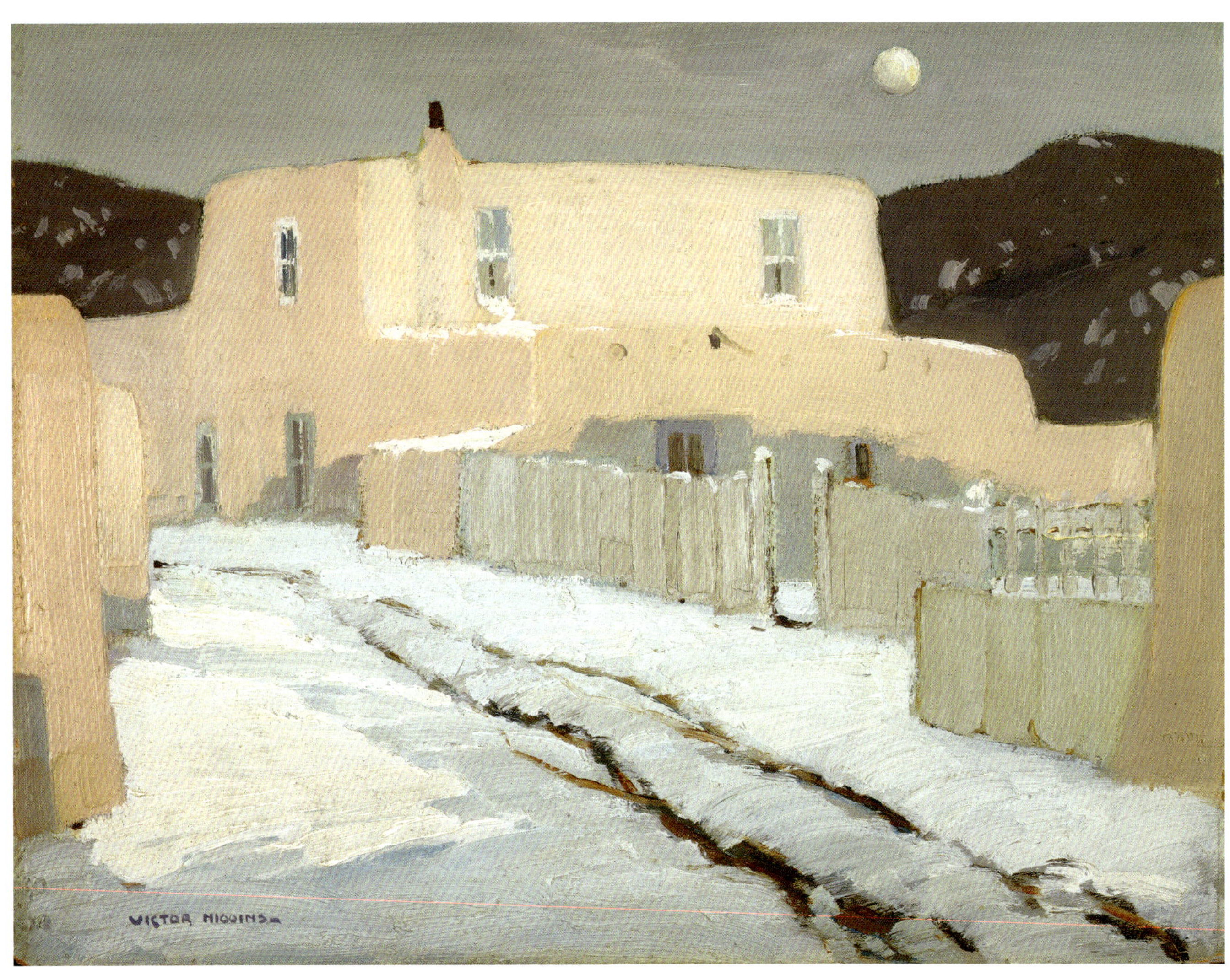

PLATE 39
Victor Higgins (U.S., 1884–1949)
Ledoux Street (My House), c. 1918. Oil on panel, 20 × 24 in.
Fred Jones Jr. Museum of Art
A2007.0044

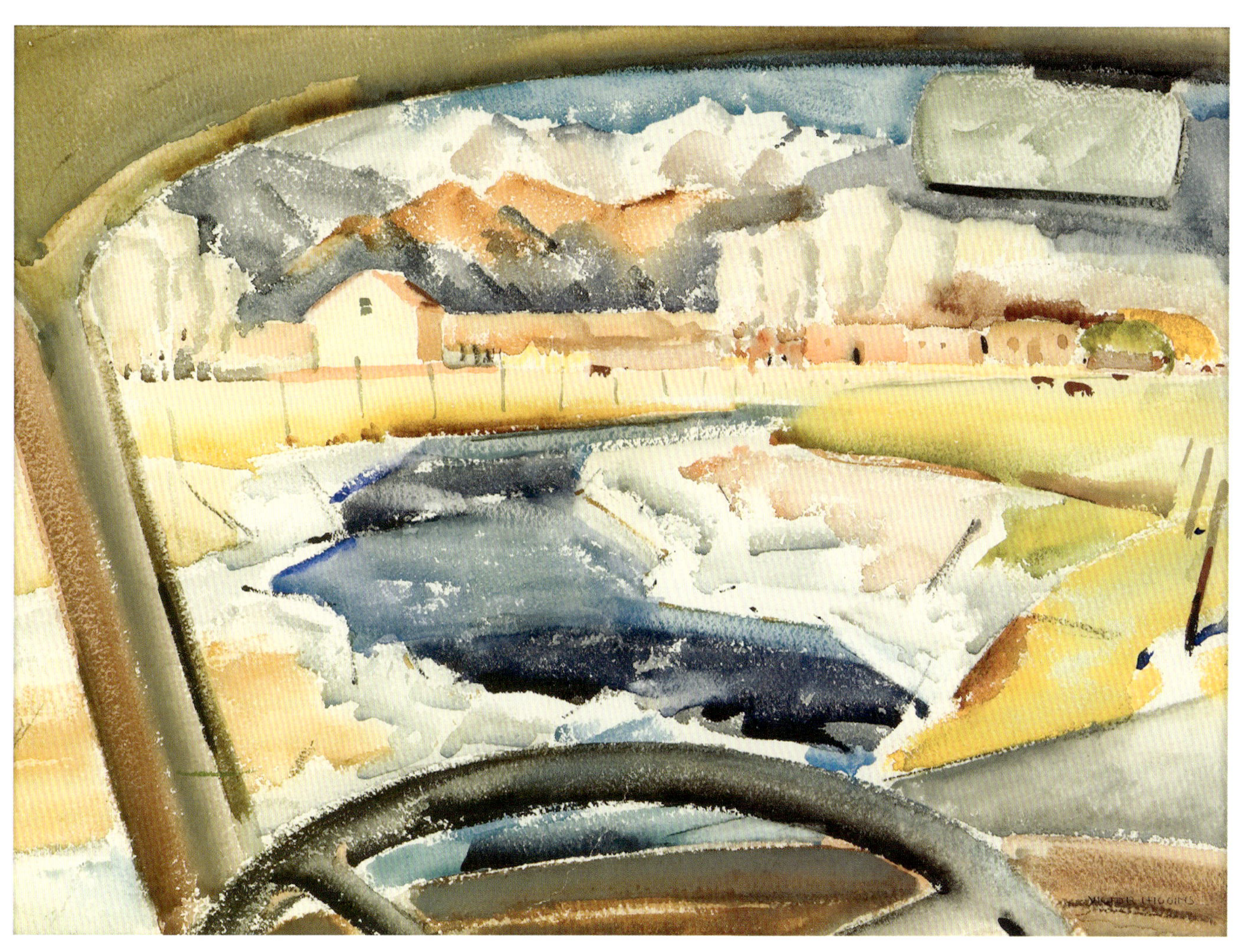

PLATE 40
Victor Higgins (U.S., 1884–1949)
New Mexico Landscape Through Auto Window, c. 1935–1937
Watercolor on paper, 15 × 21 in.
Philbrook Museum of Art
A2007.0559

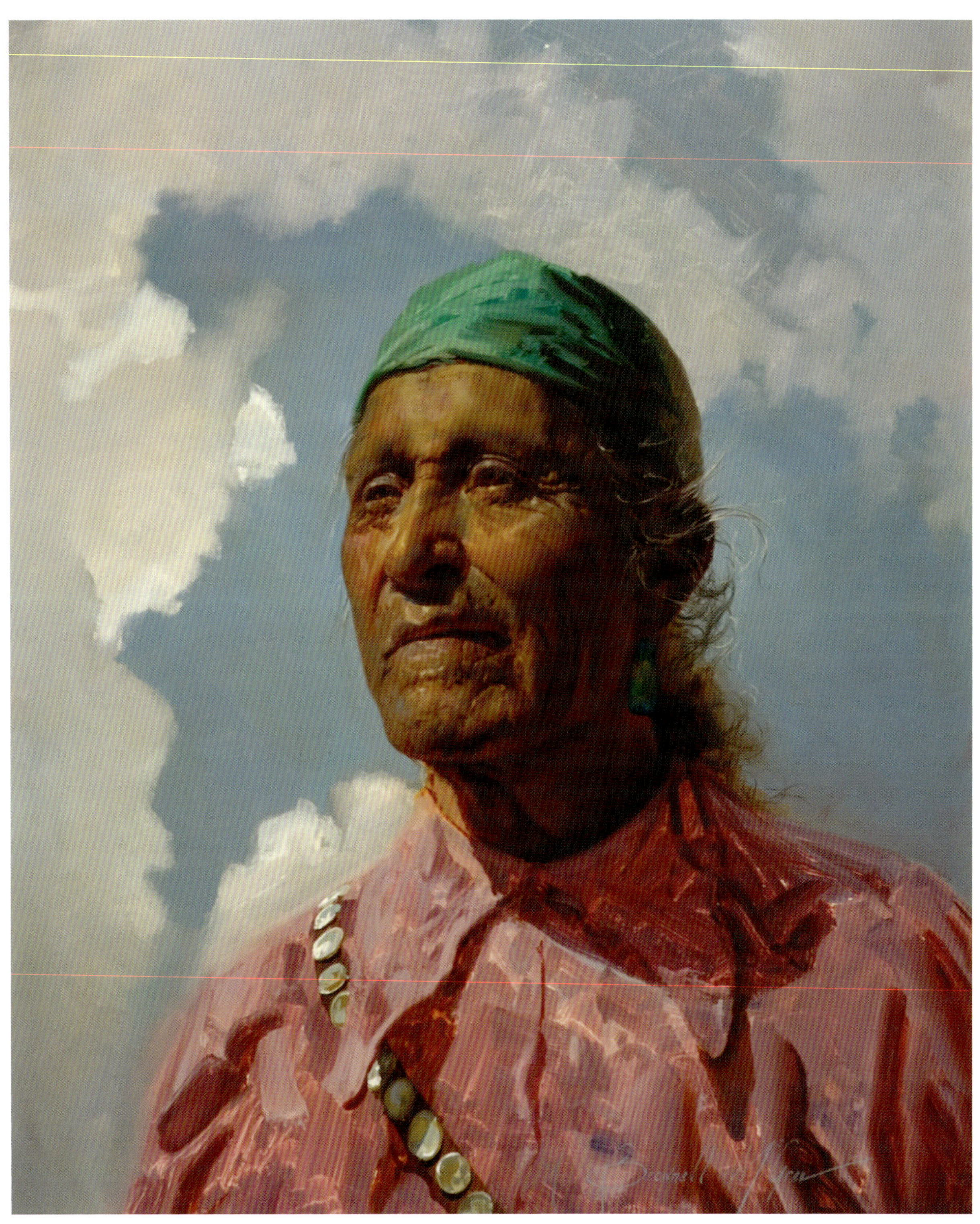

Plate 41
R. Brownell McGrew (U.S., 1916–1994)
Hosteen, n.d. Oil on board, 24 × 20 in.
Fred Jones Jr. Museum of Art
A2007.0158

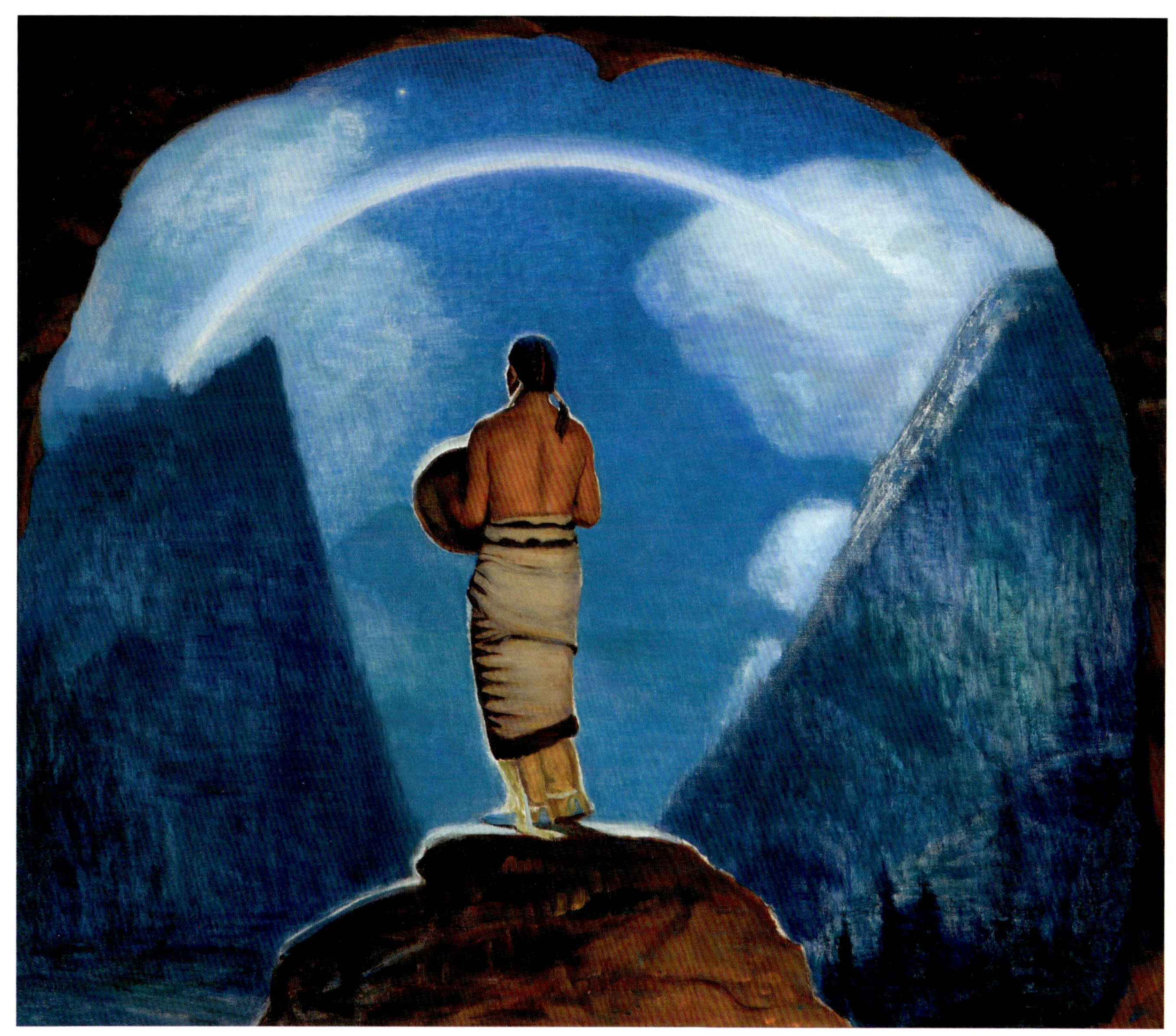

PLATE 42
Bert Geer Phillips (U.S., 1868–1956)
Song to the Moonbow, n.d. Oil on canvas, 34 × 40 in.
Philbrook Museum of Art
A2007.0195

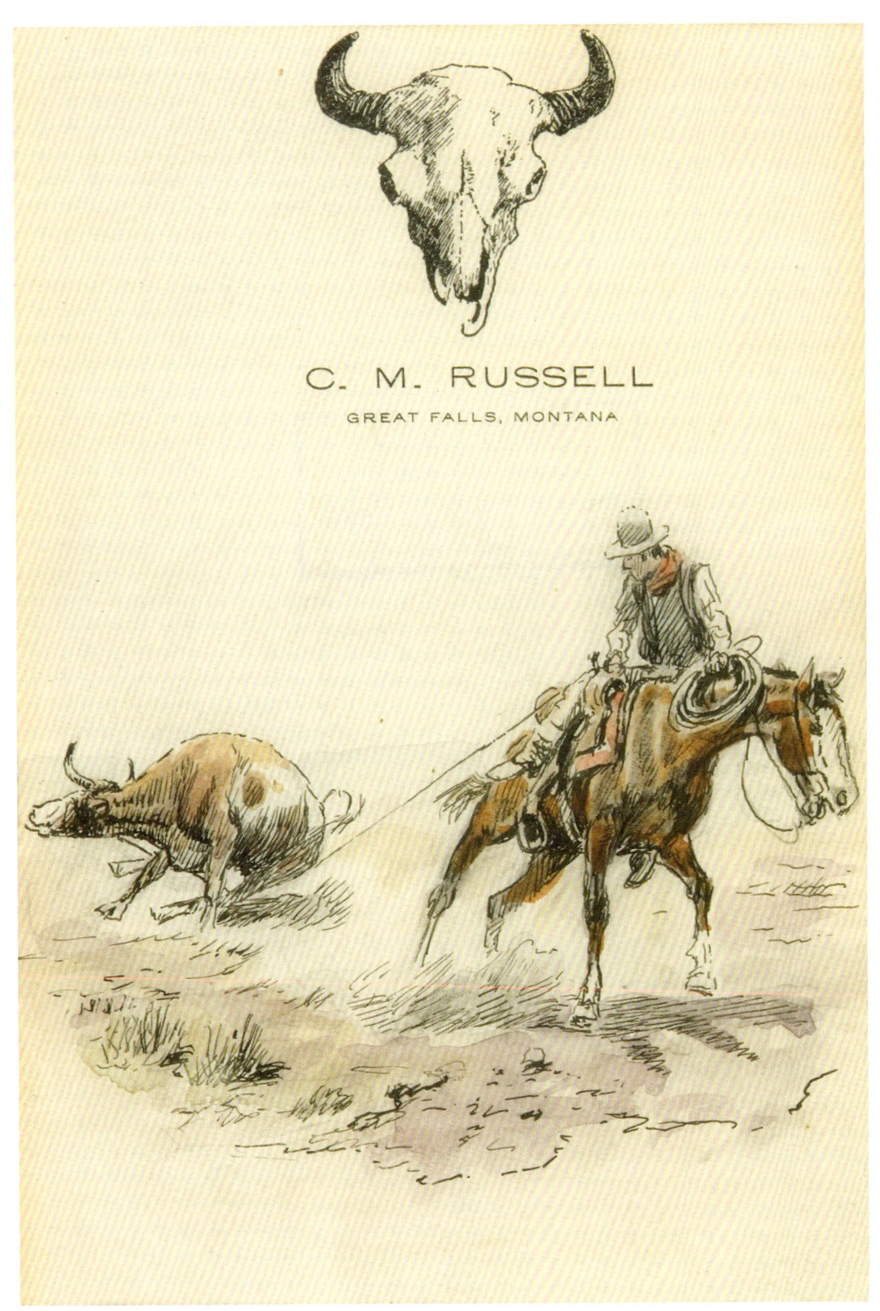

Plate 43
Charles M. Russell (U.S., 1864–1926)
Ropin', n.d. Ink and watercolor on paper, 6½ × 4½ in.
Fred Jones Jr. Museum of Art
A2007.0053

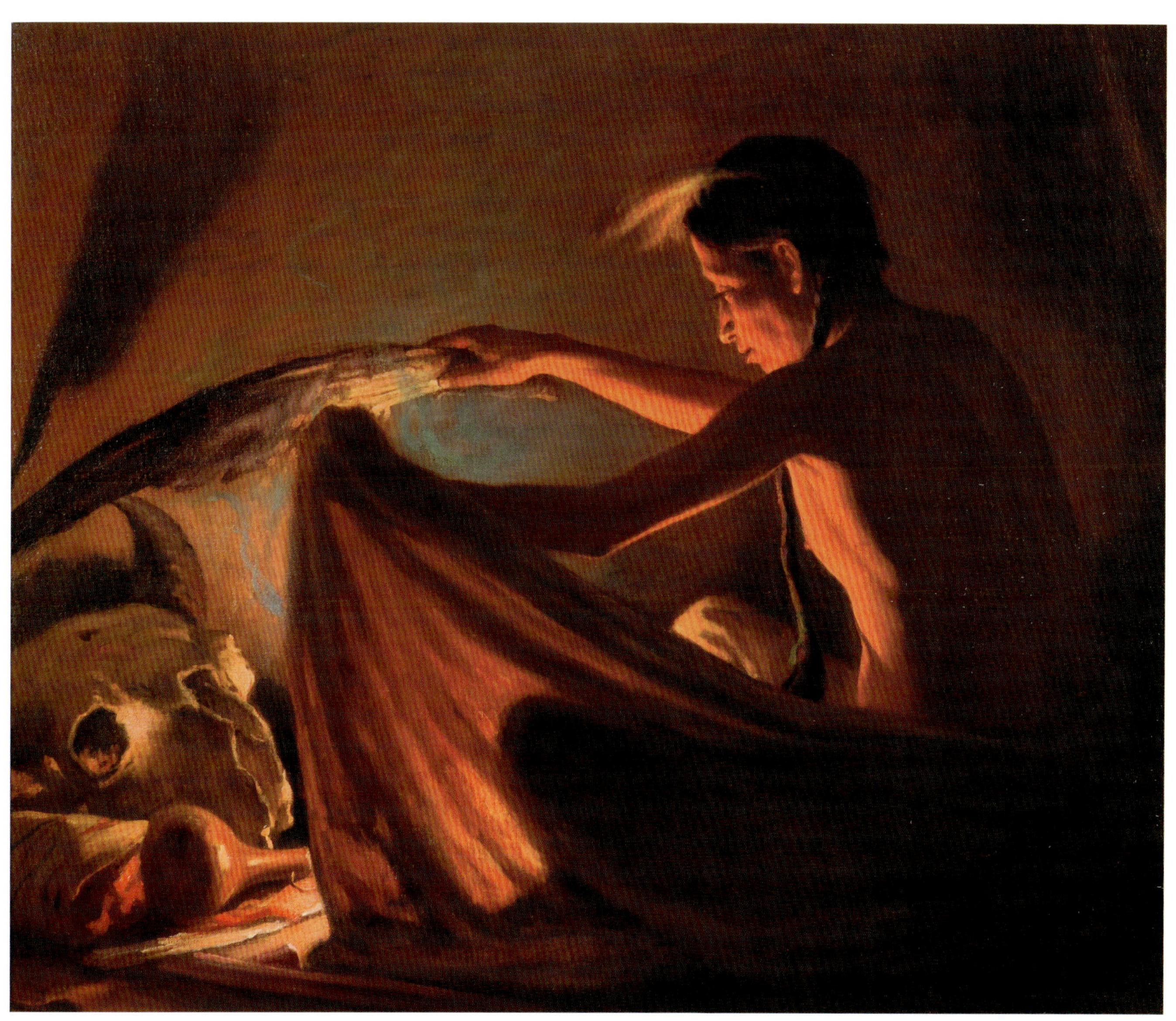

Plate 44
Joseph Henry Sharp (U.S., 1859–1953)
El Greco, n.d. Oil on canvas, 30 × 36 in.
Philbrook Museum of Art
A2007.0007

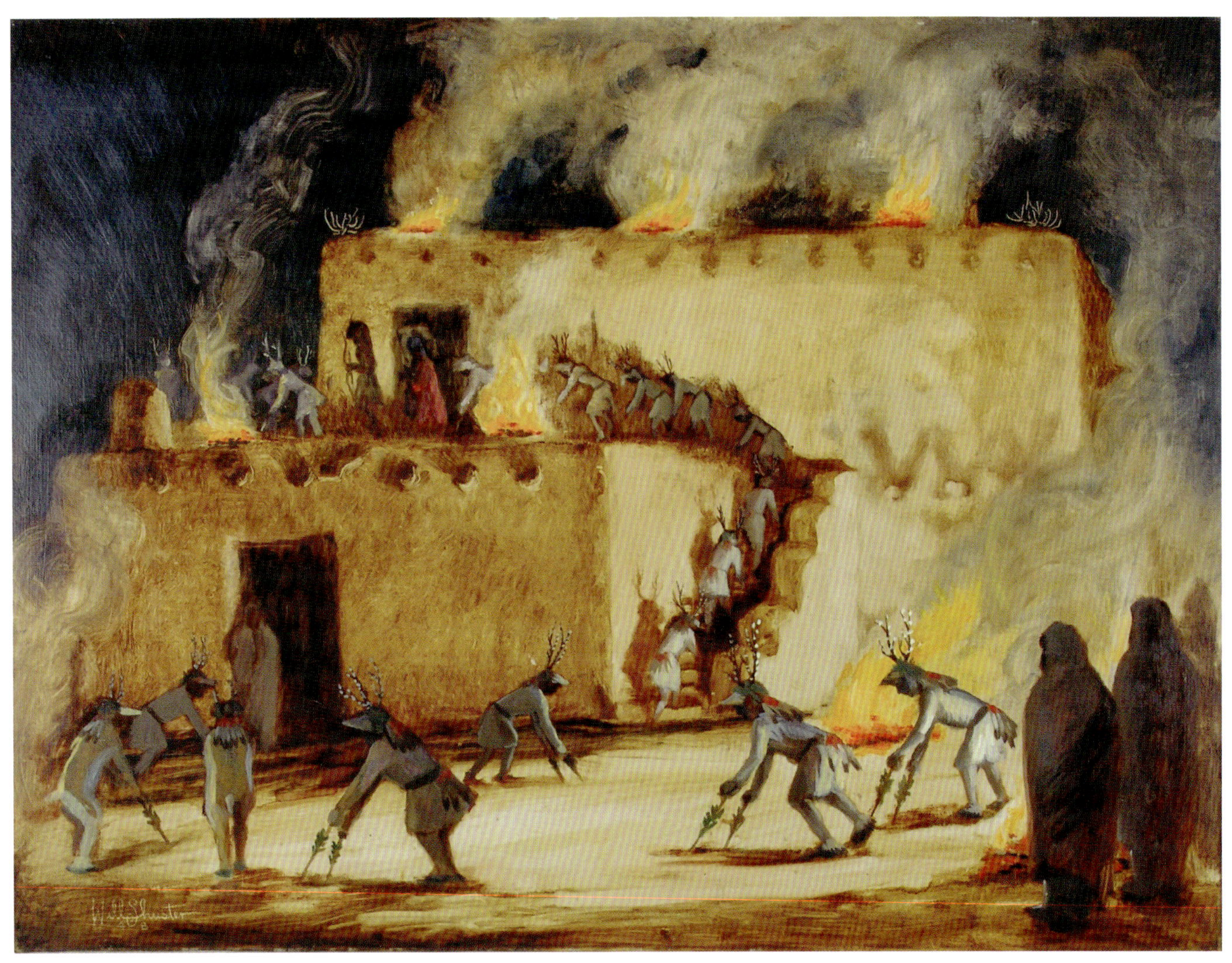

Plate 45
Will Shuster (U.S., 1893–1969)
Eve of the Deer Dance, 1948. Oil on board, 30 × 40 in.
Courtesy The Owings Gallery, Santa Fe, N.Mex.
Fred Jones Jr. Museum of Art
A2007.0171

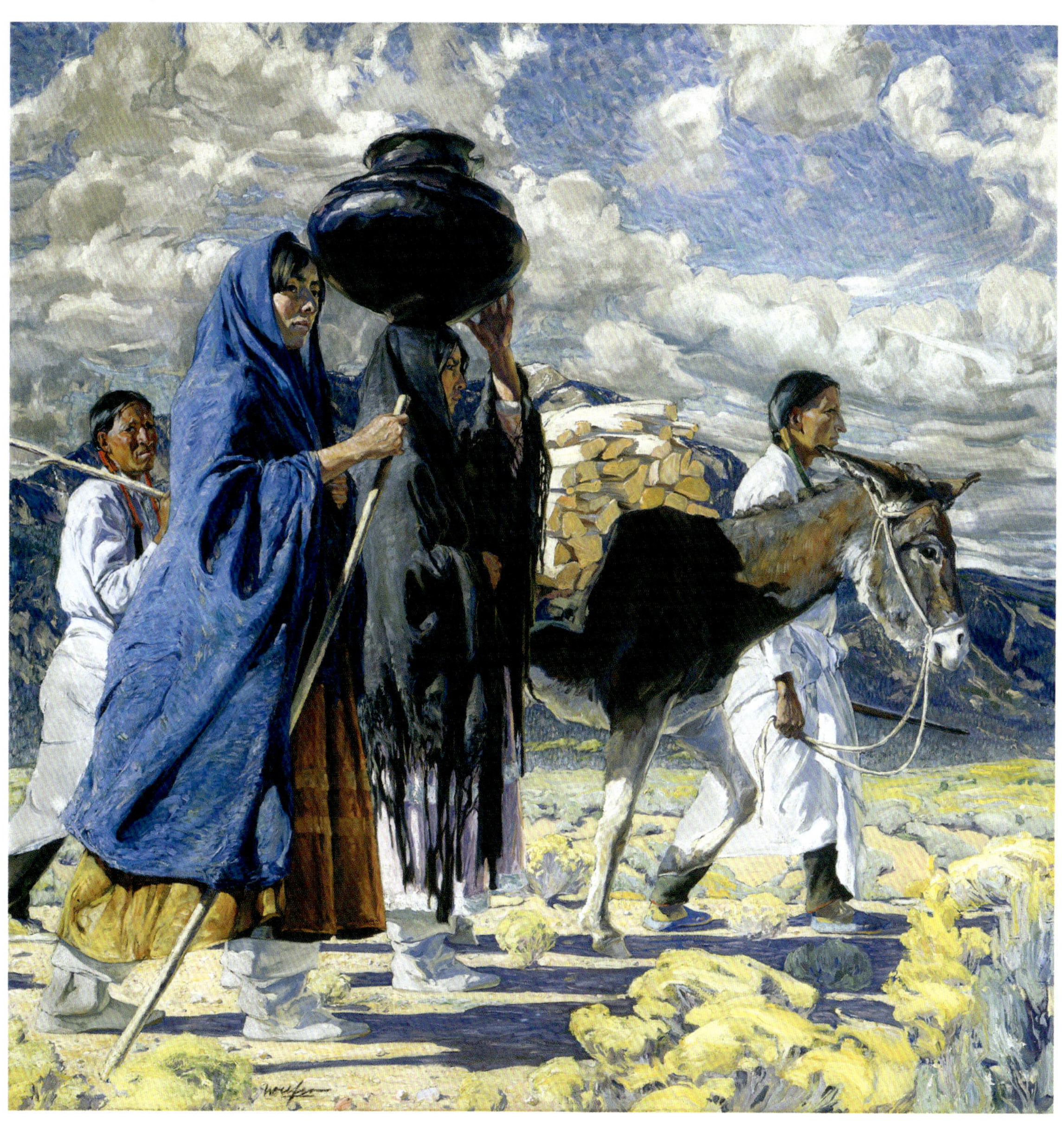

PLATE 46
Walter Ufer (U.S., 1876–1936)
Going East, 1917. Oil on canvas, 50 × 50 in.
Fred Jones Jr. Museum of Art and Philbrook Museum of Art
A2007.0125

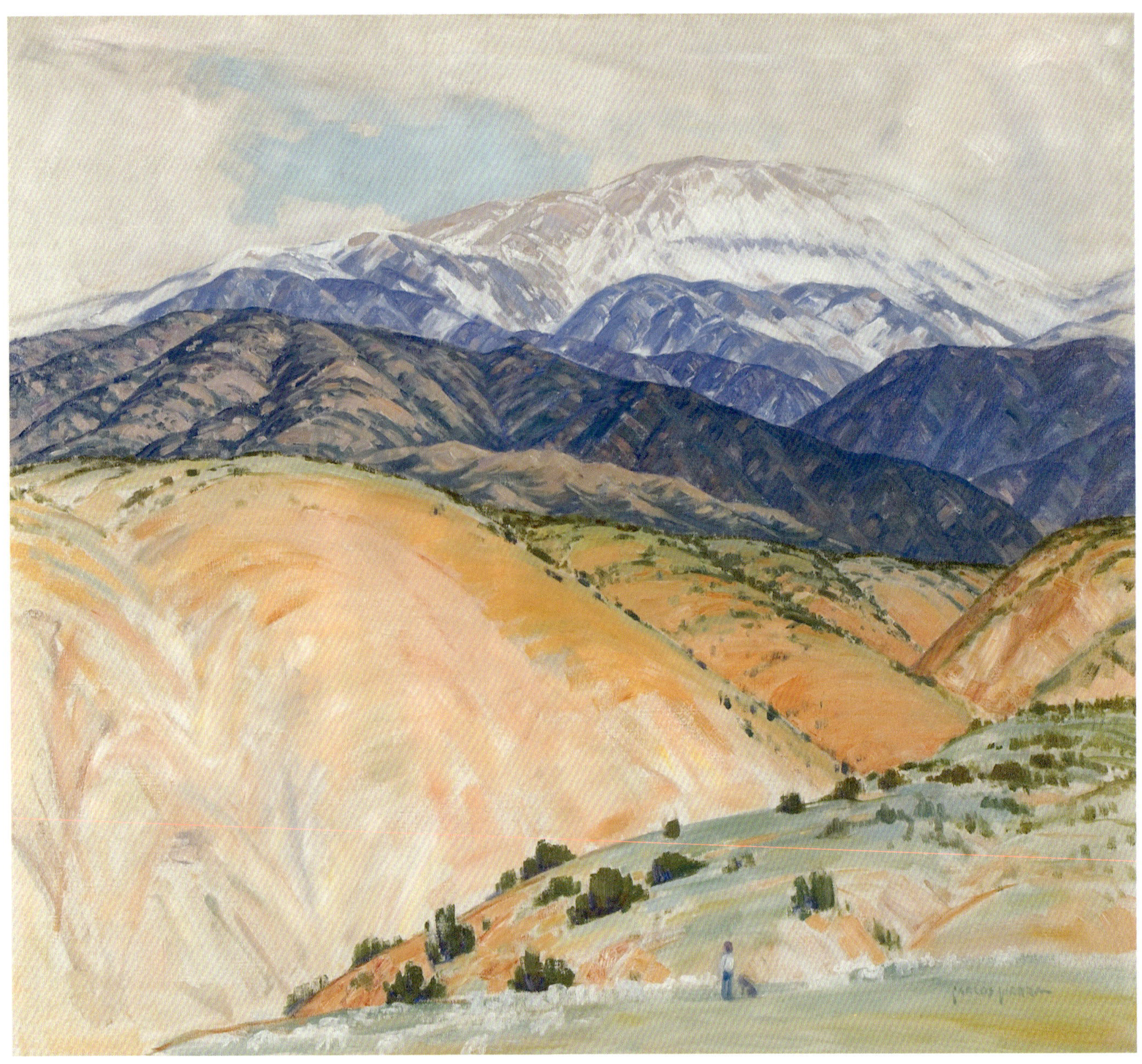

PLATE 47
Carlos Vierra (U.S., 1876–1937)
Sangre de Cristo Dawn, n.d.
Oil on canvas, 35 × 39½ in.
Fred Jones Jr. Museum of Art
A2007.0128

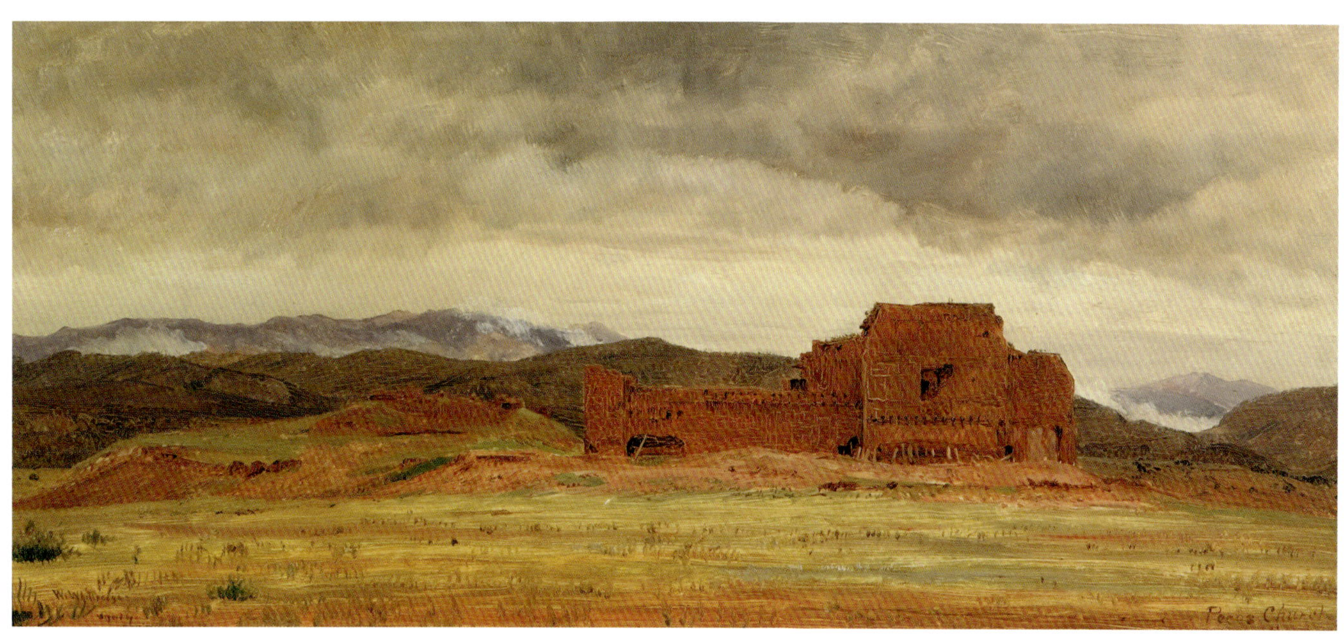

Plate 48
Thomas Worthington Whittredge (U.S., 1820–1910)
Old Pecos Pueblo Church, New Mexico, 1866
Oil on board, 10 × 22 in.
Fred Jones Jr. Museum of Art
A2007.0042

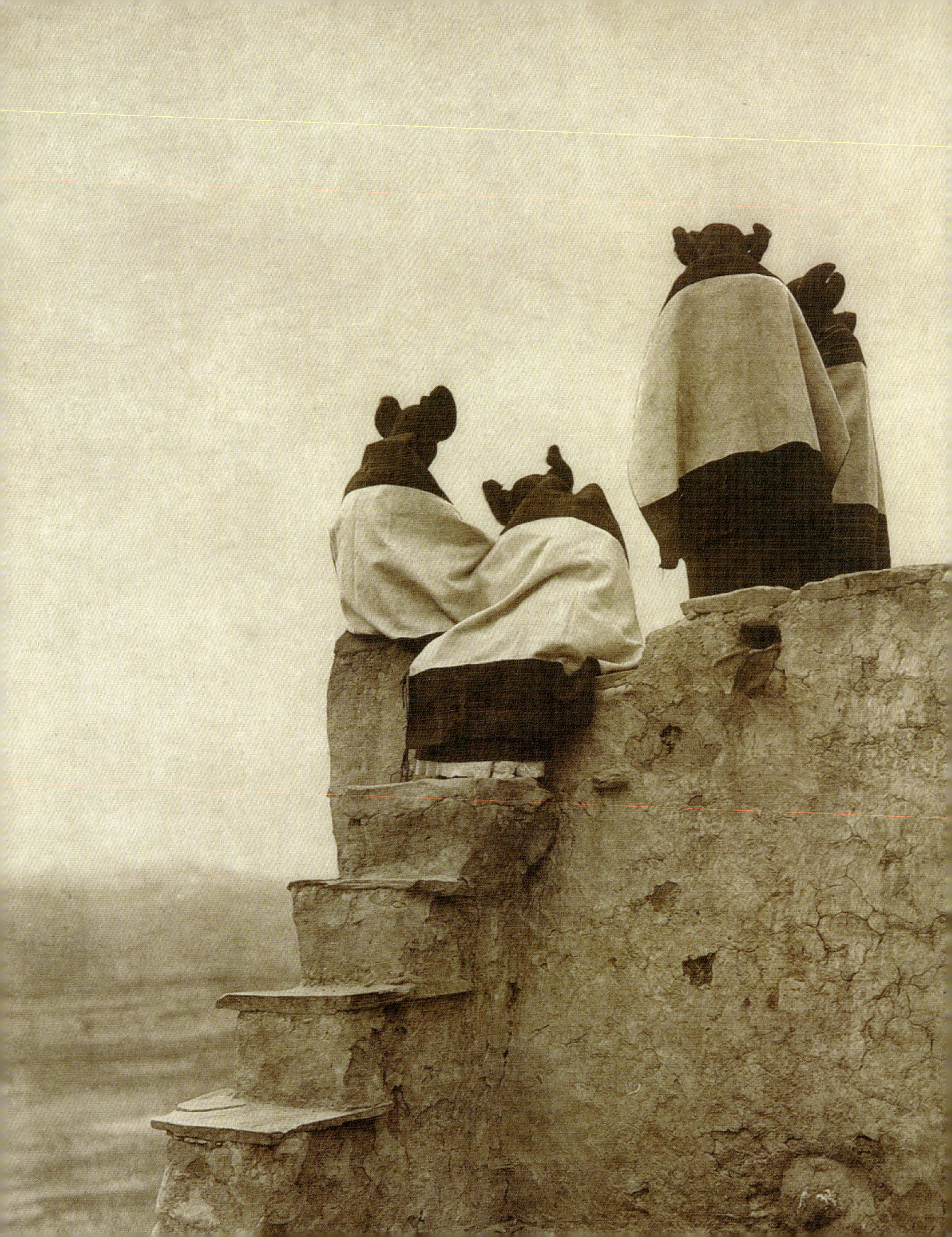

The Aesthetic and the Ethnographic

Photography of the American Southwest

Mark A. White

Chapter Three

As artistic interest in the Southwest began to increase in the 1890s, Charles F. Lummis offered a dire prediction for photography's role: "New Mexico, like the dearest women, cannot be adequately photographed. One can reproduce the features, but not the expression—the landmarks, but not the wondrous light which is to the bare Southwest the soul that glorifies a plain face."[1] Numerous photographers, as if to prove Lummis wrong, visited the Southwest in the coming decades to capture both the distinctive landscape and its people.

Adam Clark Vroman was among the early generation of photographers in the Southwest. He settled in Pasadena, California, in 1892 and sold his collection of fine books to help establish a bookstore with J. S. Glasscock. Under the influence of Lummis, he began experimenting with photography in 1894 and then visited Hopi the following year to see the snake dance. He returned to the Southwest routinely until 1904, and it was likely his 1901 visit that produced *Hopi Sash-Weaver* (c. 1901, plate 56). Vroman's intent was ethnographic; he hoped to capture distinctive aspects of Hopi life, such as aesthetic manufacture.

Vroman's final visits to Hopi coincided with those of his contemporary Edward S. Curtis, who was compiling photographs for his thirty-volume portfolio, *The North American Indian*. Curtis believed that Native cultures were vanishing under the pressure of assimilation, and he hoped to document architecture, dances, and other significant aspects of Native life. Curtis's *Watching the Dancers* (1906, plate 49) depicts a group of Hopi girls at Walpi as seen from the topmost roof. Although Curtis may have been interested in the architecture, dress, and even hairstyles of the girls, the photograph also demonstrates his interest in pictorialist photography, a style that used soft focus and other technical manipulations to emulate the expressive effects of late nineteenth-century painting. Aesthetic appreciation of the tonal

Plate 49
Edward S. Curtis (U.S., 1868–1952)
Watching the Dancers, Plate 405, 1906
Photogravure, 15 × 11 in.
Philbrook Museum of Art
A2007.0736

contrasts, the flow of line, and the massing of volumes was equally, if not more, important than the ethnographic details in *Watching the Dancers.*

The balance of aesthetic pleasure and the ethnographic impulse would continue to concern photographers in the Southwest in following decades. Laura Gilpin worked in a pictorialist style during her early career, but by the late 1920s, she preferred an approach consistent with straight, or pure, photography, which emphasized the flattening of space and clarity of line intrinsic to the art. Her *Ranchos de Taos Church* (1930, plate 52) depicts the exterior apse of the iconic St. Francis of Assisi Church, which also attracted the attention of artists such as Paul Strand and Georgia O'Keeffe. Like those artists, Gilpin emphasizes the flat, irregular planes of the adobe church and suggests, through similar tonality, that the church has risen metaphorically from the earth that surrounds it.

Gilpin had visited Taos as part of a tour of northern Arizona and New Mexico to photograph both archaeological ruins and the northern pueblos. In 1931, her companion Elizabeth Forster took a job as a field nurse for the Navajo community at Red Rock, Arizona. The visit would begin Gilpin's lifelong interest in the Navajo and their land. Photographs such as *Portrait of a Navajo Boy* (1932, plate 54) became part of her seminal manuscript *The Enduring Navajo,* eventually published in 1968 under the University of Texas Press. This photograph, when considered with others in the project, explored the continuity in Navajo traditions, despite changes modernization brought to the reservation, and insisted that their core values and mores endured.[2]

Gilpin's interest in the Navajo continued past the publication of the book, and she continually returned to families and sites she had once visited in her early career. She first photographed Shiprock, a geological formation of religious importance to the Navajo, in 1926, but returned over the decade to capture it from different angles, even from above, as in *Summit of Shiprock, New Mexico* (1973, plate 53). She had begun taking aerial photographs in the early 1940s while working as department photographer for Boeing in Wichita, Kansas, and then made several flights over the Navajo Reservation in the late 1960s and early 1970s to photograph its terrain.

The coarse beauty of the southwestern landscape attracted other photographers over the decades, including William Clift. Born in Boston, he began his career in 1962 with architectural and marine subjects, and upon his move to Santa Fe in 1971, he was attracted by the archaeological ruins and geological formations of the Southwest. A sense of quiet solitude permeates his work, and he sought a tranquility in his New Mexico photographs comparable to his earlier marine images: "The landscape of New Mexico, in particular, reminds me of the ocean spaces I grew up with: It offers the freedom to look at great distance and rest inside."[3] Photographs such as *Sheep and Petroglyphs, Canyon del Muerto, Arizona* (1975, plate 50), and *White House Ruin, Canyon de Chelly* (1975, plate 51), capture the silence and grandeur of the desert, offering a sense of peace and repose.

The landscape and Native peoples of the Southwest drew numerous artists and cultural personalities over the century, and many would eventually become national celebrities. For instance, New York socialite Mabel Dodge Luhan became a legendary figure in Taos and drew numerous artists there, including portrait painter John Young-Hunter, who took an informal photograph of her sometime after his arrival in 1917. Another amateur photographer, B. Schroeter, aimed his lens at famed San Ildefonso potter Maria Martinez and her son Popovi Da in 1957 (plate 55). The photograph depicts the transmission of culture between generations in the form of the pottery that had become nationally famous by the 1950s.

While Lummis may have doubted photography's future in the Southwest, it is abundantly apparent that the landscape and its people offer unlimited artistic inspiration, and photography continues to play a dominant role in the arts of the Southwest.

Plates 50–57

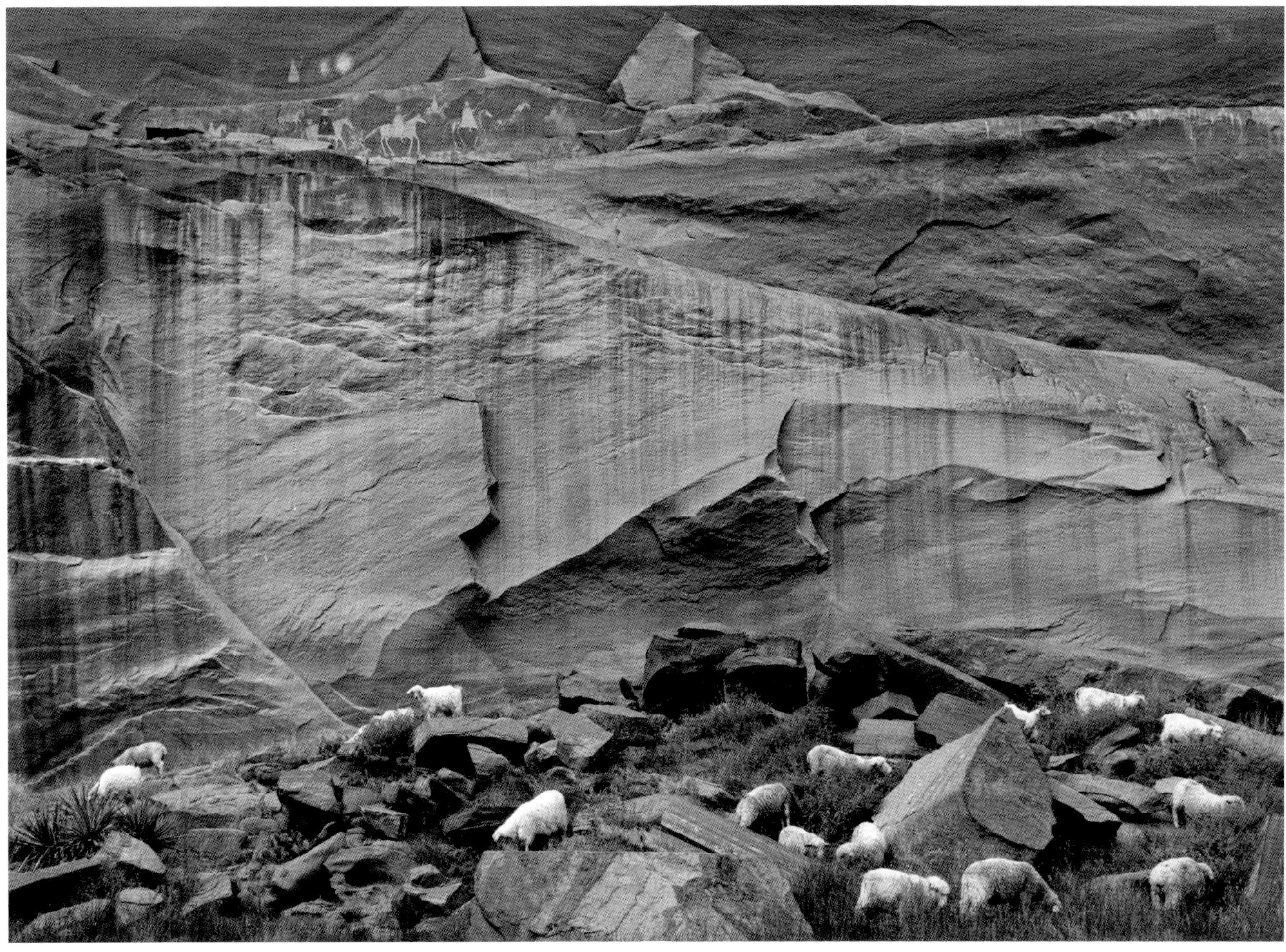

Plate 50
William Clift (U.S., b. 1944)
Sheep and Petroglyphs, Canyon del Muerto, Arizona, 1975
Gelatin silver print, 6½ × 9½ in.

Fred Jones Jr. Museum of Art
A2007.0497

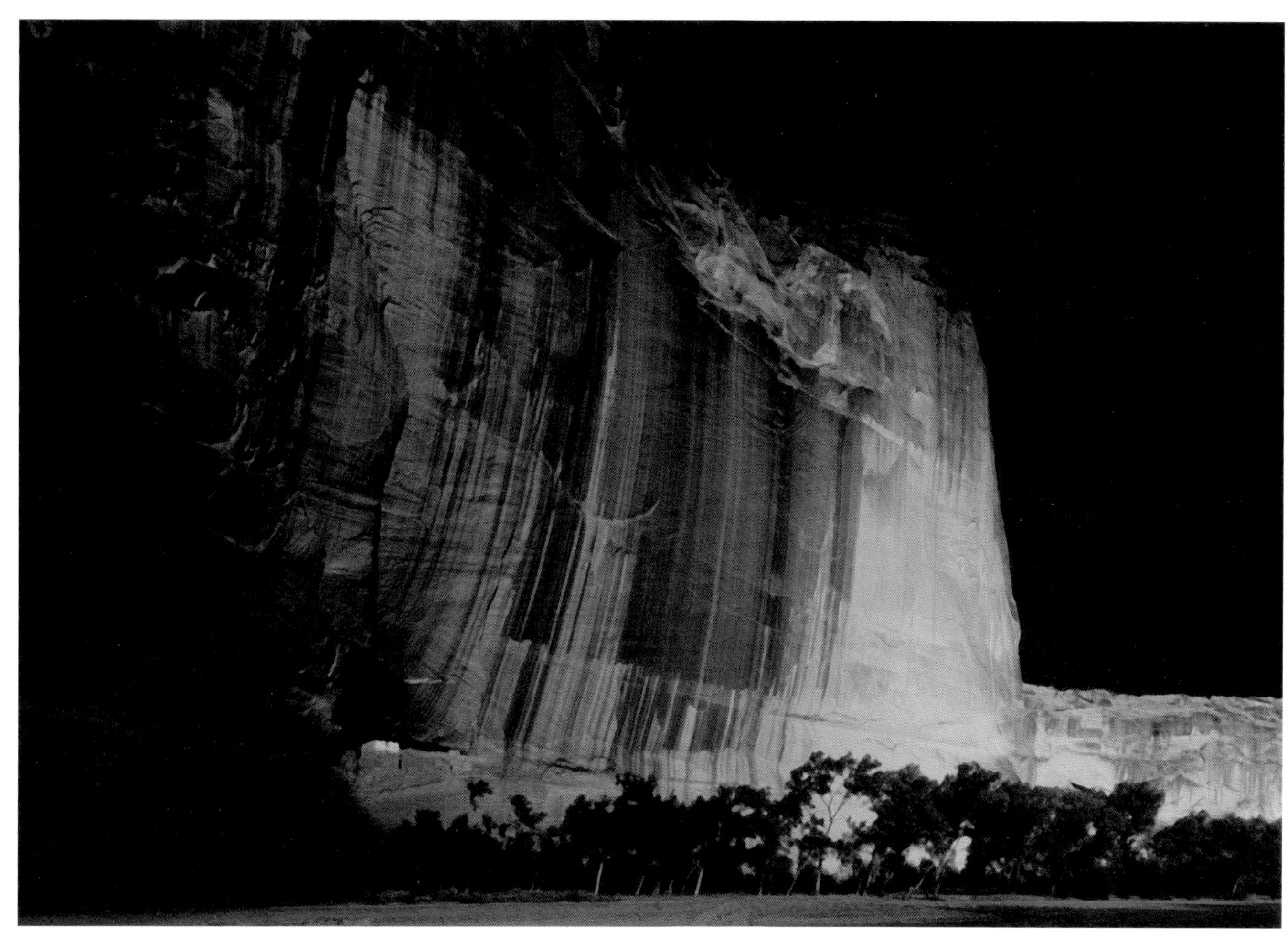

Plate 51
William Clift (U.S., b. 1944)
White House Ruin, Canyon de Chelly, Arizona, 1975
Gelatin silver print, 10 × 14½ in.

Fred Jones Jr. Museum of Art
A2007.0506

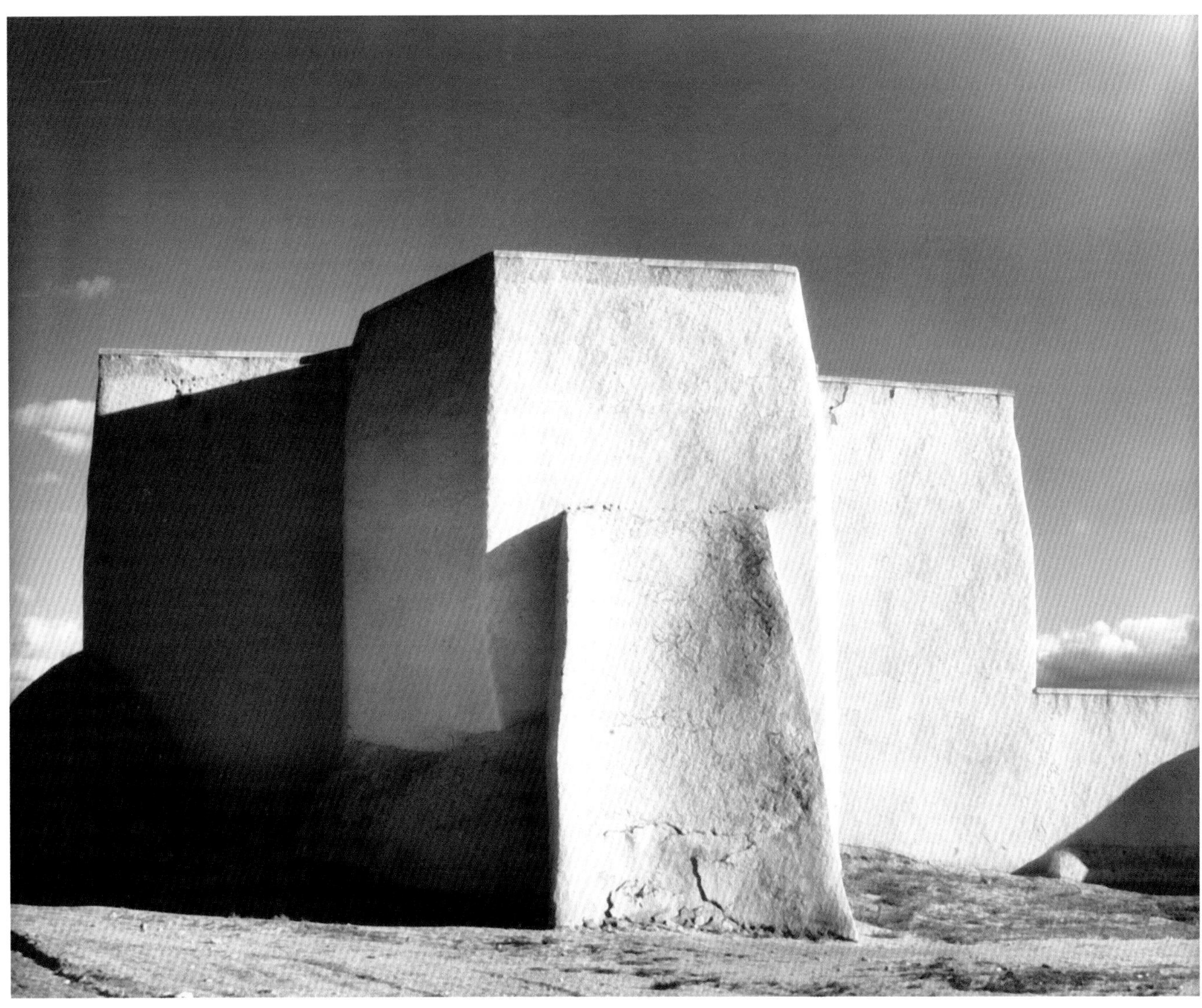

Plate 52
Laura Gilpin (U.S., 1891–1979)
Ranchos de Taos Church, 1930
Gelatin silver print, 7½ × 9 in.
© 1979 Amon Carter Museum of American Art, Fort Worth, Texas
Fred Jones Jr. Museum of Art
A2007.0463

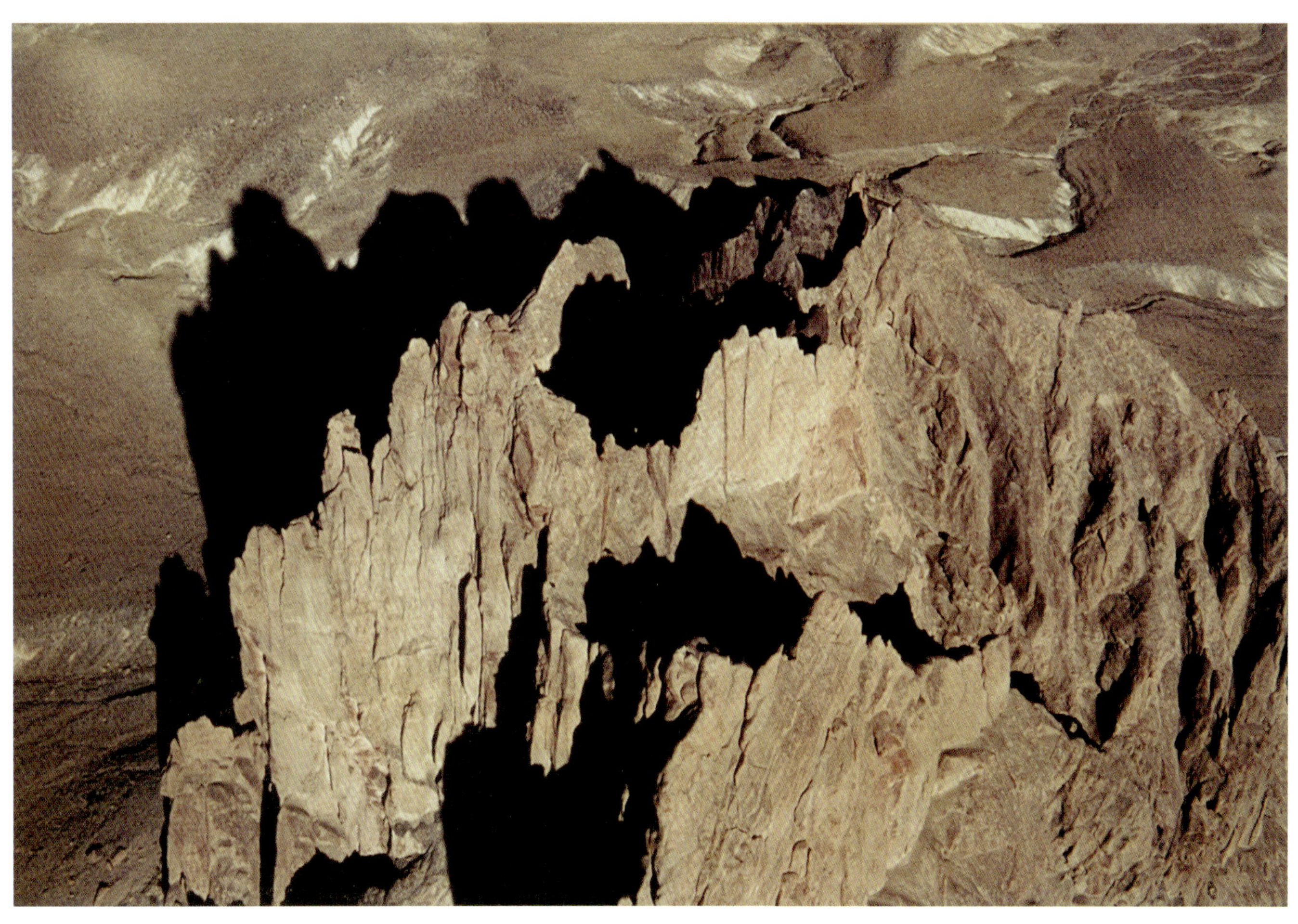

Plate 53
Laura Gilpin (U.S., 1891–1979)
Summit of Shiprock, New Mexico, 1973
Color photograph, 6½ × 10 in.
© 1979 Amon Carter Museum of American Art, Fort Worth, Texas
Fred Jones Jr. Museum of Art
A2007.0505

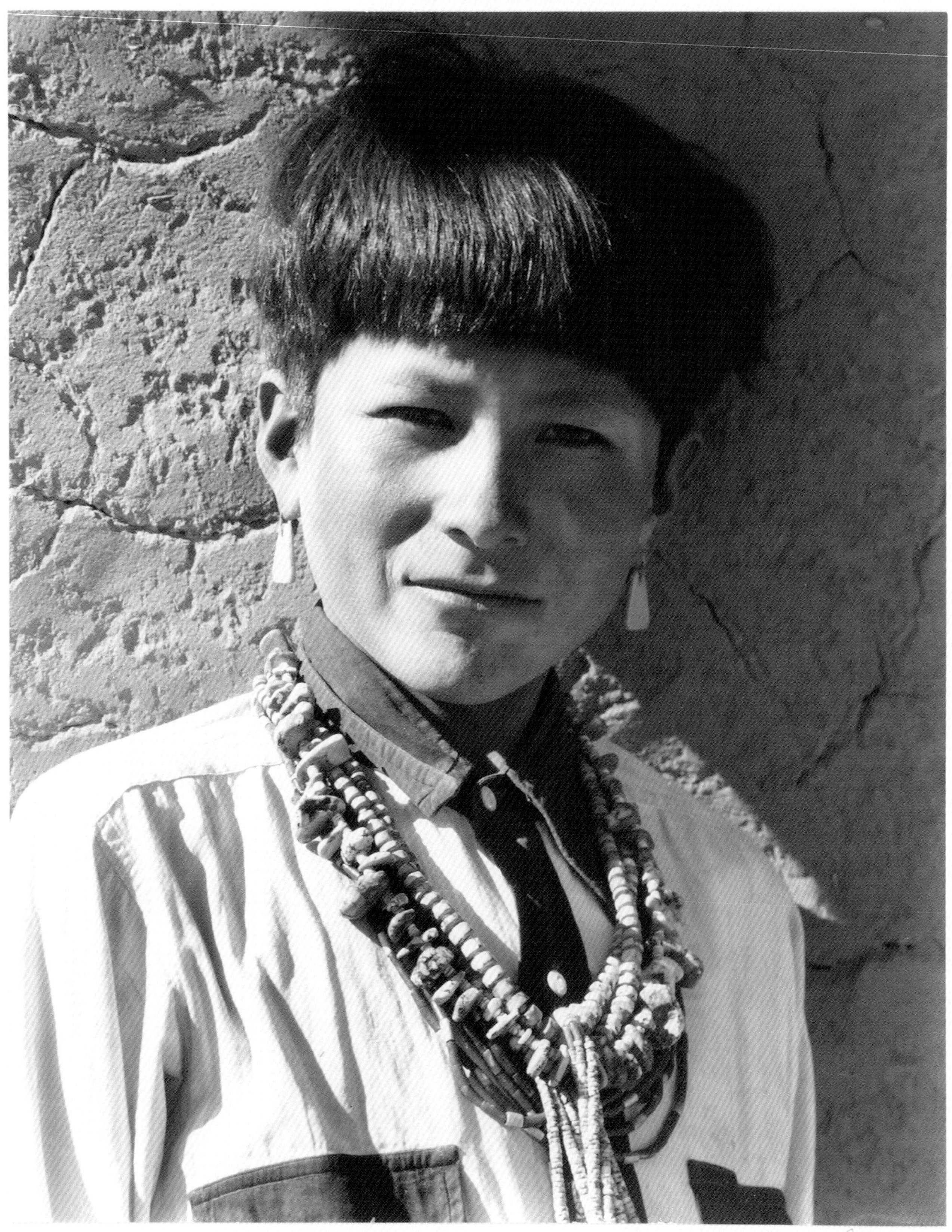
Laura Gilpin
1932

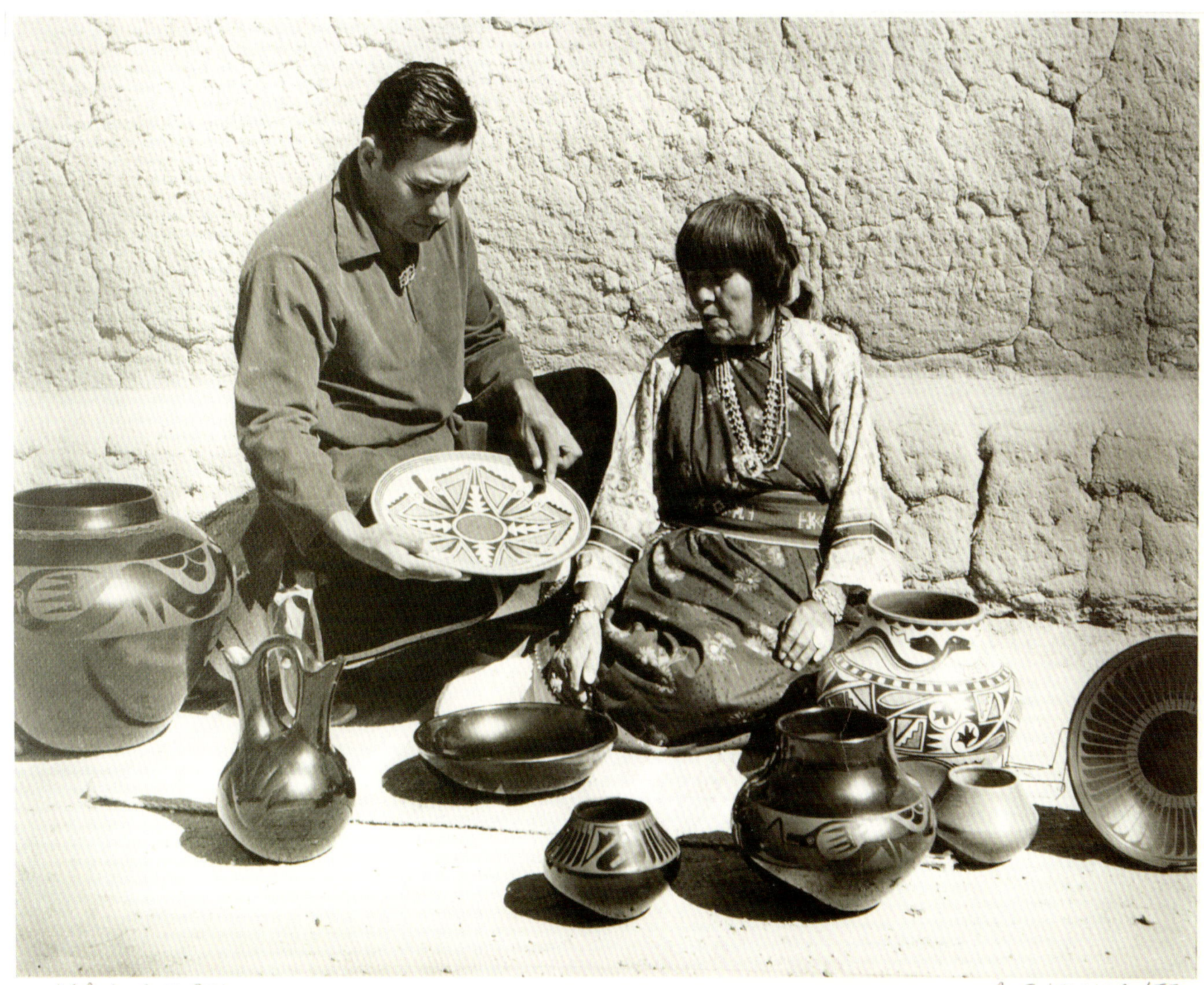

Plate 54 (facing page)
Laura Gilpin (U.S., 1891–1979)
Portrait of a Navajo Boy, 1932
Gelatin silver print, $9\frac{11}{16} \times 7\frac{3}{4}$ in.
© 1979 Amon Carter Museum of American Art, Fort Worth, Texas
Philbrook Museum of Art
A2007.0757

Plate 55 (above)
B. Schroeter (Unknown)
Maria and Son, 1957
Gelatin silver print, $10\frac{1}{2} \times 13\frac{1}{4}$ in.
Fred Jones Jr. Museum of Art
A2007.0789

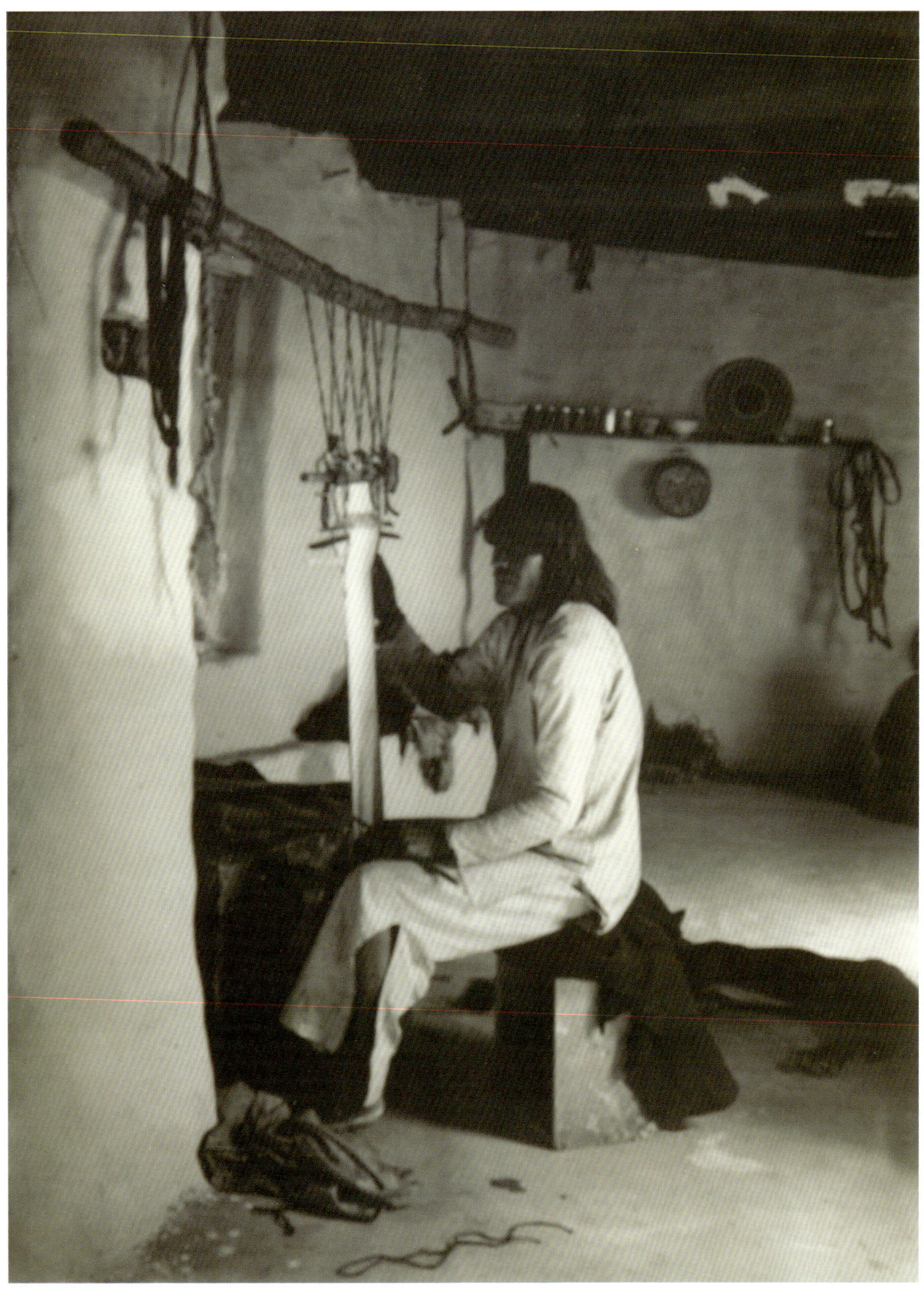

Plate 56 (above)
Adam Clark Vroman (U.S., 1856–1916)
Hopi Sash-Weaver, c. 1901
Gelatin silver print, 8 × 6 in.
Fred Jones Jr. Museum of Art
a2007.0717

Plate 57 (facing page)
John Young-Hunter (U.S., b. Scotland, 1874–1955)
Mabel Dodge Luhan, n.d.
Gelatin silver print, 20 × 16 in.
Philbrook Museum of Art
a2007.0809

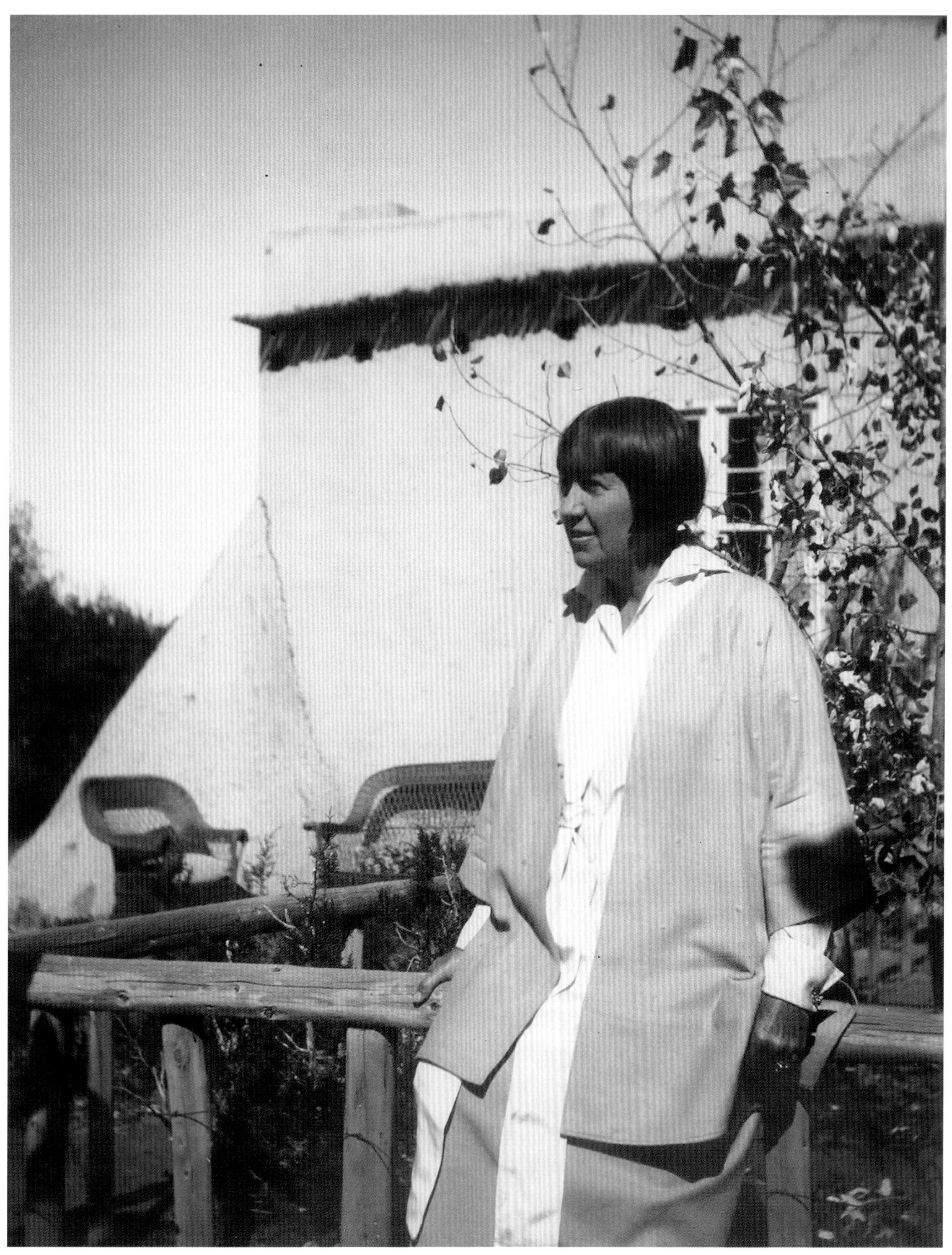

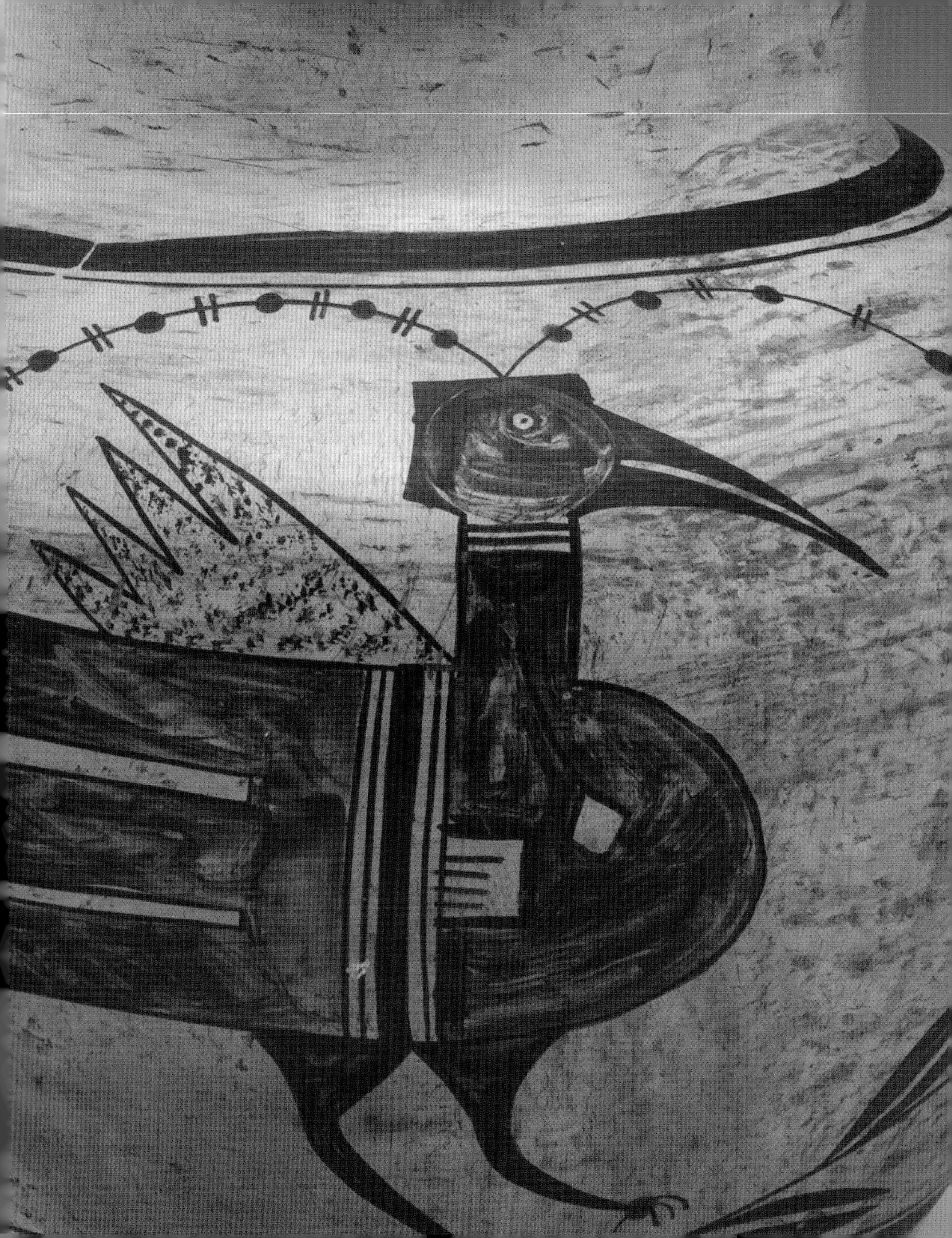

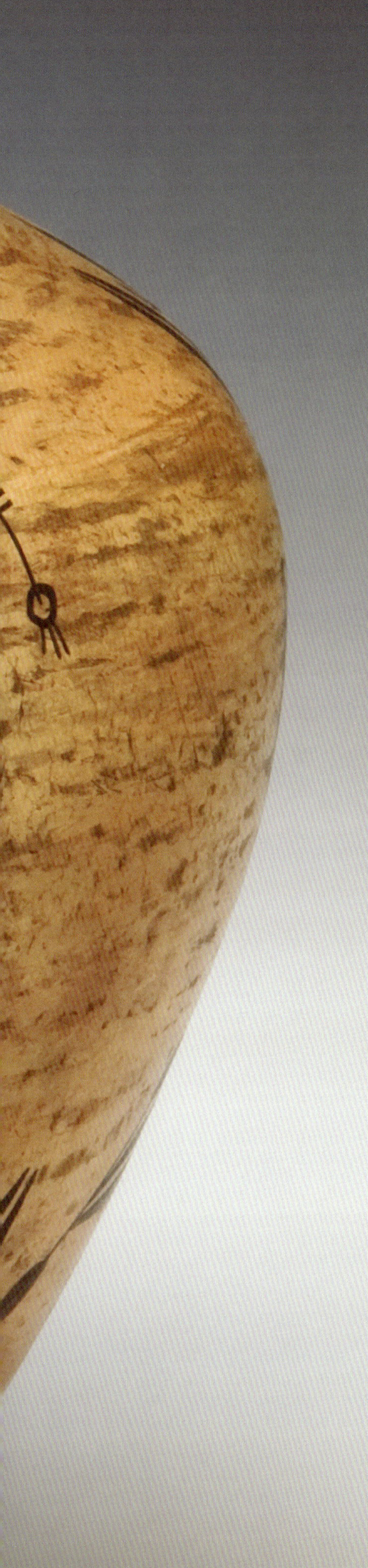

Native American Art

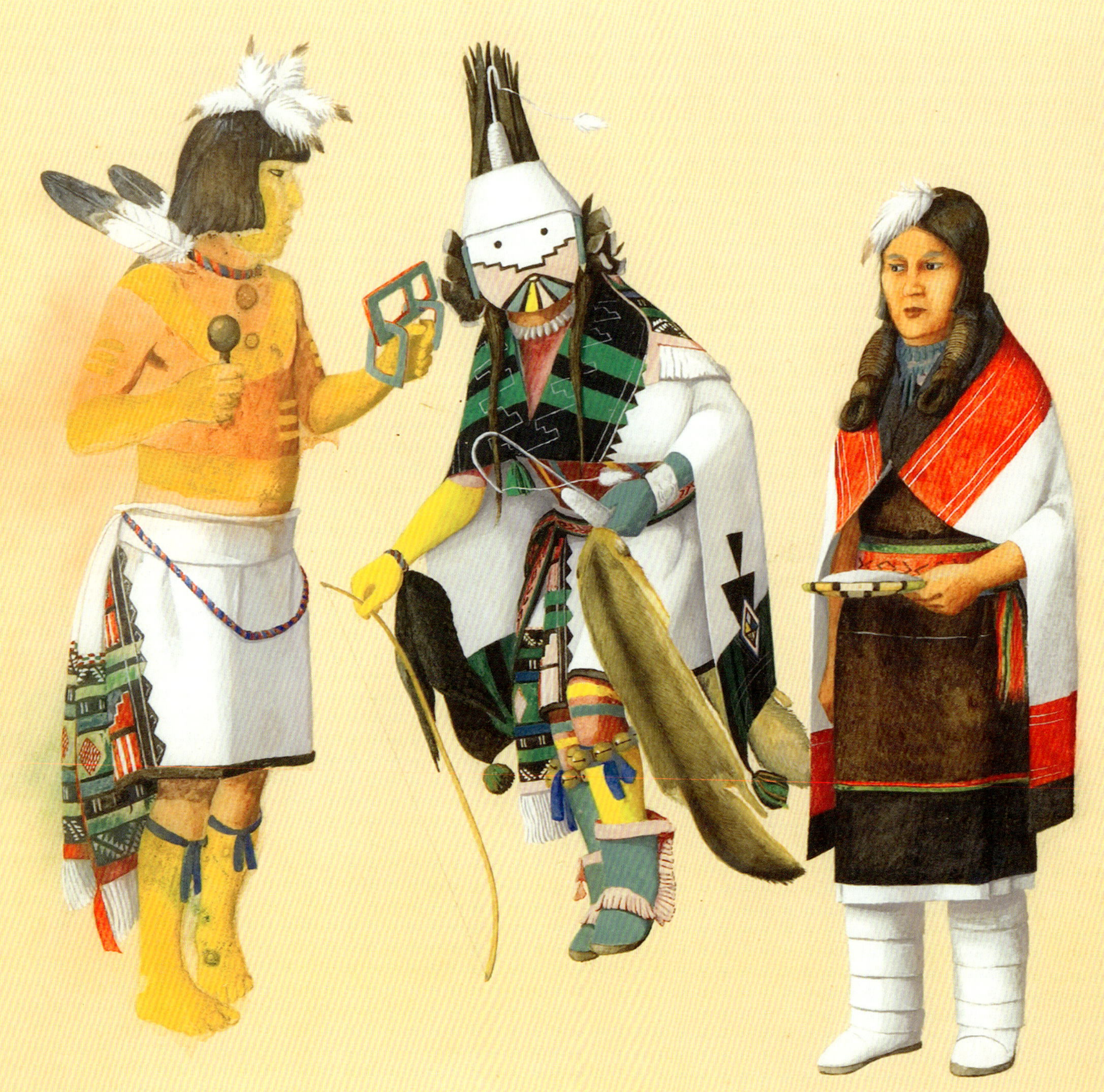
Fred Kabotie
Katchina Mana.
Shumai'koli
(Yaya Priest).

Influence and Invention
Native American Painting and Sculpture

W. Jackson Rushing III

CHAPTER FOUR

As a collector, Oklahoma native son Eugene B. Adkins was blessed with a concentrated vision. He focused almost exclusively on two aesthetic regions that have long captivated a wide audience: Oklahoma, with its plains and woodlands, and the American West. Adkins had a connoisseur's eye for quality and a scholar's knowledge of art historical significance. As a result, he collected wisely and well. The remarkable legacy of his acquisitive hunger—which was tempered by informed research—includes an outstanding assemblage of twentieth-century Native American painting and sculpture, selected highlights of which are featured in this book. In its entirety, the Adkins Collection includes fifty-three indigenous painters associated with the Southwest, seventeen with Oklahoma, and one Mission Indian—the eccentric and eclectic Fritz Scholder, always the odd man out in the history of modern Native painting.[1]

Even the short list examined in this essay reveals the complex relationships and histories contained within the Adkins Collection. Some of the stories told by these pictures and objects are familial, tribal, and institutional, while others are about the "call and response" we understand as stylistic evolution. For example, San Ildefonso Pueblo near Santa Fe, New Mexico, was one of the birthplaces, along with Anadarko, Oklahoma, of modern Native painting, and four of the artists highlighted in this book (representing three generations) were born there: Tonita Peña (1895–1949), J. D. Roybal (1922–1978), Gilbert Atencio (1930–1995), and Tony Da (1940–2008). Similarly, the Santa Clara painters Pablita Velarde (1918–2006) and Helen Hardin (1934–1984) were mother and daughter. Velarde and four other eminent second-generation modern Native artists were all students at the Studio of the Santa Fe Indian School (SFIS) in the 1930s: Allan Houser (Apache, 1914–1994), Harrison Begay (Navajo, b. 1917), Andrew Tsihnahjinnie (Navajo, 1918–2000), and Quincy Tahoma

Plate 58
Fred Kabotie (U.S., Hopi, 1900–1986)
Yaya Priest, n.d. Gouache on paper, 14⅝ x 10⅜ in.
Philbrook Museum of Art
A2007.0442

(Navajo, 1921–1956). For almost thirty years, the painting instructor at the SFIS, following Dorothy Dunn's departure, was the San Juan artist Geronima Cruz Montoya, whose son, Robert Montoya (Sandia/San Juan Pueblo, b. 1947) is included in this catalogue's selection. Hardin and Mary Morez (Navajo, 1946–2004) both participated in the Southwest Indian Art Project, the forerunner of the Institute of American Indian Arts in Santa Fe, where T. C. Cannon (Kiowa/Caddo/Choctaw 1946–1978), Bill Glass (Cherokee, b. 1950), Dan Namingha (Tewa-Hopi, b. 1950), and Tony Abeyta (Navajo, b. 1965) were all students. The Oklahoma counterpart to the Studio at the SFIS was the Art Department at Bacone College in Muskogee, whose director from 1947 to 1970 was the Cheyenne artist Walter Richard (Dick) West (1912–1996), who earned a BFA (1941) and an MFA (1950) at the University of Oklahoma. Like Houser, his generational peer, West studied with Olaf (Olle) Nordmark at the Fort Sill Indian School Art Center in the late 1930s and early 1940s. Other relationships can be teased out of the larger collection from which these highlights were culled, but this précis indicates the importance of family and village networks and the critical role played by art schools, teachers, and mentors.

The locus of the emergence of modern Native painting in the Southwest was Santa Fe, where the first generation of self-taught artists were supported by the culturati, such as the poet Alice Corbin Henderson, and by cultural institutions, including the Museum of New Mexico and the School of American Research, both founded by Edgar L. Hewett.[2] In this context, "modern" isn't meant to signify style, but signifies instead a commingling of social and aesthetic practice: the creation of nonritualistic pictures that were sold to white collectors, many of whom were engaged in salvage anthropology. Thus Peña's untitled, undated gouache painting of a Pueblo dance (plate 62) is driven by an emic, documentary impulse, as is *Yaya Priest* (plate 58), an undated gouache by Fred Kabotie (Hopi, 1900–1986). The point of intersection between these painters and their patrons was a belief in the necessity of indigenous art forms and a compelling need to record them for posterity. That is, Peña, the only female painter of her generation, was engaged in what David W. Penney and Lisa A. Roberts have described as auto-ethnography. A subject matter or image that was *natural* for Peña (who was also known as Quah Ah, or White Coral Beads) was *exotic* for her collectors, and thus she was picturing for outsiders "what is normally only enacted."[3] Like Peña's and Kabotie's pictures of cultural life, *The New Bride Woman* (plate 63), an undated work on paper by Otis Polelonema (Hopi, 1902–1981), is characterized by fastidious brushwork and attention to detail. Both Kabotie and Polelonema began painting as teenagers at the SFIS with the encouragement of Elizabeth DeHuff, wife of the school's superintendent, and their genre paintings constitute an indigenous naturalism.

Although artists who trained at the Studio at the SFIS under Dunn and Montoya typically worked in the "house style," virtually all of them managed to give it personal inflection. Begay's untitled, undated image of Navajo men performing a round dance is a classic example: the colors are flat and the pictorial space almost nonexistent; no extraneous details detract from the gestalt of the image; and the details that are given (clothing and jewelry) are meant to establish ethnicity, or "Navajoness," which the figures are performing for the viewer (plate 64). Tsihnahjinnie's undated gouache, *Navajo Thinking of His Horse* (plate 65), is less anthropological, more imaginative, with its apparitional horse and arcing, decorative image of a supernatural being. The Navajo man, a tall vertical form positioned just slightly off the central axis, is framed by a series of curves in the middle register and by spindly plants in the lower register. Simultaneously active and still, the painting pictures "thinking" and spirit for us, just as it unifies supernatural, human, land, animal, and plant forms into a quiet narrative moment. Although they were created thirty years apart, Tahoma's untitled gouache (1952, plate 66) and Velarde's *Mealtime on the Mesa* (1982, plate 67) are instructive in comparison. The former is explosively dynamic, with three powerful horses flying through the air seemingly into our space. With manes and tails whipping in the wind, the horses are the epitome of untamed energy. By contrast, Velarde gives us a charming genre scene, with roadrunners standing in for a human family. Precisely drawn, with indigenous designs decorating their bodies, the birds forage for food in a fantastic landscape.

Although J. D. Roybal (Oquwa, or Rain God), from San Ildefonso, was, in terms of age set, a member of the second, or Studio-style, generation of southwestern painters, he wasn't schooled there. His uncle, however, was Alfonso Roybal (Awa Tsireh, or Cattail Bird), a member of the first generation, who, along with Fred Kabotie, Julian Martinez, and Tonita Peña, helped establish the criteria for quality in modern Pueblo painting. In the nephew's untitled, undated (perhaps after 1955) tempera on paper, at the very front of the picture plane, a line of dancers and musicians follow a Koshare (or sacred clown). In the background, echoing the entrance of their ancestors into this world, more Koshares emerge from a kiva (sacred, subterranean space). The figures in the foreground perform on a stylized design, as if it were the apron of a stage. The design symbolizes survival in the high desert, implying that nature is literally the foundation of culture (plate 68). We see a rather different approach in the mid-career work of Gilbert Atencio (Wah Peen, 1930–1995), who was governor of San Ildefonso in 1966 and the nephew of Julian and Maria Martinez. Certainly, Atencio made "traditional" genre paintings of dancers and dancing, but he is best remembered, perhaps, for large, realistic portraits of single figures, such as the tempera and the gouache, both from 1964, featured here: *The Flute Player* (plate 69) and *Untitled* (*Pueblo Woman with Pot,* plate 51). Using strong drawing and spatial perspective, Atencio allows his volumetric figures to occupy pictorial space. Boldly colored and emphasizing ethnographic details, both figures are given cultural specificity by the presence of pottery, a textile, or a glimpse of architecture. These "props" function compositionally even as they mark the statuesque figures as San Ildefonsans. A similar realism and dramatic presence often characterized the work of the Oklahoma painter Valjean Hessing (Choctaw, 1934–2006), whose gouache *Allotment Paper for Rock and Candy* (1977, plate 70) shows an autochthonous and statuesque male figure with his

Plate 59
Gilbert Atencio (Wah Peen) (U.S., San Ildefonso, 1930–1995)
Untitled (*Pueblo Woman with Pot*), 1964. Gouache on paper, 16½ × 11 in.
Philbrook Museum of Art
A2007.0929

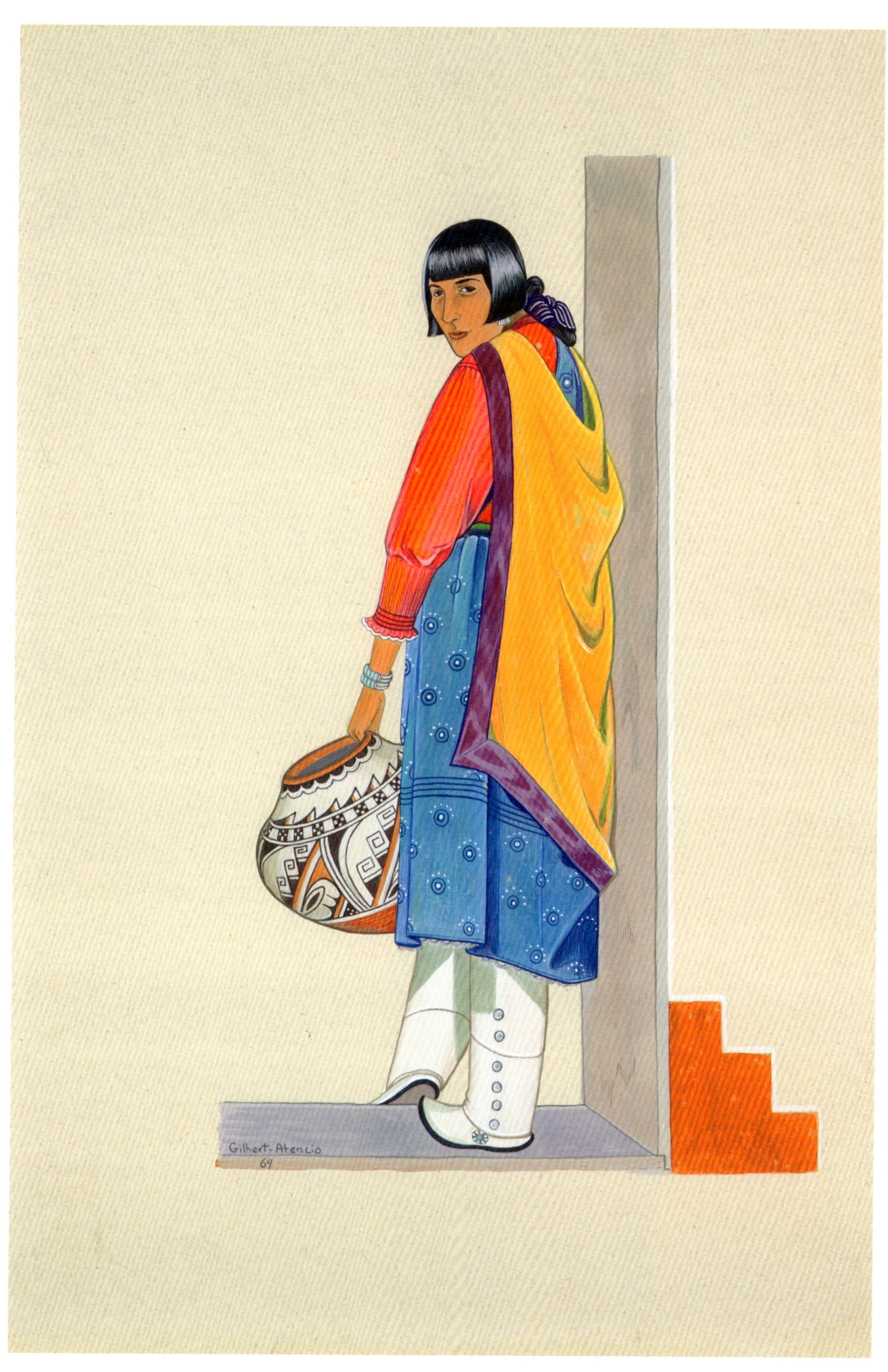
Gilbert-Atencio
64

extended family behind him. His rhetorical posture and the piece of paper he clutches in his hand are all that's necessary to establish the forced removal of the Choctaws from their traditional woodland home in the southeastern United States as the raison d'être for this gripping painting.

If the institutional loci of modern Native painting before the 1960s were the Studio at the SFIS and the Art Department at Bacone College, the closing of the Studio and the simultaneous opening of the Institute of American Indian Arts (IAIA) in Santa Fe in 1962 was the catalyst for radical change. The Southwest Indian Art Project, an experimental summer school for Native artists at the University of Arizona in Tucson, was a dress rehearsal for the new IAIA. In 1960 both Hardin and Morez were enrolled in the summer project, where their painting instructor was Tonita Peña's son, Joe Herrera (Cochiti), the inventor of Pueblo modernism.[4] Herrera had been celebrated in the early to mid-1950s for fusing designs and images from ancient pictography, kiva murals, pottery, and textiles with modernist influences (Paul Klee, cubism, art deco). The resultant paintings, which extended and transformed Studio genres, and which demonstrated the compatibility of Pueblo and modernist geometry, showed a generation of southwestern Indian painters the way forward. *The Four Worlds* (tempera, c. 1954), a recent gift to the Fred Jones Jr. Museum of Art from noted collector Rennard Strickland, is a fine example of this period in Herrera's career. Hardin's undated (probably c. 1975–1977) oil on board *Vision of a Ghost Dance* (plate 71) shares with Herrera's Pueblo modernism a spattered, atmospheric background and emphasis on geometry and aboriginal decorative forms. Figurative but semiabstract—again, a hallmark of Herrera's mature work—Hardin's dancers are but specters and appropriately so, given the subject matter. Morez's oil on canvas *Father Sky and Mother Earth* (1970, plate 72) may have been inspired by an iconic watercolor reproduction of a Navajo sandpainting in the collection of the Wheelwright Museum of the American Indian in Santa Fe and published by the Museum of Modern Art in 1941. As in many classic Herrera paintings, Morez recontextualizes traditional imagery: on an abstract color field that evokes the heat and scintillating colors of Navajo country, she floats a pair of cosmological figures in an indeterminate space. As Nancy J. Parezo has observed, Father Sky and Mother Earth figures are popular in commercial sandpaintings.[5] Although not an IAIA student, Tony Da's masterful untitled drawing and painting in casein on paper (1971, plate 73) relates both to Herrera's style *and* to the fantastic stylized birds painted in the 1920s by his grandfather, Julian Martinez. Da's bird is constructed from basket and pottery designs and decorated with clan symbols and a scroll motif that signifies, perhaps, the emergence and journey of the ancestors. All the parts are unified in a configuration that is linear, balanced, and notable for its clarity and precision. In its articulation and sublimation of part to whole, Da's image speaks to the harmony of Pueblo culture in its ideal form.

Other southwestern Indian painters in the Adkins Collection who studied at the IAIA include Dan Namingha and Tony Abeyta. Namingha's *Night Singer* is an undated early work (c. 1975 perhaps), painted in a fluid, gestural style (plate 74). The horizontal striations of landscape are balanced by the emphatic verticality of the female figure, and the natural texture of the jute picture support establishes a telluric character. Abeyta's *Yeis in Chanting Procession* (a mixed media work from 1994) is striking for its scale and vibrant, dynamic surface (plate 75). Both artists come from artistic families: Namingha's great-great-grandmother Nampeyo initiated the Hopi Pottery Revival in the late nineteenth century, and his mother, Dextra Quotskuyva, is a celebrated potter; Abeyta's father, Narciso Abeyta (Ha So De), was a psychologically expressive painter and classmate of Herrera and Tsihnahjinnie at the studio.[6] Similarly, Robert Montoya (Soe Khuwa Pin) is the son of the distinguished painter and teacher Geronima Cruz Montoya.[7] Although not an IAIA student, he did earn a master's degree at the University of Oklahoma. Montoya's *Pueblo God Mother* (watercolor,

1985, plate 76) in the Adkins Collection, which is remarkably similar in style to his *Winter and Summer Pueblo Corn Dancers* (also 1985) in the Avery Collection of American Indian Paintings at the University of Arizona, suggests a keen awareness of his mother's work, as well as that of Herrera and Hardin. Mixing transparency, planarity, and geometry with more atmospheric passages, Montoya demonstrates a masterful control of watercolor, which is a difficult and unforgiving medium. With it he achieves here both delicacy and fidelity.

The most innovative artist to emerge from the IAIA in its early years was inarguably T. C. Cannon, who, like his teacher Fritz Scholder, used historical photographs, pop art, and various expressionist tendencies to create memorable images that investigated the very nature of what Native American painting could, should, and would be. A Native son of Oklahoma and a Vietnam veteran, his tragic death at age thirty-two in 1978 robbed the world of a prodigious talent. Cannon is represented in the Adkins Collection by a pair of small ink drawings, including an untitled self-portrait (1976, plate 60), which uses an elegant, almost calligraphic line to represent himself as an Indian cowboy dandy. *Indian and Tipi (Study for Lonely Indian)* (1972, plate 77) reveals an early stage in the creative process, in which a historical image is put into play in a notational sketch.

In addition to a stellar selection of paintings, Adkins also collected some sixteen Native American sculptures, including works by Doug Hyde (Nez Perce), Bruce Wynne (Spokane), and the legendary Zuni fetish carver Leekya Deyuse (1889–1966). Dick West's undated *Nostalgia* will be a revelation for those who know him only as a painter (plate 78). Expertly carved in wood, a male figure turns his body in space and looks back over his shoulder (at the past, perhaps), allowing West to show his ability to explore solid and void and to demonstrate his mastery of anatomy. Polished to a high sheen, the work is a fine marriage of subject matter and sculptural form. Bill Glass's *Buffalo* (1975, plate 79), which he carved

Plate 60
T. C. Cannon (U.S., Kiowa Caddo, Choctaw 1946–1978)
Self-Portrait, 1976. Ink on paper, 8 × 5 in.

Philbrook Museum of Art
A2007.0515

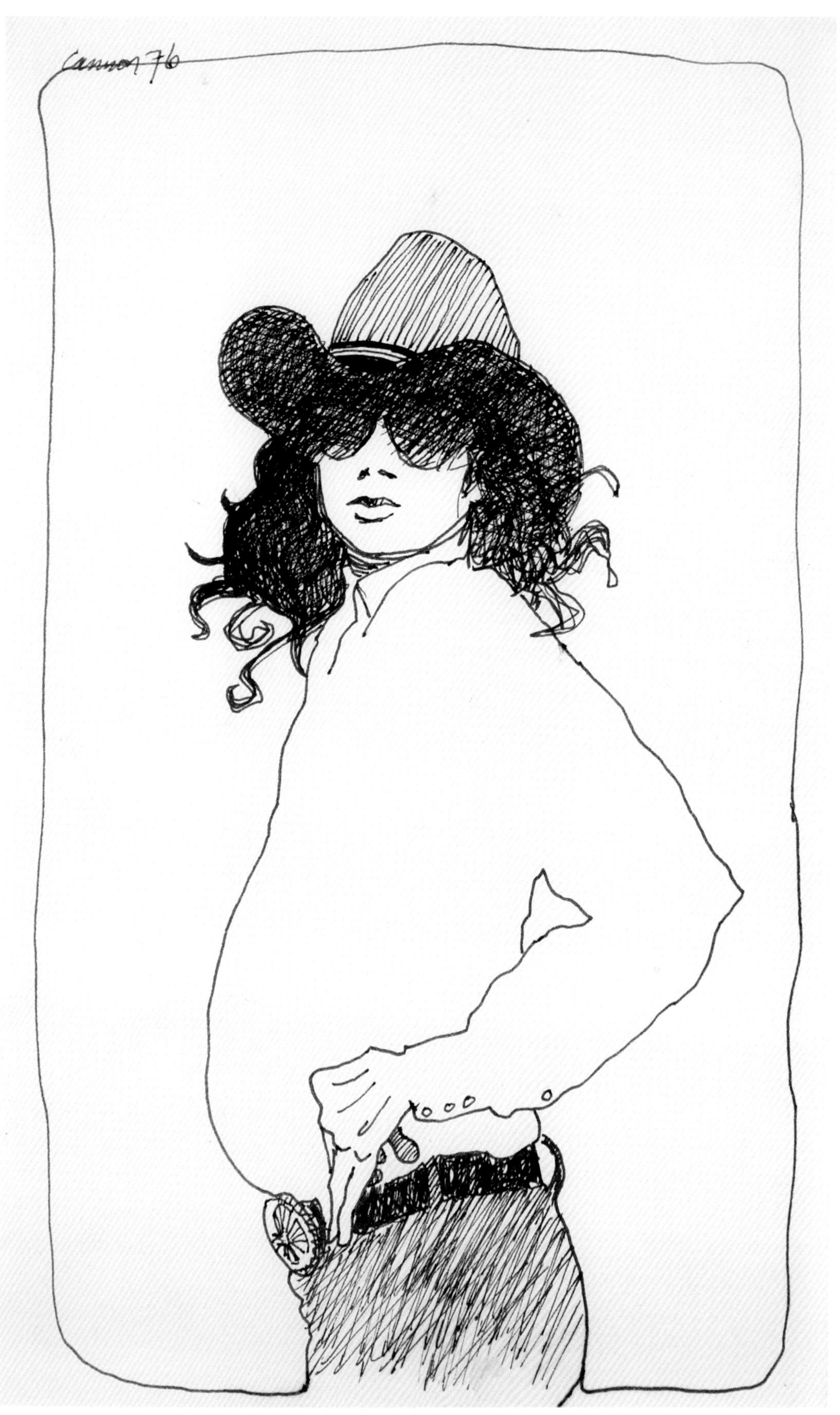
Cannon 76

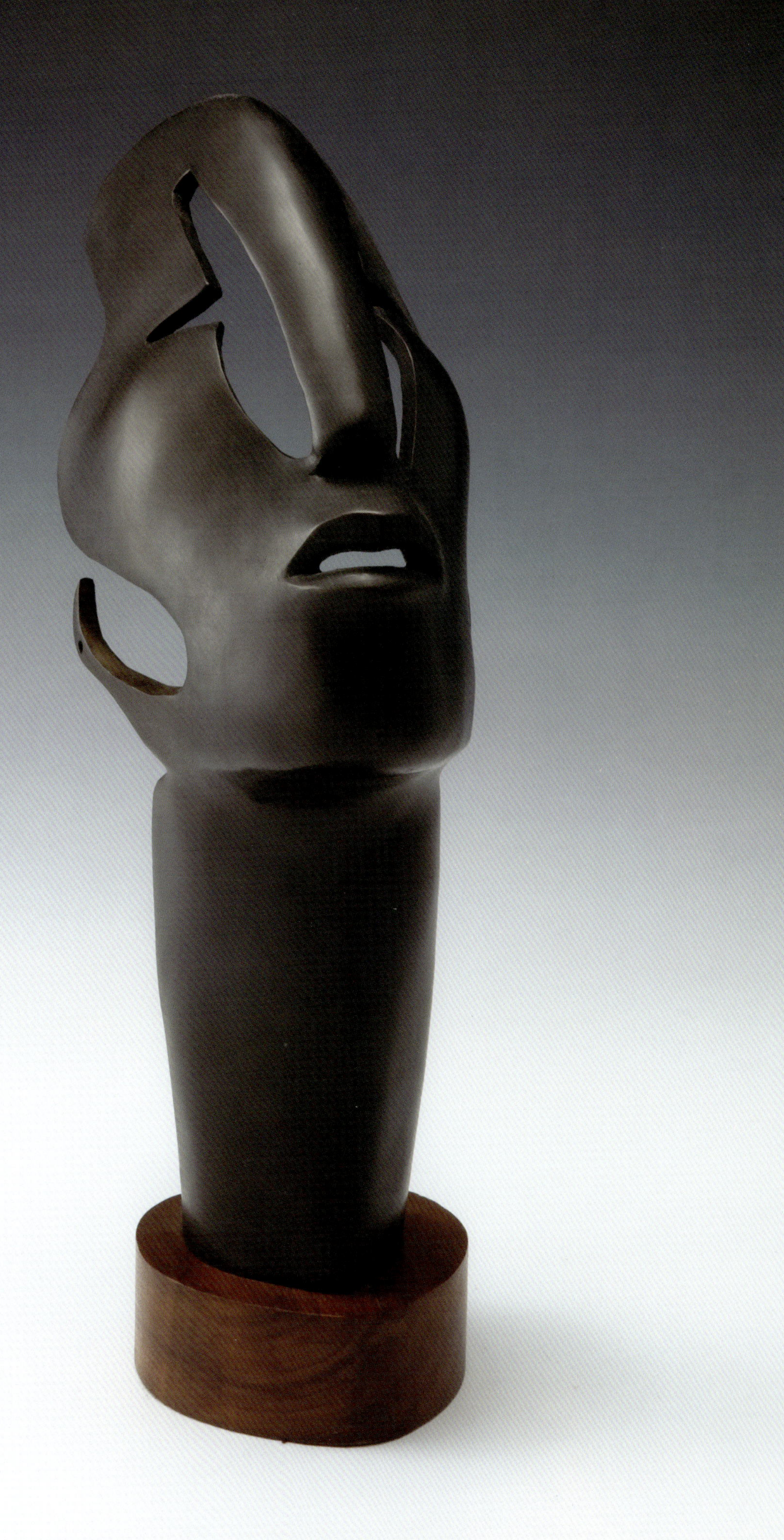

from white stone when he was only twenty-five years old, objectifies for us the relationship between hunter and animal. Glass, who studied with Allan Houser at the IAIA (1971–1973), has been recognized as a Master Artist by the Five Civilized Tribes Museum in Muskogee, Oklahoma. The four Houser sculptures in the Adkins Collection enhance the already strong holdings of his work in the Fred Jones Jr. Museum of Art. Houser, who was the first Native American to receive the National Medal of Art (1992), was among the most celebrated artists of the twentieth century. He established his critical reputation with direct stone carvings and cast bronzes in the 1970s, although he had been receiving awards and important commissions as a painter since the late 1930s. His dreamlike *Apache Mask* (bronze, 1976, plate 61) is a sleek, euphoric, open-work figure that embodies a feeling of universal spirituality.[8] It is a classic example of his inner vision and his refined sensitivity to materials and plastic form.

Eugene B. Adkins was clearly a prescient and progressive collector of Native American painting and sculpture. Even this brief overview indicates that he was not conceptually constrained by such categories as "traditional," "authentic," or "avant-garde." On the contrary, he acquired art across a wide aesthetic spectrum, leaving for posterity a collection ripe with curatorial and educational possibilities.

Plate 61
Allan C. Houser (U.S., Chiricahua Apache, 1914–1994)
Apache Mask, 1976. Bronze, 14½ × 5½ in.
© Chiinde LLC
Fred Jones Jr. Museum of Art
A2007.B32

Plates 62–79

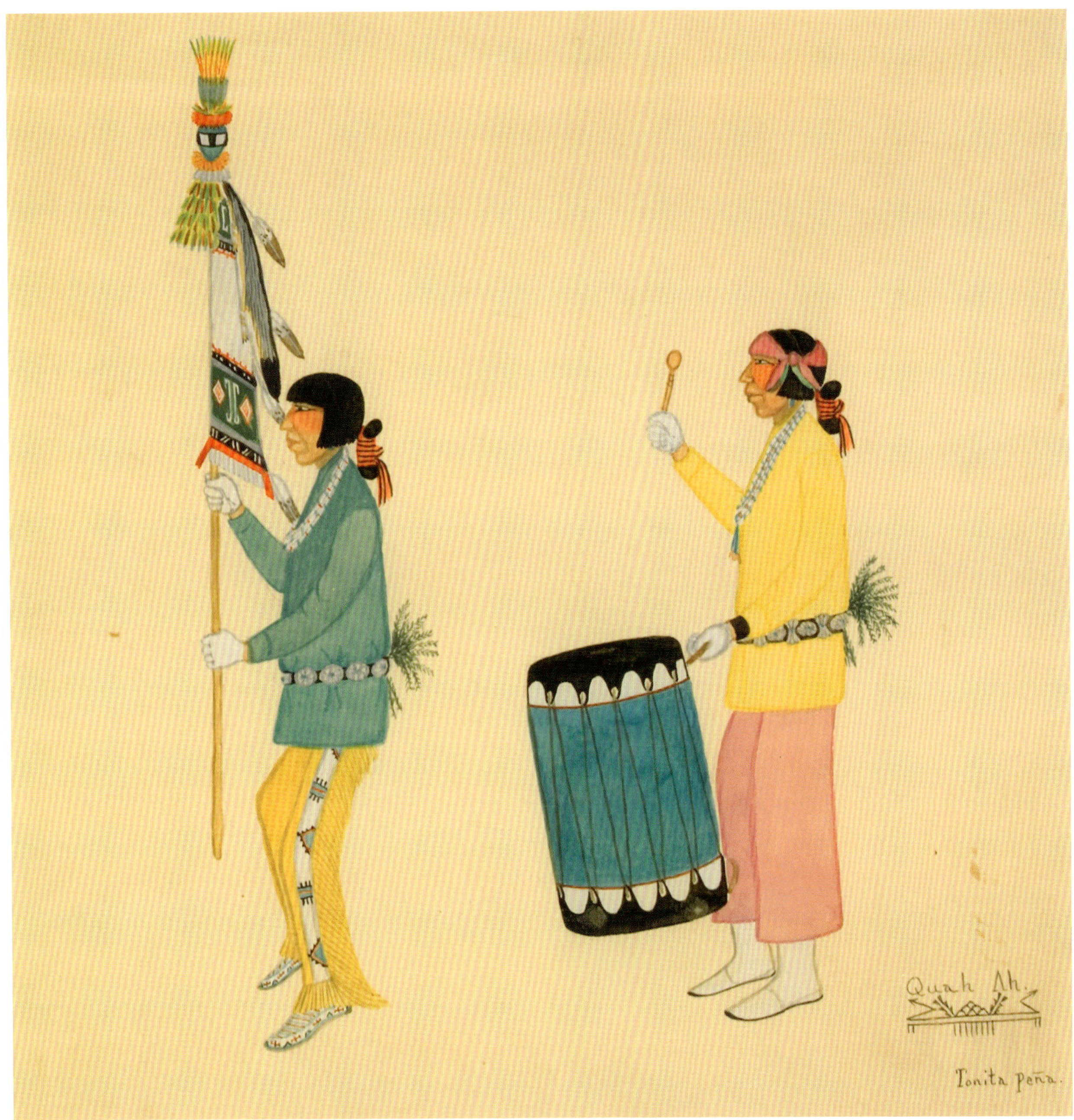

Plate 62
Tonita Peña (Quah Ah) (U.S., San Ildefonso, 1895–1949)
Untitled (Corn Dance), n.d. Gouache on paper, 12 × 12 in.
Fred Jones Jr. Museum of Art
A2007.0432

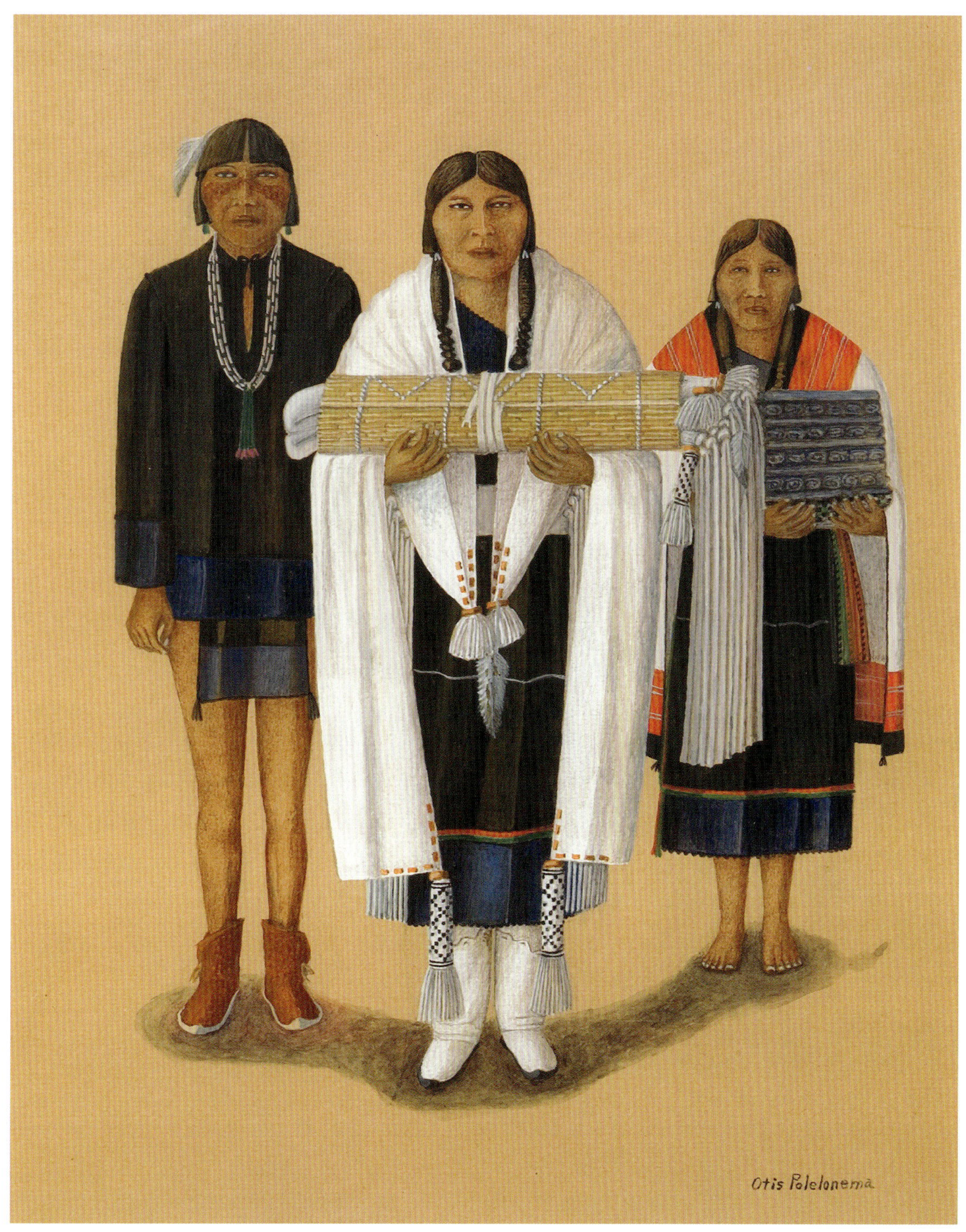

Plate 63
Otis Polelonema (U.S., Hopi, 1902–1981)
The New Bride Woman, n.d. Mixed media on paper 13 × 11 in.
Fred Jones Jr. Museum of Art
A2007.0318

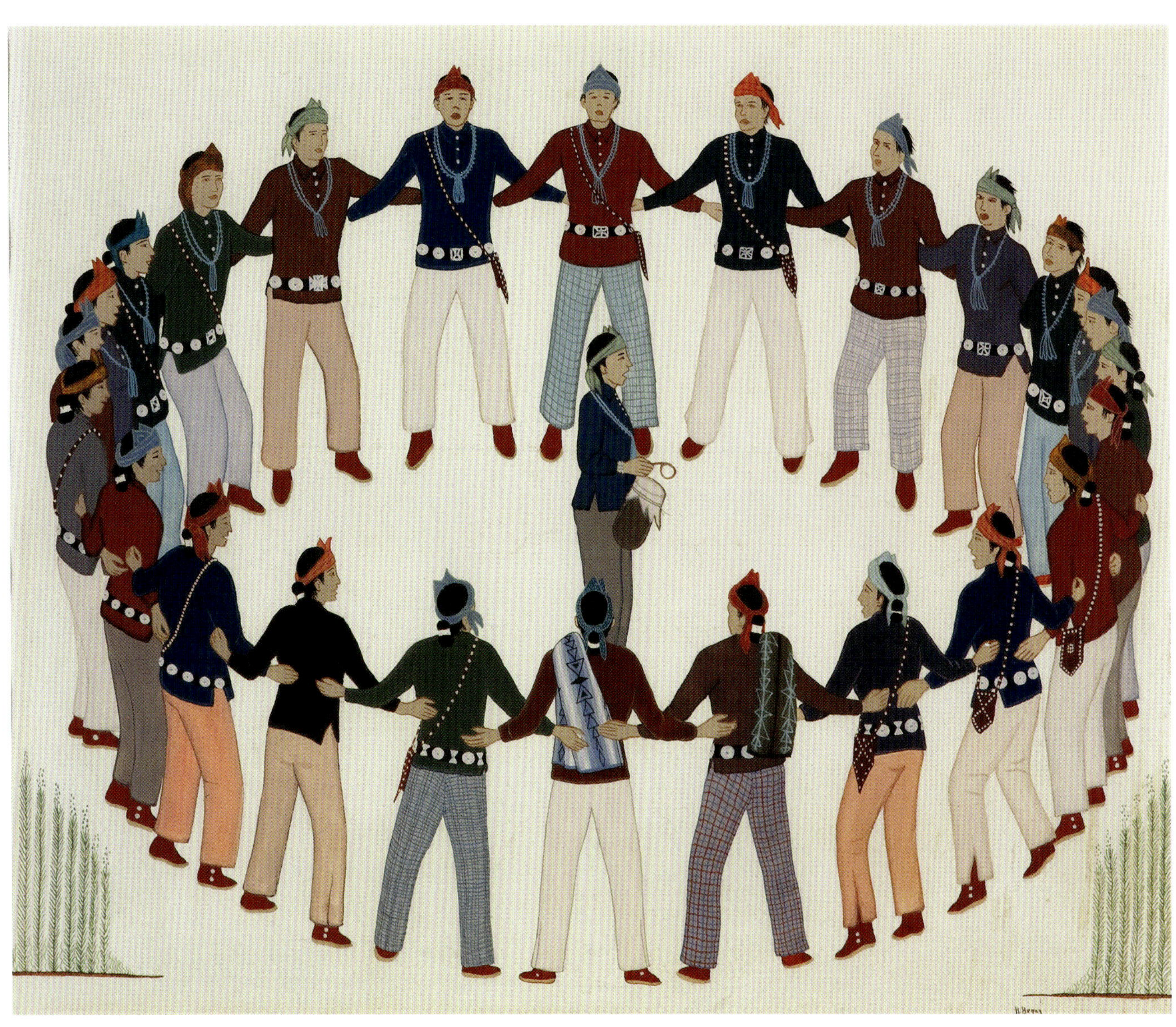

Plate 64
Harrison Begay (U.S., Navajo, b. 1917)
Untitled, n.d. Gouache on paper, 11 × 14 in.
Fred Jones Jr. Museum of Art
A2007.0539

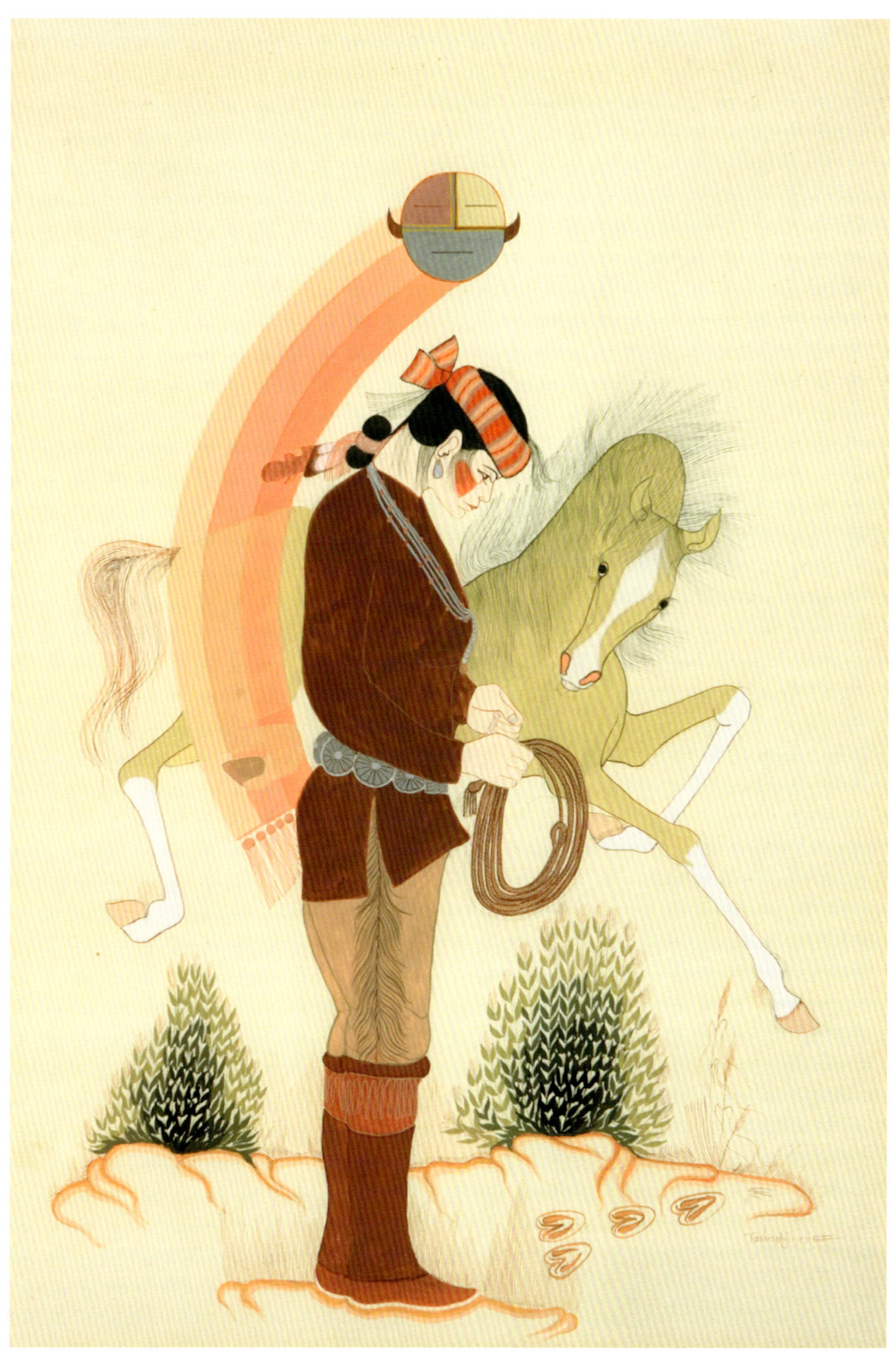

Plate 65
Andrew Tsihnahjinnie (U.S., Navajo, 1918–2000)
Navajo Thinking of His Horse, n.d. Gouache on paper, 19 × 13 in.
Fred Jones Jr. Museum of Art
A2007.0953

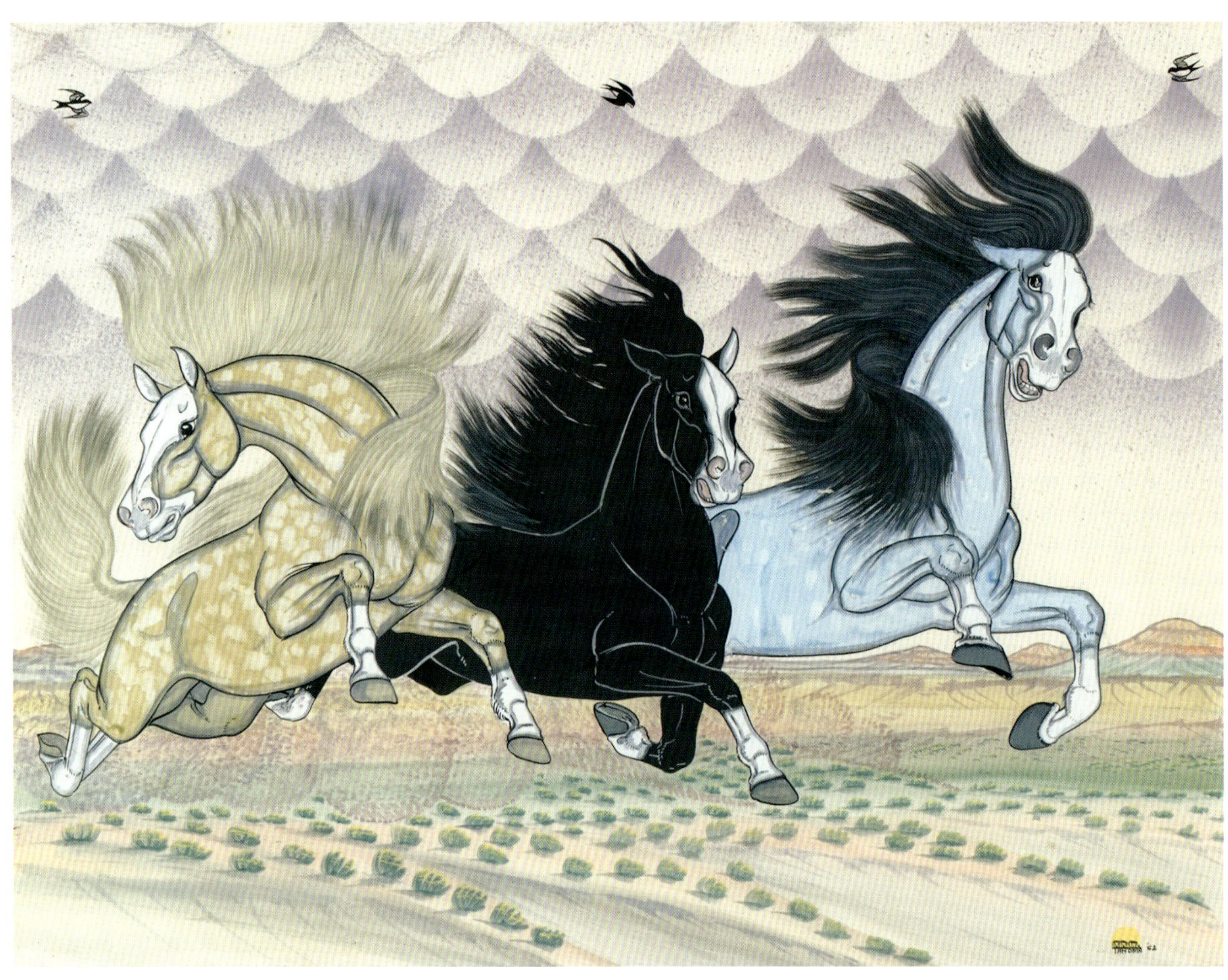

Plate 66
Quincy Tahoma (U.S., Navajo, 1921–1956)
Untitled, 1952. Gouache, 21 × 28 in.
Philbrook Museum of Art
A2007.1017

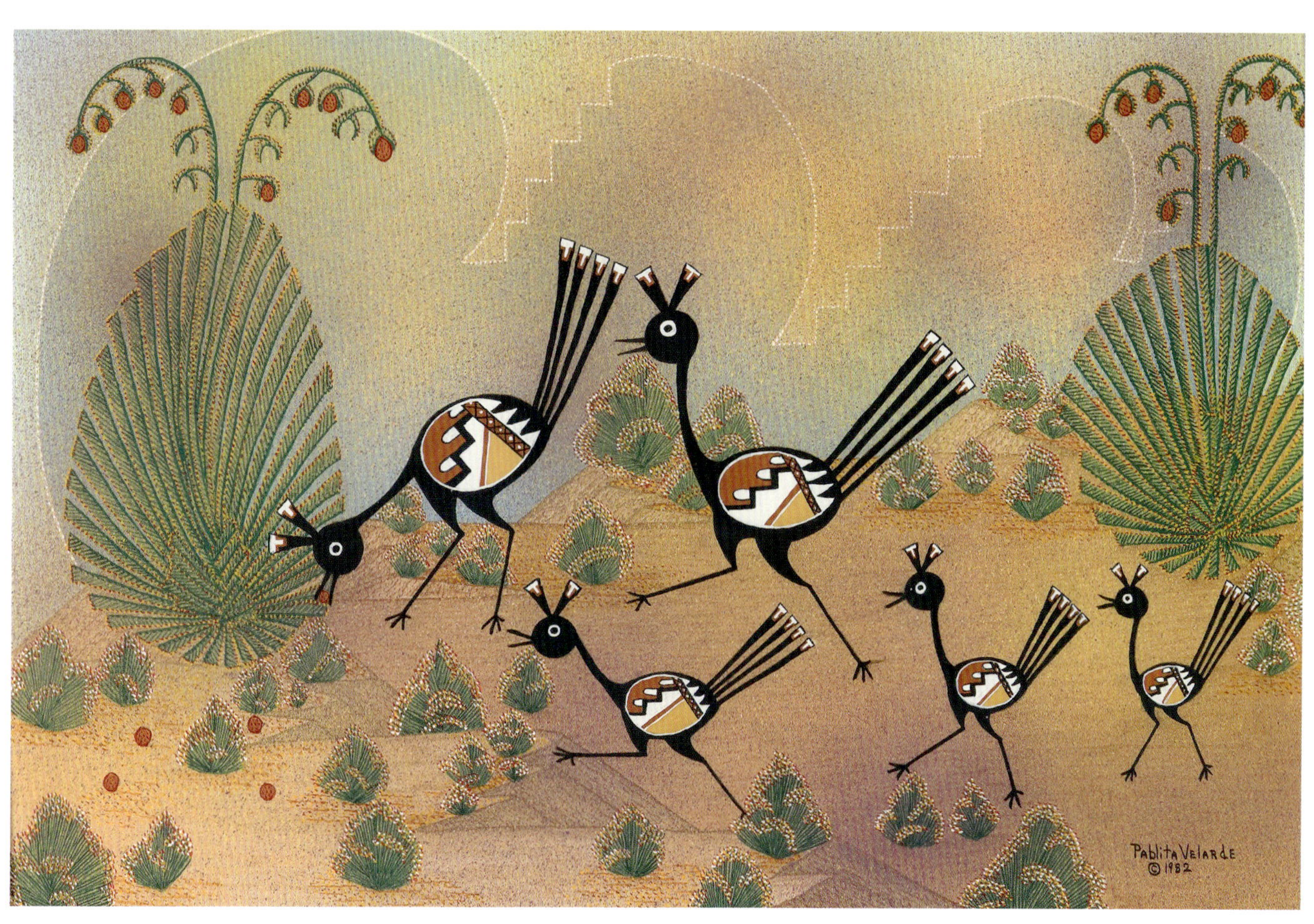

Plate 67
Pablita Velarde (U.S., Santa Clara, 1918–2006)
Mealtime on the Mesa, 1982. Casein on board, 11½ × 17 in.
Philbrook Museum of Art
A2007.0918

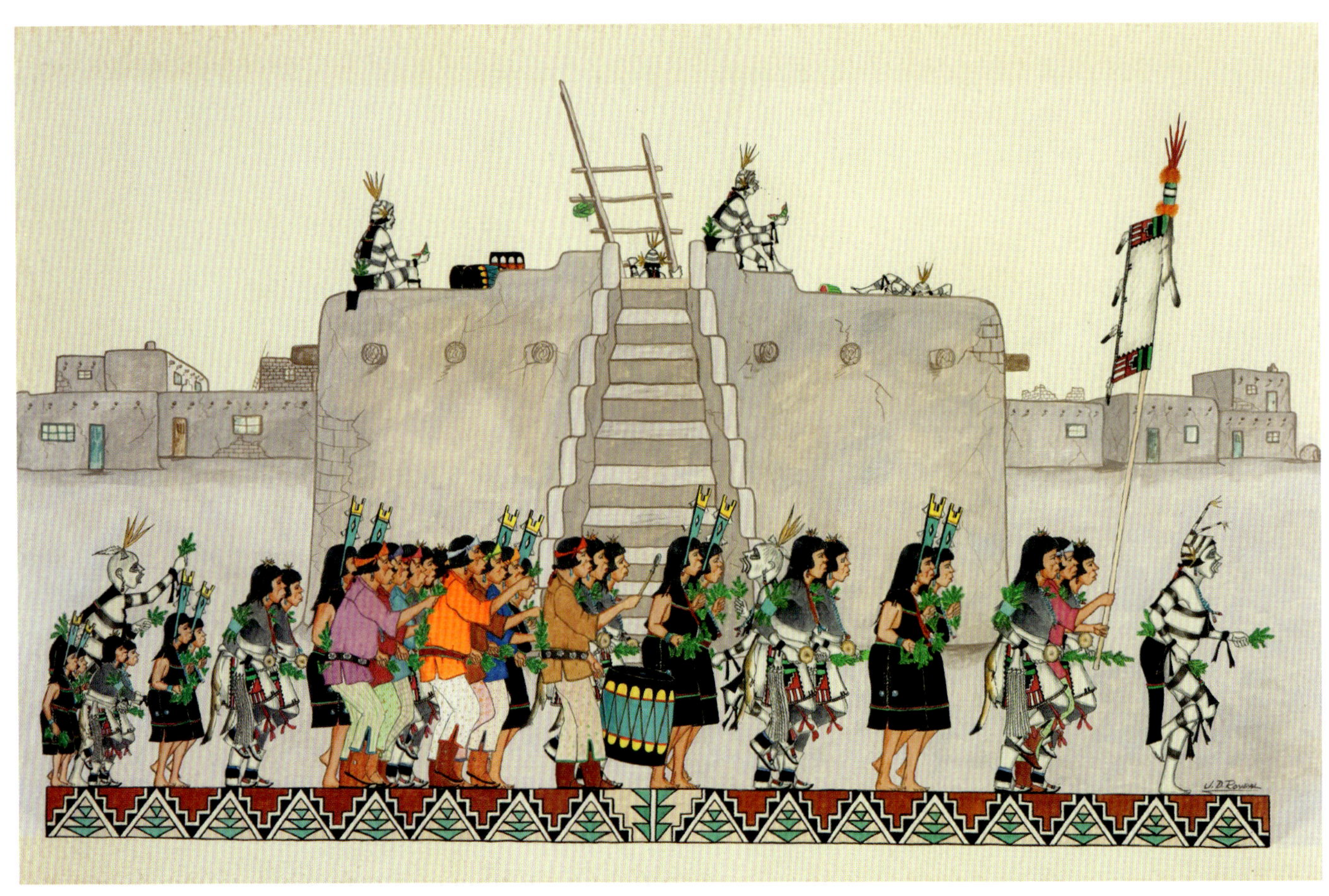

Plate 68
J. D. Roybal (U.S., San Ildefonso, 1922–1978)
Untitled, n.d. Tempera on paper, 13 × 21 in.
Philbrook Museum of Art
A2007.0374

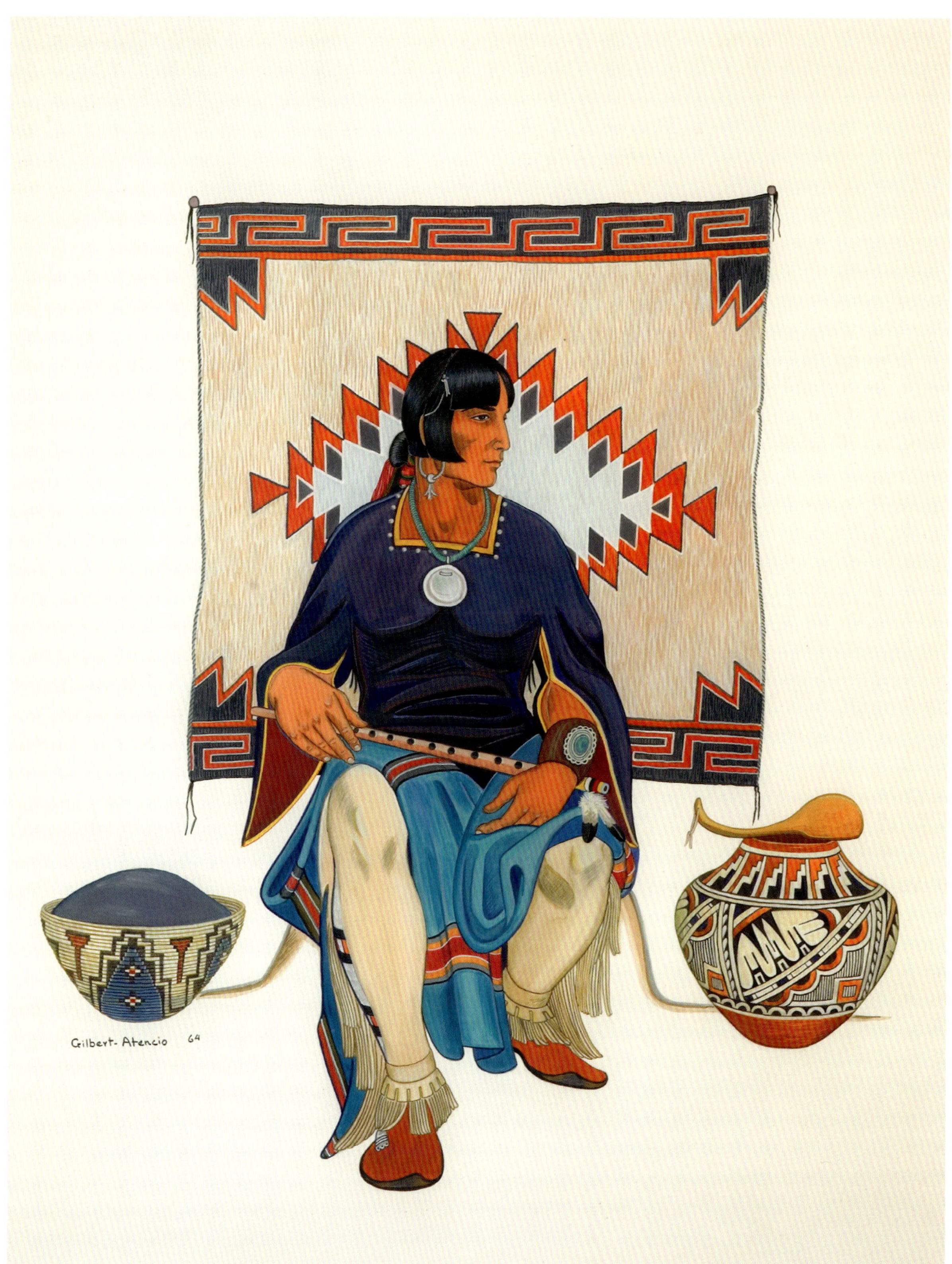

Plate 69
Gilbert Atencio (Wah Peen) (U.S., San Ildefonso, 1930–1995)
The Flute Player, 1964. Gouache on paper, 27 × 20 in.
Fred Jones Jr. Museum of Art
A2007.1015

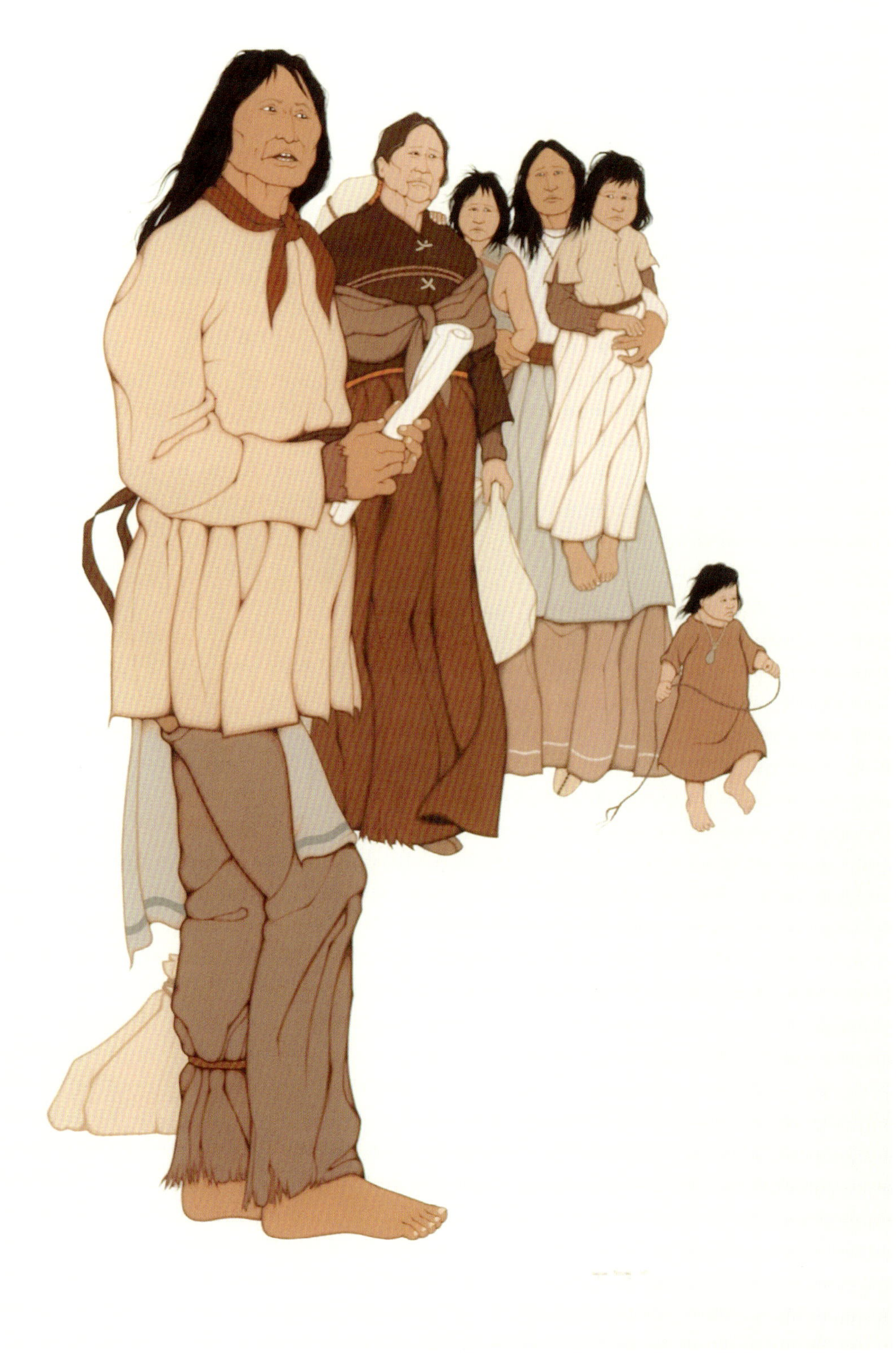

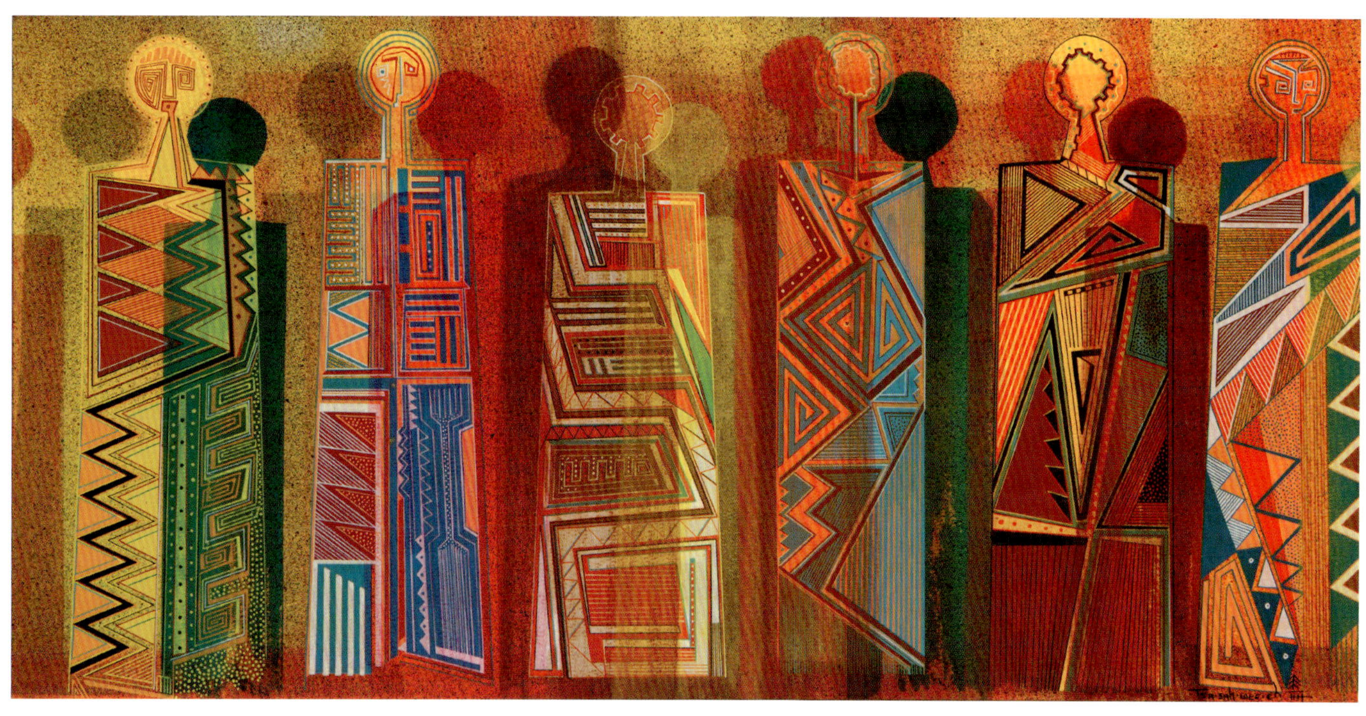

Plate 70 (facing page)
Valjean Hessing (U.S., Choctaw, 1934–2006)
Allotment Paper for Rock and Candy, 1977. Gouache, 30 × 19 in.
Fred Jones Jr. Museum of Art
A2007.1018

Plate 71 (above)
Helen Hardin (Tsa-Sah-Wee-Eh) (U.S., Santa Clara, 1943–1984)
Vision of a Ghost Dance, n.d. Oil on board, 12 × 24 in.
Philbrook Museum of Art
A2007.0189

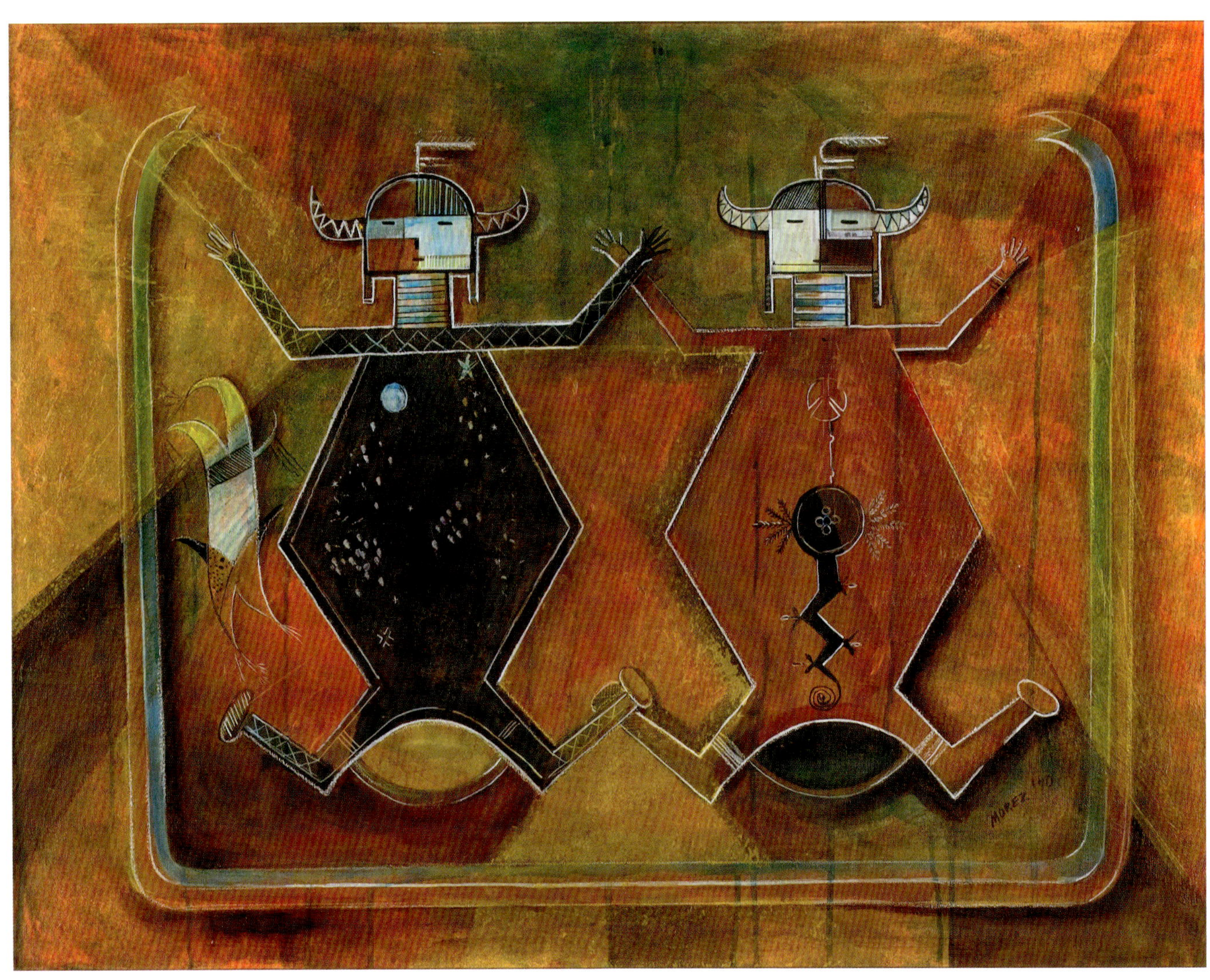

Plate 72
Mary Morez (U.S., Navajo, 1946–2004)
Father Sky and Mother Earth, 1970. Oil on canvas, 30 × 40 in.
Fred Jones Jr. Museum of Art
A2007.0210

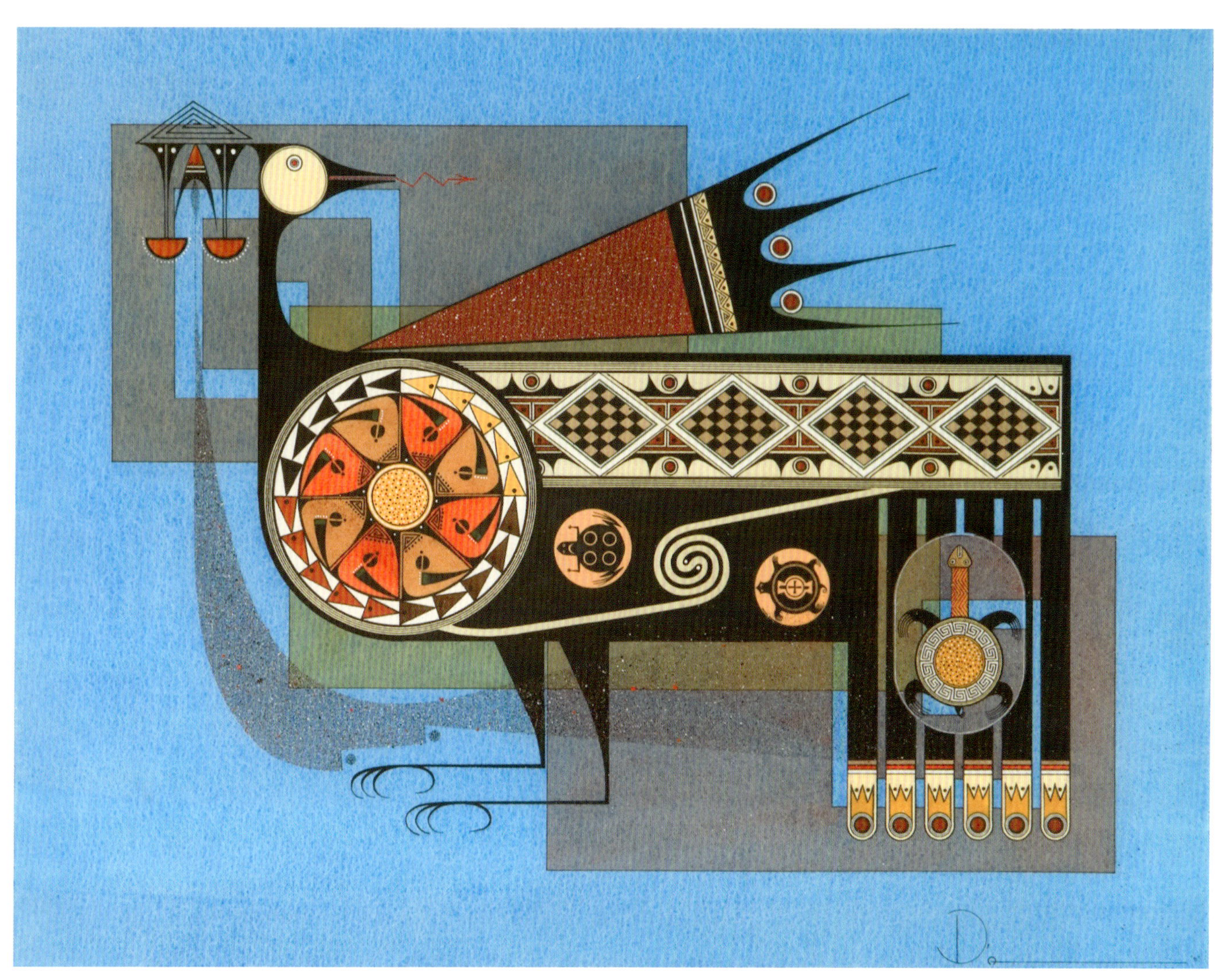

Plate 73
Tony Da (U.S., San Ildefonso, 1940–2008)
Turkey, 1971. Casein on paper, 14 × 18 in.
Fred Jones Jr. Museum of Art
A2007.0639

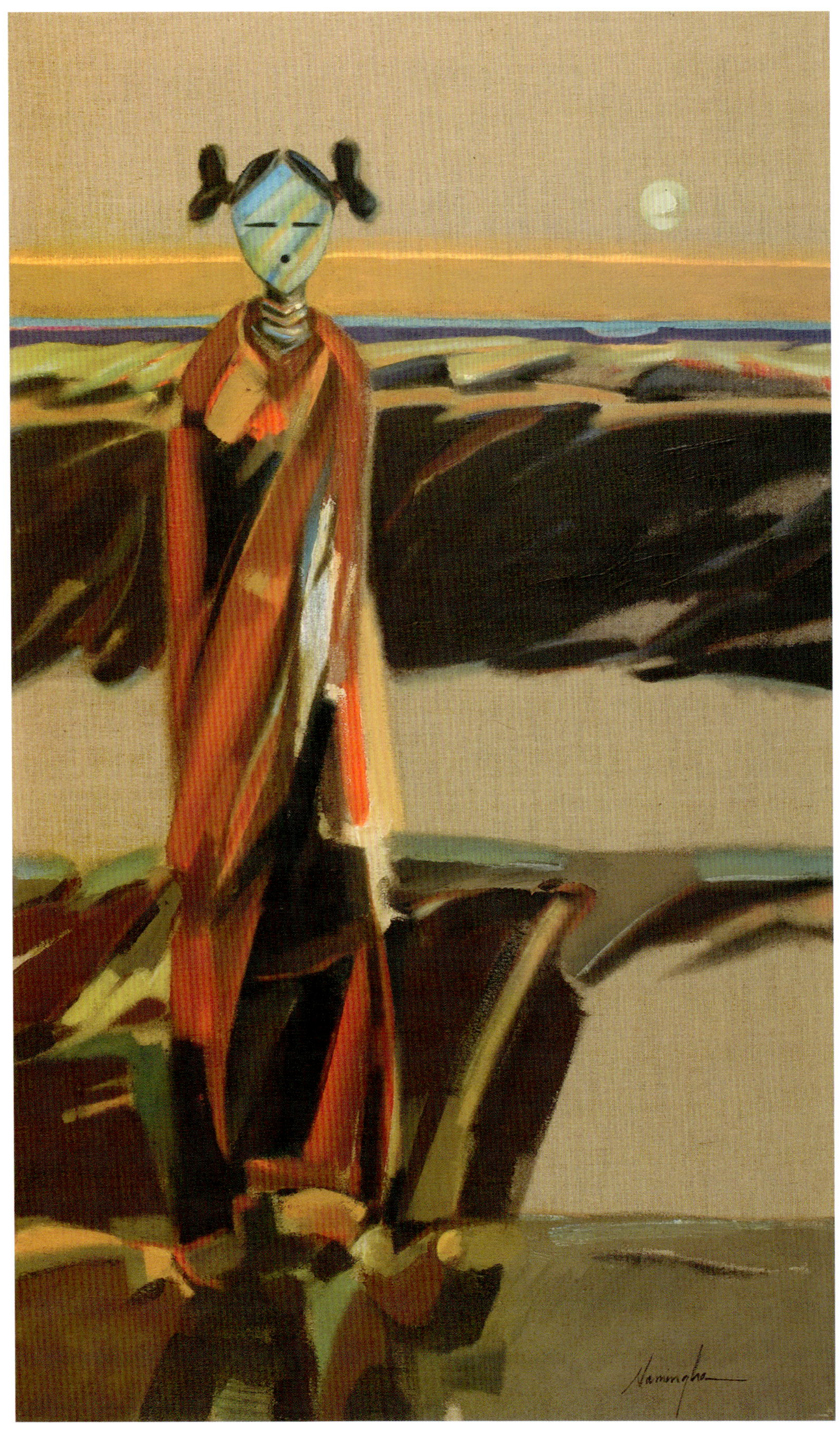

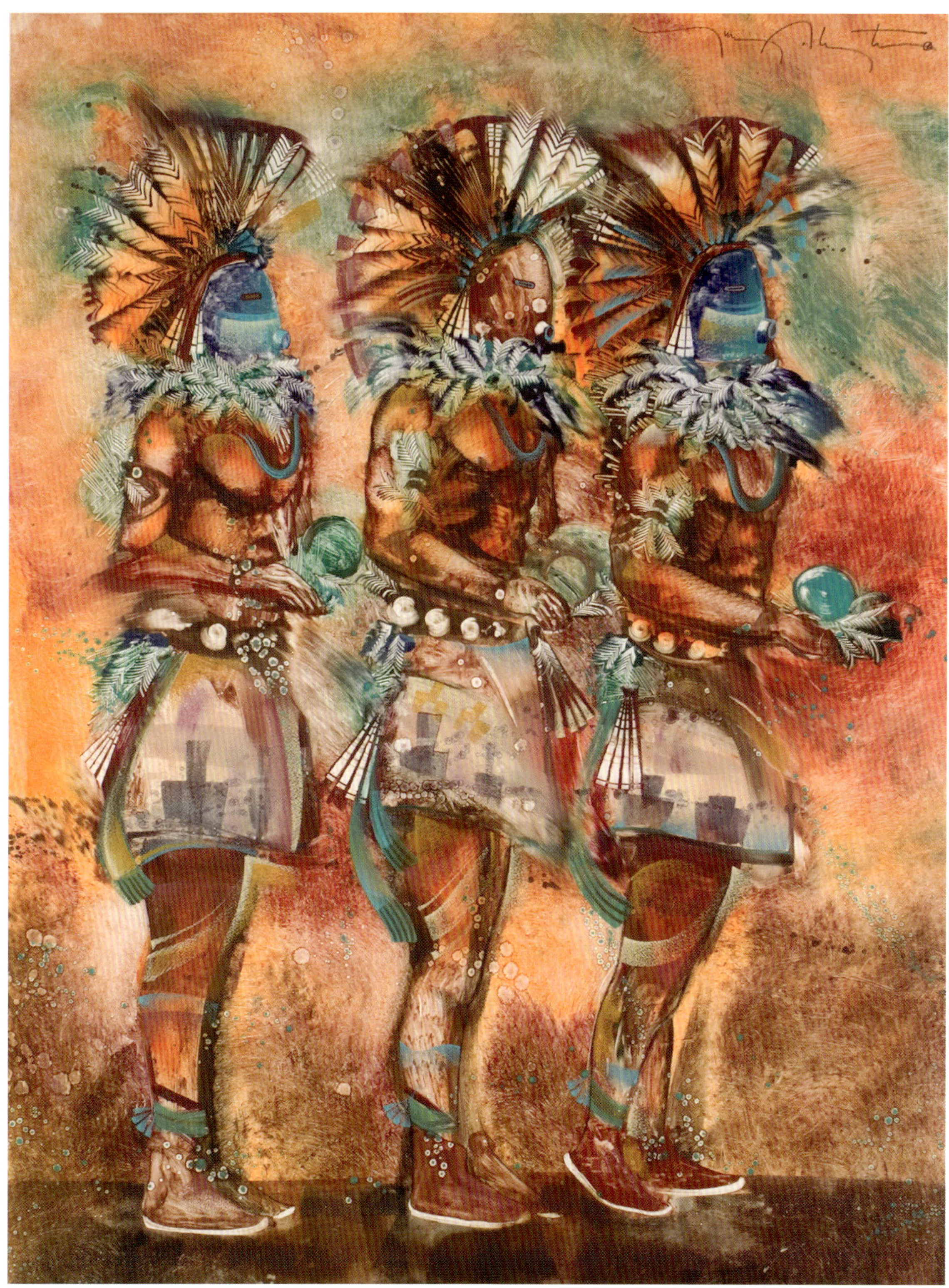

Plate 74 (facing page)
Dan Namingha (U.S., Tewa-Hopi, b. 1950)
Night Singer, n.d. Acrylic on jute, 54 × 32 in.
Philbrook Museum of Art
A2007.0226

Plate 75 (above)
Tony Abeyta (U.S., Navajo, b. 1965)
Yeis in Chanting Procession, 1994
Mixed media monotype, 48 × 36 in.
Fred Jones Jr. Museum of Art
A2007.1039

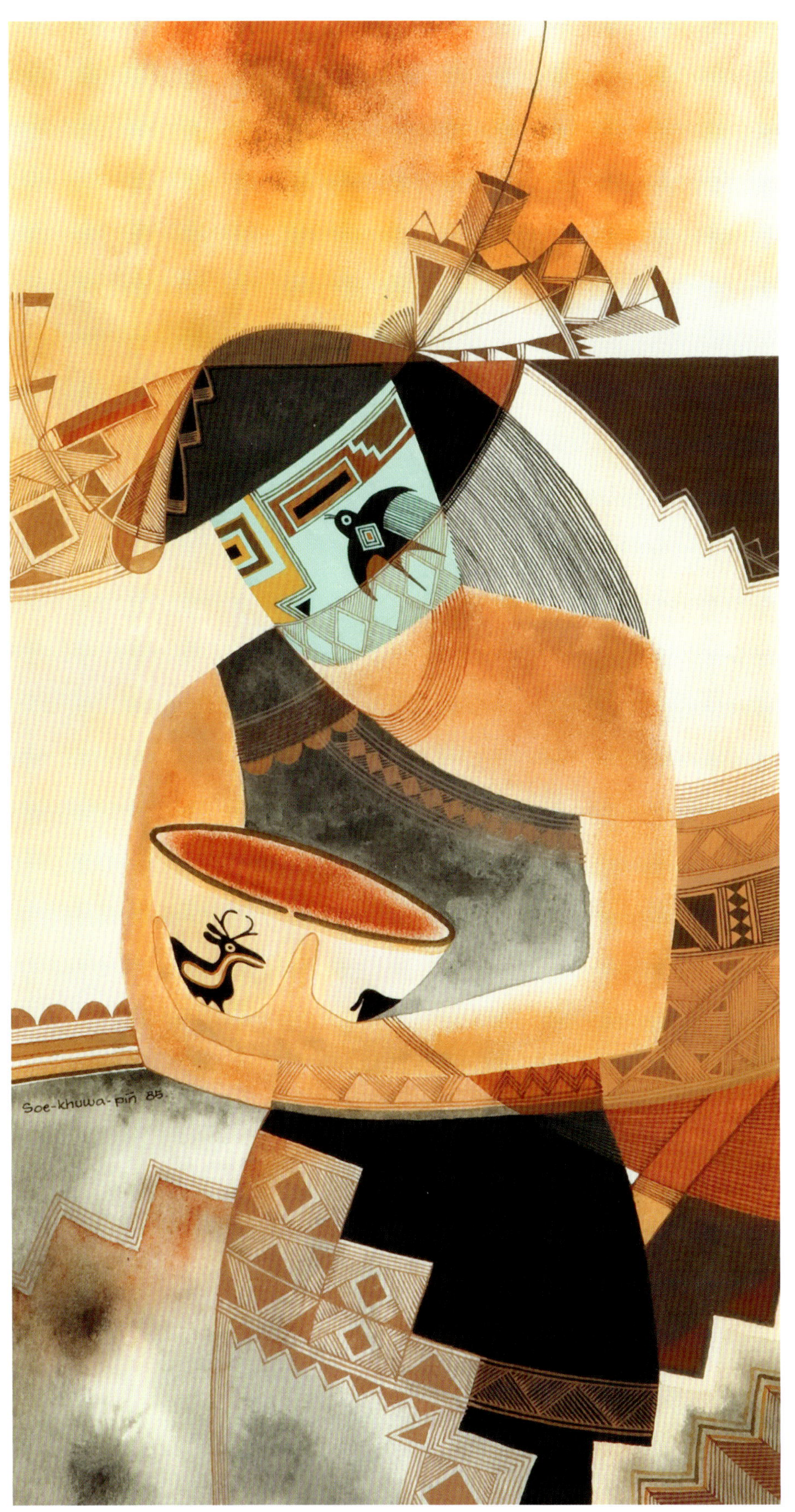

PLATE 76
Robert Montoya (Soe-Khuwa-Pin)
(U.S., Sandia, San Juan, b. 1947)
Pueblo God Mother, 1985
Watercolor on board, 15 × 7¾ in.
Philbrook Museum of Art
A2007.0344

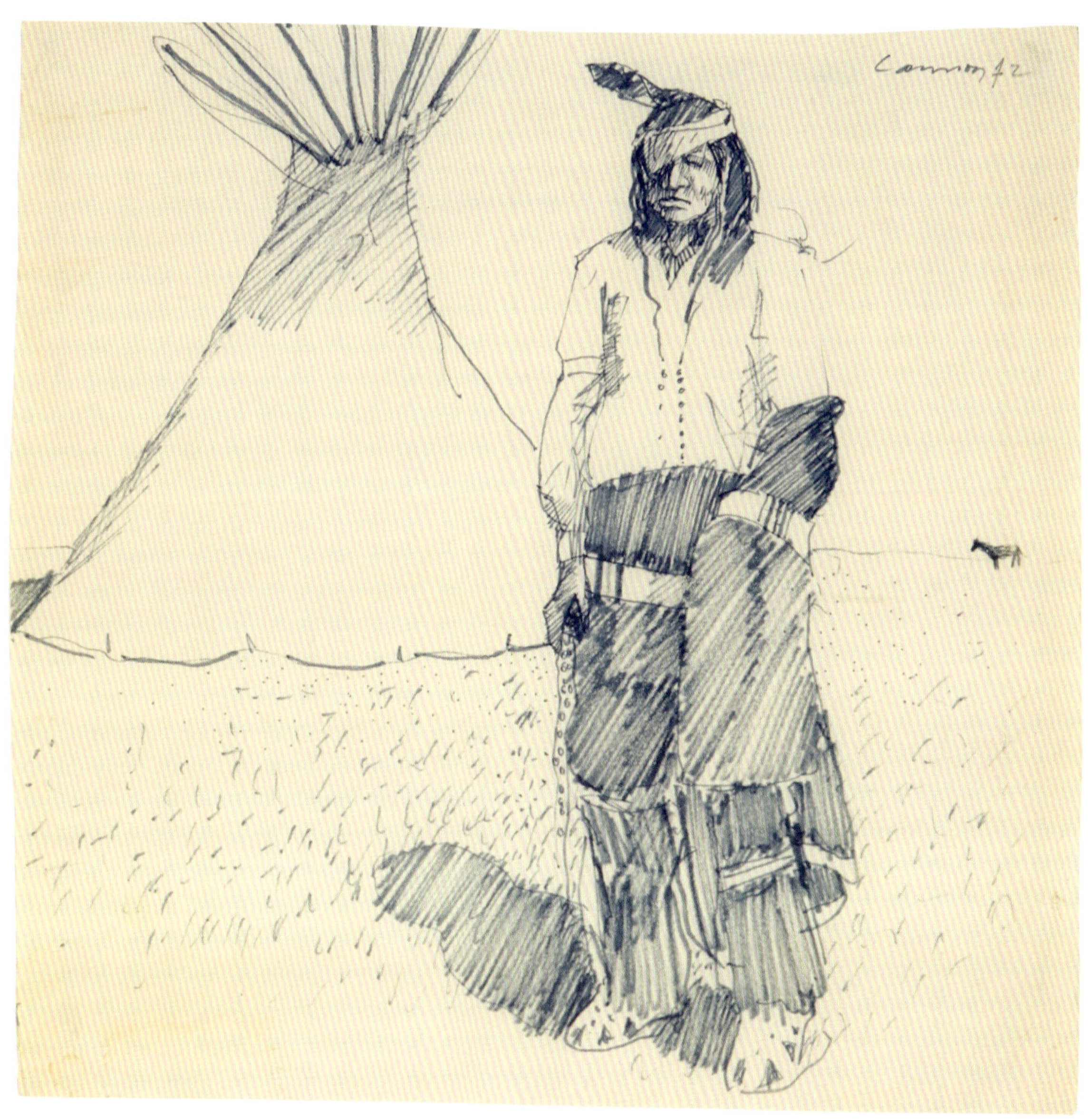

PLATE 77
T. C. Cannon (U.S., Kiowa Caddo, Choctaw 1946–1978)
Indian and Tipi (Study for Lonely Indian), 1972
Blue ink on paper, 11 × 11 in.

Fred Jones Jr. Museum of Art
A2007.0434

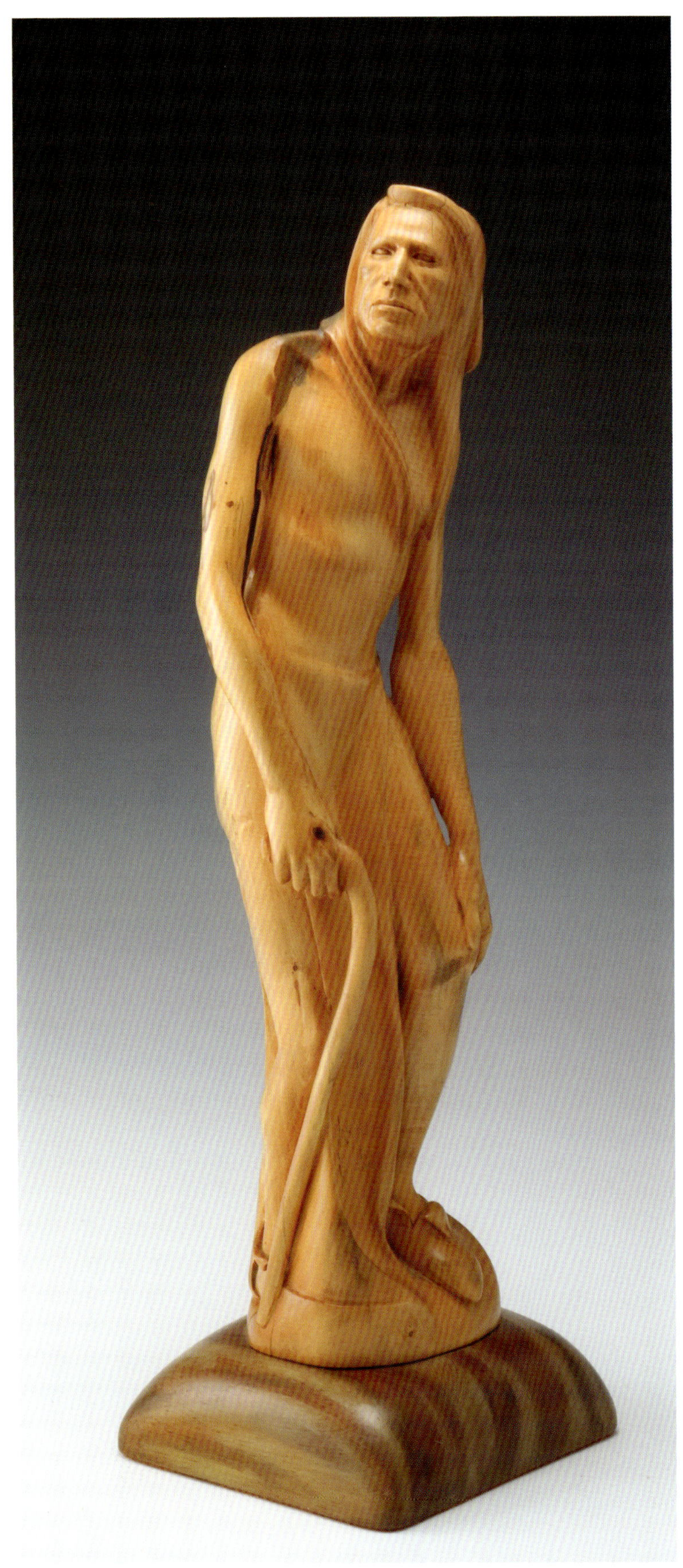

Plate 78
Walter Richard (Dick) West (Wap-pah-nah-yah)
(U.S., Cheyenne, 1912–1996)
Nostalgia, c. 1966. Buckeye, 19¾ × 6½ in.
Fred Jones Jr. Museum of Art
a2007.m12

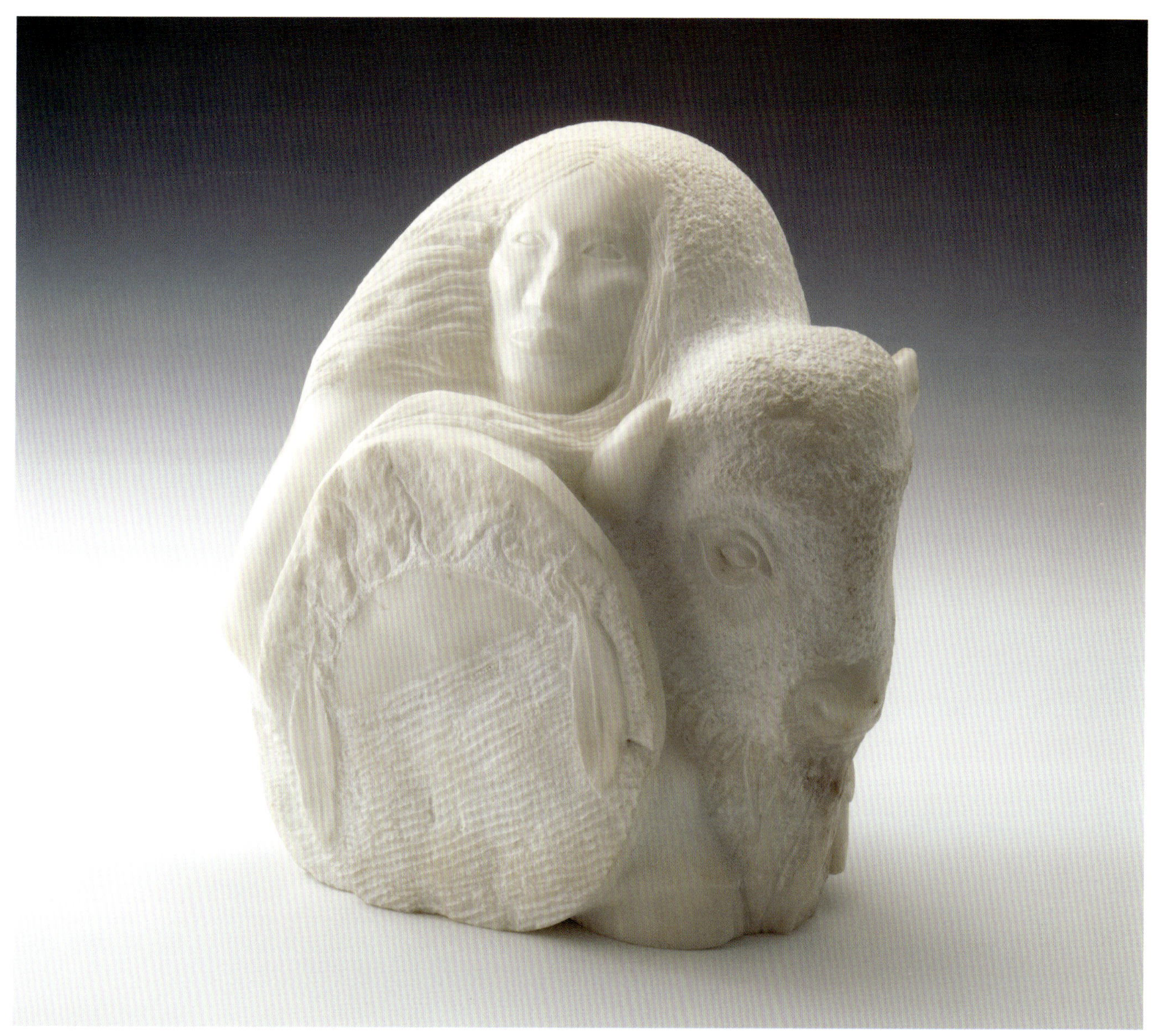

PLATE 79
Bill Glass (U.S., Cherokee, b. 1950)
Buffalo, 1975. White stone, 13½ × 13 in.
Fred Jones Jr. Museum of Art
A2007.M10

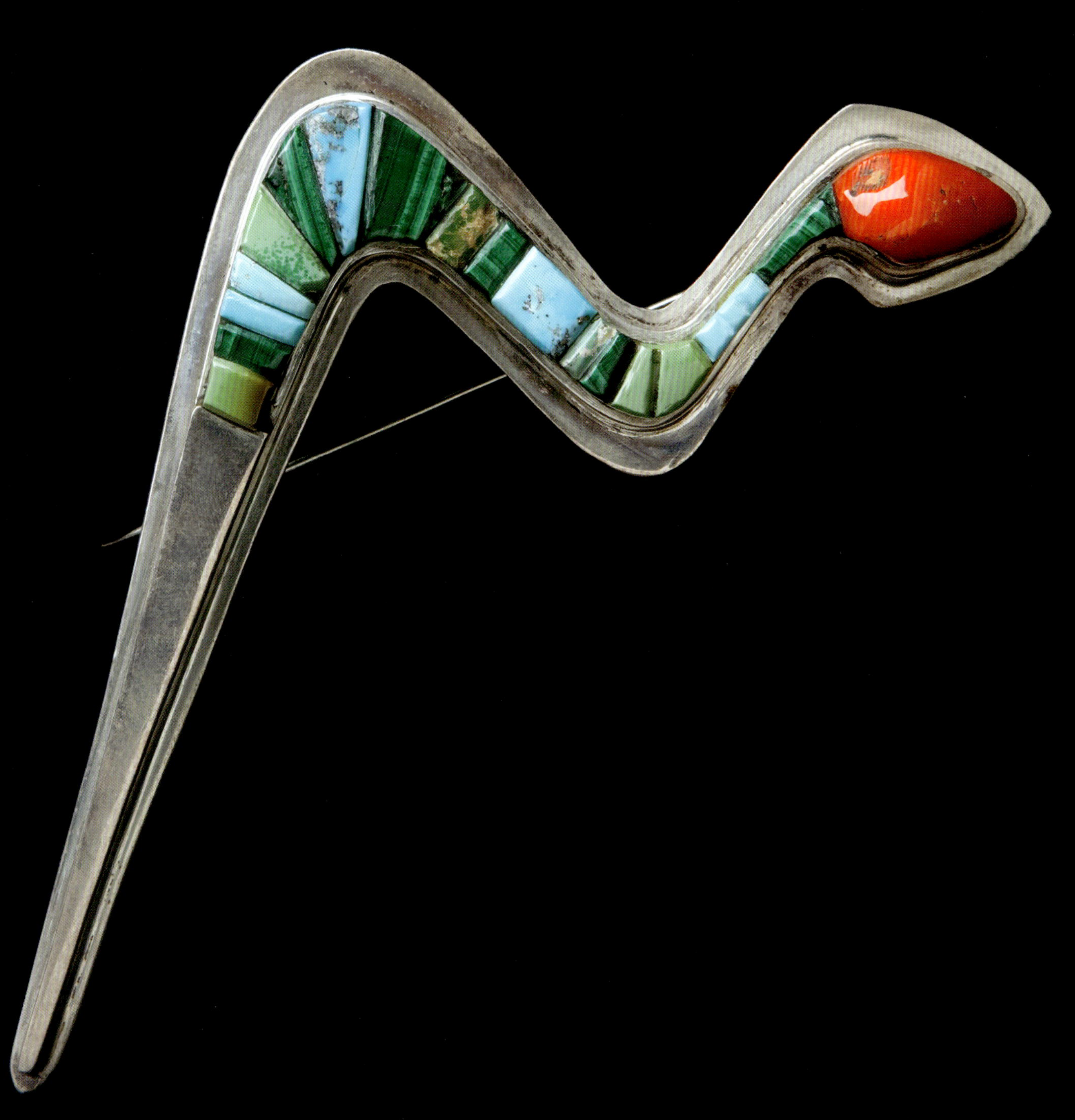

Tradition and Innovation

Native Jewelry, Silverwork, and Fetishes

Christina E. Burke

Chapter Five

Jewelry, silverwork, and carved fetishes compose the single largest category of art, Native or non-Native, in the Adkins Collection.[1] This jewelry collection is also one of the single largest ever amassed, rivaling that of famed trader C. G. Wallace as well as those of the Fred Harvey Company and School of American Research.[2] Not only is this grouping large, it is also diverse and contains pieces of exquisite craftsmanship, creativity, and historical significance. Although most of the work in the collection can be categorized as jewelry meant to be worn as adornment (bracelets, necklaces and pendants, rings, pins, earrings, buckles), the collection also features various types of objects and serviceware, including teapots, trays, and boxes. Many of the pieces represent distinctive cultural traditions developed by southwestern jewelers in the late 1800s and passed on through the generations. Other pieces highlight the bold innovations that characterized the modern era of Native design in the 1960s and '70s.[3]

During this time, many of the most important contemporary jewelers, including Charles Loloma (Hopi), Preston Monongye (Mission, adopted Hopi), and Kenneth Begay (Navajo), were experimenting with new materials and techniques, developing unique styles that would set the stage for innovation in Native fine art from the late twentieth century through today.[4] Adkins began collecting in the early 1960s, and by the end of the 1970s, he had already acquired many significant pieces by these master jewelers among others. He bought pieces from the artists directly at market shows in Santa Fe, Gallup, and Scottsdale, and through galleries and dealers. He even purchased several pieces from the Sotheby's-run auction of the C. G. Wallace Collection held in Phoenix in November 1975. Adkins continued collecting into the early twenty-first century, purchasing pieces from the next generation of innovators, who carried on the tradition of experimentation established by Loloma and others.

DETAIL OF PLATE 86 (p. 139)
Charles Loloma (U.S., Hopi, 1921–1991)
Snake Pin, 1970s

Within this large and diverse group of work are classic examples of such tribally specific silversmithing techniques as Navajo stampwork and repoussé as well as Hopi overlay.[5] There are also pieces that feature such lapidary skills as Zuni petit point and channel inlay, as well as Santo Domingo mosaic overlay (for example, plate 82, among others discussed below).[6] The work of hundreds of jewelers from throughout the Southwest is represented, many of whom have been identified by their hallmarks, although the process of identifying makers is ongoing.

Navajo silverwork is characterized by a simple silver form often embellished with stampwork or repoussé and inlaid with turquoise, echoing the techniques and styles first developed by Native jewelers in the late 1880s.[7] Pieces were sometimes fabricated by either cold hammering silver coins or soldering together silver wire. After learning smithing techniques from Mexican blacksmiths in the late 1800s, however, Navajo jewelers began casting by pouring molten silver into molds carved out of tufa, a brittle volcanic lava stone found throughout the Southwest. One of the most striking pieces in the collection is also one of the simplest: a silver belt buckle created from a mold made of tufa stone (plate 102). Traditionally, the silver would be polished, as in this piece, although sometimes the texture of the rough stone was left on part of the surface as a design element. Designs were also created by using repeating patterns stamped or chiseled into the silver (plate 107). Many Navajo bracelets show these traditional elements (plates 92 and 93). These two bracelets feature large pieces of turquoise as their primary focus, set in simple bands of silver, whether tufa cast or fabricated from strands of triangular wire. In other examples, the overall design is created by incorporating twisted silver wire with fabricated beads and other shapes to form an animal or insect, as in the pin shown in plate 85.

The technique known as Hopi overlay has a more recent history. It was developed in the late 1940s as a collaboration between Indian veterans of World War II and staff from the Museum of Northern Arizona in Flagstaff.[8] This technique requires at least two sheets of silver; one forms the base or background, and the other has a design cut from it. Once soldered together, the entire piece is submerged in an oxidizing liquid, such as liver of sulphur, which turns it black. The top layer is then polished to reveal a shiny silver surface, while the cut-out recess remains matte black. This contrast can be made even more pronounced by chiseling a texture into the exposed bottom layer (plates 95 and 100).

Lapidary work was common throughout the Southwest, but particularly fine inlay became associated with artists at Zuni.[9] Intricate patterns and designs are created using a variety of stones and shells, which are either inlaid directly, stone on stone (plate 87), or separated by a thin piece of silver (i.e., channel inlay). A Zuni pin representing the deity Rainbow Man (plate 99) shows both techniques. Another pin (plate 98) has both channel inlay and another traditional Zuni technique known as petit point, or needlepoint inlay, in which tiny stones (usually turquoise) are set in individual silver bezels. The result is a delicate and even lacy design used either on its own or, as in this case, in addition to other techniques.

Among many of the Pueblo in northern New Mexico, the creation of stone and shell beads dates back thousands of years.[10] Such beads, formed from turquoise, coral, and various shells, were made into jewelry and sold or traded to other tribes. Necklaces were often made from multiple strands of beads, whether large or small. One such necklace (plate 88) is made of two strands of rounded turquoise beads offset by a few oval tabs carved from spiny oyster shell. Another necklace, by Mike Bird-Romero (San Juan/Taos), is symbolic of the synthesis of Native and European cultures and religions, incorporating multiple strands of small coral beads with silver crosses (plate 83).[11] Even finer shell beads made from olivella shells, known as heishi, are used in necklaces (including as spacers in necklaces of carved fetishes), as well as in earrings and even bracelets.

Another use of stones and shells, called mosaic overlay, was developed by artists at Santo Domingo.[12] This technique is also thousands of years old, and it has had a revival since the 1980s, led primarily by jeweler Angie Reano Owen.[13] Mosaic overlay requires fine lapidary skills to work with small pieces of stone and shell that are adhered to a base of shell, wood, silver, or other material. The adhesive, usually a naturally occurring substance such as asphaltum, can be both functional and decorative, because the black lines in between the inlay often contribute to the overall design of the piece. Two early examples include a pair of earrings that feature overlaid squares of abalone and spiny oyster set on wood (plate 101) and a tobacco canteen made from two halves of a spiny oyster that have been sealed with an edging of stamped silver and embellished with overlay of turquoise at the top (plate 82).[14] A more recent piece, attributed to Reano Owen, demonstrates how this tradition has been brought into the contemporary: a complex pattern is created with small slivers of colorful materials set on a base of shell that forms the bracelet (plate 91).

Skill at carving stone and shell is also seen in the variety of fetishes in the Adkins Collection.[15] This includes not only single fetishes (plate 114), but also jewelry and silverwork that incorporate fetishes as design elements. One such piece is a multistrand necklace by Zuni carver David Tsikewa (plate 84), which won first place at the 1965 Gallup Inter-Tribal Ceremonial. Another important piece is a large silver buckle dominated by ten turquoise fetishes (plate 103). The piece was made by master carver Leekya Deyuse (Zuni) and was part of the C. G. Wallace Collection. Wallace was a long-time trader among the Zuni, and over about forty years he amassed a substantial collection of jewelry and other material. Some of this was donated to the Heard Museum in Phoenix, but the bulk of the collection was sold at an auction organized by Sotheby's in November 1975.[16] Presumably, Adkins purchased the piece at that auction.

Among the serviceware and other objects in the Adkins Collection are various sizes of boxes, from small pill boxes (plate 96) to larger containers, which perhaps were made as jewelry boxes. The serviceware includes sets of salad servers, corn cob holders, and even a single iced tea spoon by Charles Loloma (plate 111).[17] A four-piece tea set, complete with matching tray, by Kenneth Begay (plate 110), is characteristic of Begay's work, incorporating ironwood and silver, and using bold, clean lines in the design.[18]

In addition to the many pieces of traditional Native jewelry are dozens of contemporary works by such innovators as Begay, Loloma, and Monongye. These are important because they represent each of the artist's work from the 1960s through the 1980s, a time when each experimented with various materials and techniques in developing their distinctive styles, combining tradition and innovation. Charles Loloma was particularly interested in the use of various textures, often contrasting rough surfaces with polished ones.[19] His silver cuff with faceted turquoise (plate 94) was created using a mold carved out of tufa stone. Loloma left this sandy texture on the body of the bracelet, embellishing it with an oxidizing agent, and then contrasting it by polishing the smoothed edges of the piece. In addition, the large turquoise piece has been cut into an asymmetrical shape and faceted, as opposed to being smoothed and polished into a round or oval cabochon, as is typical of traditional pieces.

Loloma was also among the first Native jewelers to work in gold and incorporated such nontraditional materials as lapis lazuli, ironwood, and even fossilized mammoth ivory in what became known as his characteristic stacked inlay (plate 89). Other classic Loloma pieces in the Adkins Collection include a ring (plate 81) and buckle (plates 104A and 104B). These two illustrate several of Loloma's unique design elements, including the use of gold and the addition of inlay on the inside or reverse of the piece.

Preston Monongye was prolific in his work, and Adkins collected dozens of his pieces, from pins and pendants to bracelets and chalices. One piece that Adkins wore was an inlaid bolo of a Zia sunface (plate 108). It is tufa cast and has stone-on-stone inlay of shell, turquoise, coral, and jet. Monongye also created a large bracelet, a silver cuff, on which he strung multiple strands of heishi beads accentuated with a row of turquoise and coral (plate 90).

In addition to the tea set mentioned above, Adkins also collected many pieces by Kenneth Begay. Among these are two asymmetrical "swirl" bracelets embellished with traditional repoussé, in which the silver is stamped from the reverse side (plate 97).

Other innovative work in the collection is by such artists as Gail Bird (Santo Domingo) and Yazzie Johnson (Navajo), who have collaborated to create unique jewelry for the past thirty years. Adkins acquired only two of their pieces, one of which is a reversible pendant (plates 80A and 80B). This is from a series created in the 1980s that features traditional Navajo basketry designs on one side and such materials as jasper and agate on the other. The work of Bird and Johnson, like that of Loloma, Monongye, and Begay, combines both traditional materials and techniques with innovative elements to create a unique object that expands the definition of Native jewelry specifically and Indian art in general.

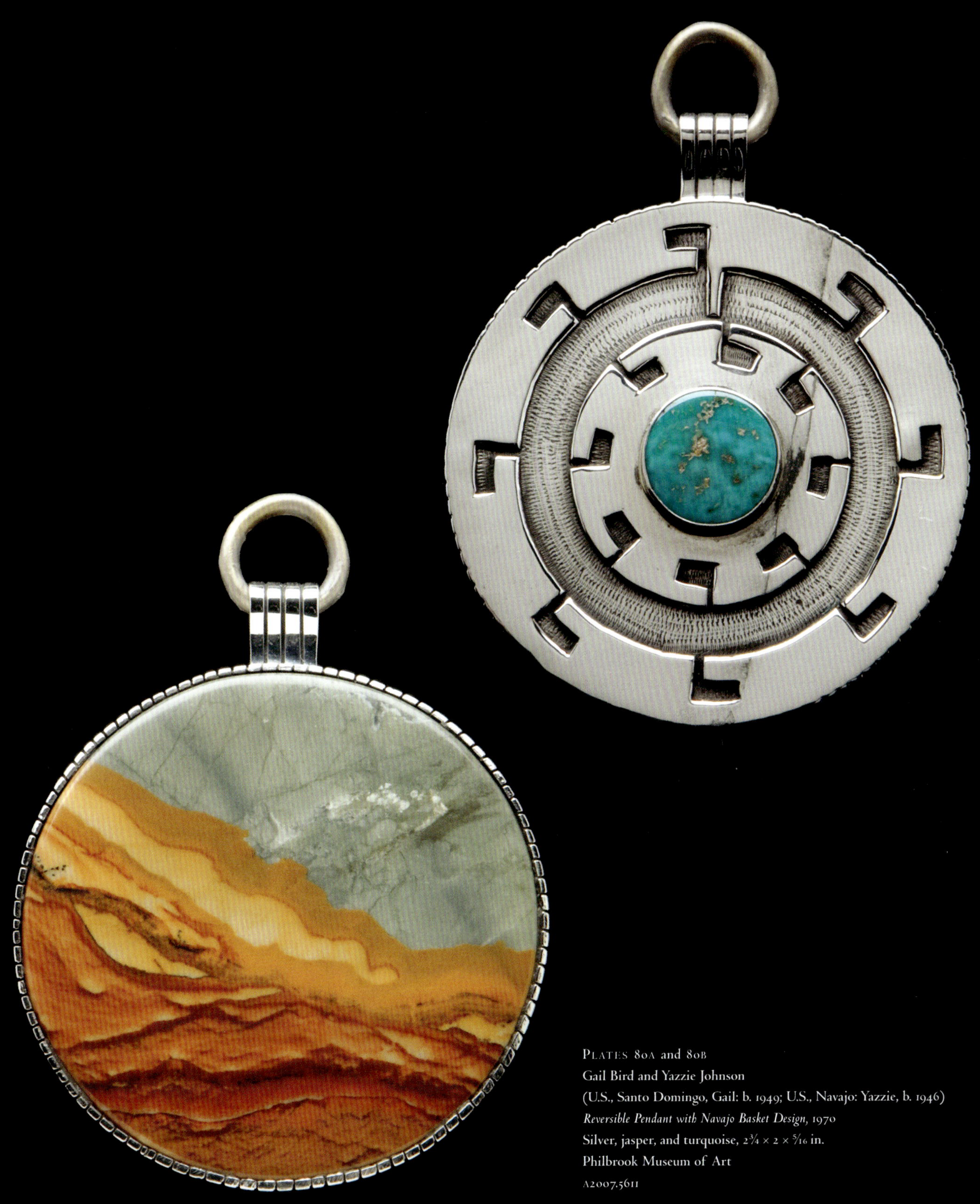

Plates 80a and 80b
Gail Bird and Yazzie Johnson
(U.S., Santo Domingo, Gail: b. 1949; U.S., Navajo: Yazzie, b. 1946)
Reversible Pendant with Navajo Basket Design, 1970
Silver, jasper, and turquoise, 2¾ × 2 × 5/16 in.
Philbrook Museum of Art
A2007.5611

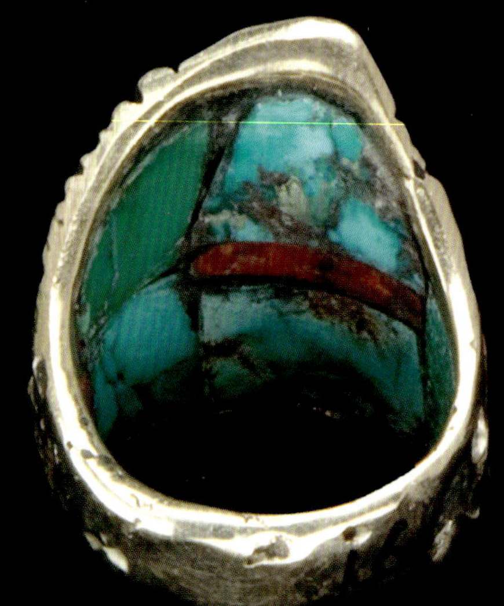

Plate 81
Charles Loloma (U.S., Hopi, 1921–1991)
Lost-Wax-Cast Ring with Interior Inlay, 1970s
Gold, lost-wax cast, with black sapphire in turquoise and gold inlay on the inside, 1 × 1 × 1 in.
Philbrook Museum of Art
A2007.5838

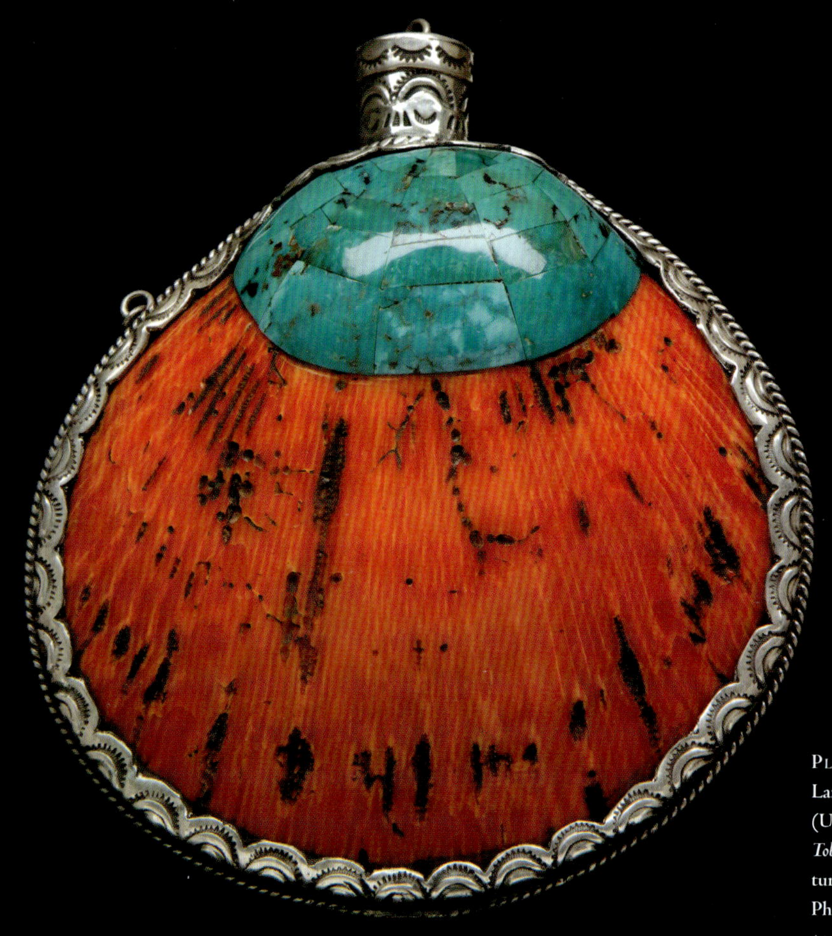

Plate 82
Lambert Homer, Sr. (attributed)
(U.S., Zuni/Navajo, 1917–1972)
Tobacco Canteen, n.d. Spiny oyster, turquoise, and silver, 4 × 3½ × 1½ in.
Philbrook Museum of Art
A2007.9039

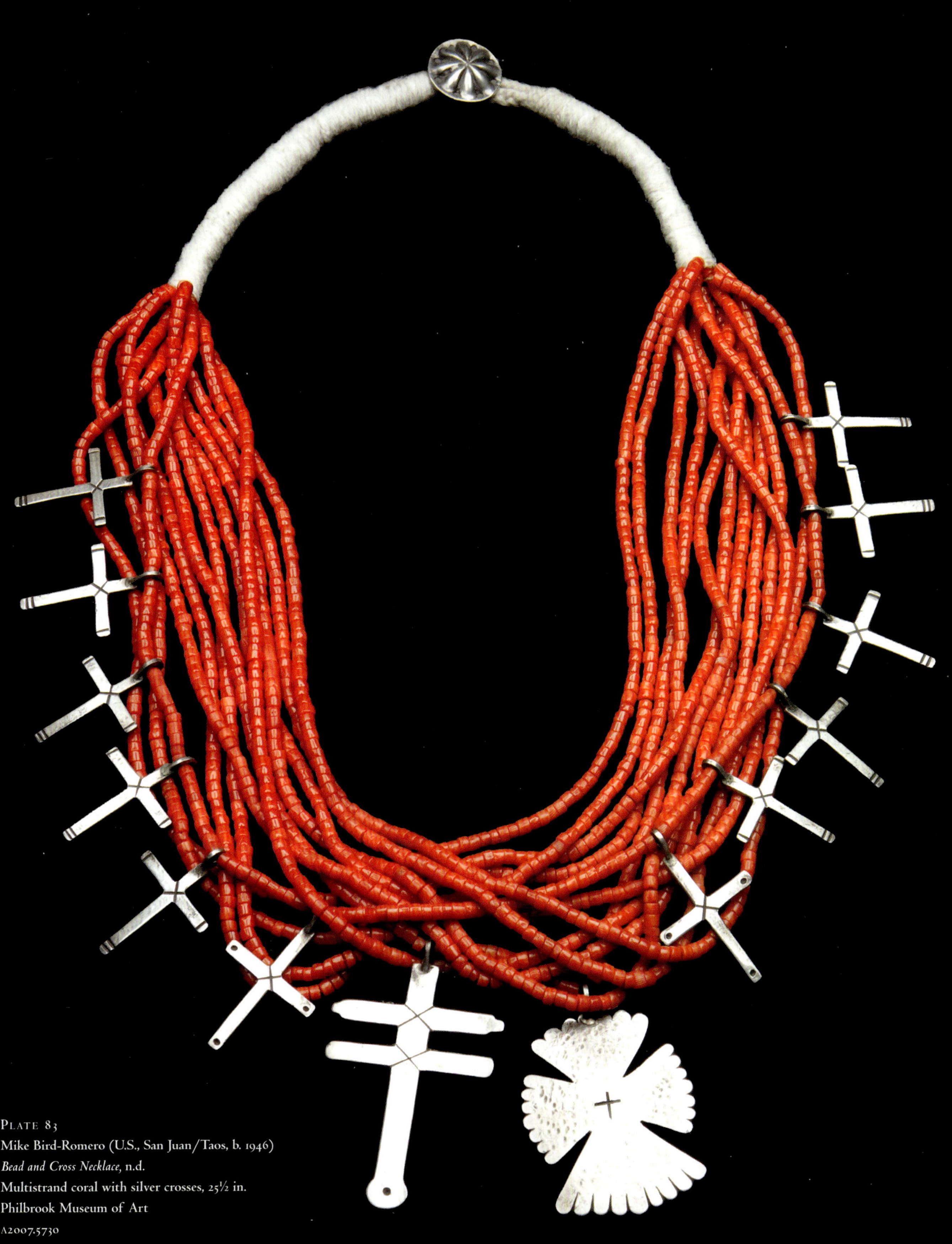

PLATE 83
Mike Bird-Romero (U.S., San Juan/Taos, b. 1946)
Bead and Cross Necklace, n.d.
Multistrand coral with silver crosses, 25½ in.
Philbrook Museum of Art
A2007.5730

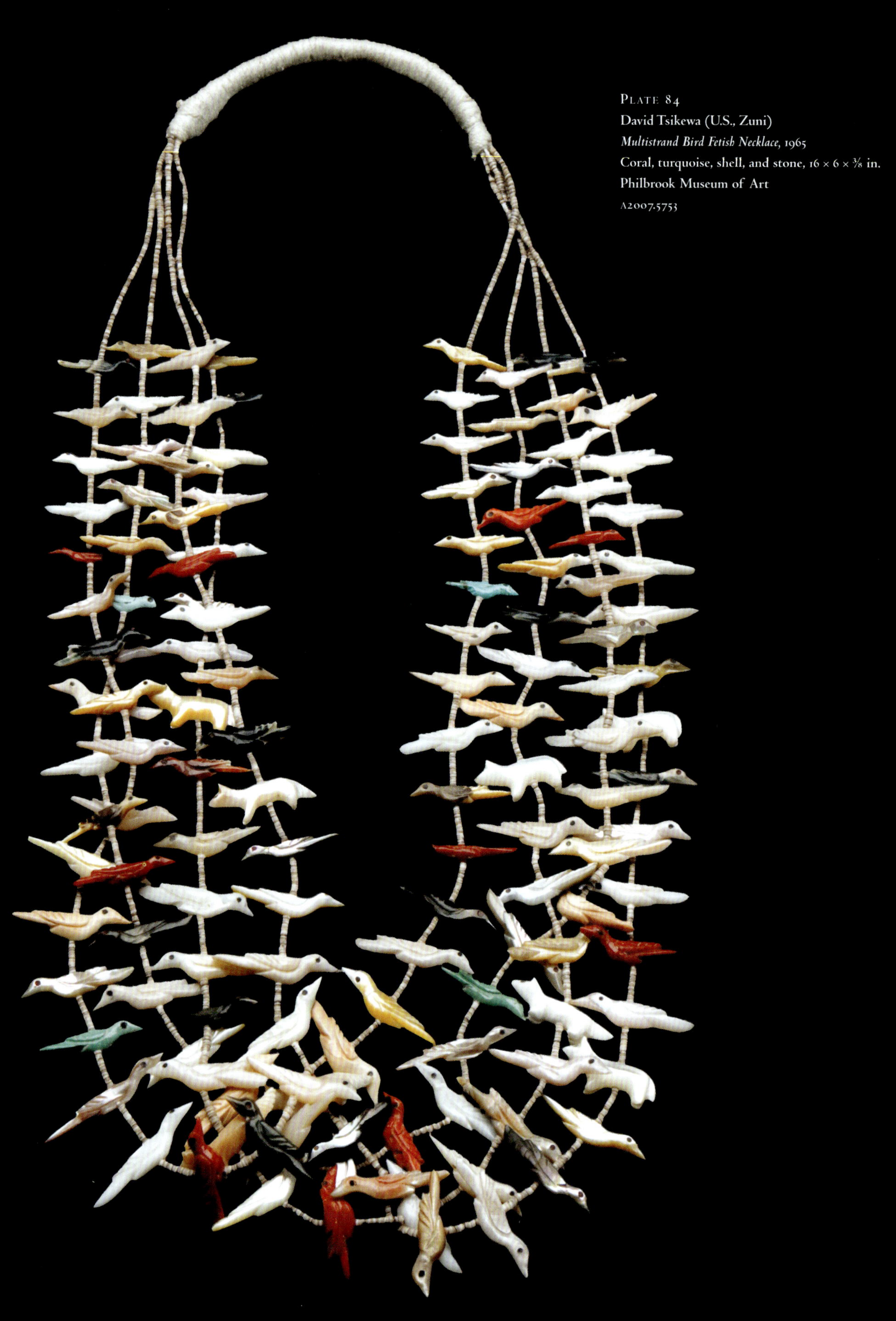

PLATE 84
David Tsikewa (U.S., Zuni)
Multistrand Bird Fetish Necklace, 1965
Coral, turquoise, shell, and stone, 16 × 6 × ⅜ in.
Philbrook Museum of Art
A2007.5753

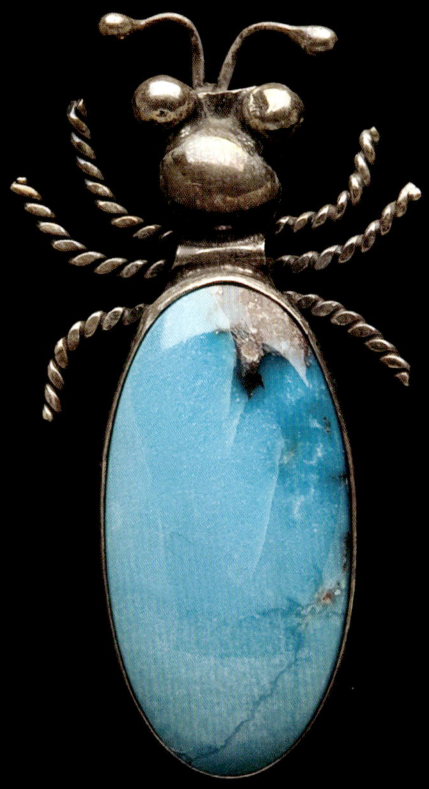

PLATE 85
Unknown (U.S., Navajo)
Insect Pin, n.d. Silver and turquoise, 1⅝ × ⅝ × ⅜ in.
Fred Jones Jr. Museum of Art
A2007.5382

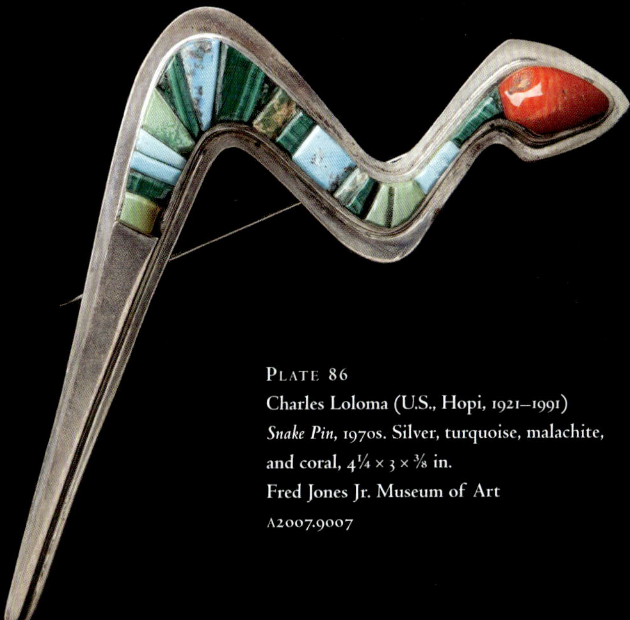

PLATE 86
Charles Loloma (U.S., Hopi, 1921–1991)
Snake Pin, 1970s. Silver, turquoise, malachite, and coral, 4¼ × 3 × ⅜ in.
Fred Jones Jr. Museum of Art
A2007.9007

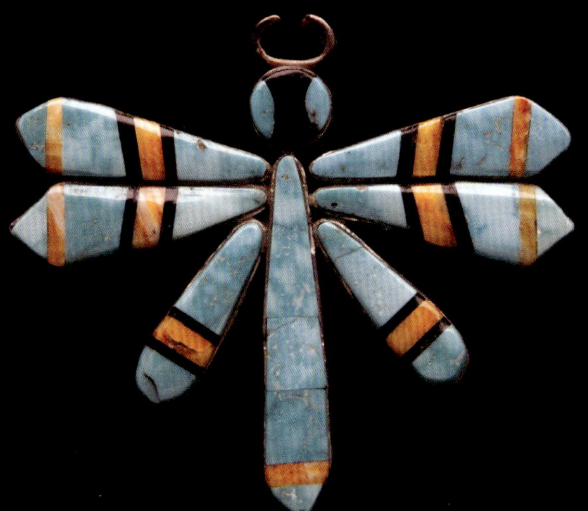

PLATE 87
Unknown (U.S., Zuni)
Dragonfly Pin, n.d.
Silver, turquoise, spiny oyster, and jet, 2 × 2⅛ × ⅜ in.
Fred Jones Jr. Museum of Art
A2007.5404

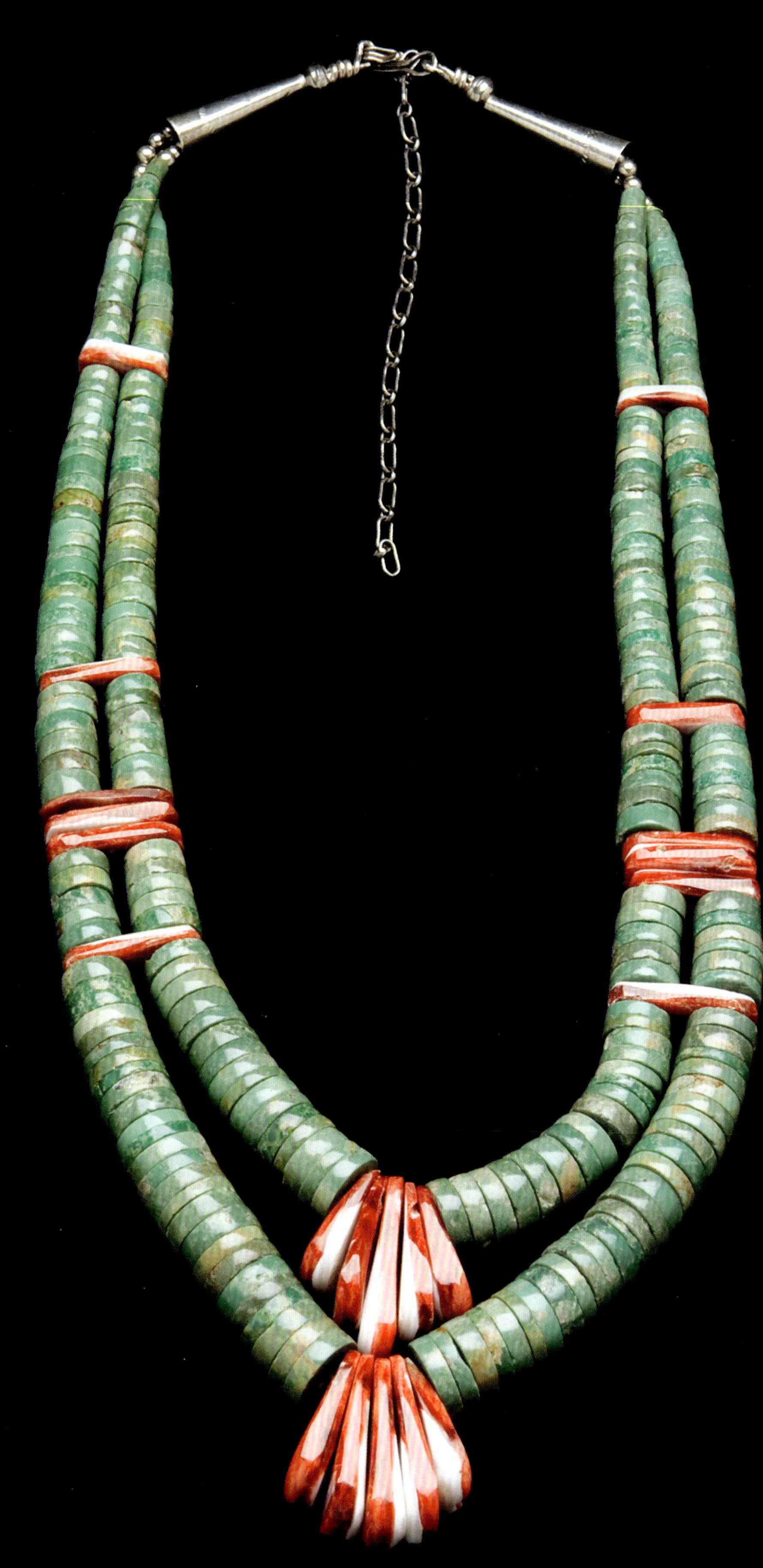

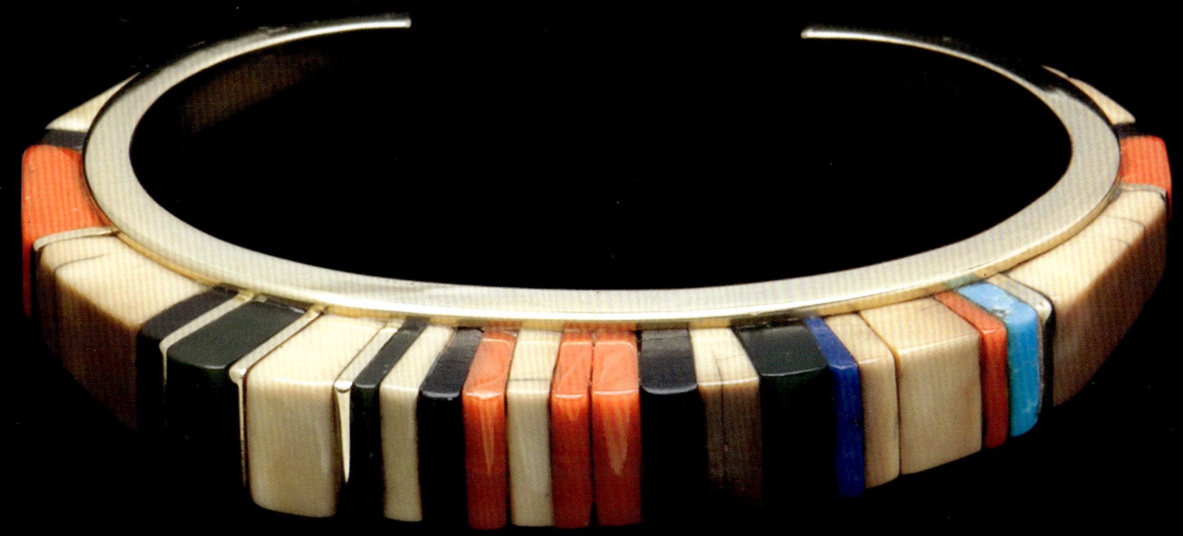

Plate 88 (facing page)
Unknown (U.S., Santo Domingo)
Two-strand Necklace, n.d.
Turquoise and spiny oyster, 22⅜ × 3¼ × 5/16 in.
Philbrook Museum of Art
A2007.5613

Plate 89 (above)
Charles Loloma (U.S., Hopi, 1921–1991)
Bracelet with Stacked Inlay, 1970
Gold, turquoise, fossilized ivory,
ironwood, and coral, ⅜ × 2¾ × 2¼ in.
Philbrook Museum of Art
A2007.5814

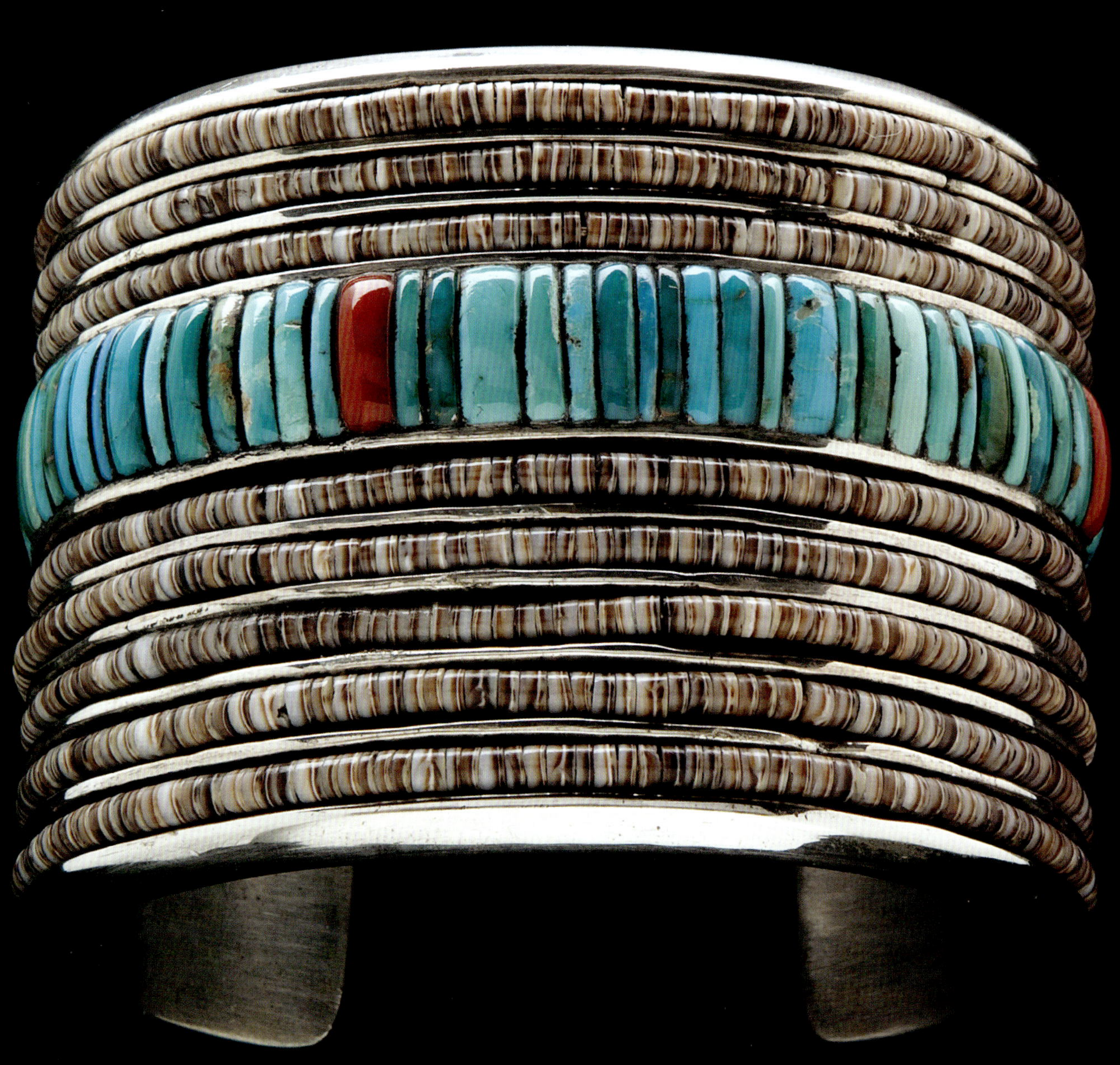

PLATE 90
Preston Monongye (U.S., Mission/Mexico, adopted Hopi, 1927–1987)
Cuff Bracelet, n.d.
Silver, heishi shell beads, turquoise, and coral, 2 × 2¾ × ⅛ in.
Philbrook Museum of Art
A2007.5184

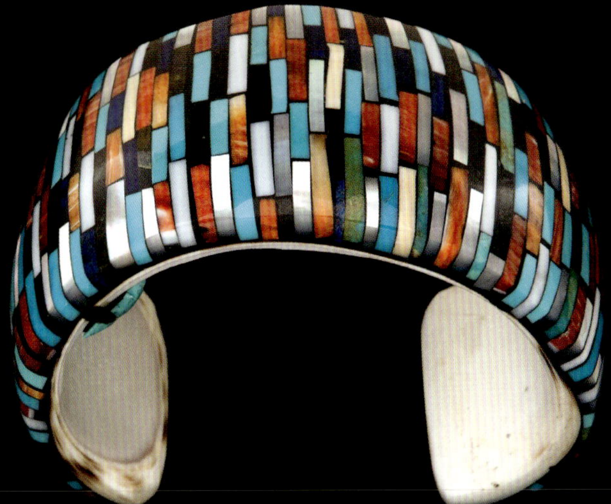

Plate 91
Unknown (U.S., Santo Domingo)
Bracelet with Mosaic Inlay, 1980s. Shell, turquoise, coral, and mother-of-pearl, 1 7/16 × 2 7/8 × 2 7/16 in.
Philbrook Museum of Art
A2007.5128

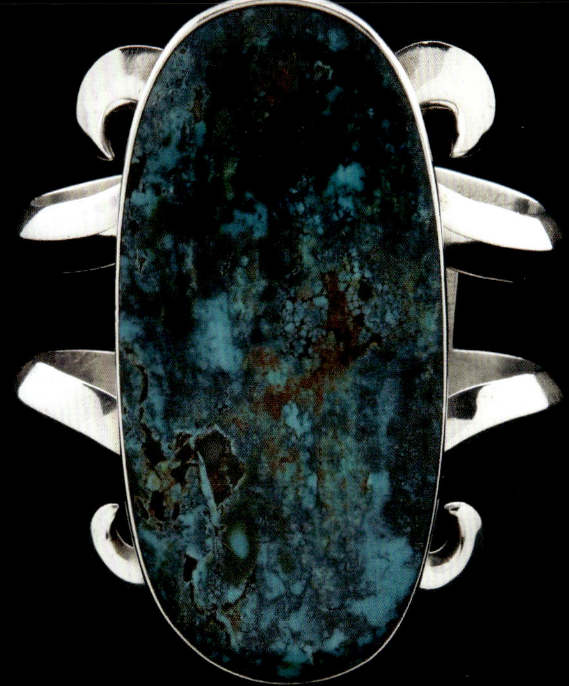

Plate 92
Unknown (U.S., Navajo)
Tufa-Cast Bracelet with Large Oval Turquoise, 1940
Silver and turquoise, 3 1/8 × 2 7/8 × 2 1/8 in.
Fred Jones Jr. Museum of Art
A2007.5082

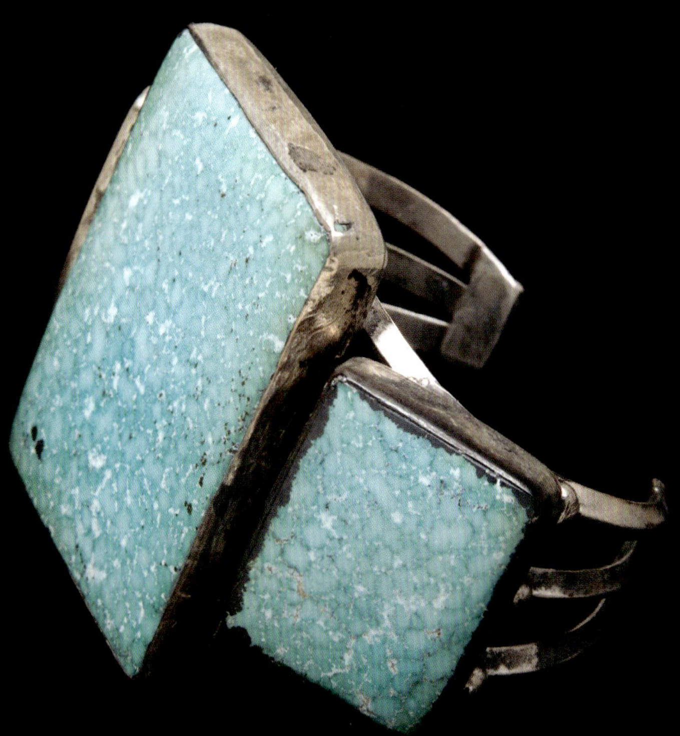

Plate 93
Unknown (U.S., Navajo)
Tufa-Cast Bracelet with Three Pieces of Turquoise, n.d.
Silver and turquoise, 2 × 3 1/2 × 2 1/2 in.
Fred Jones Jr. Museum of Art
A2007.5088

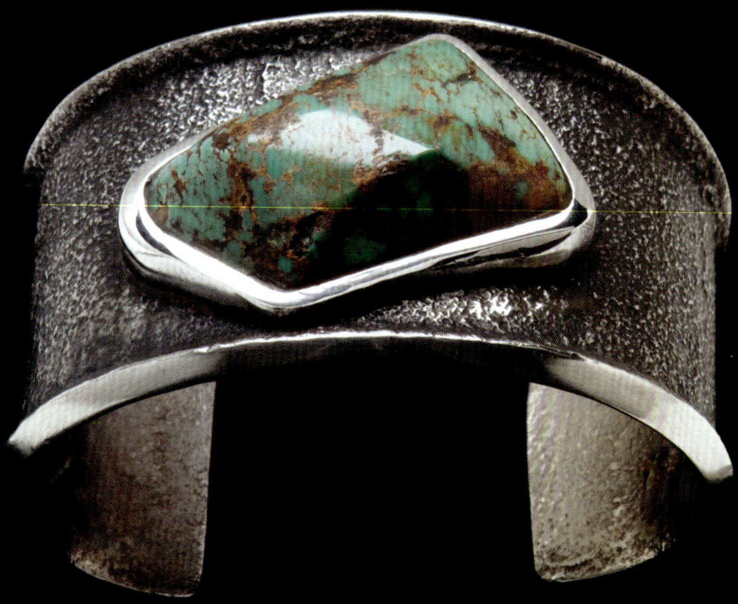

Plate 94
Charles Loloma (U.S., Hopi, 1921–1991)
Tufa-Cast Bracelet with Faceted Turquoise, 1970s
Silver and turquoise, 1⅝ × 2¾ × 2⅜ in.
Philbrook Museum of Art
A2007.5100

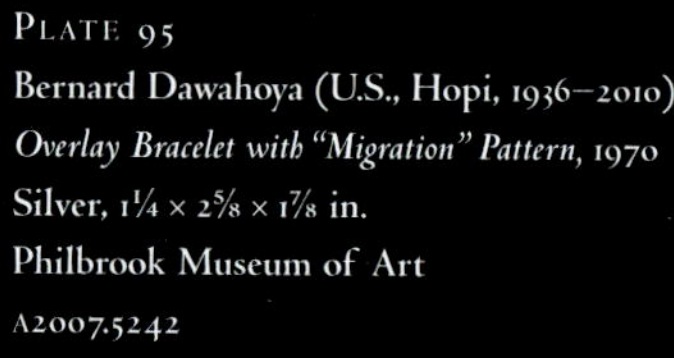

Plate 95
Bernard Dawahoya (U.S., Hopi, 1936–2010)
Overlay Bracelet with "Migration" Pattern, 1970
Silver, 1¼ × 2⅝ × 1⅞ in.
Philbrook Museum of Art
A2007.5242

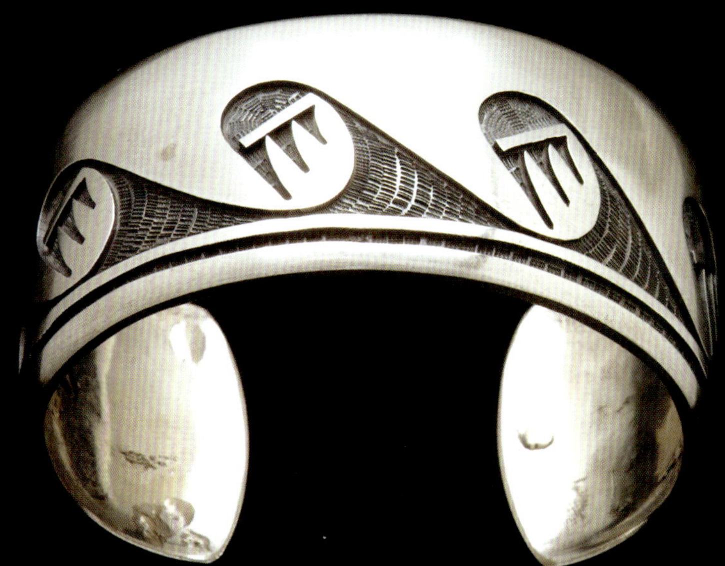

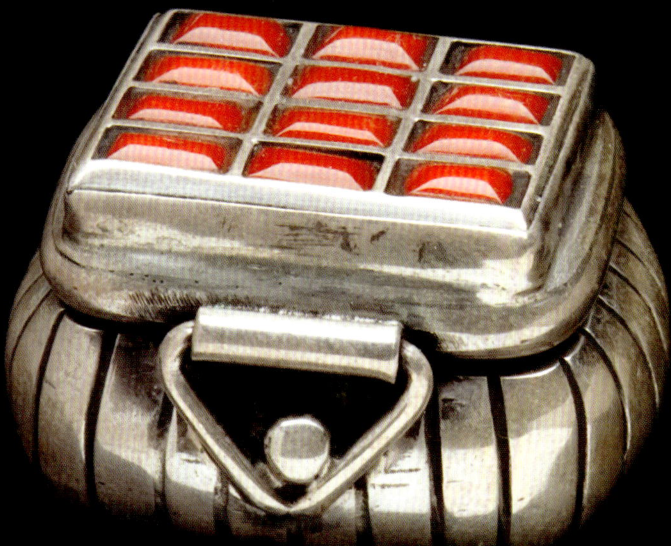

Plate 96
Unknown (U.S., Zuni)
Pillbox, n.d. Silver and coral, ¾ × 1 7/16 × 1¼ in.
Philbrook Museum of Art
A2007.6220

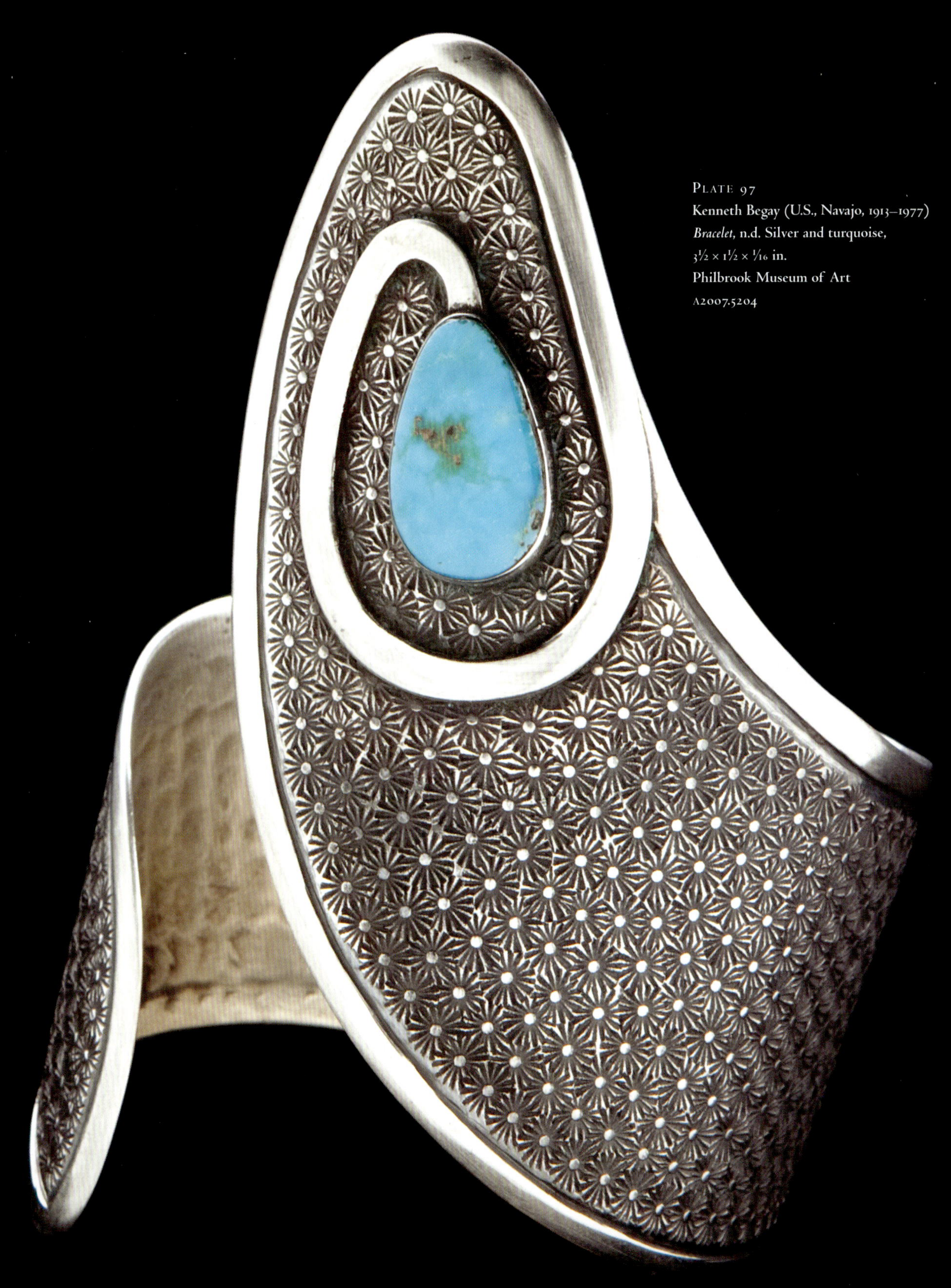

Plate 97
Kenneth Begay (U.S., Navajo, 1913–1977)
Bracelet, n.d. Silver and turquoise,
3½ × 1½ × 1/16 in.
Philbrook Museum of Art
A2007.5204

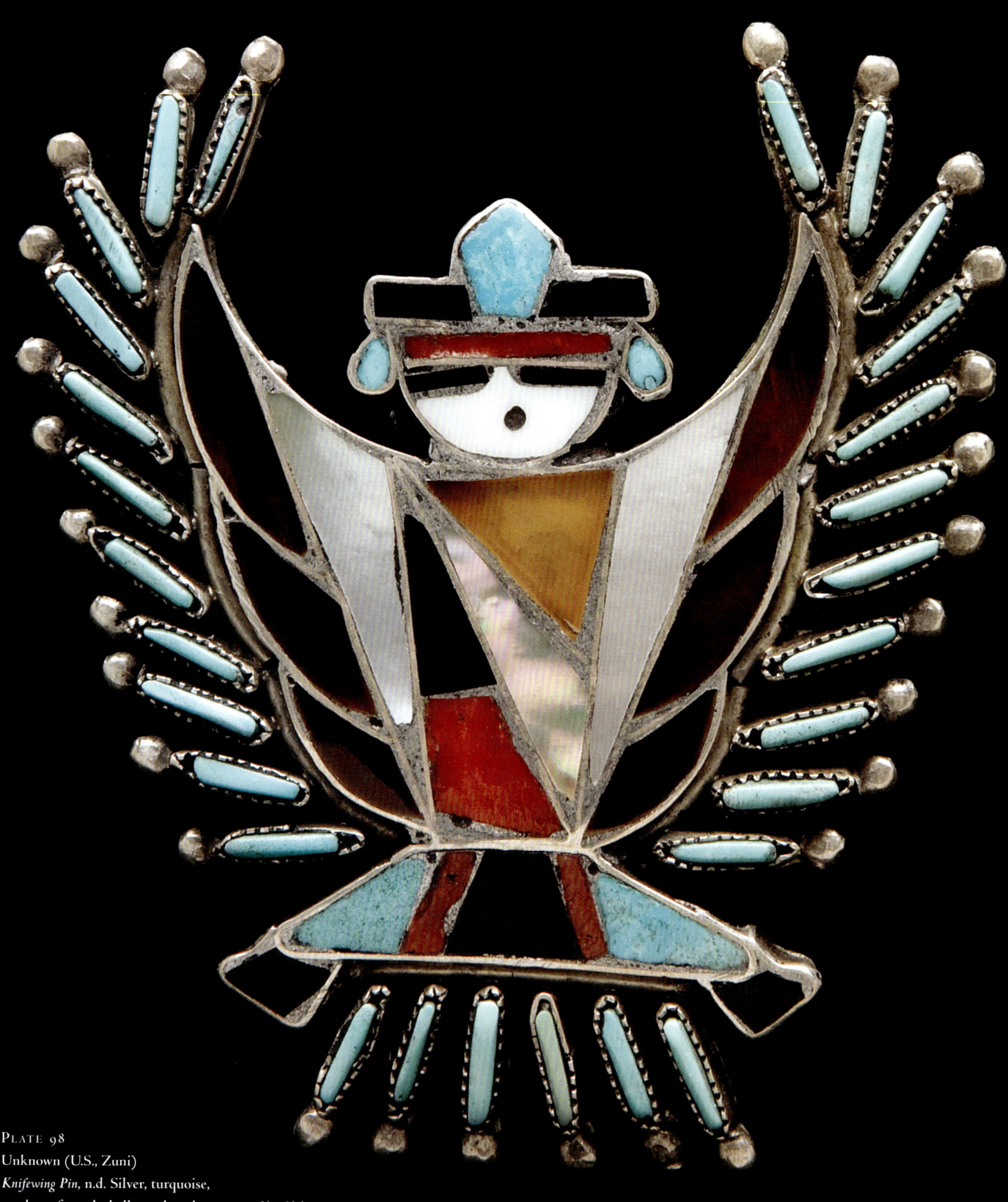

PLATE 98
Unknown (U.S., Zuni)
Knifewing Pin, n.d. Silver, turquoise, mother-of-pearl, shell, coral, and onyx, 2 × 1¾ × ¼ in.
Philbrook Museum of Art
A2007.7140

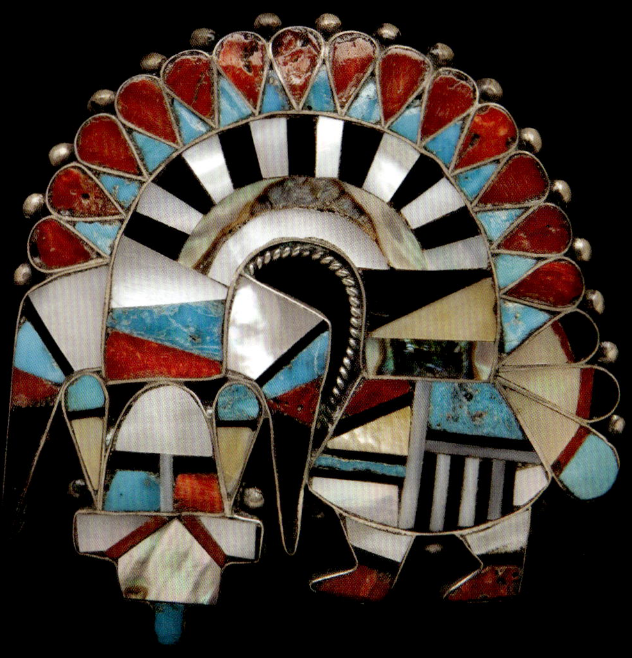

Plate 99
Unknown (U.S., Zuni)
Channel Inlay Pin of Rainbow Man, n.d.
Silver, turquoise, coral, jet, abalone, mother-of-pearl, and tortoise shell, 2½ × 2½ × ¼ in.
Fred Jones Jr. Museum of Art
A2007.5386

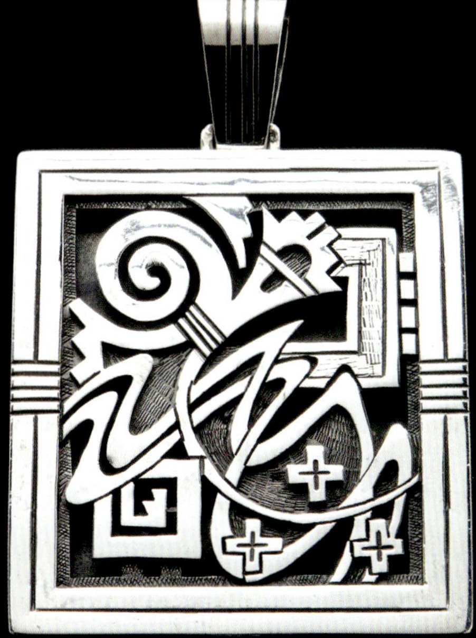

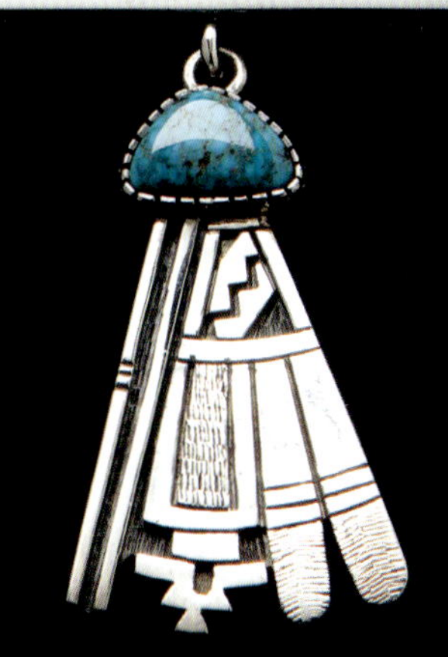

Plate 100
Michael Kabotie (Lomawywesa)
(U.S., Hopi, 1942–2009)
Pendant with Hopi Overlay, 1987
Silver and turquoise, 5¾ × 2¼ × ½ in.
Philbrook Museum of Art
A2007.6405

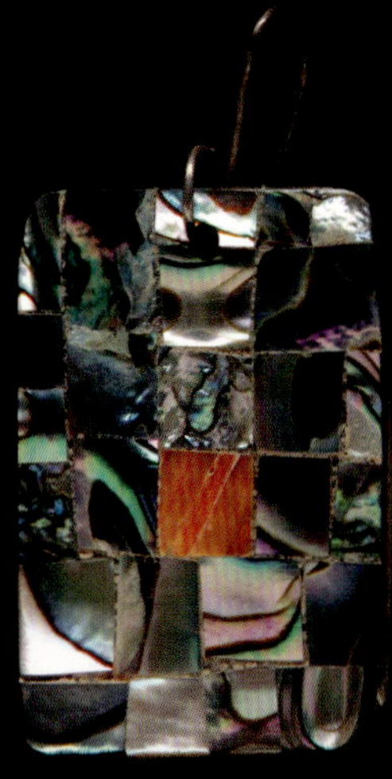

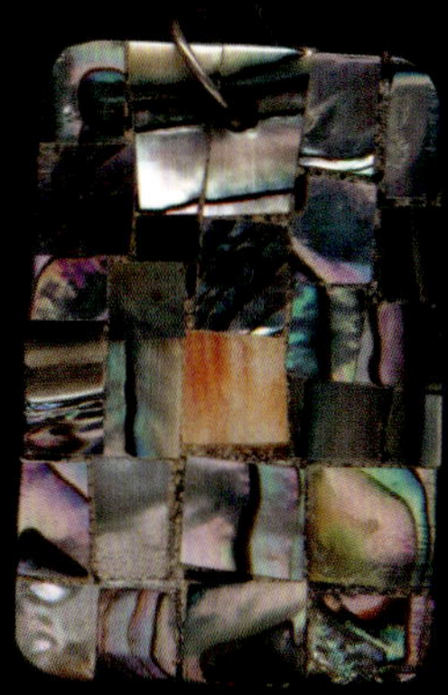

Plate 101
Unknown (U.S., Santo Domingo)
Earrings, n.d. Wood, abalone, spiny oyster, and turquoise, 2 3⁄16 × 1 × ½ in.
Philbrook Museum of Art
A2007.5311

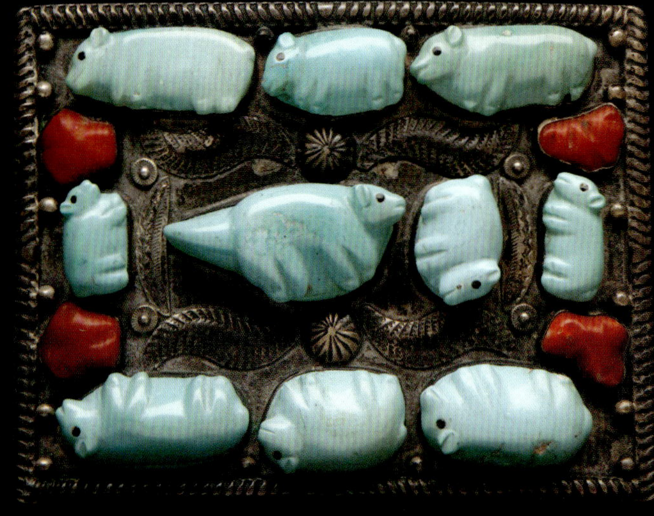

Plate 103 (detail, facing page)
Leekya Deyuse (U.S., Zuni, 1889–1966)
Large Silver Belt Buckle with Fetishes, 1938
Silver, turquoise, and coral, 4 × 5¼ × ½ in.
Philbrook Museum of Art
A2007.5889

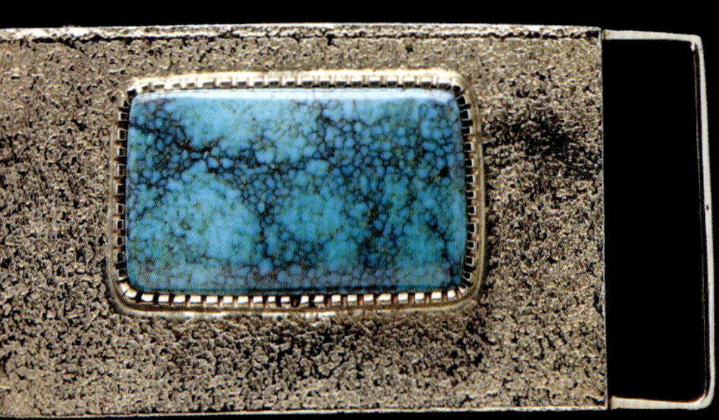

Plate 104A and 104B
Charles Loloma (U.S., Hopi, 1921–1991)
Gold Buckle with Turquoise Inlay, 1970s
Gold, turquoise, coral, and lapis lazuli, 1½ × 3 × ¾ in.
Philbrook Museum of Art
A2007.5827

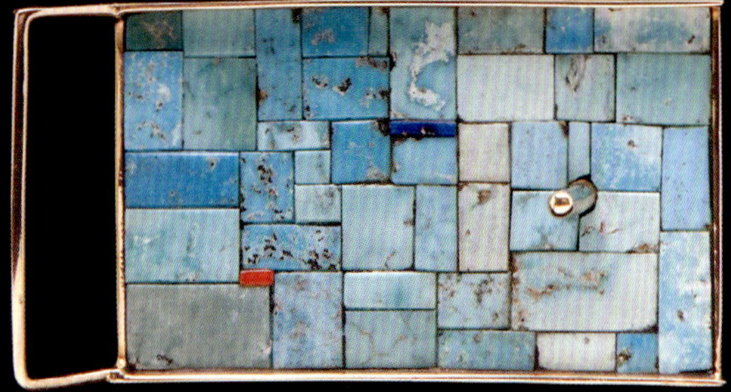

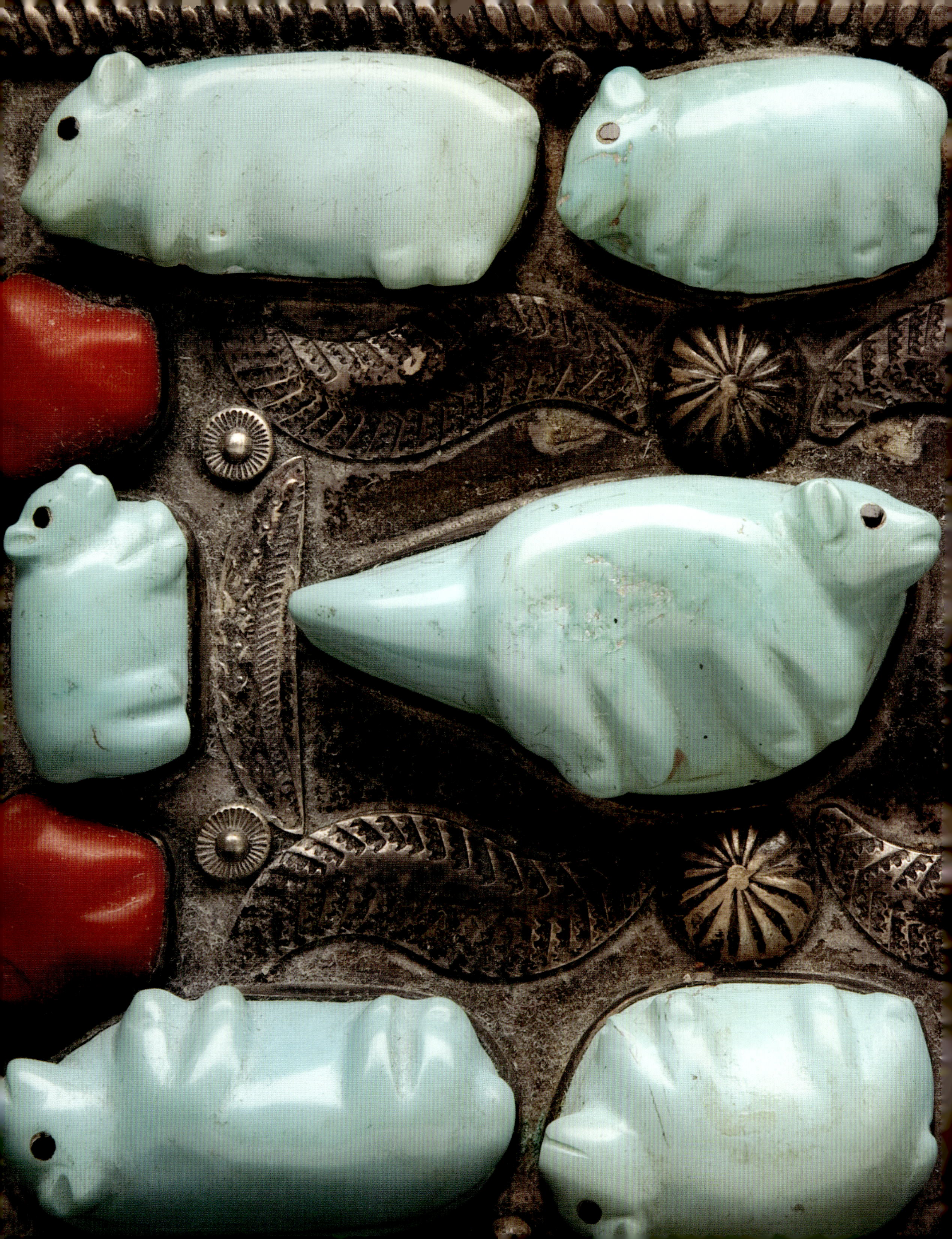

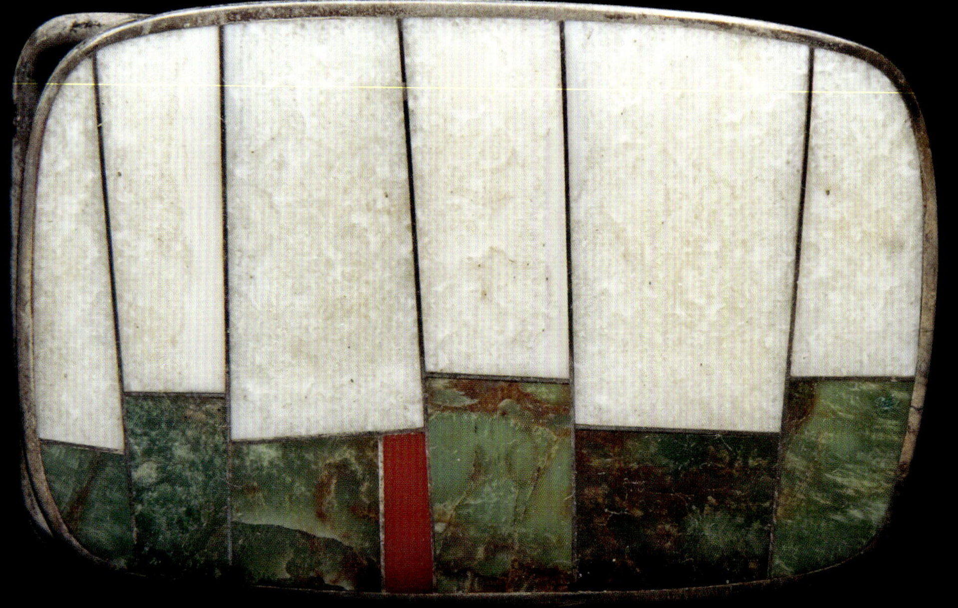

Plate 105
Unknown (U.S., Hopi)
Buckle, n.d. Silver, fossilized ivory, turquoise, and coral, 1⅞ × 3 × ⅝ in.
Philbrook Museum of Art
A2007.5878

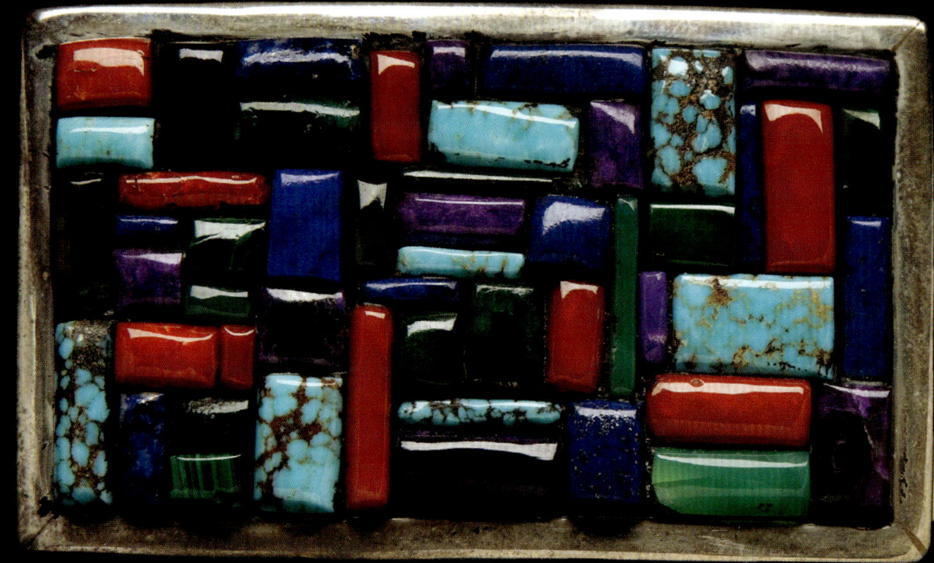

Plate 106
Yellowhorse (U.S., Navajo)
Belt Buckle, n.d. Silver, turquoise, serpentine malachite, coral, sugalite, and lapis lazuli, 2½ × 1½ × ½ in.
Fred Jones Jr. Museum of Art
A2007.5896

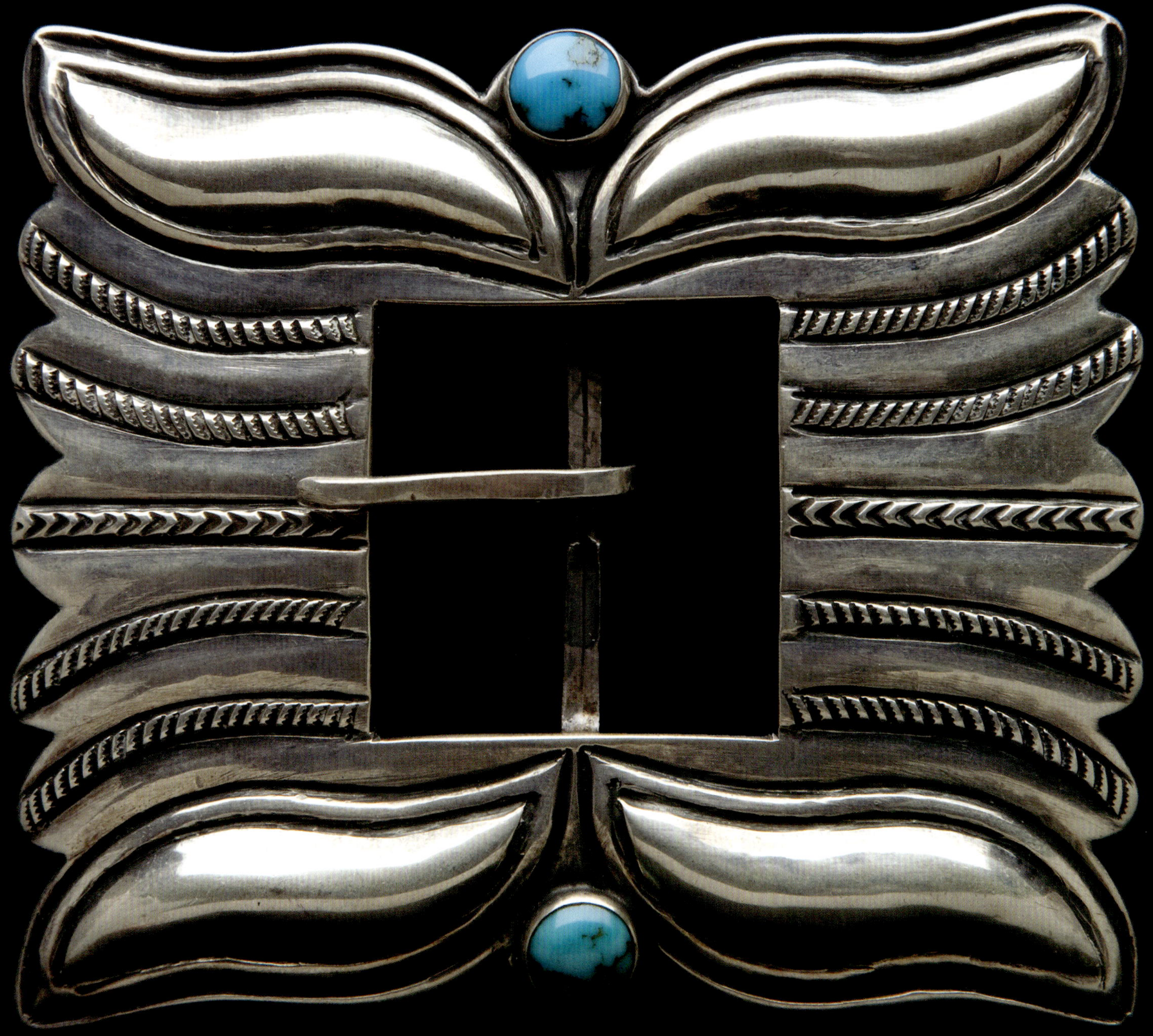

PLATE 107
Austin (Ike) Wilson (U.S., Navajo, ?-1960)
Belt Buckle, 1950. Silver and turquoise, 3 × 3⅜ × ¼ in.
Philbrook Museum of Art
A2007.5907

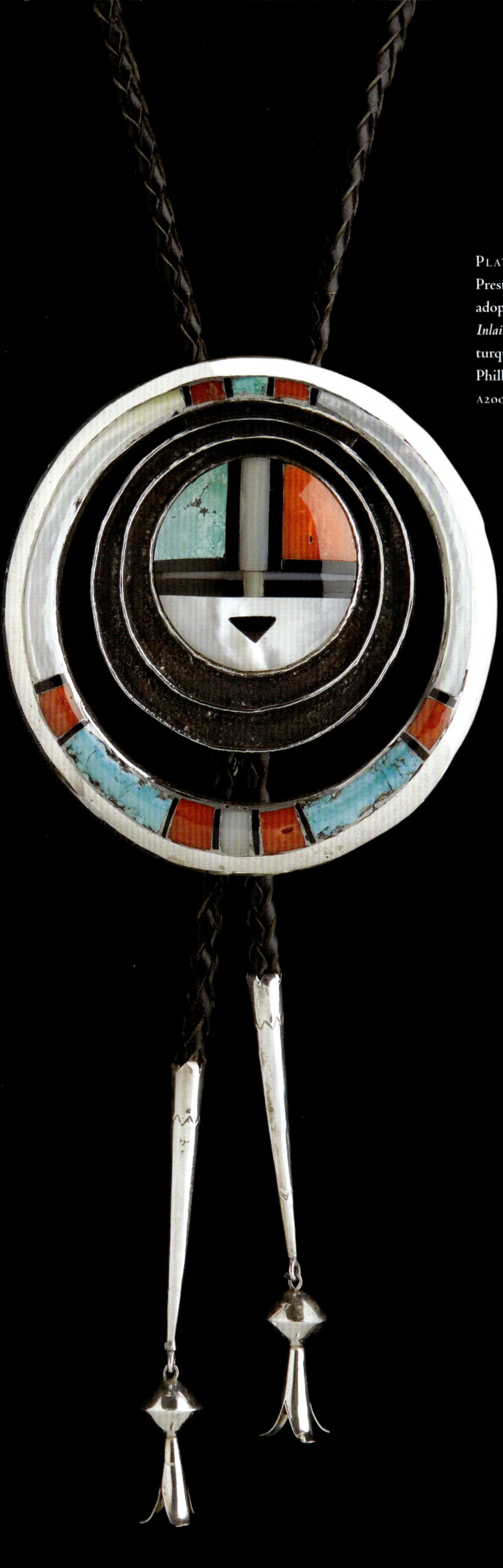

Plate 108
Preston Monongye (U.S., Mission/Mexico, adopted Hopi, 1927–1987)
Inlaid Bolo Tie, c. 1970. Silver, shell, turquoise, coral, and jet, 3½ × ⅜ in.
Philbrook Museum of Art
A2007.5988

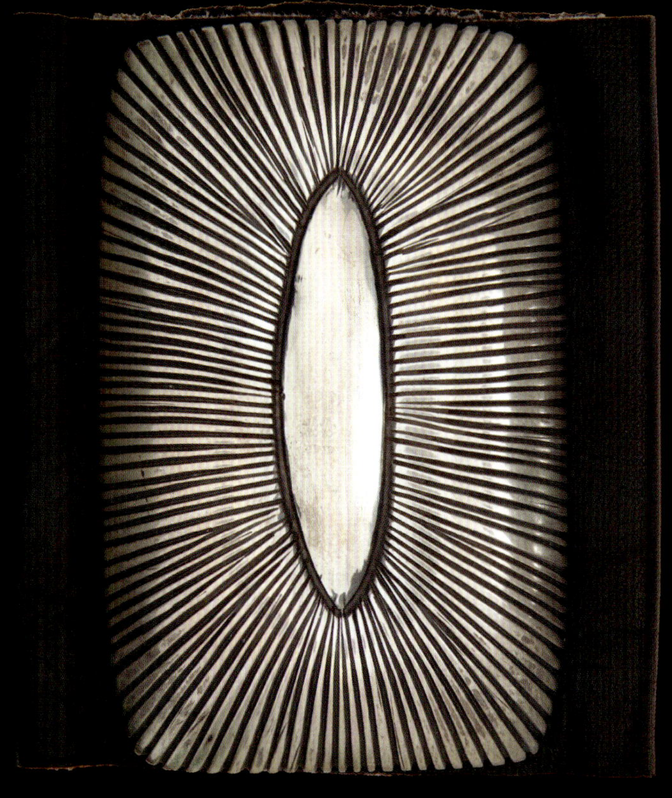

Plate 109 (detail, facing page)
Unknown (U.S., Navajo)
Bow Guard, n.d. Leather and silver, 4 × 3½ × 9/16 in.
Philbrook Museum of Art
A2007.6310

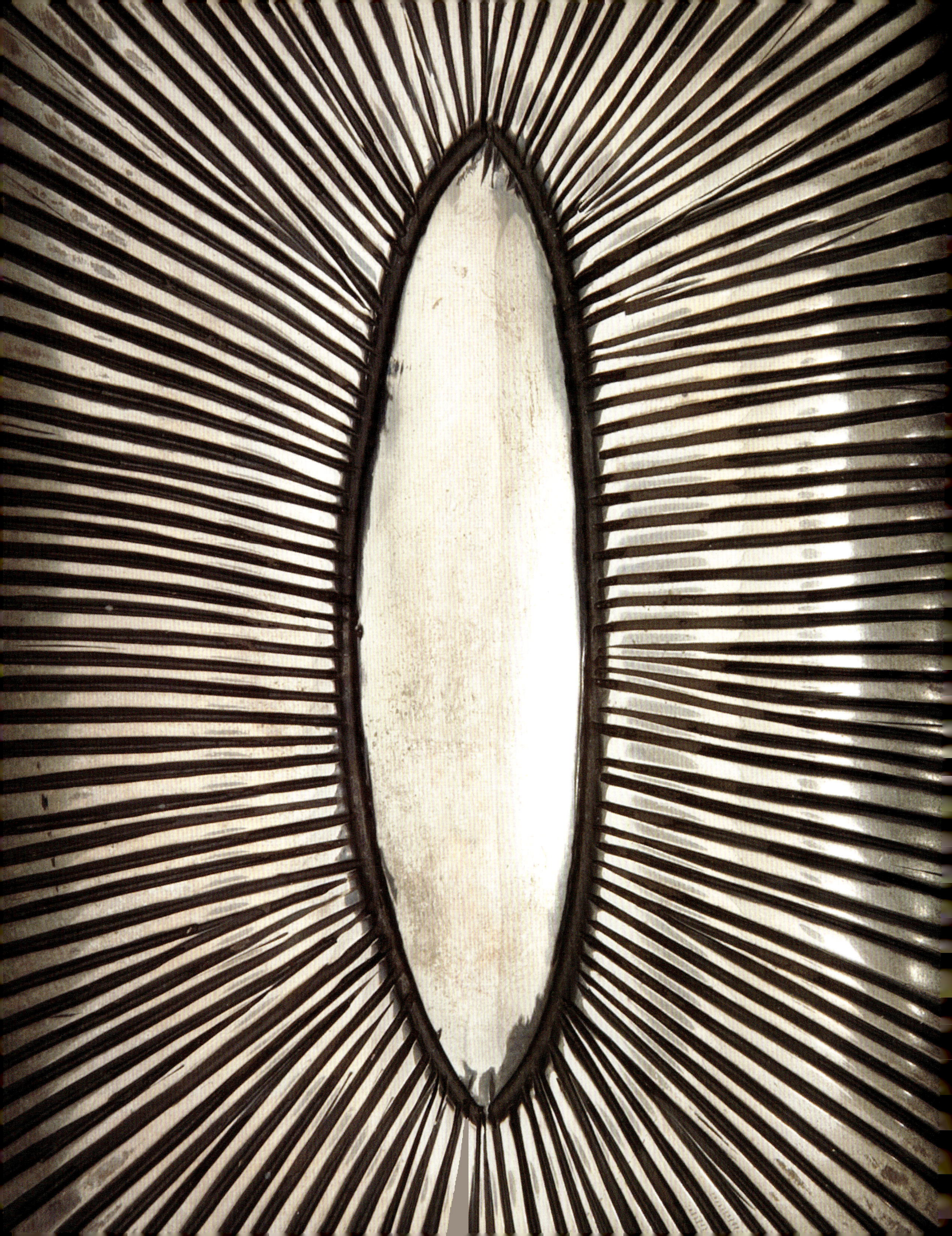

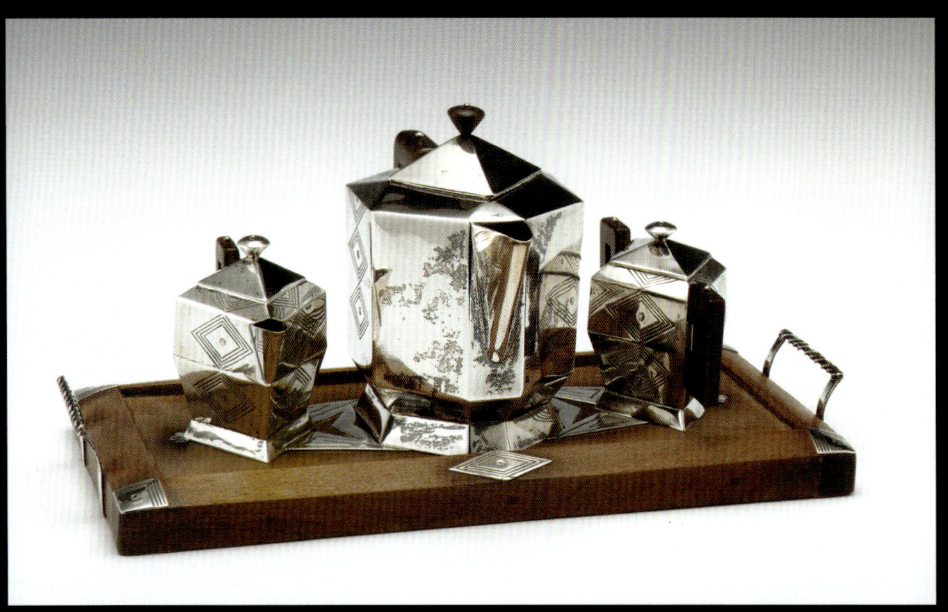

PLATE 110
Kenneth Begay (U.S., Navajo, 1913–1977)
Teaset and Tray, n.d.
Silver and ironwood, 3¾ × 5½ × 3½ in.
Philbrook Museum of Art
A2007.6333

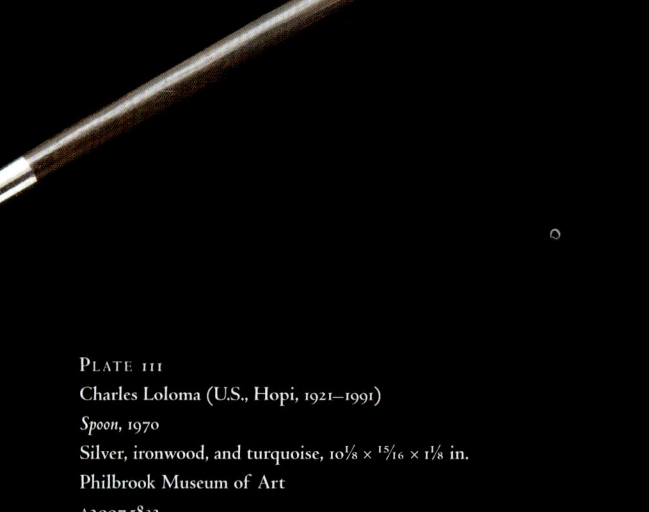

PLATE 111
Charles Loloma (U.S., Hopi, 1921–1991)
Spoon, 1970
Silver, ironwood, and turquoise, 10⅛ × 15/16 × 1⅛ in.
Philbrook Museum of Art
A2007.5832

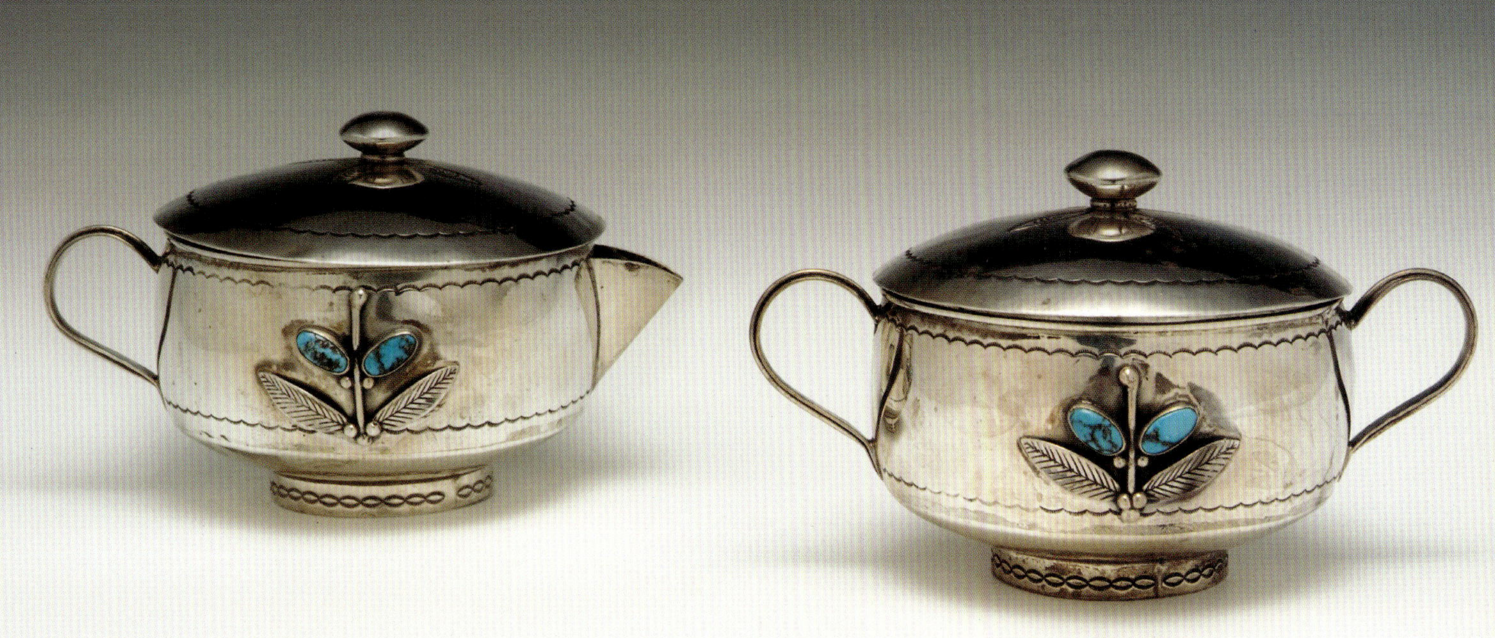

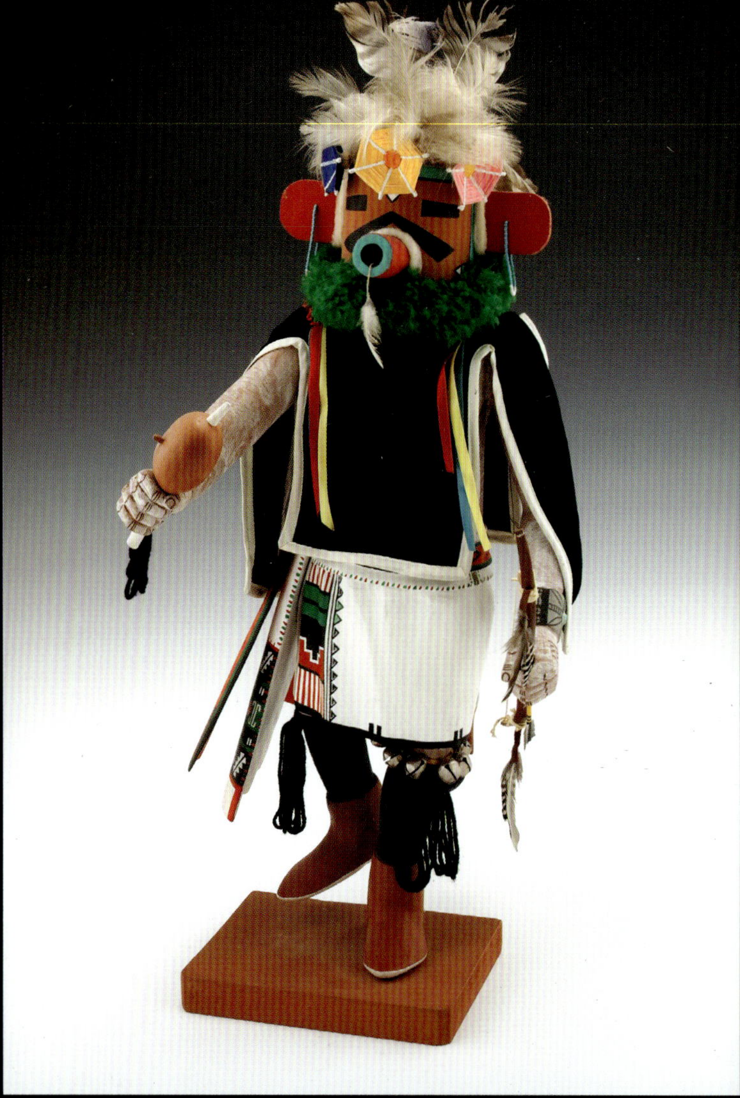

Plate 113
Henry Shelton (U.S., Hopi, b. 1929)
Velvet Shirt (Navan) Kachina, n.d.
Wood, paint, velvet, bells, ribbon, yarn, and feathers, 30 × 12⅜ × 15 in.
Fred Jones Jr. Museum of Art
A2007.6825

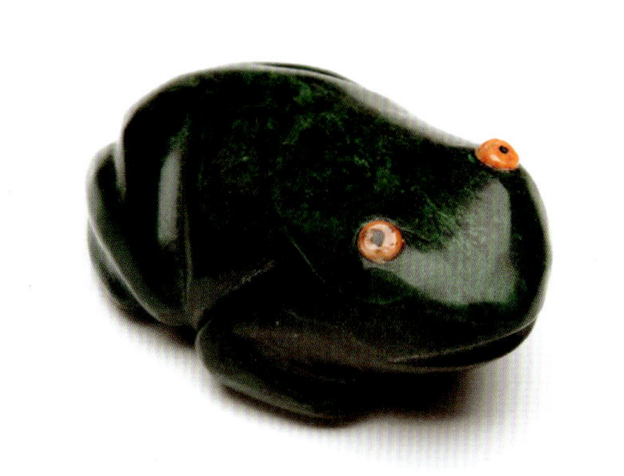

Plate 114
Unknown (U.S., Zuni)
Frog Fetish, n.d.
Serpentine and spiny oyster, 3½ × 2½ × 1½ in.
Fred Jones Jr. Museum of Art
A2007.6370

Plate 115 (facing page)
Henry Shelton (U.S., Hopi, b. 1929)
Hemis (Jemez) Kachina, 1967
Wood, paint, and feathers, 28 × 8 in.
Philbrook Museum of Art
A2007.6809

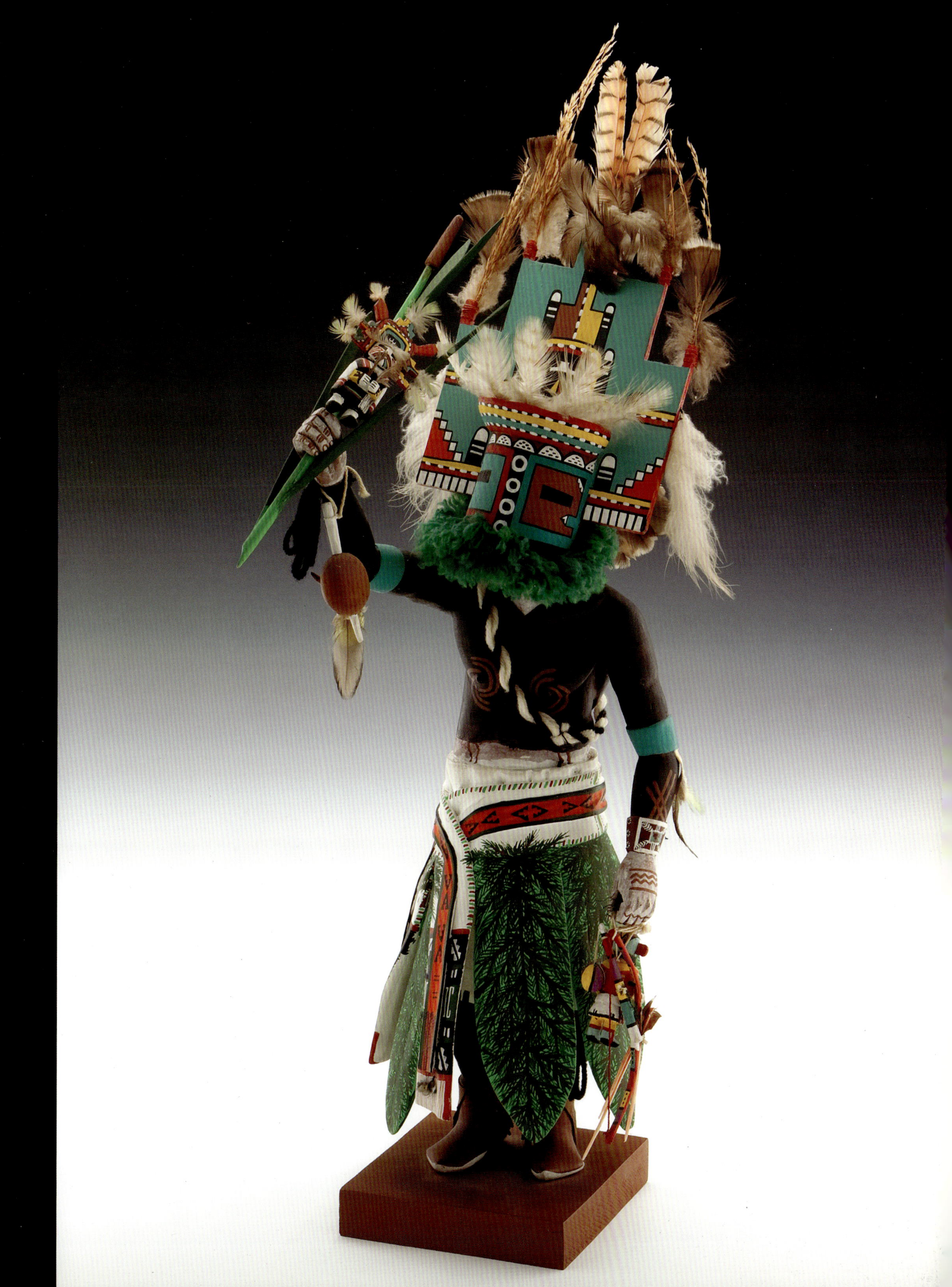

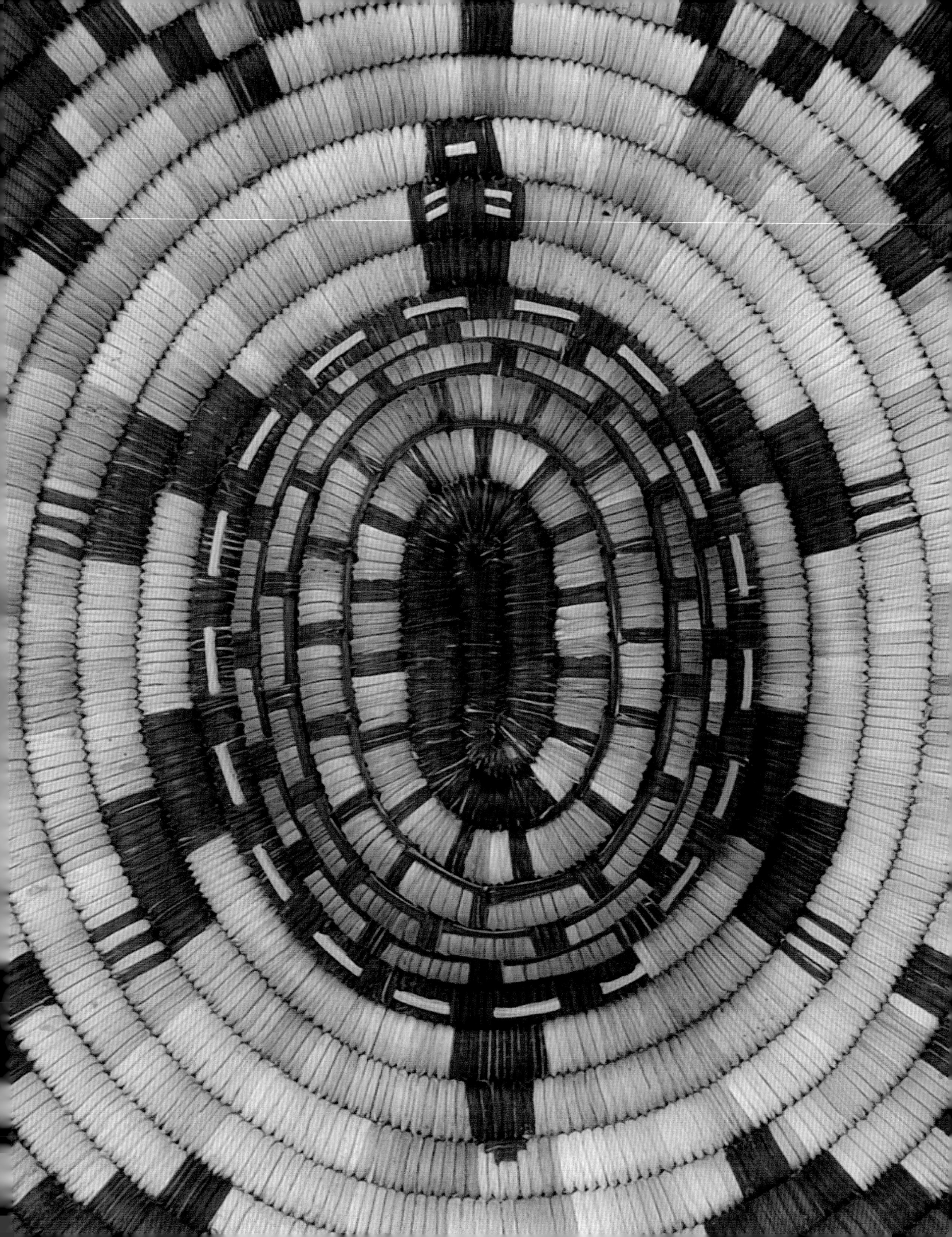

Materials of the Earth and Its People

Baskets and Textiles in the Adkins Collection

Mary Jo Watson

CHAPTER SIX

BASKETS

Basketry is perhaps the most important form of the craft arts as it is, apparently, the oldest of all with the exception of tool making. . . . Among the Anasazi of the Southwest, some of the earliest ceramic pieces were formed inside baskets, thus effecting form. Also many of the earliest pottery designs were taken directly from baskets.

CLARA LEE TANNER

Eugene B. Adkins was fascinated with Native American arts, especially those of the American Southwest. North American Indian arts in each geographic area are related to their environment, their available materials for manufacture, and their iconography and iconology. The desert area of North America was the origin of brilliant, specialized architecture, painting, pottery, and weaving. Distinct forms, designs, and symbols give insight into the lives, economies, and cultures of the people in this area. Many of the earlier designs and forms are now represented with new media and materials, yet the new art maintains a close relationship to the beliefs, cosmos, and ideals of earlier artists and circumstances. All this can be seen in Adkins's collection of baskets and weavings.

Throughout the centuries in the great American desert Southwest, baskets were developed based on the need for containers, storage, gathering, cooking food, and numerous other uses.[1] Practical items included trays, jars, bowls, mats, burden baskets, and sifters, and later baby carriers and plaques were developed. Gift baskets, made for special occasions, were found in many tribes, and miniature baskets, many as small as a sewing thimble, gave the artists an opportunity to demonstrate superior skills.

DETAIL OF PLATE 117 (p. 171)
Remalda Lomayestewa (U.S., Hopi, b. 1938)
Raised Turtle Plaque, 1969

Basket making is generally considered a woman's art, although among earlier Pueblo people, men occasionally constructed baskets.[2] In the twentieth century, baskets were primarily made by women; however, some men wove.[3] Regardless, weavers were important to the well-being of the tribe because the baskets contained cultural information and later earned income. Weavers whose techniques and forms were especially skillful were awarded prestige and became a source of pride for the people; many of their baskets became central in sacred ceremonies.[4] Today, families continue to pass down baskets from one generation to the next and remember the makers.

Common throughout the Adkins Collection are baskets that reflect a strong knowledge of tribal history, environment, and cultural designs and symbols. "Each basket expresses a subtle dialogue between the individual weaver's creativity and his, or more often, her cultural traditions."[5] Part of that tradition includes gathering the correct materials. This long process, covering several seasons of a year, requires knowing when to cut, extract, strip, cut into weavers, and dye as well as drying out the reeds until the materials are finally woven together. Depending on location, some common basket-making materials of the Southwest include alder bark, bear grass, desert willow, cattail stems, martynia, devil's claw, sumac, and yucca, to name a few. Serious attention is given to the spiritual connection between the weavers and the materials of the earth. In this art form, "collecting materials for use in basketry reflects an intimate relationship between human society and the natural world."[6]

Once the materials are ready, the process of weaving a form is completed using four basic techniques: plaiting, wicker, twining, and coiling. These techniques are then elaborated on, with dyed materials, mixed colors, and a regularity of patterns—sets of geometric designs and human and animal forms, many arranged symmetrically and asymmetrically.

Triangles, diamonds, circles, steps, frets, straight lines, squares, and meanders and variations on all of these can be found on many woven baskets.[7] The complexity, mental acuity, and creativity of Native artists evident in these baskets is astonishing.

During the latter part of the nineteenth century and well into the twentieth, much of this knowledge was diminished and in some cases lost. Over the centuries, weavers adapted their baskets to changing needs and forms as large and small storage baskets were replaced with pottery vessels. During the nineteenth century two events occurred, even greater than centuries of trading and contact with other tribes, that changed the course of basket making and other arts in the Southwest. In the 1880s trains began running through the region, bringing in yarn and bolts of cloth, "which curtailed weaving, and framing tools, which affected the economy, but also pots and pans which took the place of baskets in many tribes."[8] In 1901, closely following the advent of imported goods to the Southwest, the national superintendent of Indian Schools, Estelle Reel, was rethinking the course of study for Indian students. Reel felt that retention of the older crafts was important and would become a viable means of income.[9] She put out a call to find Indian experts to teach the craft skills, including basket making, in Indian schools, but technology, government policies of the nineteenth century, and influence from outside cultures of the early twentieth century continued to bring changes to tribal arts. These changes created challenges for Indian basket makers and, in some cases, because of limited production in many tribes, caused serious decline in the knowledge and understanding of basket-making processes.

These changes brought about a significant transition among all tribal artists in the first half of the twentieth century. The ability of Native people to respond to new ideas, sometimes new media, created a sense of survival for the people and their arts. The Adkins basket collection fits into this aspect of twentieth-century Indian art and features adaptations associated with the new direction of combining economic appeal with older traditions.

Trains also brought tourists, Americans and Europeans interested in myriad Indian-made items, echoing the new Indian policy of support for Indian crafts. This propelled a bourgeoning attitude about sales of "authentic" Indian items, which eventually created a dynamic industry in tribal communities. In the Southwest, particularly, an invigorated tribal art industry included basket making. Adkins's collection of baskets and weaving includes many representatives of tribes and artists able to rethink the rationale for basket making beyond practical needs and to develop concepts outside their tribal venue. "There were those weavers who were able to make the transition from producing pieces made for domestic use or trade to those made for sale."[10]

In many instances, it is difficult to know whether the early twentieth-century artists were making baskets for sale or for the tribe or whether they were influenced by government policy or the new era of Indian art for sale. Artists did respond to the tourist market with new basket designs and materials. One of the earliest baskets in the Adkins Collection is dated 1920, by a named artist, Mary Snyder (1870s–1951), of the Chemehuevi, a tribe related to southern Nevada and southwestern Paiutes.[11]

Snyder's coiled bowl basket is probably made with willow, sumac, and devil's claw (plate 118). She used geometric designs and naturalistic images, as did other weavers in her small group. The latter designs "included butterflies, snakes, plants, trees, lizards, birds and insects."[12] The polychrome basket bowl in the collection was formed with a contrasting background of very light cream willow and intricately spaced and staggered sections of a darker brown material. Starting with a small coil in the lower center of the bowl, the sides flare out to the rim, and the basket is finished with stitches in a light cream color with intervals of darker beige.

Floating across the interior surface of this flared bowl are fifteen images of bugs and lizards. The two-dimensional lizards and bug images in the weaving are composed in a rich dark brown, situated in two rings around the bowl interior. Their sizes differ somewhat, with six large lizards in the upper ring and plump four-legged bugs interspersed throughout the top of the second ring, which is closer to the bottom.[13] These same images appear on the exterior of the woven basket and echo an environment that contains both the colors and the materials of a special desert world. According to Schaaf, Snyder's favorite designs included rattlesnakes, which "had to be treated with great respect or snake sickness might result."[14] Mary Snyder was considered the only Chemehuevi weaver with power enough to portray realistic rattlesnakes.[15] Of two Chemehuevi shallow bowls by Mary Snyder in the Clark Field Collection at the Philbrook Museum in Tulsa, one design includes rattlesnakes, and the other, stinkbugs. Snyder traveled throughout the Southwest and was credited with originating several designs.[16] One can imagine how plentiful snakes, insects, and lizards are in parts of the great American desert and why the artist added them to her basket. Other favorite images for her to weave were ants, bees, whirlwinds, cats, and mice.[17]

All these images reflect an understanding of the environment and her attachment to all the elements of her particular world. The design selections in this basket are personal, and her association with nature is vivid, intimate, and knowledgeable. At the same time, she demonstrates remarkable skill. Hundreds of stitches are involved within the coiled basket form. This expertise could come only with training and knowledge about gathering and processing materials taught to her by her elders. Her evenness of stitching, placement of color, and bold designs provide evidence of the quality of fine art. Eugene Adkins was drawn to quality, which he found in the work of Mary Snyder.

Another of his expert choices was a Paiute lidded bowl made in 1960. This coiled and beaded basket is remarkable in its overall design and color (plate 116). The artist, Clara Castillo (dates unknown), a Northern Paiute, was awarded the Folklife Apprenticeship Masters and Apprentices Award by the Nevada Arts Council in 1986.[18]

In the 1870s the Northern Paiute were settled in several reservations throughout eastern California, Nevada, Utah, southern Idaho, and southeastern Oregon. Beaded baskets became popular with tourists, and "by 1908 Mono Lake Paiute women started to place the designs from these bands, loom woven beaded bands, on coiled baskets using a netted overlay of glass beads."[19]

Glass beads were introduced to Native people by Europeans, and the artistry of adaptation became apparent when jewelry, clothing, horse apparel, and eventually baskets provided an avenue of beaded artistic expression. Until the sixteenth century, American Indians used jade, turquoise, freshwater pearls, mica, copper, shells, porcupine quills, and numerous other materials for artistic purposes. The Adkins *Beaded Lidded Bowl* offers a vibrant experience of color, form, and design and the fully realized intent of tourist and government interventions.

Prior to the 1960s, it was evident from earlier paintings, such as murals, and pottery, that American Indians were adept at the use of color and color combinations. Clara Castillo was likely trained in the western ideal of color theory taught to all American art students. Her use of the colors blue and orange in this woven lidded bowl confirm either a learned or inherent color sensitivity that Natives used with complimentary colors of the traditional western color wheel.

The body of the bowl is divided into three circular registers and is composed of diamond patterns, one large and two small. A bright sky blue background covers the basket as a base for all the designs and patterns. Dark blue, orange, red, black, and light blue beaded outlines of the larger diamond in the middle of the basket surround a dark blue center with double diamonds, one on top of the other.

A characteristic of this delightful and arduously beaded basket is the size of the central band that exhibits the widest designs placed on and around the central body. Indian artists knew that the larger width of patterns in the center of the basket bowl accentuated the width of the bowl. In this instance, a diamond pattern was larger in the center and decreased in size at the base and the rim of the bowl. This method allowed the round middle shape to "expand" the central areas of the basket. This sophisticated knowledge is seen throughout the centuries of Native arts.

Another sophisticated and elite basket in the Adkins Collection is one made by an unknown Washoe artist. The small Washoe tribe is recognized by many basket experts as making some of the finest baskets in American Indian art history. The Washoe once lived on the lands where Reno, Carson City, and Gradnerville/Minden in Nevada and South Lake Tahoe in California now stand. In 1917 the tribe was provided a reservation in Carson City.[20]

The most famous of all the Washoe basket weavers was Louise Keyser, whose relationship with Abe and Amy Cohn in the late nineteenth and early twentieth centuries promoted Washoe basket making.[21] Washoe baskets became prominent because of the "increased popularity of Indian baskets with collectors and tourists; the patronage and business skills of Abe and Amy Cohn; and the talented weaver Louisa Keyser."[22] The success of the Washoe basket makers was due not only to the Cohns's promotion of one basket maker but to the talent and creative ability of many in the Washoe basket-making community, who were adept and superb artists. A tight, well-presented basket was completed with twenty stitches per inch. "The most popular new shape was a compressed globular jar called a 'degikup.'"[23] Created by Keyser, the degikup was "a spheroid-shaped, small mouthed basket patterned after the Pomo Treasure Basket."[24]

The Adkins Washoe basket is a superior representation of a degikup coiled basket, with elegant and refined designs (plate 123). There are three circles on the surface of the tightly coiled golden yellow basket. True to Washoe traditions, the maker added a different shape of design on these three circles, one toward the base, one in the middle, and one connected to the rim of the basket. On the lower end toward the base are multiple dark brown designs

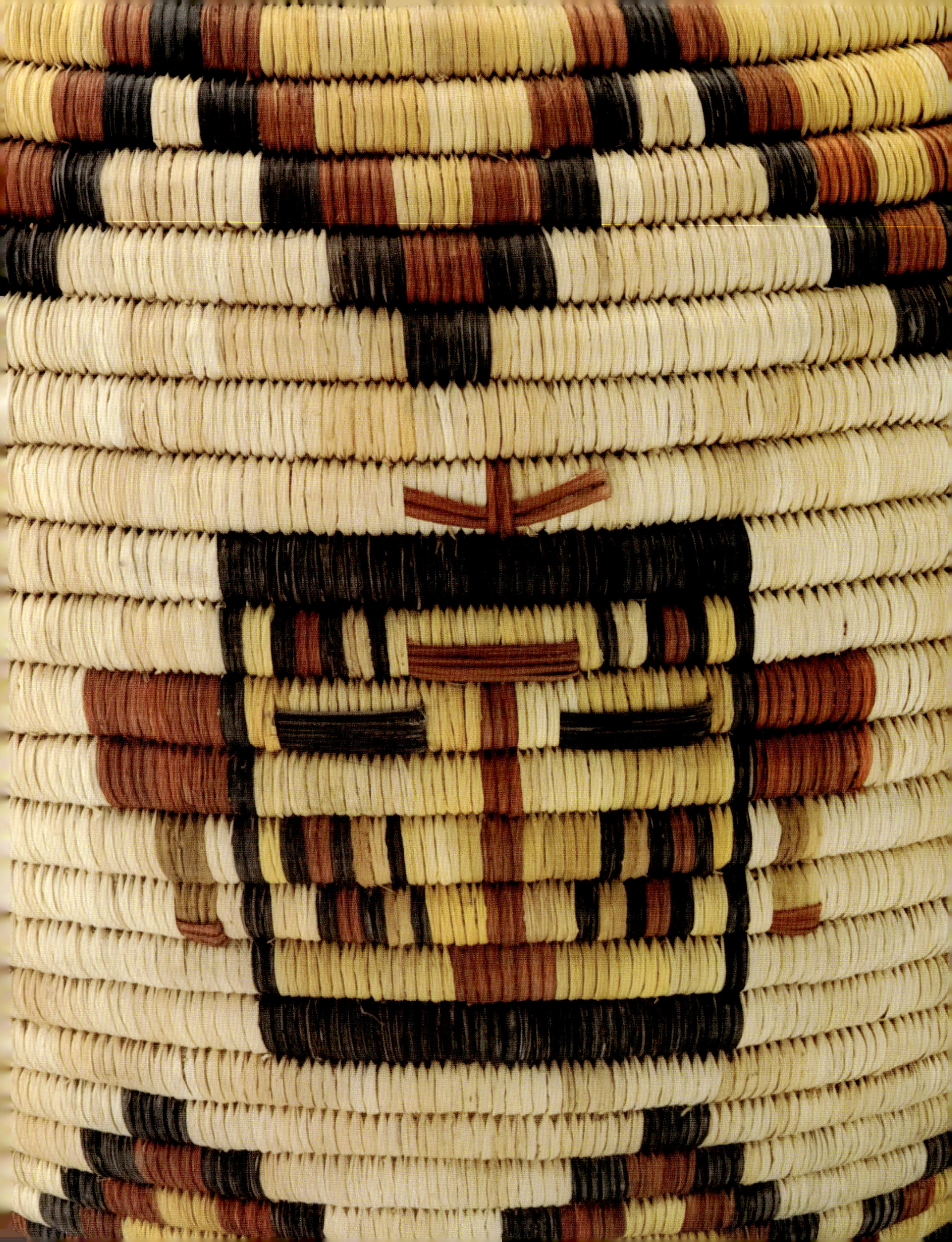

of an elongated diamond pattern, small in size. In the center of the basket, constrained yet complex designs of dark brown shapes resembling the letter H are found in even distances around the main body of the form, covering seven of the coiled rows. The H patterns are interspersed in the middle of the design with a fourth row of the golden background, creating an interruption and interesting design feature. At the top is a row of more elongated diamond patterns found on five rows of coils proceeding to the rim at the top. The interior of the basket exhibits the same exact design. The features of this finely coiled Washoe basket make it a superior representative of Washoe baskets in the Eugene Adkins Collection.

Several baskets in the Adkins Collection are from the Hopi tribe. "Hopi Indian basketry probably has the longest continuous life of any in the Southwest today, for its heritage can be traced back 1500 years and possibly much more."[25] Numerous women and men in the Hopi tribe made baskets of exquisite quality and designs, winning top prizes for their superb basket making at various markets in the twentieth century. Each area of the Southwest creates specific and singular designs of iconographic and internal meaning special to the individual tribes. Although the Hopi weaving techniques were similar to others, they made creative and exceptional contributions in designs, colors, and forms.

Remalda Lomayestewa (b. 1938) of Second Mesa, an active basket maker of the Bearstrap/Spider Clan, is renowned for her coiled baskets, which "she makes for paybacks, gifts, and Basket Dances. If she has additional time, she also makes baskets for sale."[26] Some of her favorite designs include clouds, corn, kachinas, butterfly maiden, Mudhead, turtle, whirlwind, and spiders.[27] In her Adkins basket, created in 1969, the raised turtle is central in the coiled plaque (plate 117). The basket is likely made of yucca and rabbit brush, with a mixture of natural and aniline dyes.[28]

DETAIL OF PLATE 120 (p. 174)
Unknown (U.S., Hopi)
Coiled Polychrome Jar with Kachina Head Design, 1970s

The turtle is woven with dark and light brown to emphasize the raised position of the turtle's back, which is pushed through by the artist. The turtle is surrounded with a neutral color that is outlined toward the top with fourteen pointed black inverted Vs, and situated in between are seven red and seven reversed neutral Vs. The rim is finished in black.

From the arid areas of northern Mexico into the American Southwest, Indian people continually give special attention to clouds, lightning, dragonflies, frogs, turtles, and other symbols associated with water. Small images, including tadpoles, are placed on pottery, and tiny images of frogs were carved to help summon rain. Gourds and turtle shell rattles are also symbolic of water.

Another Hopi bowl in the Adkins Collection, the *Polychrome Coiled Shallow Bowl,* (1970), is a coiled series of starlike forms with eight lines radiating to the rim (plate 119). The forms are outlined with black diamonds, complementing the natural and dyed fibers. A superb set of small Hopi coiled containers is also included, such as a polychrome jar featuring a kachina head design (plate 120) and a small coiled basket encircled by four Mudhead figures in natural fibers included in the basket design, accentuated with black on the rim (plate 122). Another example of Hopi basketry is the polychrome wicker *Peach Basket* (1970, plate 121).

Wicker work is found throughout Hopi country, but several women who specialize in wicker weaving are from Third Mesa, in the villages of Hotevilla, Bacavi, and Kykotsmovi. Wicker is a different type of weaving, using rabbit brush and a fiber the Hopi call *sivi.*[29] Wicker baskets are filled with bright colors. Because of the weaving technique, a vertical and horizontal ripple effect is seen on the polychrome wicker peach basket, an example of beauty in form and precise weaving. Unfortunately, the maker is unknown.[30]

Compared with other tribes, Navajos began weaving relatively recently. "At this time it is somewhat difficult to determine how and when ancestral Puebloan basketry and pottery designs found their way into Navajo basketry. Few examples of Navajo baskets made prior to the nineteenth century exist."[31] The reasons for the paucity of Navajo basket making are complex, but it is thought by many that during the early parts of the twentieth century, the Navajo depended on their neighbors, the Paiutes, among others, to supply them with ceremonial baskets. Since the mid-twentieth century, however, Navajo baskets artists have emerged as some of the more artistically engaging, creative, and bold contemporary basket makers.

Chester Yellowhair's handsome *Coiled Plaque* (1967) is woven with three colors—yellow, black, and red—arranged with a solid red circle enclosed by black triangles on both sides, with a split, or opening, found at the top of the basket (plate 124). This is an example of a wedding, or ceremonial, basket. Eugene Adkins's eye for quality had rested on a new trend in Navajo artistry. Yellowhair's basket, made of yucca fibers, has a commanding presence because of the exacting coil weaving and the mixture of strong colors.

The Adkins Collection's sampling of fine baskets also includes work from the Pima, Apache, and Papago, now known as the Tohono O'odham tribe, in Arizona, and from the Pomo, Mission, and Yokut Indians from California. There is a superb basket from Alaska, a finely woven basket from the southeastern United States, and one from the Northeast made of birchbark. Basket making continues to be an important part of tribal life. Several weavers continue in the traditional manner of their grandmothers and other elders. Many, like the Hopi artist Remalda Lomayestewa, are committed to teaching the knowledge of materials and processes to the next generation. Baskets hold a spiritual and cultural significance and survive in a great many tribes. This significance is perhaps best expressed by the Navajo philosophy concerning baskets, as told to Molly Yellowman by her mother, Gladys Yellowman: "The basket is a representation of this earth. The start is the emergence place. The white in the middle is the earth. The first black designs are the mountains. The red is the rainbow. The outside black designs are clouds and the outside white design represents the waters of the world."[32]

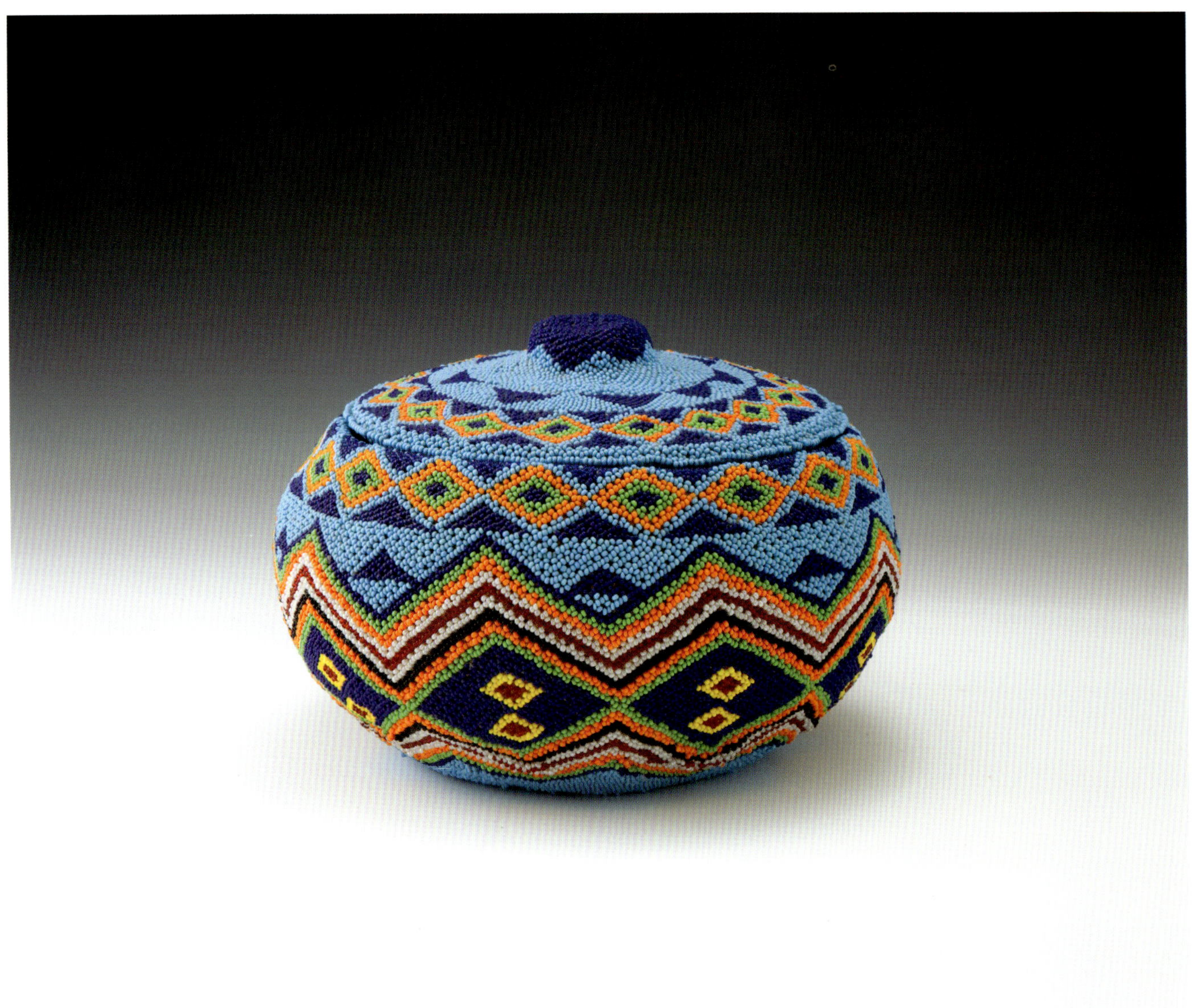

Plate 116
Clara Castillo (U.S., Paiute, dates unknown)
Beaded Lidded Bowl, 1960s. Willow, tule, and glass beads, 9 × 9 × 6 in.
Fred Jones Jr. Museum of Art
A2007.7829

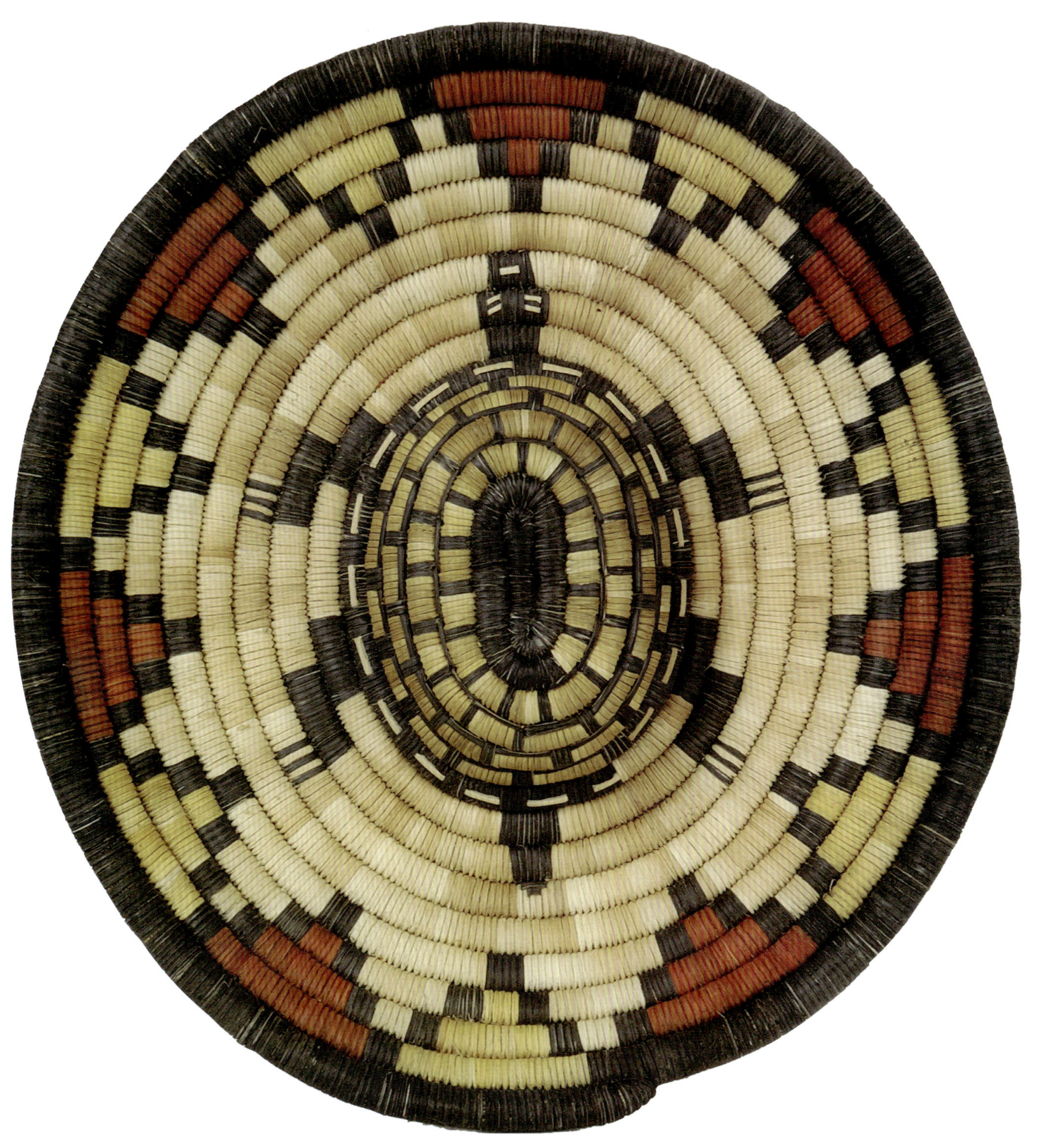

Plate 117
Remalda Lomayestewa (U.S., Hopi, b. 1938)
Raised Turtle Plaque, 1969. Yucca fibers, galetta grass, and natural dyes, 1¾ × 10¾ × 9¾ in.
Fred Jones Jr. Museum of Art
A2007.7815

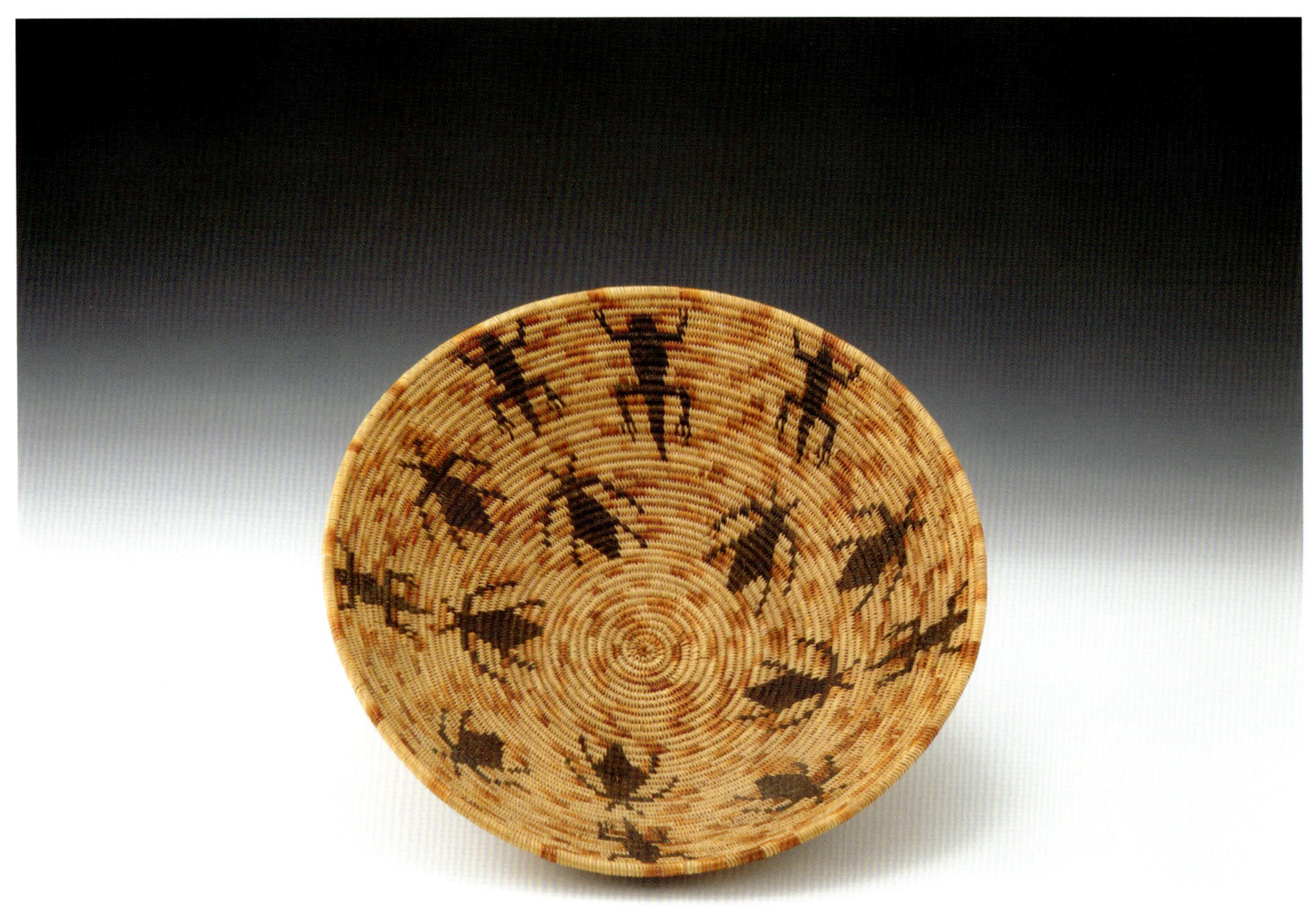

Plate 118 (above)
Mary Snyder (U.S., Chemehuevi, 1870s–1951)
Polychrome Coiled Basket with Bugs and Lizards, 1920s
Juncus and dyed juncus, 14 × 13¾ × 3½ in.
Fred Jones Jr. Museum of Art
A2007.7821

Plate 119 (facing page)
Talitha (U.S., Hopi, unknown)
Polychrome Coiled Shallow Bowl, 1970s
Yucca, galetta grass, and natural dyes, 18½ × 18½ × 3 in.
Fred Jones Jr. Museum of Art
A2007.7818

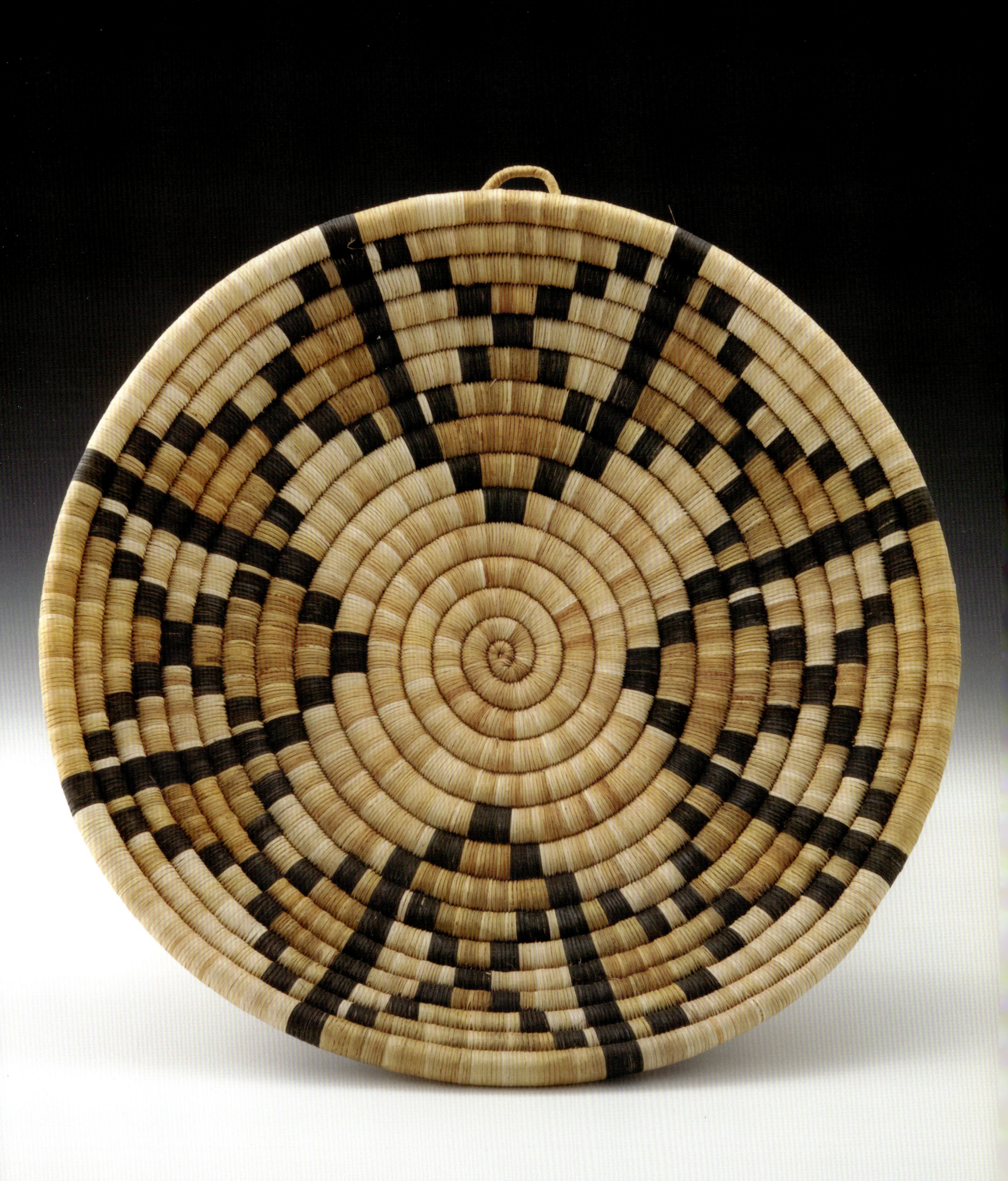

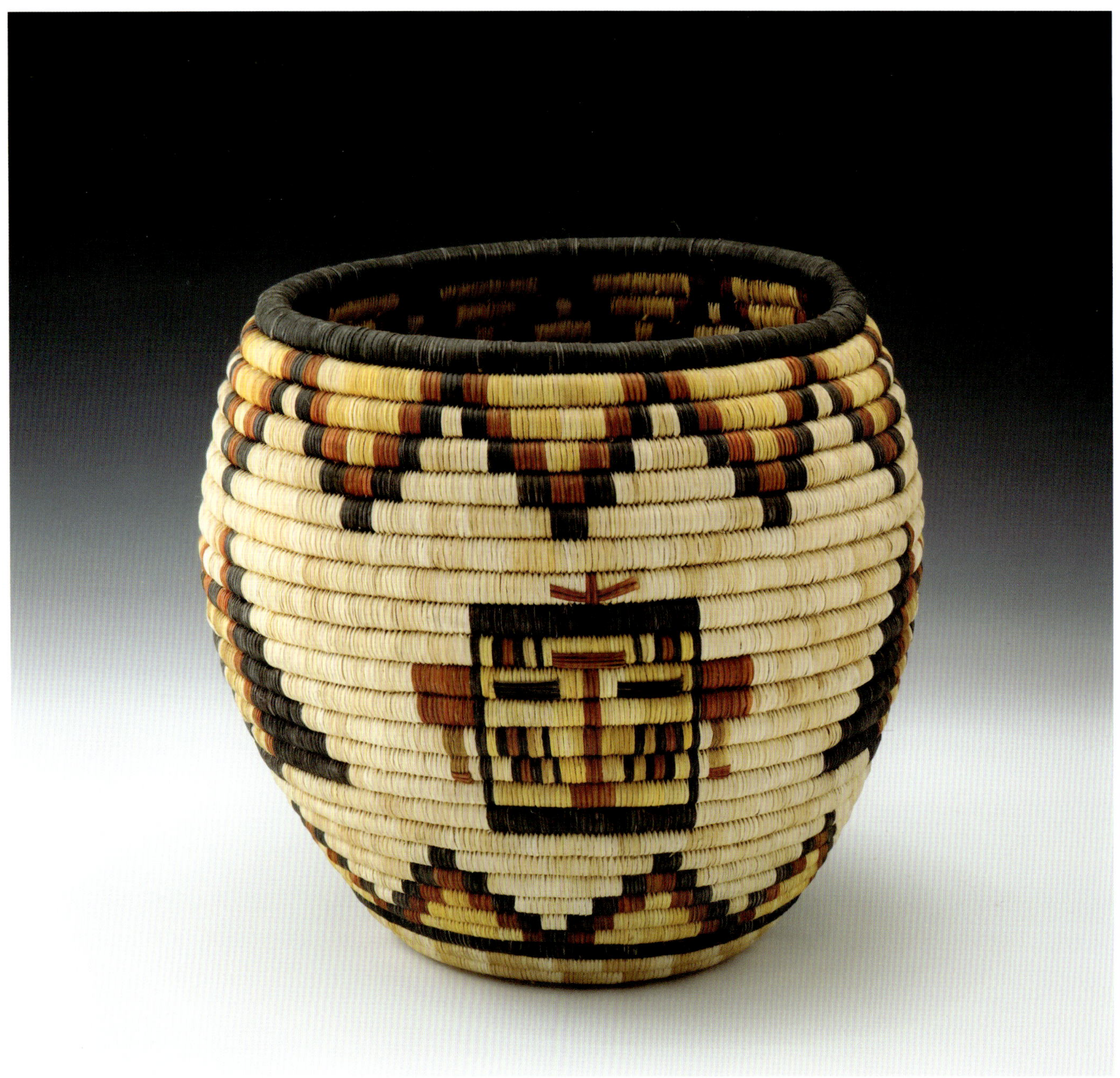

PLATE 120
Unknown (U.S., Hopi)
Coiled Polychrome Jar with Kachina Head Design, 1970s
Yucca, galetta grass, and natural dyes, 9¾ × 10¾ in.
Philbrook Museum of Art
A2007.7806

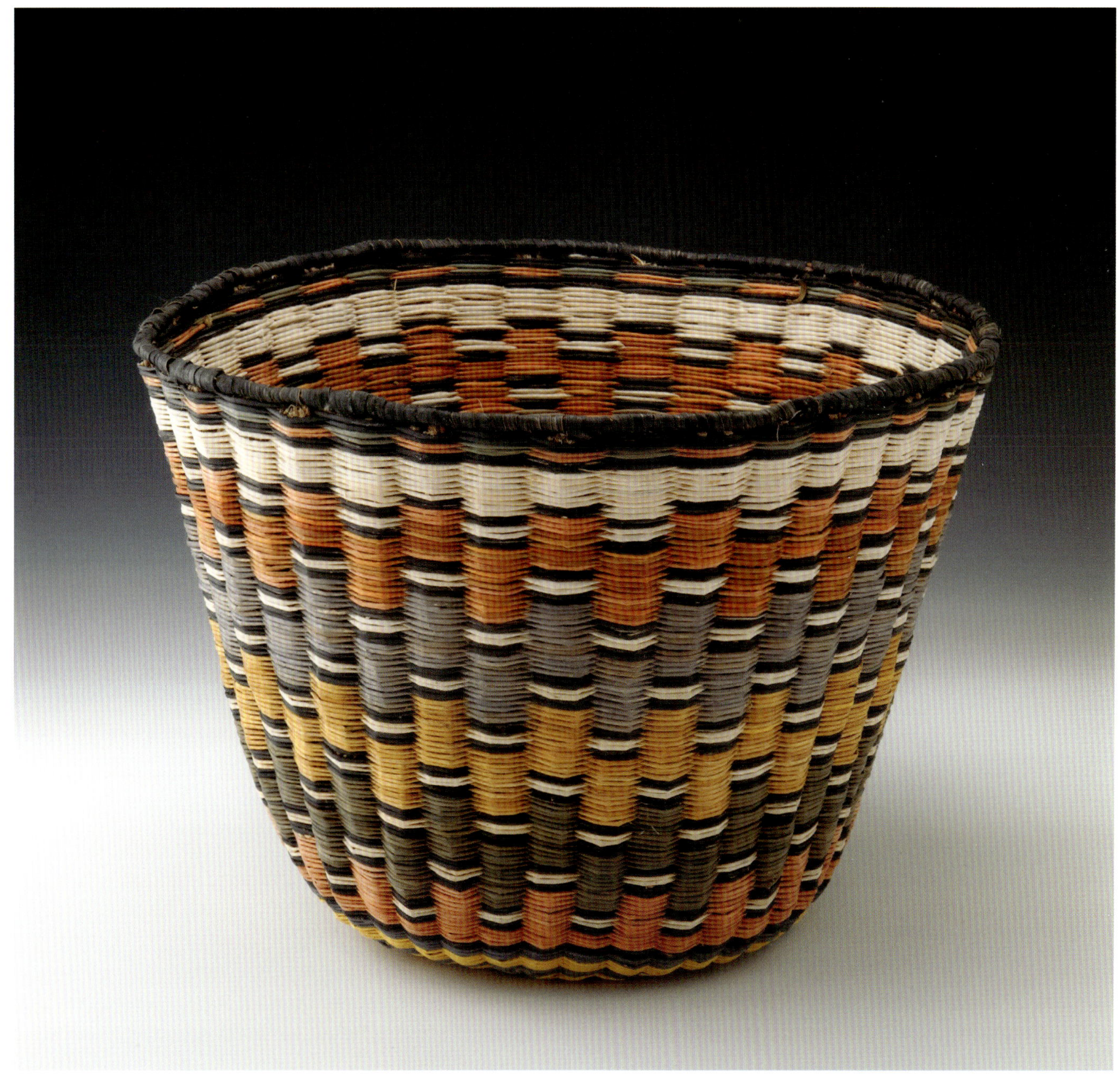

Plate 121
Unknown (U.S., Hopi)
Peach Basket, 1970s
Yucca, galetta grass, and natural dyes, 11 × 15 in.
Philbrook Museum of Art
A2007.7808

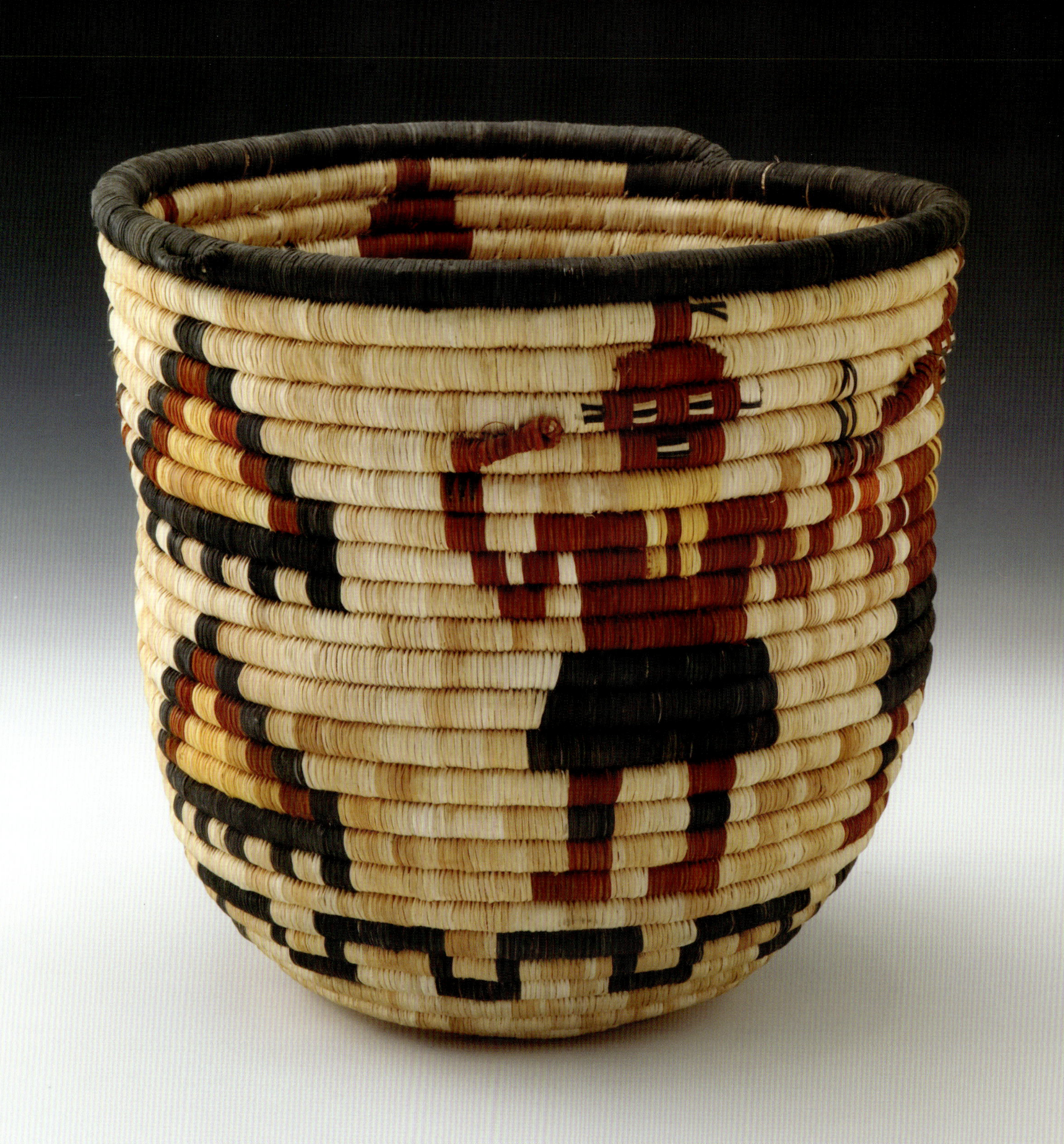

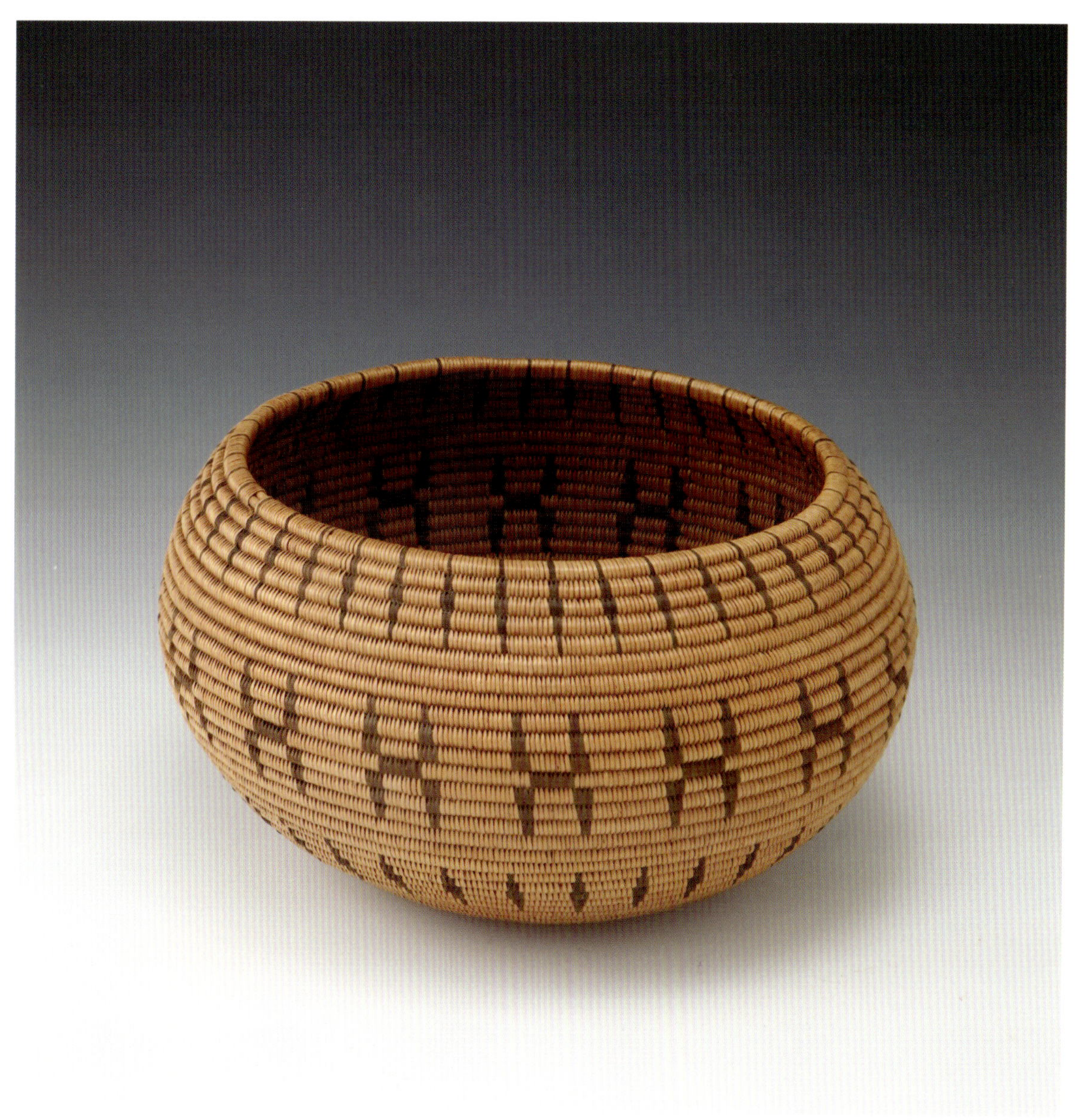

Plate 122 (facing page)
Unknown (U.S., Hopi)
Polychrome Coiled Basket with Four Mudheads, 1970s
Yucca, galetta grass, and natural dyes,
10½ × 11¾ × 10¾ in.
Fred Jones Jr. Museum of Art
A2007.7810

Plate 123 (above)
Unknown (U.S., Washoe)
Degikup Three Rod Coiling, 1920s
Willow and braken fern roots, 8½ × 8½ × 5 in.
Fred Jones Jr. Museum of Art
A2007.7824

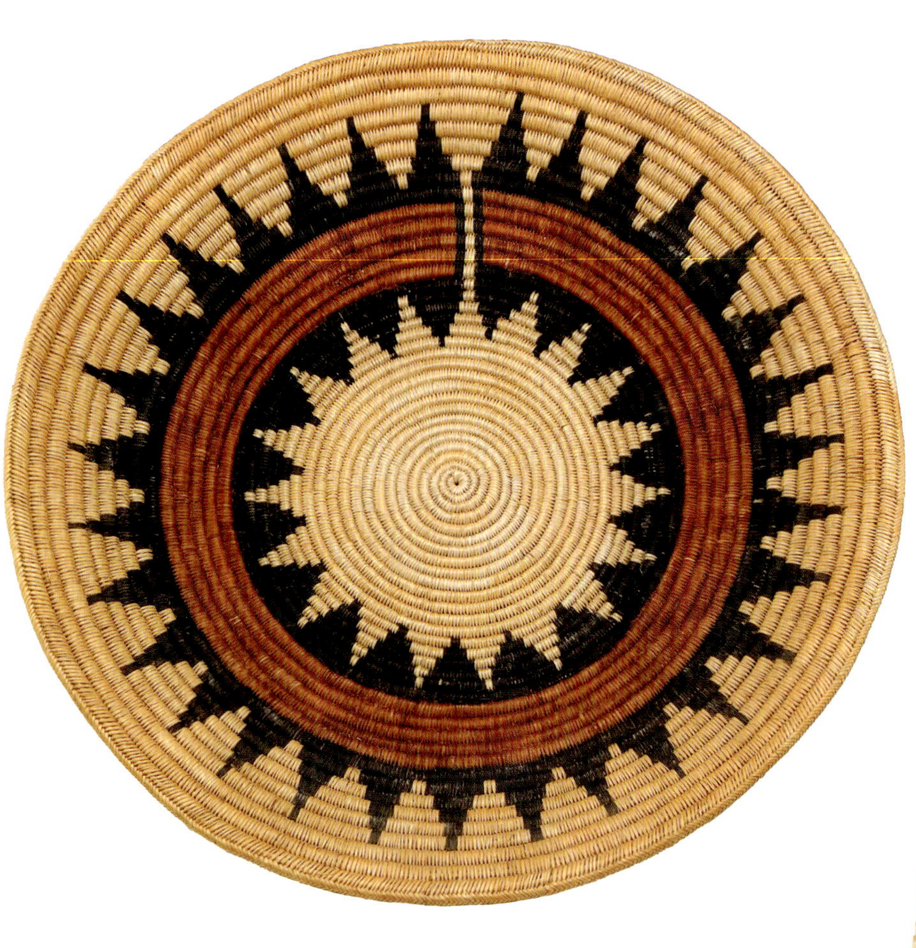

Plate 124 (detail, facing page)
Chester Yellowhair (U.S., Navajo, 1912–1990)
Coiled Plaque, 1967
Yucca, galetta grass, and natural dyes, 3 × 20½ in.
Philbrook Museum of Art
A2007.7819

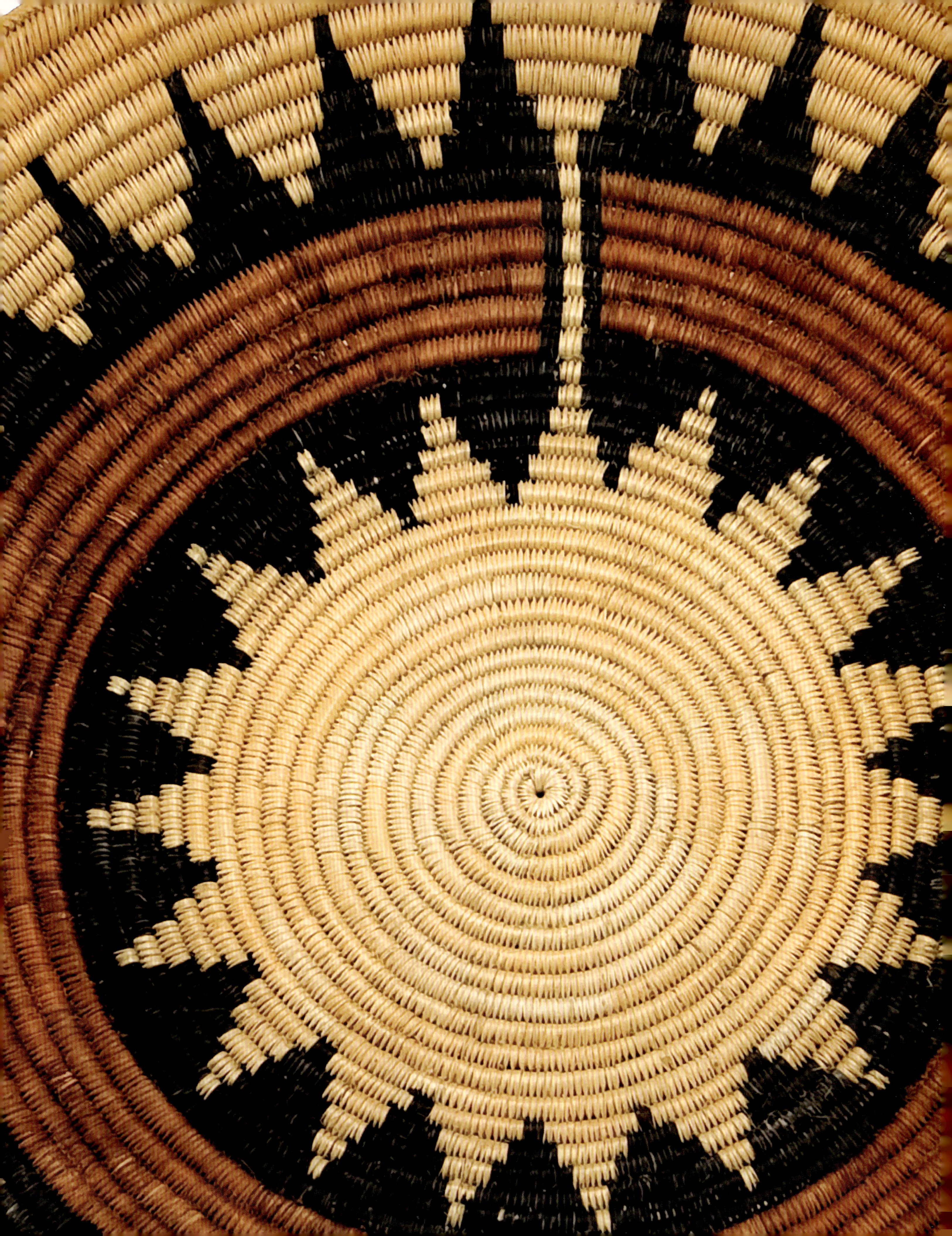

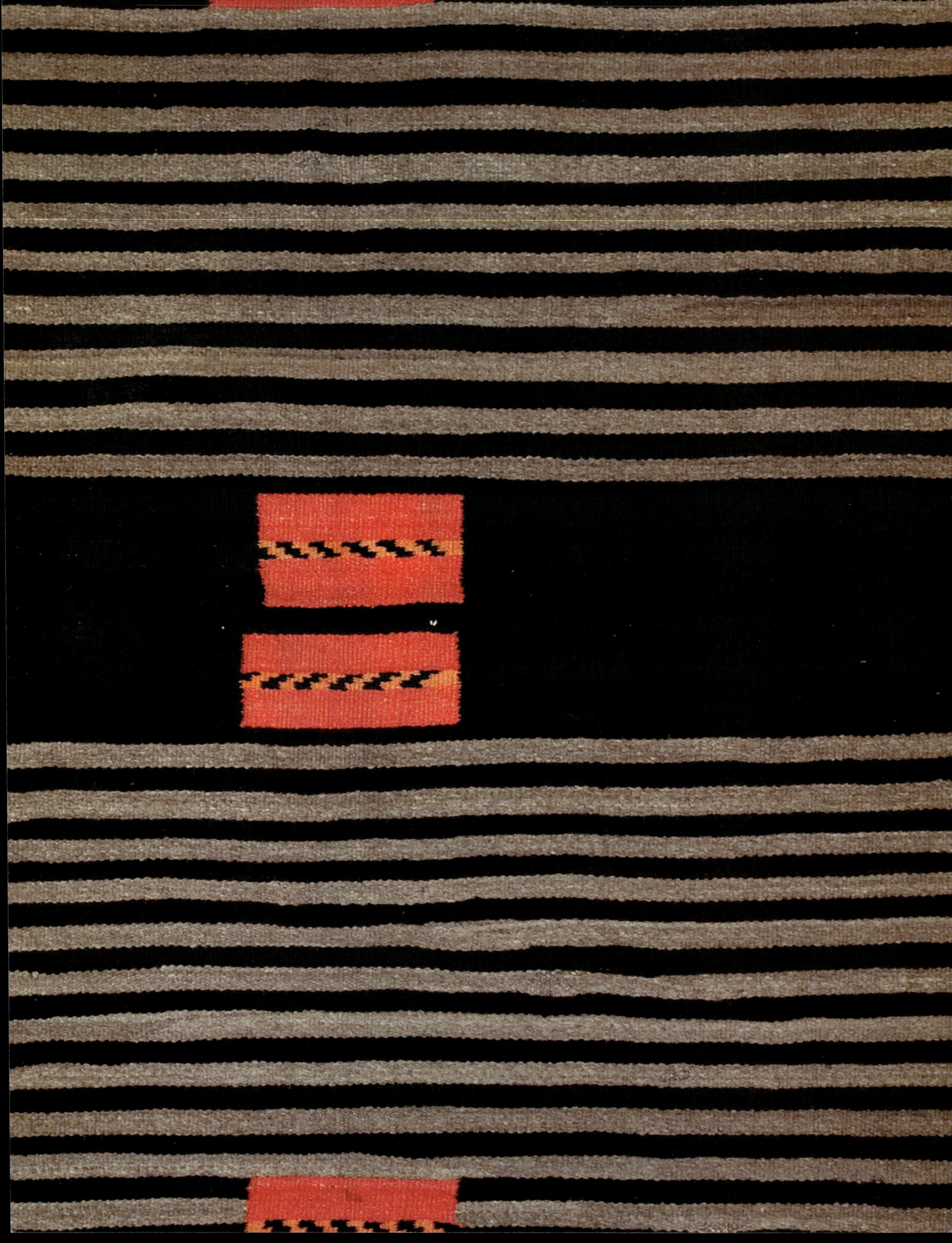

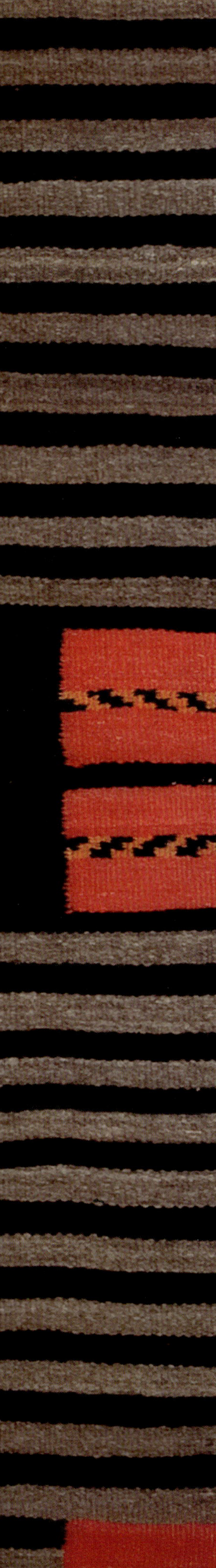

TEXTILE WEAVING

Clara Lee Tanner asks, What, then, is a true textile? How do textiles differ from basketry? Are there transitional pieces of weaving? What is the real difference between bast fiber textiles and cotton textiles?[33]

Tanner answers these questions by saying that unlike basket weaving, textiles are produced from

> the manipulation of the materials so fine and flexible that some device is necessary to hold certain of the filaments in position during the process of weaving. Although it took centuries to develop the processes, the devices or tools are the whorls, spindle sticks, a belt loom, an upright loom, a true loom, with heddle and held rod in position, accompanied by weaving tools including a batten stick, comb, needle threader, a bodkin or a needle. As in basketry there are wide arrays of techniques including, a. plain weave, single warps and wefts, b. Twill weave, under-one-over -two. c. Gauze weave two warps are crossed and held in this position as more wefts pass through them, making an open-work effect in the fabric.[34]

Later techniques of weave include tapestry, twill, warp float, and now numerous other techniques used by Pueblo and Navajo weavers.[35]

Textile weaving materials, like those of basket making, were gathered from the earth. "Bast or woody fibers on the whole are coarser and seldom are or can be prepared to equal the fineness of cotton, flax, or other such materials."[36] Cotton appeared in the Southwest after A.D. 700. Signs, such as seeds and matted fibers, of cotton use among the Hohokam appear between A.D. 700 and 1100.[37] In Tularosa Cave, Catron County, New Mexico, was found a fragment of a piece of woven cotton cloth with a green, black, and natural geometric design.[38]

DETAIL OF PLATE 125 (p. 186)
Unknown (U.S., Navajo)
Second Phase Chief's Blanket, 1880

Weaving developed and changed among the early cultures in the American Southwest. The early periods as seen in the murals at the precontact Hopi village of Awatovi record woven sashes, belts, ties, and kilts.[39] One example is an exquisite blanket from Hidden House, which presents a sophisticated offset quartered layout.[40] Many of the same designs are part of the traditional dress of the Pueblo and the Navajo. Yucca and apocynum, called Indian hemp, or dog bane, were important materials for the weaver. Among the ancient items made were sandals, woven bags, and trump bags or straps. Lacelike shirts from Tonto Ruins and twined plaited cotton and blankets were finely woven.[41]

The distinction between tribes, techniques, and iconic designs is a subject far too lengthy for this summation. According to Joe Ben Wheat, the Pueblo Indians began to use the large upright loom around A.D. 800. The work of the Navajo consists of the tapestry weave, which is more complicated.[42] These two groups form the profound center of Southwest textile weaving, which developed over the centuries into a nationally and internationally known industry of Indian and individual art.

A typical Pueblo technique was "50/50 plain weaves and warp faced weaves. . . . These weaves produce fabrics that make a suitable background for embroidery."[43] In the nineteenth century, weaving forms of Zuni, Jemez, Hopi, Acoma and Rio Grande included mantas, blankets, kilts, skirts, blouses, and dresses, all woven by men except at Zuni, where women were the weavers.[44] According to Rodee, the Rio Grande Pueblo developed weaving based on the heavy looms of the Spanish. "The combined production of both Indian and Spanish looms soon made textiles one of the province's chief exports."[45]

The fascinating history of weaving is told through many perspectives, including that of the traders, who occupied an important and historical place in the production and sales of woven materials.[46] After long periods of changes stemming from outside influences—earlier the Spanish, later the Anglo-Americans, and then the designated traders—the Southwest tribes continue to weave. As with basket weaving, the use of woven materials has changed, largely because the tourist consumer wanted an authentic Indian weaving with recognizable Indian designs and symbols.

The Navajo developed numerous styles of blankets, including a series of chief's blankets with special patterns, which are classified by dates. Important to their weaving were women's dresses, rugs, saddle blankets, wearing blankets, belts, and sashes. Especially important were those woven for ceremonial purposes, those that reflect the Navajo cosmos. In the Adkins blanket collection are many Navajo blankets and other weavings, primarily rugs, from the Hopi, the Pueblo (such as San Juan), and the Rio Grande region of 1930.

The blanket shown in plate 125 was woven by an unknown Navajo in approximately 1880. This wearing blanket, *Second Phase Chief's Blanket,* was part of the classic textiles period, which included the pattern called first phase chief's blanket. The second phase pattern was dominant from the 1850s and 1860s and is recognized by "small blocks of crimson bayeta . . . inserted at the ends and centers of each of the narrow blue stripes."[47] In this particular blanket are twelve blocks of the red color—three at the top, three on the bottom edge, and six in the middle. The blanket is bordered on either end with a small row of dark blue, with a wide dark blue in the center. Third phase chief's blankets have the addition "of a center diamond, with side half diamonds."[48]

In June 1995, the National Museum of the American Indian produced an exhibition titled *Woven by the Grandmothers.* The catalogue has images of nineteenth-century Navajo wearing blankets woven between 1840 and 1880. The blankets include "the Navajo woman's two-piece dress; early chief blankets; finely woven serapes, mantas, worn as shawls or wrapped around the body as dresses; women's striped shoulder blankets; and thick, everyday blankets, or *diyogi,* translated as 'soft and fluffy.'"[49] The Navajo weavers have different districts, where they are known for special styles and types of patterns. Some of these areas are Ganado, Tees Nos Pos, Two Grey Hills, Crystal, Chinle, Burntwater, and Blue Canyon.

One of the later developments in weaving includes what is referred to as pictorial weaving: "Pictorial rugs began appearing in the late nineteenth century. Perhaps the best selling style of nineteenth century pictorials were small, partially completed rugs on looms, often depicting railroad trains and sold along the tourist route developed by the Fred Harvey Company. Yei rugs began to be produced around the late 1890s and were the most popular pictorials made to be sold to the tourist trade during the first half of the twentieth century."[50] Early on there were prohibitions against weaving images of deities, sacred places, and scenes that were concerned with the cosmos of the people. After this changed, some weavers gave insight into sacred ceremonies. Other pictorials were lighthearted, sometimes humorous, and included images of cows, chickens, 1920s Ford automobiles, rabbits, and horses, to name a few.[51]

The Adkins Collection holds a remarkable and powerful pictorial, the image of Neil Armstrong, the American astronaut, descending the ladder to set foot on the moon. The weaving also includes the famous statement, "One small step for man, one giant leap for mankind," and the date July 28, 1969. The unknown Navajo weaver completed this in 1970.

A more prosaic pictorial is the *Pictorial Rug with Hogans* (plate 126). Included in this weaving are the images of twelve hogans in rows of six. The double horizontal hogans are woven in different colors. From the bottom up, the hogans are red, yellow, gray, brown, black, and blue at the top of the rug. The roofs of the houses have different colors in each set, and six of the hogans have crosses at the top center, possibly representing the four directions. The cosmology of the Navajo world is expressed in the shape of the hogan. The doorway always faces east; the roof supports are clustered in the region of the four directions; and the hearth is like the sun, in the center of the hogan.[52] Other patterns and weaving areas are well represented in this collection.

Many of the Hopi weavings are wedding robes, which are completed in a cream-colored field with edges filled with dramatic designs and colors. An exquisite San Juan-Tewa rug woven by Geronima Montoya also displays dramatic colors and designs on the borders. All the Adkins weavings reflect the care and interest seen throughout the Adkins collections, whether painting, jewelry, or pottery.

The University of Oklahoma is pleased to have the stewardship for so much of this fine Native American art. This collection will be an illuminating subject of study for the twenty-first century and help educate the public, scholars, students, the proud people of Oklahoma, and visitors from around the world.

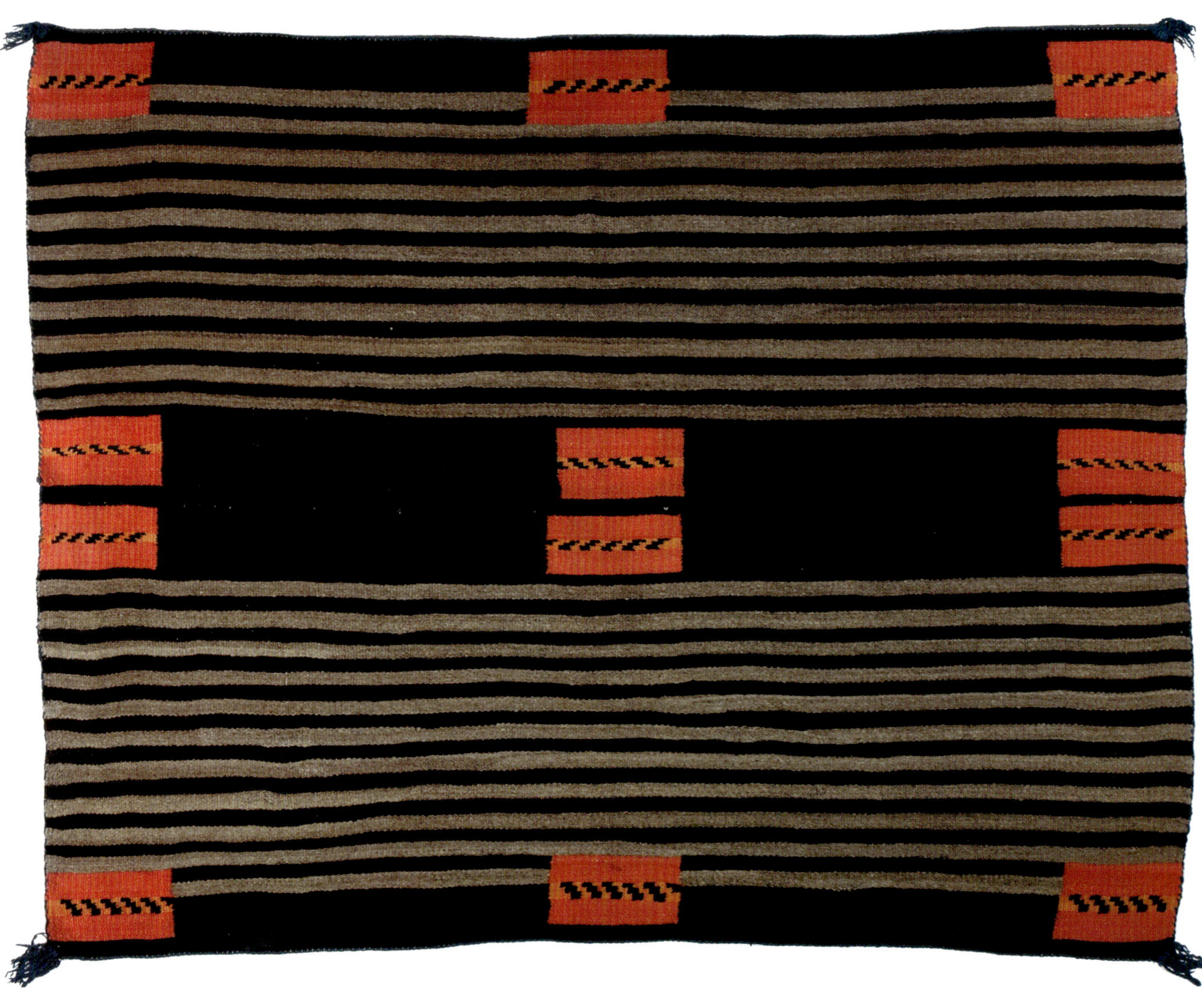

Plate 125 (above)
Unknown (U.S., Navajo)
Second Phase Chief's Blanket, 1880
Wool, 44 × 56 in.
Fred Jones Jr. Museum of Art
A2007.7526

Plate 126 (facing page)
Unknown (U.S., Navajo)
Pictorial Rug with Hogans, n.d.
Wool, 49 × 33 in.
Fred Jones Jr. Museum of Art
A2007.7544

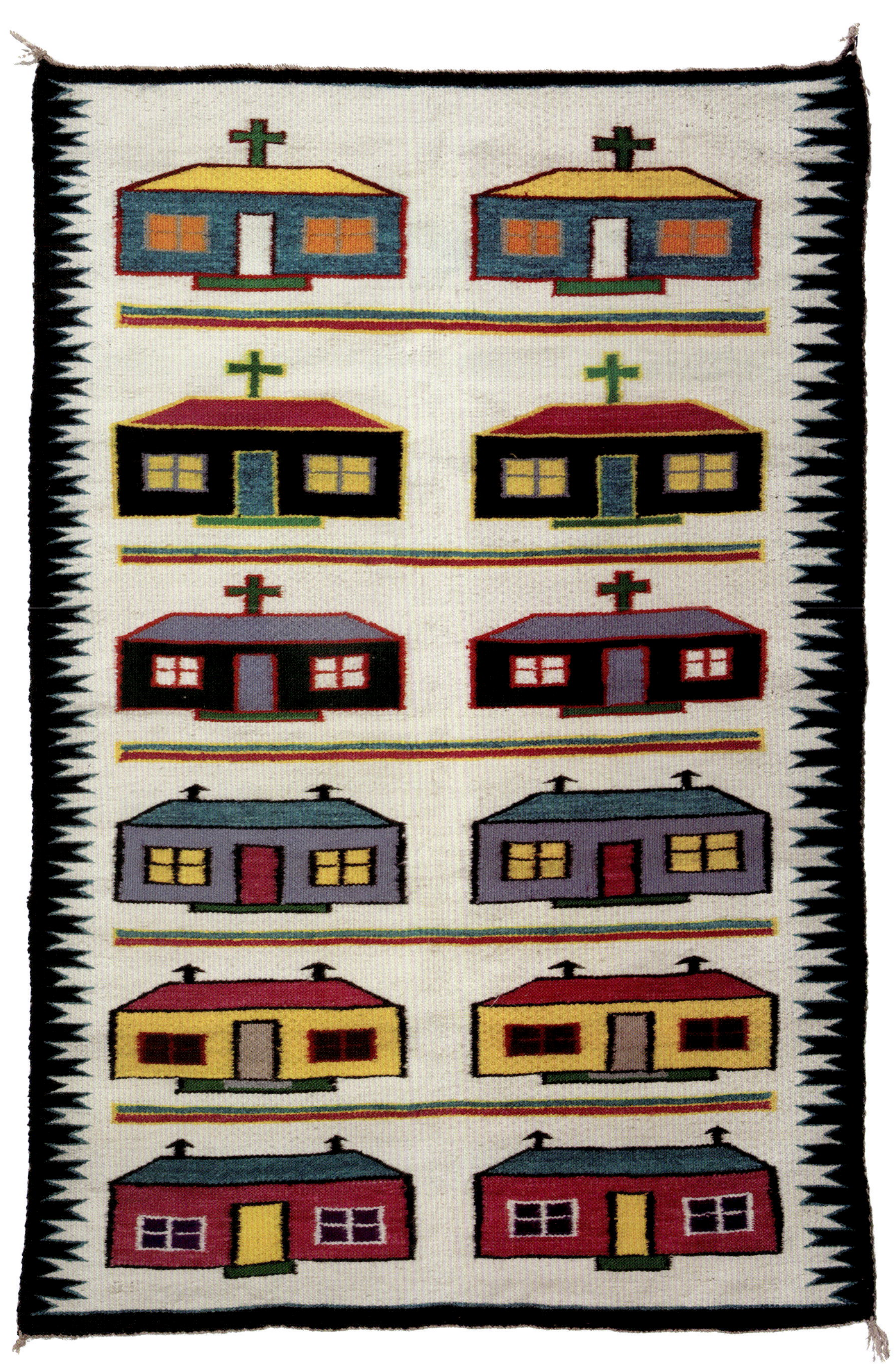

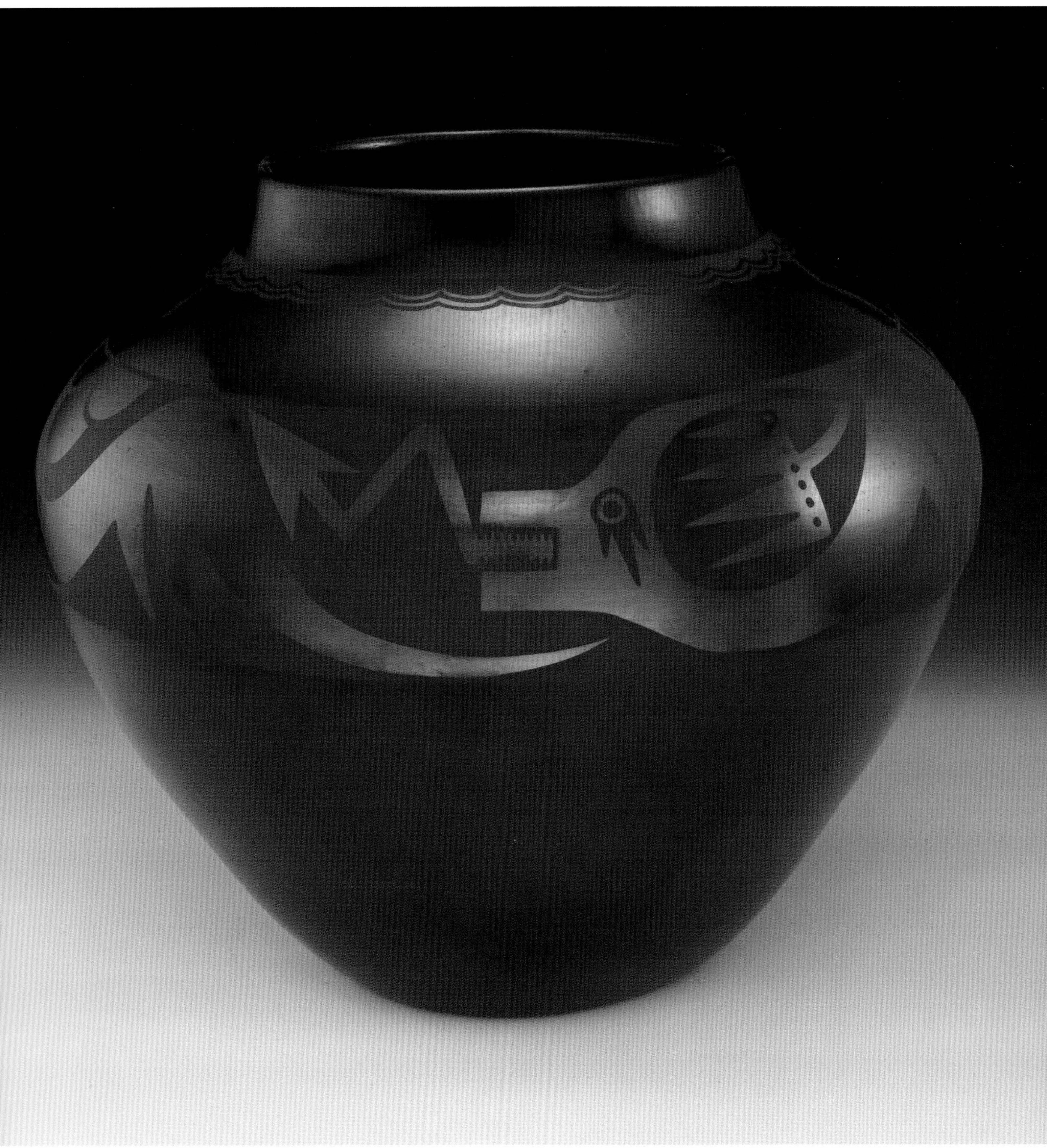

Authenticity and Change
Native American Pottery

Jane Ford Aebersold

Chapter Seven

The American Indian pottery tradition is one of the world's grand ceramic traditions, complex and fascinating. Inextricably interwoven within the culture, the pottery of the southwestern pueblos reflects the experiences of the familiar; more broadly ranges across the larger canvas of native society; is multilayered and episodic; and becomes intimate in spirituality to pueblos and villages, then to families, tracing through history to contemporary modes.

At the turn of the twentieth century, several women from southwestern pueblos and villages began a great renewal of traditional styles of Native American pottery. In the middle of the century, Eugene Adkins of Tulsa, Oklahoma, began to build an extraordinary collection of the pottery of these women, their families, and their neighbors. His collection, moving across tribal and pueblo boundaries, is formed of the work of modern-era potters (from the 1880s through the 1990s) and shapes a cohesive account of the spiritual, cultural, and artistic heritage of southwestern Pueblo people. Adkins collected across tribal and pueblo boundaries, extensively in Hopi, San Ildefonso, Santa Clara, and Acoma; less extensively in Zuni and Cochiti; and in smaller numbers the pottery of the Navajo, Taos, Picuris, Jemez, Pojoaque, Maricopa, Ohkay Owingeh (San Juan), Nambe, Santo Domingo, and Zia.

Plate 127
Maria Martinez and Popovi Da
(U.S., San Ildefonso, Maria: 1881–1980; Popovi: 1922–1971)
Black on Black Jar with Avanyu, 1957
Fred Jones Jr. Museum of Art
A2007.7064

As fascinating as the art itself is the determination of one man to acquire work over such a broad expanse of the American Indian pottery landscape, particularly with the quality of the works collected. Composed of both masterworks and simple pieces, this collection is a celebration of the vitality, skill, and creativity of American Indian potters. It is also a testimony to a man whose collection was shaped by deep respect for Native cultures, acknowledgement of the historical significance of the pottery tradition in telling the story of those cultures, and of course, his enormous aesthetic joy in the work. A collection such as this one, carefully chosen, reflects artistic vision and cultural history and presents invaluable ongoing documentation of a group of people and an era.

American Indian pottery has traditionally been a family affair. The studio was in the home; pottery making was interspersed with daily life; and family members added their particular expertise as makers, painters, and polishers. The signature of an individual potter has historically been in the handling and shaping of the clay and in the details of design; artists today can identify the work of their elders by the feel of a pot and the burnished, painted, or carved elements. The addition of the signature name is a fairly recent development, coming about when the distribution of wares moved outside the pueblos.

The magnificent *Black on Black Jar with Avanyu* (1957, plate 127, see also plate 55), made by Maria Martinez and her son Popovi Da, represents the zenith of elegance and sophistication in the work of the legendary potter of San Ildefonso. The articulation of the expansive curve of the body, the grace of the Avanyu design, and the superb burnishing and polishing echo Maria's work begun in partnership with her husband, Julian Martinez, and continued in collaboration with other family members until her passing in 1980. The Adkins Collection holdings include eighty pieces, primarily pottery but also painting and jewelry, by this remarkable family.

The mix of the elements clay, water, and fire mingled and formed by human hands represents a special harmony with nature and opens the way to communication with others socially, spiritually, and politically. The spiritual element of American Indian pottery making is seminal and shared throughout the pueblos, in times past and today. Clay dug from Mother Earth is treated with utmost care and respect by the potters—always before digging, there are prayers to Mother Earth accompanied by the sprinkling of cornmeal. Contemporary potters indicate that this spiritual connection extends to the forming, painting, and firing of the clay work, as was the ancestors' way.

The potter Lonnie Vigil left pueblo life for university and then for the business world. Coming to the realization that he needed to reconnect to the spiritual and cultural life of the pueblo, he came home to Nambe and set about learning the methodology of forming pottery from micaceous clay. Now, his work (plate 177), built and imagined in tradition, exemplifies the aesthetic choices open to the contemporary American Indian potter.

Over centuries, styles evolve and change, and production levels ebb and flow as transformative societal events occur. Though reasons for making pottery in a particular way change from one era to another, they are always embedded in the potter's contemporary culture. Archaeologists and ethnologists have traced patterns of materials used, forms created, and surface embellishments to establish a time frame of pottery types and to build narratives about civilizations and about the evolution of the art form. Clay fragments, pottery, and clay figures have been found in abandoned sites at Awatovi, Pajarito Plateau, Chaco Canyon, and Mesa Verde; these excavated pieces can be linked in form, decoration, and material to modern Pueblo pottery. Authentic continuance from prehistoric to contemporary work is found in elements of form, interpretation of design elements through a narrative story line, and symbolic patterns derived from interactions with nature and spiritual life.

Lucy Lewis and Marie Zieu Chino of Acoma famously referenced pots from earlier cultures to establish the path of their own designs. Lucy Lewis is particularly associated with bird symbolism (plate 168), with the heartline deer (plate 167), and with the fine line designs derived from Mimbres pots (plate 169). Marie Zieu Chino interpreted old Acoma design and form in *Black on White Jar* (1965, plate 164). This large jar is vibrant and bold in form and, in painting, gestural and confident—an extraordinary pot. No less amazing, but completely different in presence, is the controlled form and precise, delicate line work on Chino's 1978 jar (plate 166).

Pottery provides a strong and consistent record of southwestern Native customs and traditions, both in previously recorded history and in the Adkins Collection. There is a wonderful constancy that comes down through the centuries of clay working, a physical language that is a communication from one potter to another through time and place. The physical way of working with clay is the same from prehistory to now: clay has to be rendered malleable by the addition of water, and usually some temper (grit), perhaps fusible material—all determined by where the clay is mined or dug, what the use is to be, what the forming method is to be, how fast or how slow the potter can work the material, a sense of oneness with the clay, an understanding of the patience and components of making, decoration to be conceptualized and stylized, how to dry, how to fire. Natural clay colors, when fired in the traditional stacked and pit-fire methods, range from black, red, orange, brown, white, off-white, golden tans, buff, peach, and green. The clay may be burnished to a fine shine or left with a satin or matte surface finish. The pots may celebrate form and function and be left without further decoration, or be embellished with line, figuration, and pattern. The language of pottery form and design is similar across the southwestern pueblos, but each potter, pottery family, and pueblo makes work distinctive to their own group.

Nampeyo of Hano incorporated stars, feathers, birds, bat wings, and other symbols from Native culture into her work, and those designs have been carried forward and further refined by the exceptionally gifted potters in the family. The migration design has become a family signature and is represented in the collection by the *Polychrome Jar, Migration Design* (1972, plate 149), by Fannie Nampeyo, a jar commissioned by Eugene Adkins.

The Tafoya family of Santa Clara descends from Sara Fina and Geronimo Tafoya. The bear paw design (plate 157), inherited from Sara Fina, is closely associated with Margaret Tafoya, one of the most important Pueblo potters of this century. The family has also maintained the tradition of deep carving, exemplified in Tafoya's *Red Wedding Vase, Carved Avanyu* (1964, plate 158).

The pueblos of the Southwest present a rich and vibrant pottery history, from prehistoric times to the present. Some innovations are embraced: Tony Da often embellished his clay forms with heishi, turquoise, flint, and silver (plate 134) and set a precedent for future artists, across pueblo boundaries. Other innovations are more controversial: Rafael Medina painted designs on his wife Sofia's traditional pottery forms, interpreting Native America's spiritual and tangible interaction with the natural world, using very nontraditional acrylic paint (plate 146).

Celebrating the metamorphosis of clay from Mother Earth into a complex body of work that reveres and expands the artistic heritage of Native American culture and recognizes personal interpretations of form and design, this collection is the legacy of the makers and of the extraordinary vision and passion of the collector. This is a glorious collection of American Indian pottery, and we are fortunate caretakers.

The plates in the following section are organized by Pueblo of origin.

Plates 128–178
San Ildefonso Pueblo

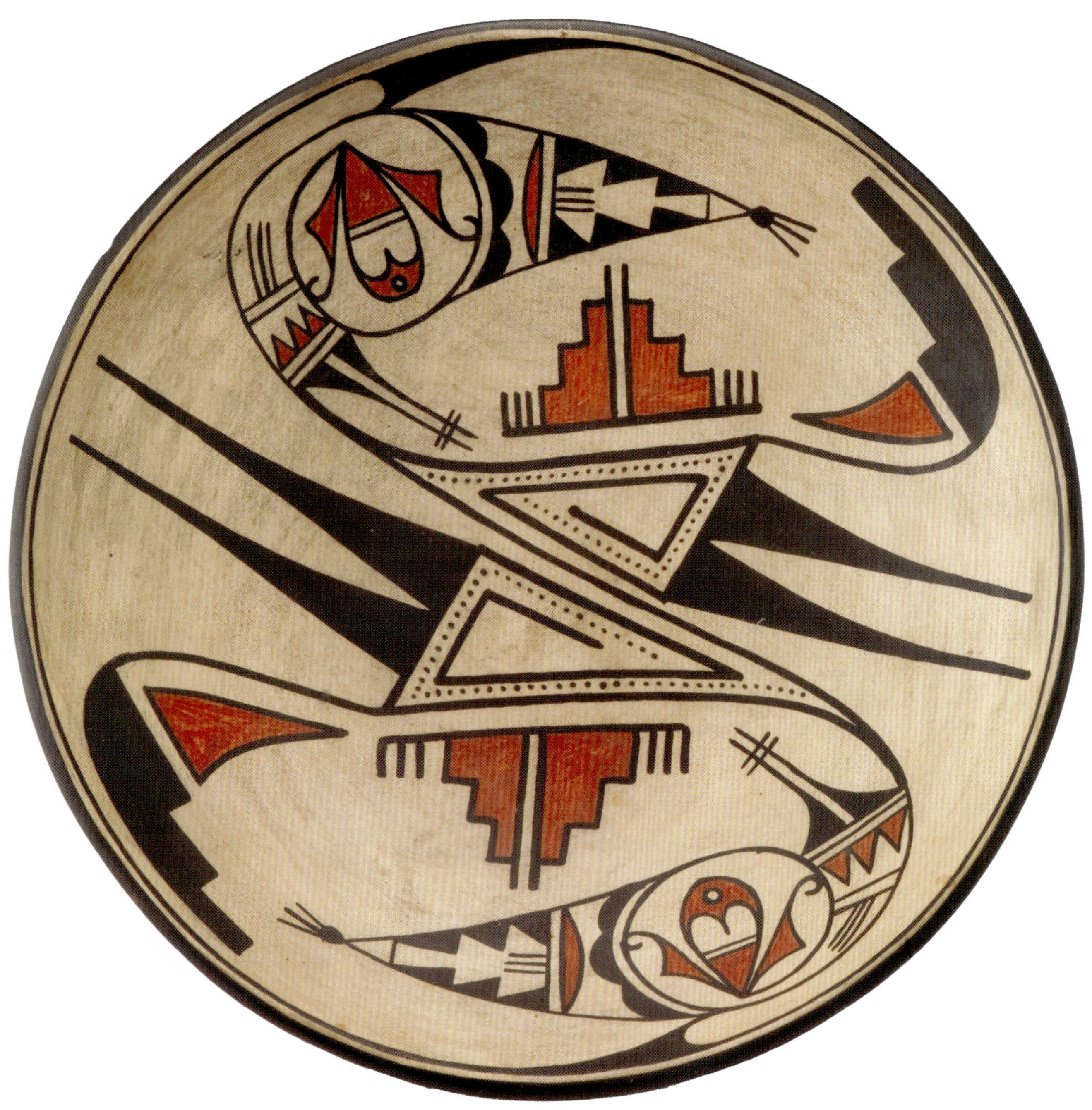

Plate 128
Maria Martinez and Julian Martinez
(U.S., San Ildefonso, Maria: 1881–1980, Julian: 1885–1943)
Polychrome Plate, c. 1930. Native clays and paints, 2½ × 13⅞ in.
Fred Jones Jr. Museum of Art
A2007.7098

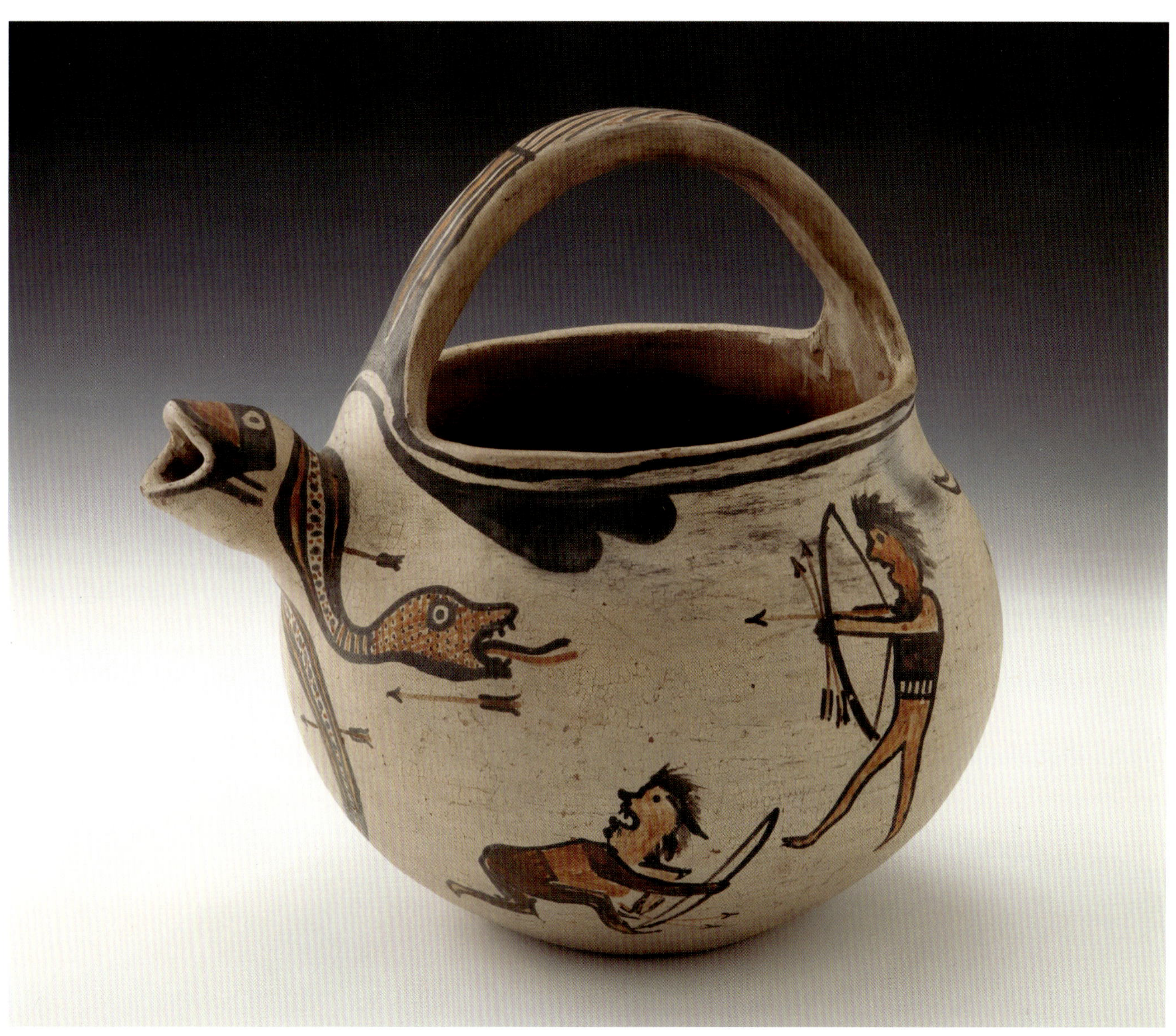

Plate 129
Unknown (U.S., San Ildefonso or Cochiti)
Effigy Pitcher, c. 1900. Native clays and paints, 9⅝ × 9³⁄₁₆ in.
Fred Jones Jr. Museum of Art
A2007.7310

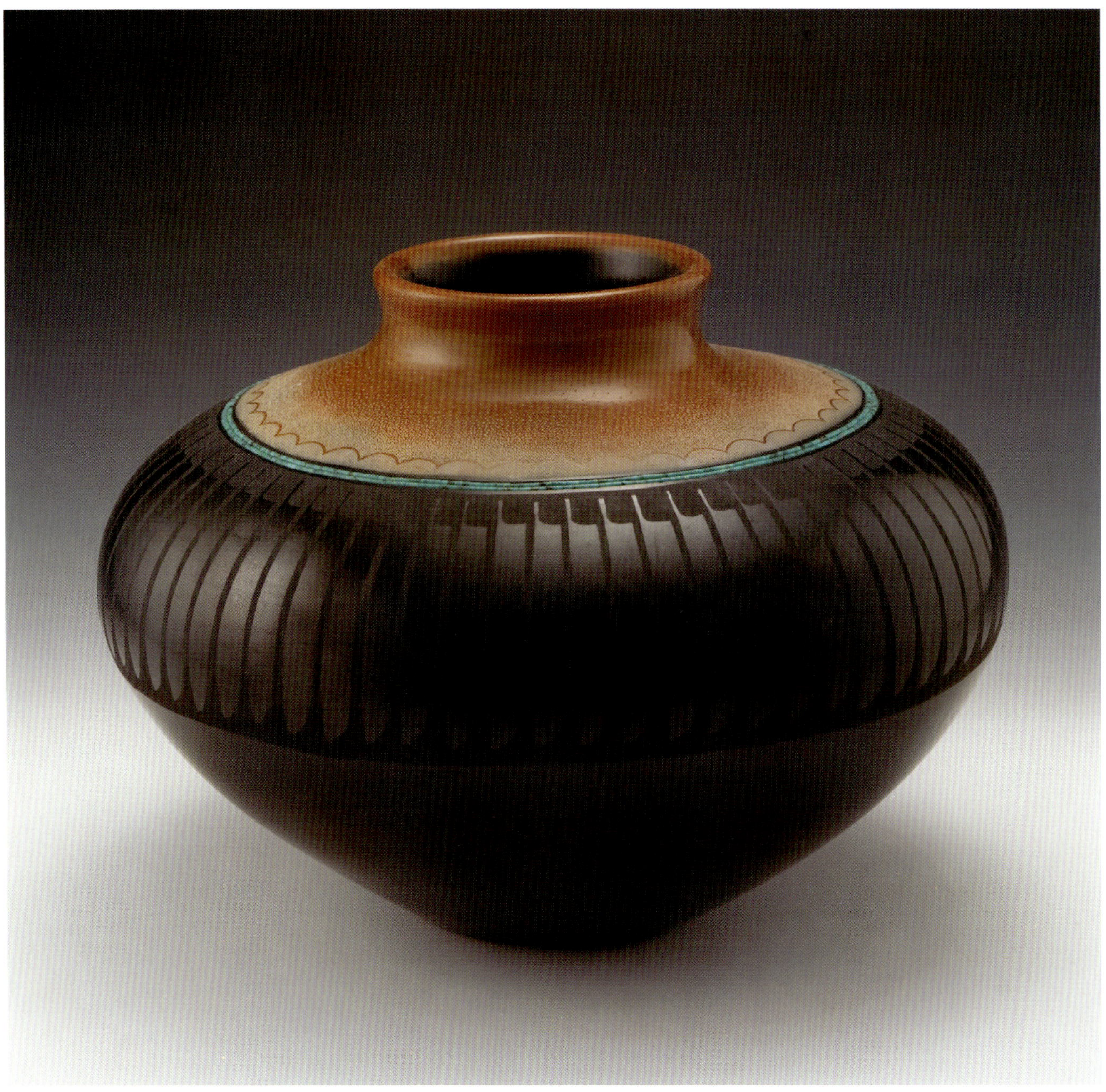

Plate 130
Popovi Da (U.S., San Ildefonso, 1922–1971)
Black and Sienna Jar, 1967
Native clays and turquoise, 8¾ × 12⁷⁄₁₆ in.
Fred Jones Jr. Museum of Art
A2007.7071

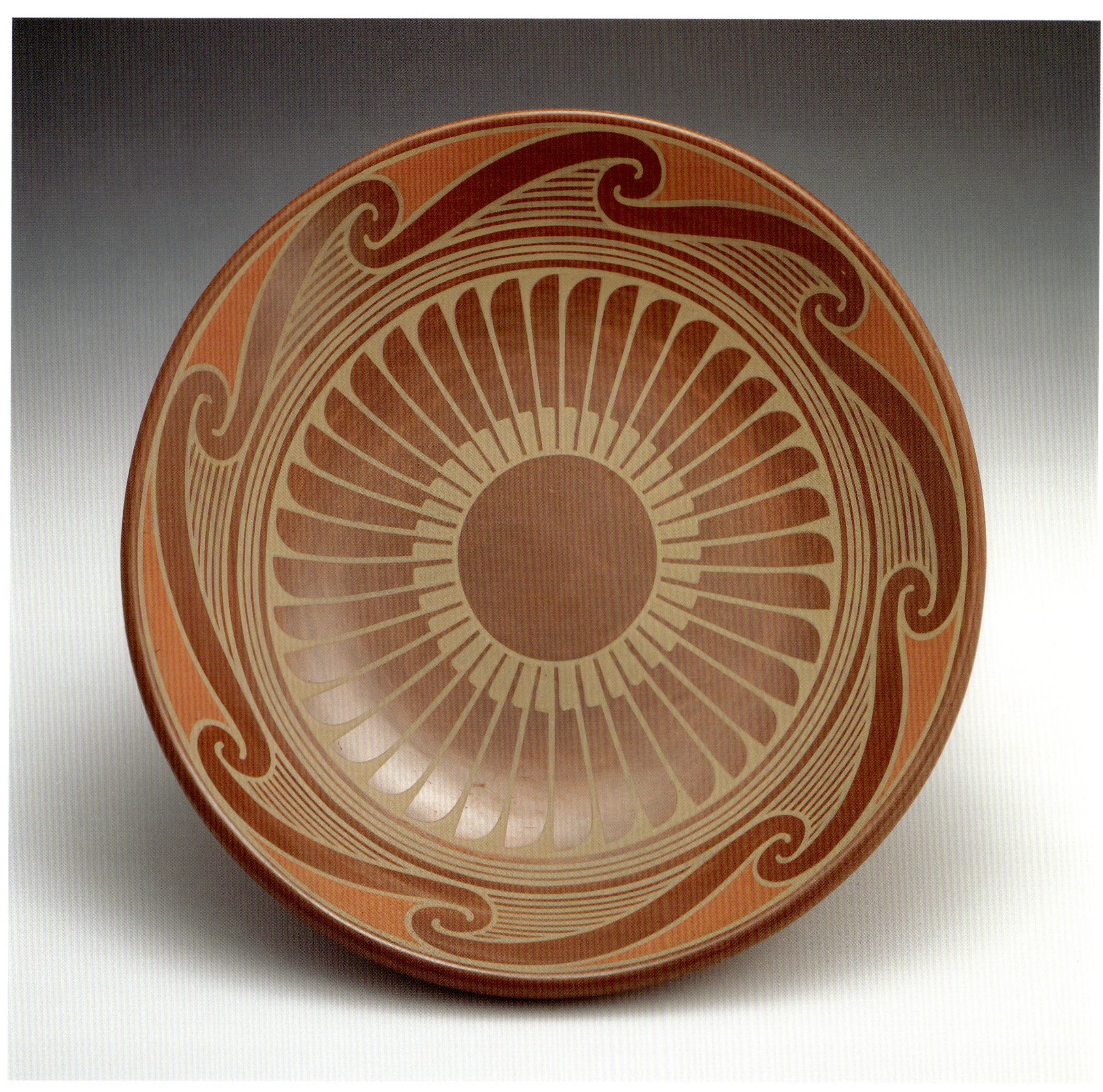

Plate 131
Popovi Da (U.S., San Ildefonso, 1922–1971)
Buff, Terra Cotta, Red Plate, 1967
Native clays, 2⅝ × 15 in.
Fred Jones Jr. Museum of Art
A2007.7072

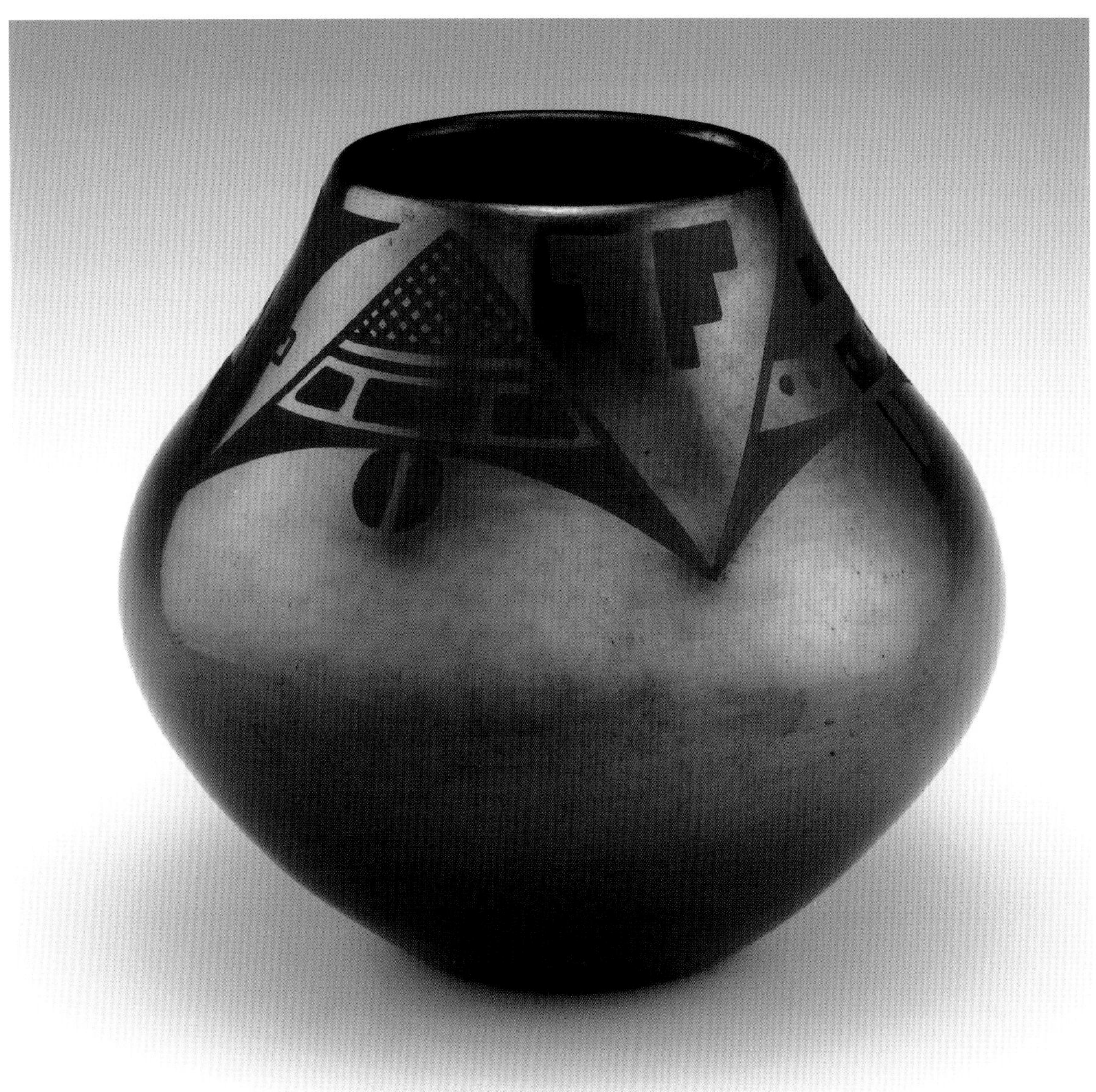

Plate 132 (above)
Maria Martinez and Popovi Da
(U.S., San Ildefonso, Maria: 1881–1980; Popovi: 1922–1971)
Black on Black Jar, 1963. Native clays, 7 × 7⅞ in.
Philbrook Museum of Art
A2007.7109

Plate 133 (facing page)
Maria Martinez (U.S., San Ildefonso, 1881–1980)
Polished Black Jar, 1963
Native clay, 9¾ × 10 in.
Fred Jones Jr. Museum of Art
A2007.7109

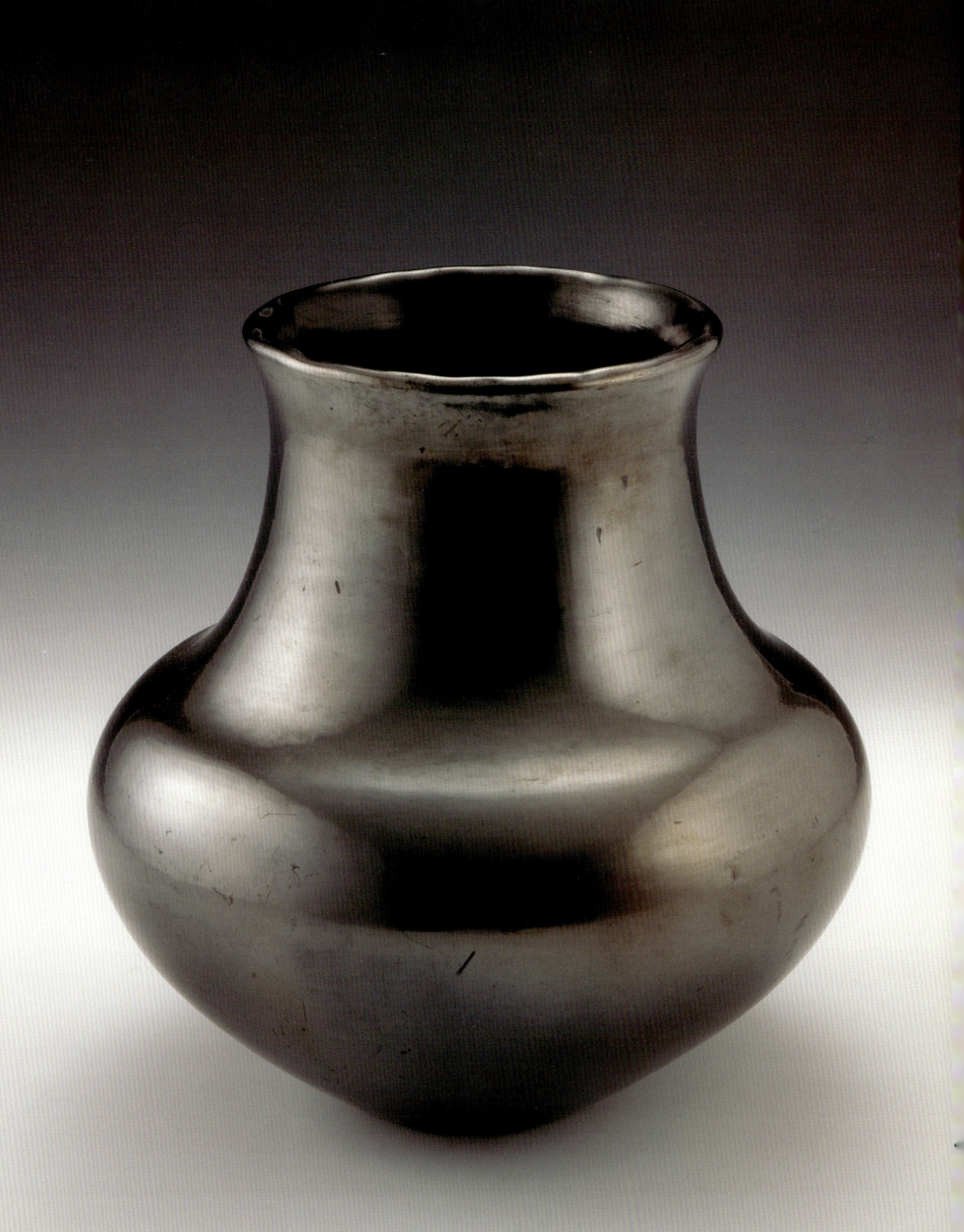

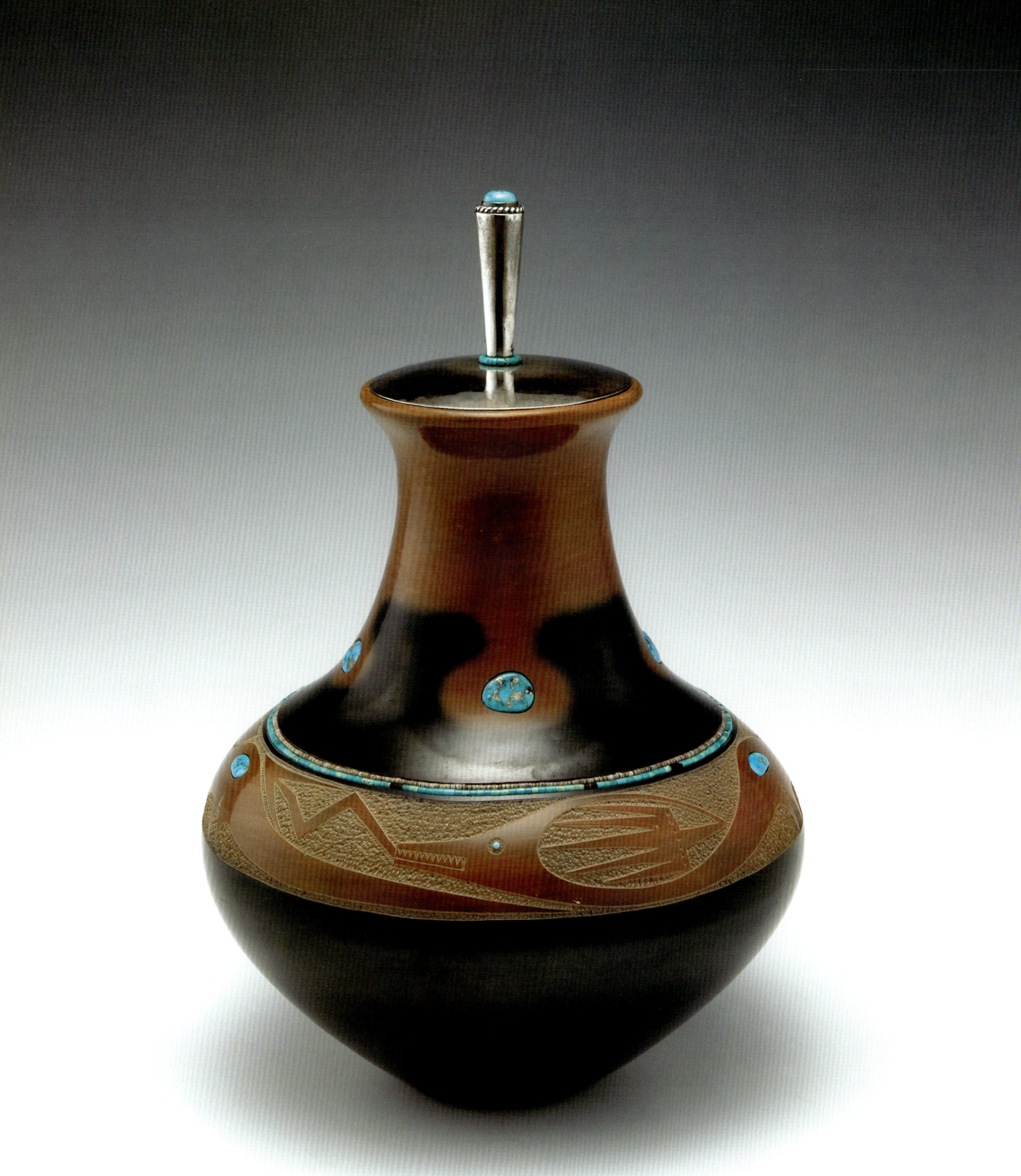

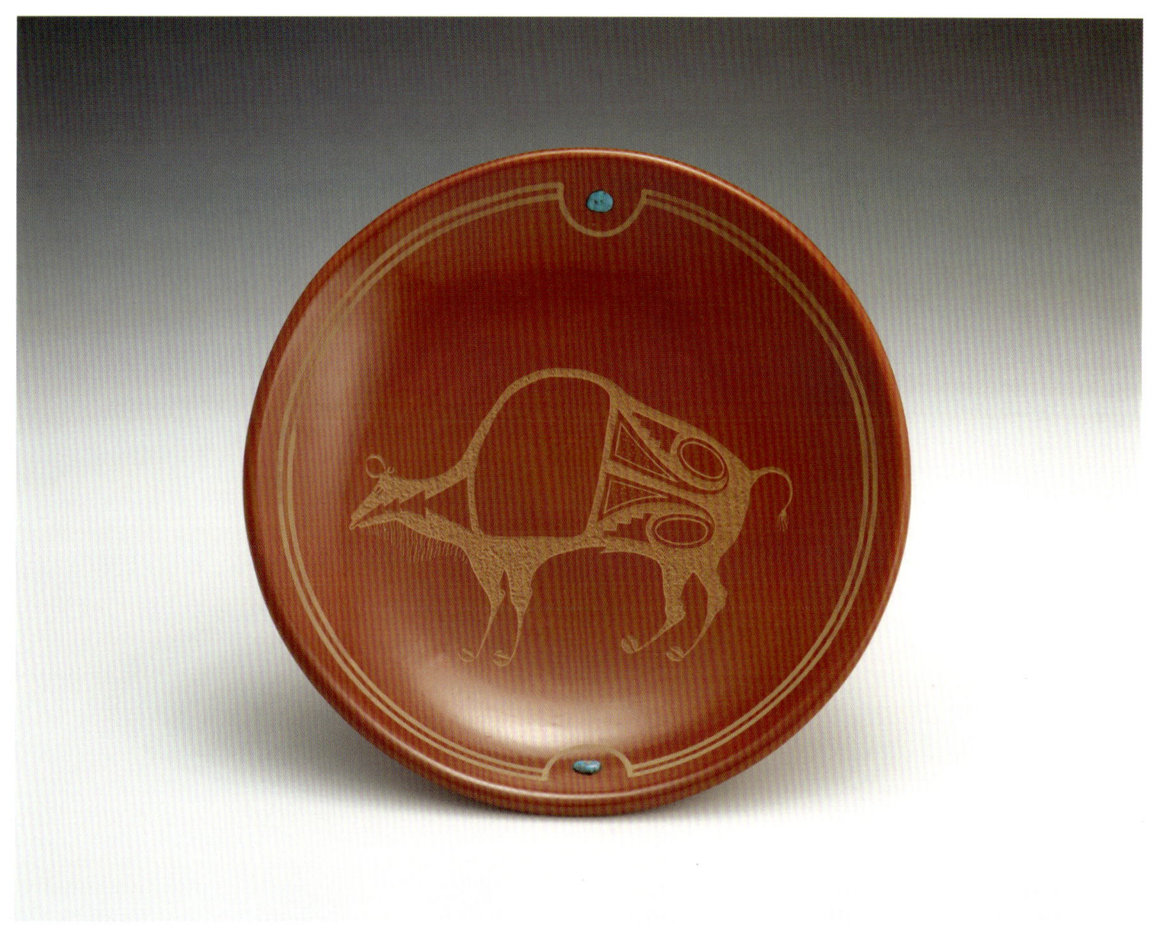

Plate 134 (facing page)
Tony Da (U.S., San Ildefonso, 1940–2008)
Lidded Jar, 1972. Native clays, turquoise, heishi, and silver, 11⅝ × 8¼ in.
Fred Jones Jr. Museum of Art
A2007.7076

Plate 135 (above)
Tony Da (U.S., San Ildefonso, 1940–2008)
Bison Plate, c. 1970. Native clays and turquoise, 2¼ × 11⅝ in.
Fred Jones Jr. Museum of Art
A2007.7077

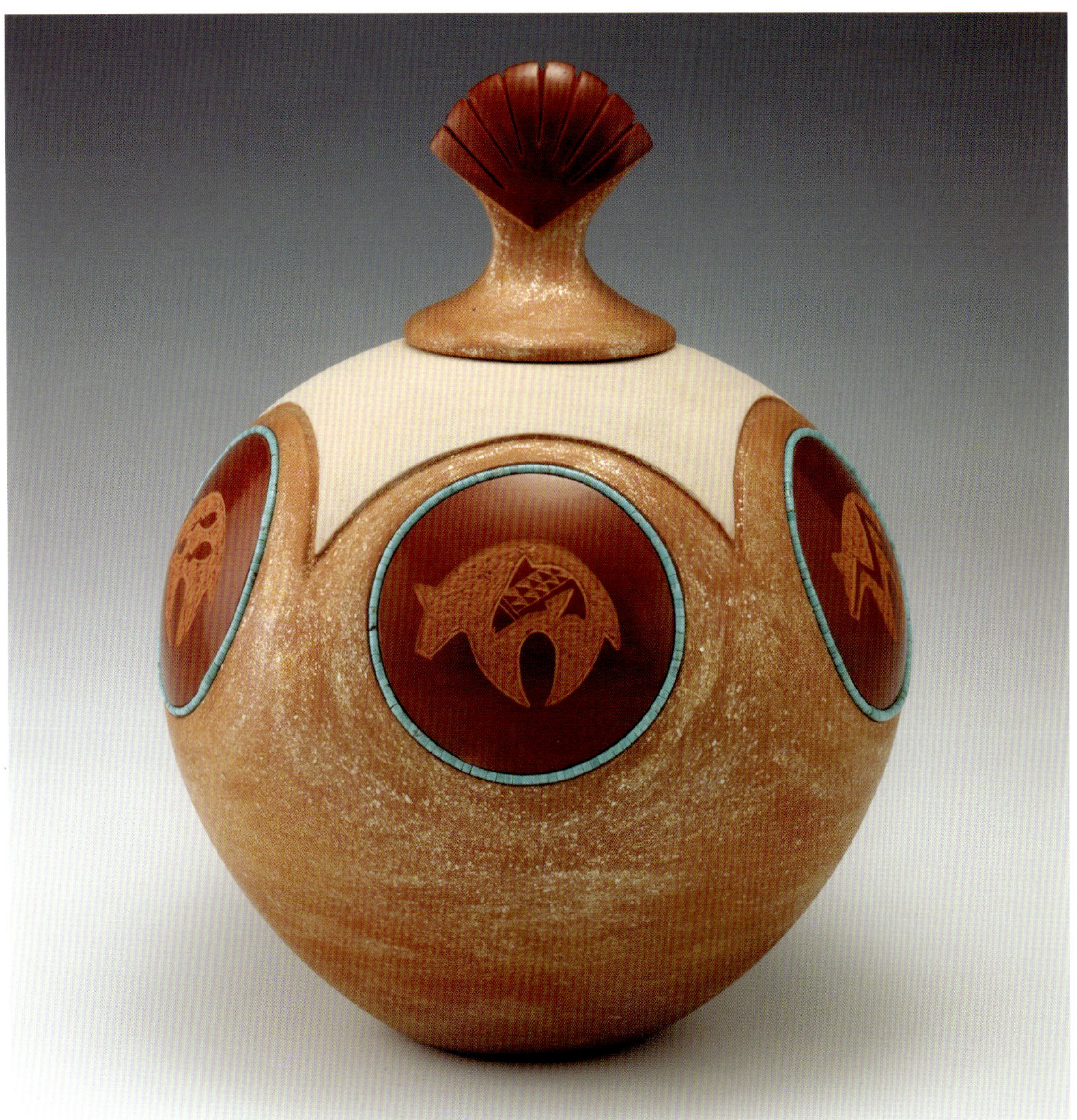

Plate 136
Russell Sanchez (U.S., San Ildefonso, b. 1966)
Lidded Jar, 1994. Native clays and turquoise, 10⅜ × 8⅛ in.
Fred Jones Jr. Museum of Art
A2007.7205

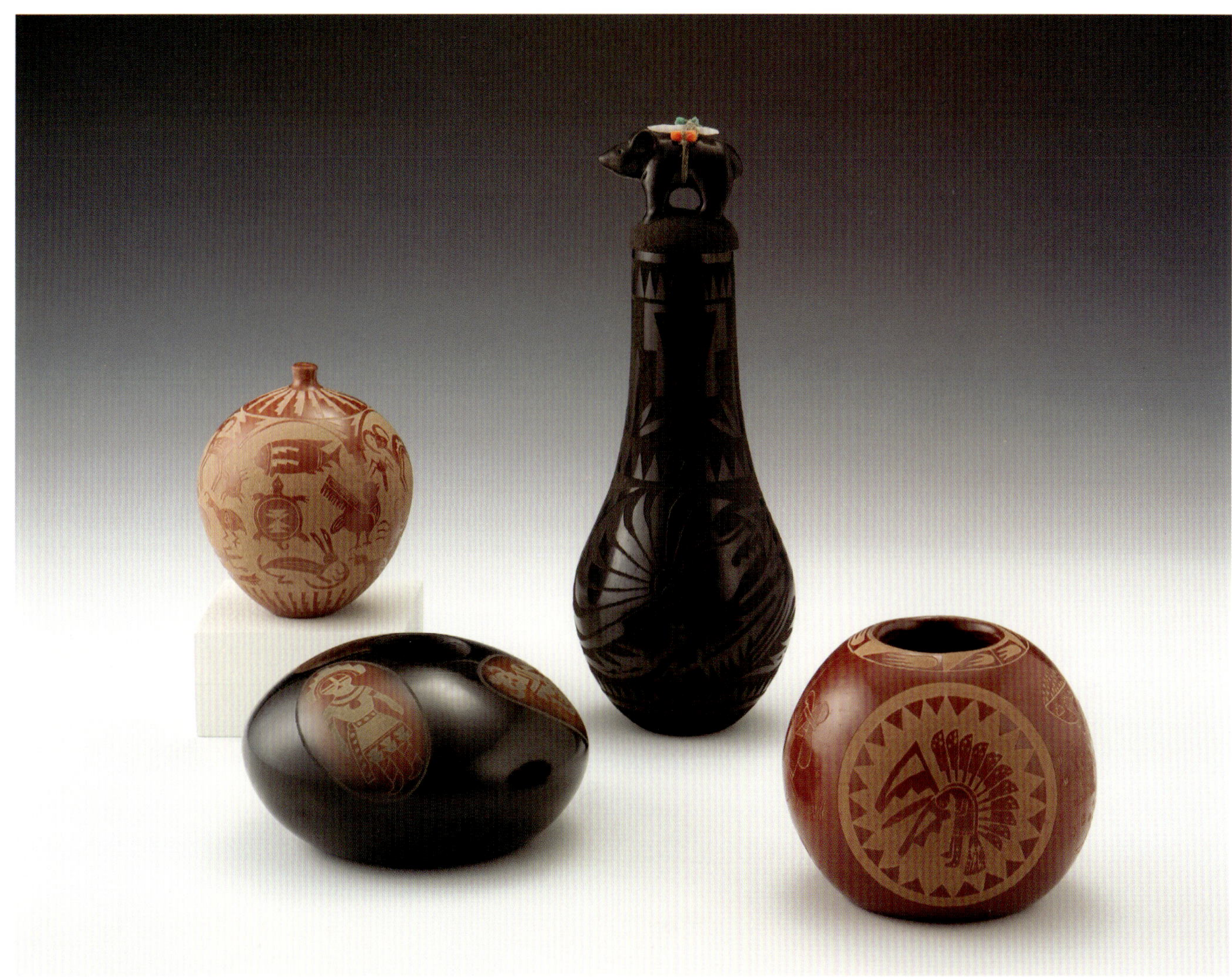

Plate 137

(left above)
Grace Medicine Flower (U.S., Santa Clara, b. 1938)
Miniature Vase, Incised Figures, c. 1970. Native clays, 3½ × 3⅛ in.
Fred Jones Jr. Museum of Art
A2007.7151

(left below)
Camilio Sunflower Tafoya (U.S., Santa Clara, 1902–1995)
and Grace Medicine Flower (U.S., Santa Clara, b. 1938)
Red and Black Seed Pot, Incised Figures, c. 1970. Native clays, 2 × 4½ in.
Philbrook Museum of Art
A2007.7150

(right above)
Joseph Lonewolf (U.S., Santa Clara, b. 1932)
Blackware Lidded Vase, Bear Fetish, 1971. Native clays, turquoise, coral, and flint, 8⅝ × 3⅜ in.
Fred Jones Jr. Museum of Art
A2007.7148

(right below)
Camilio Sunflower Tafoya (U.S., Santa Clara, b. 1938)
Miniature Jar, Incised Figures, c. 1970. Native clays, 2 × 4½ in.
Fred Jones Jr. Museum of Art
A2007.7150

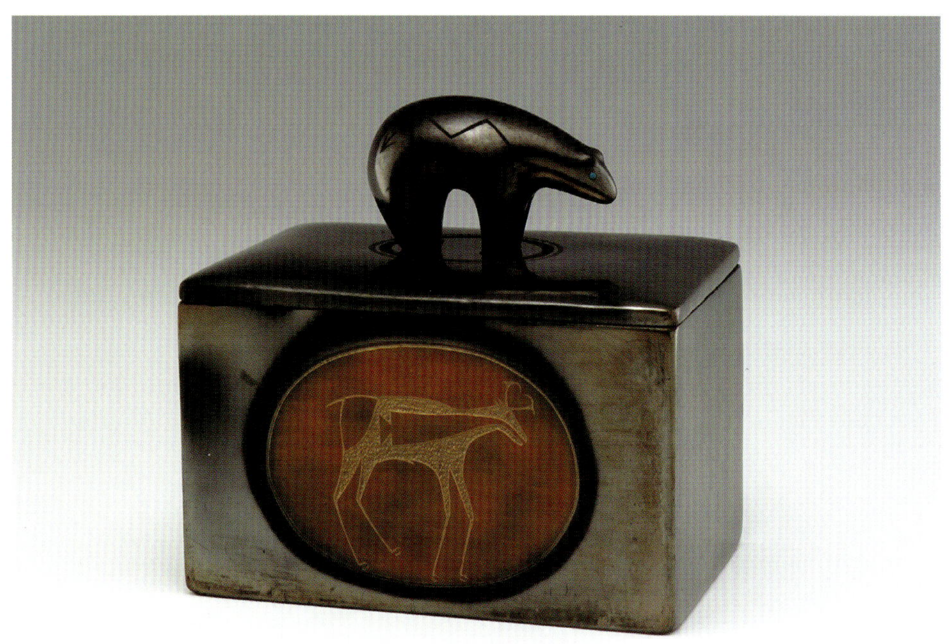

Plate 138
Tony Da (U.S., San Ildefonso, 1940–2008)
Black and Sienna Lidded Box with Bear Handle, 1968
Native clays, 5¼ x 9½ in.
Fred Jones Jr. Museum of Art
A2007.7082

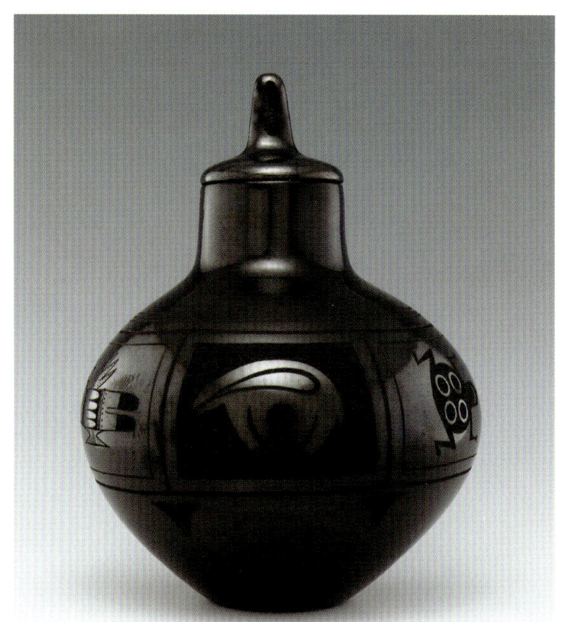

Plate 139
Maria Martinez and Tony Da (U.S., San Ildefonso, Maria: 1881–1980; Tony: 1940–2008)
Polished Black Lidded Jar with Bird, Lizard, and Bison Designs with Sgraffito, 1967. Native clays, 15 x 11⅝ in.
Fred Jones Jr. Museum of Art
A2007.7025

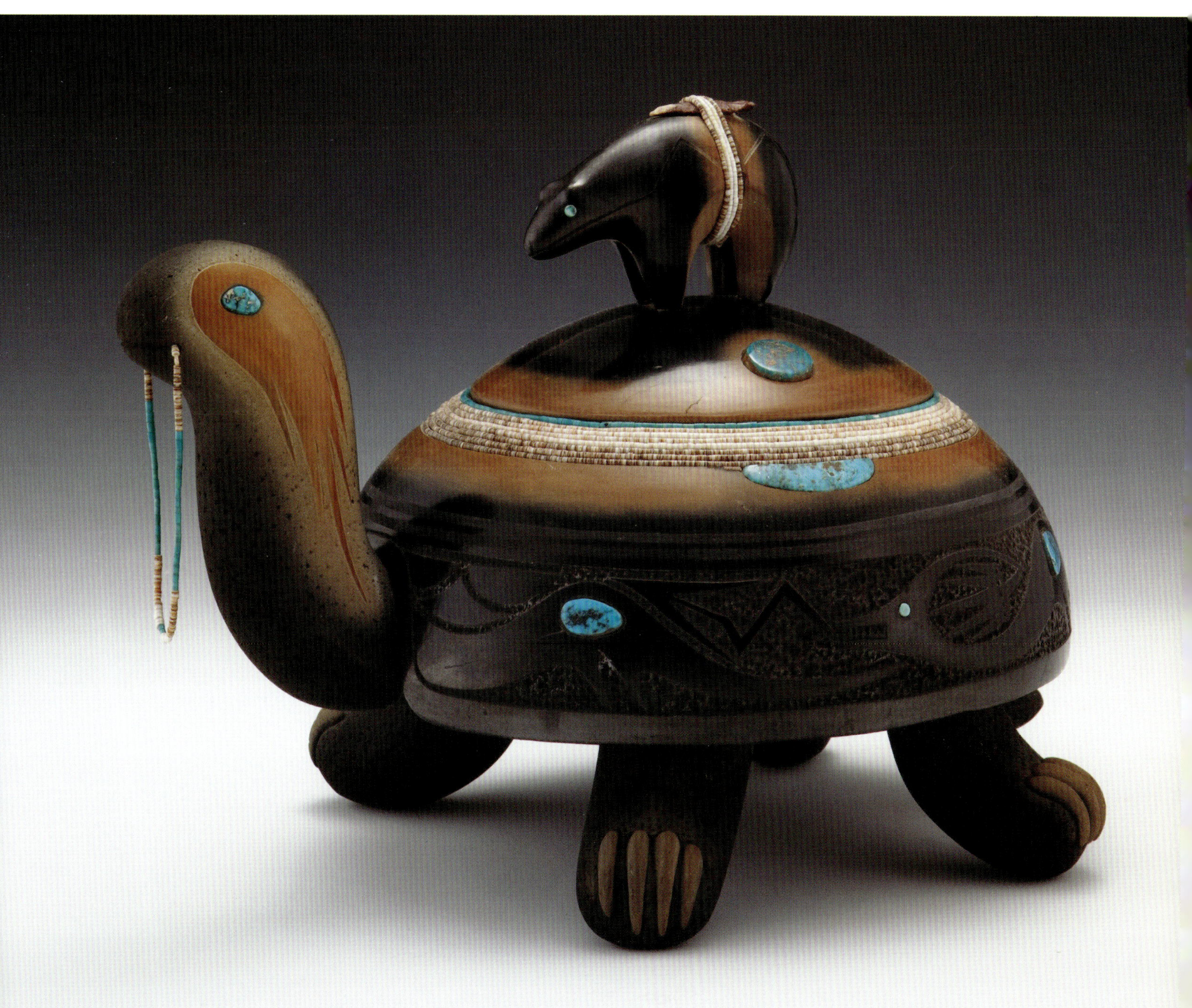

PLATE 140
Tony Da (U.S., San Ildefonso, 1940–2008)
Lidded Turtle Vessel, c. 1970. Native clays, turquoise, heishi, and flint, 8¼ × 8 in.
Fred Jones Jr. Museum of Art
A2007.7078

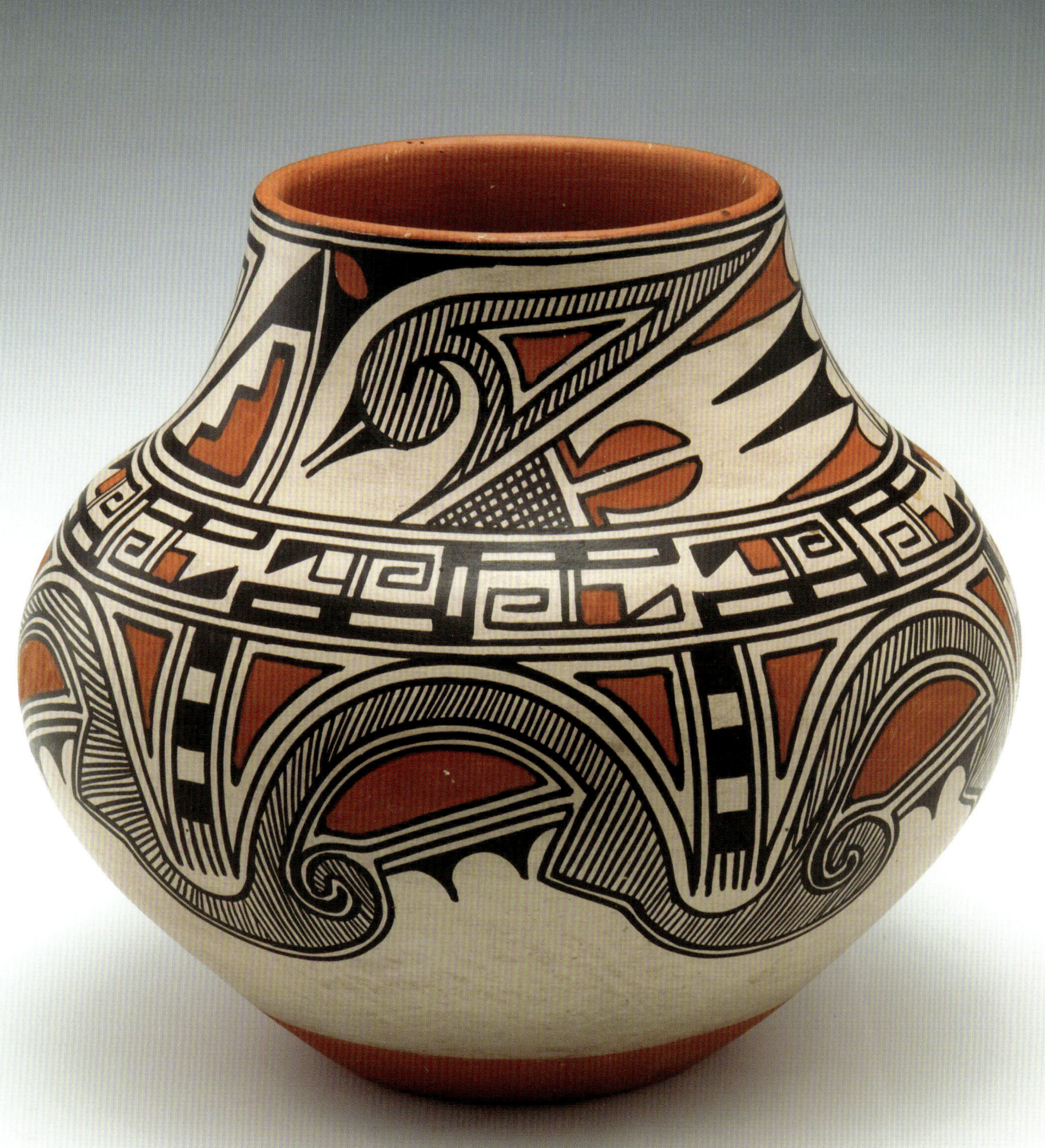

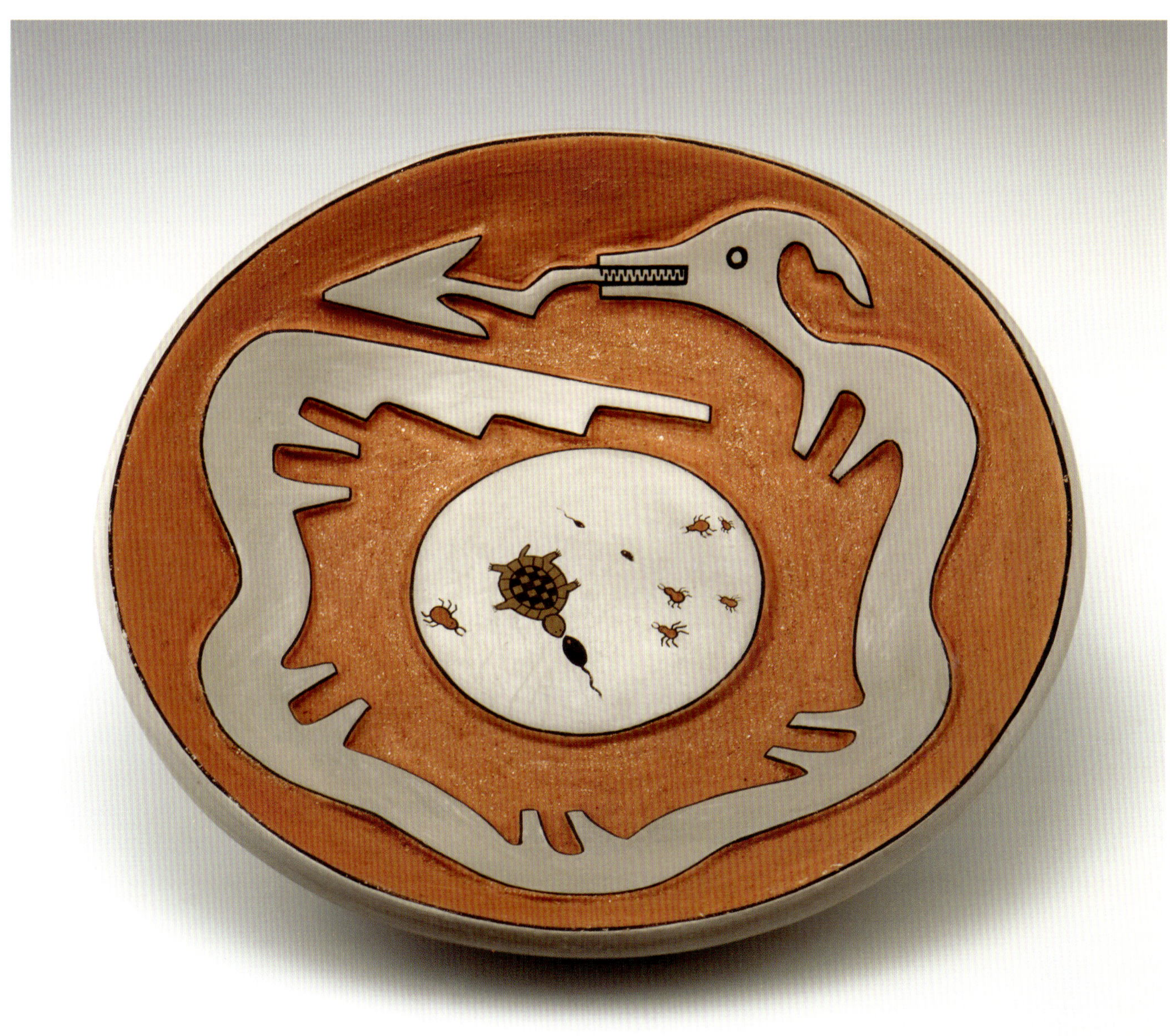

Plate 141 (facing page)
Maria Martinez and Popovi Da
(U.S., San Ildefonso, Maria: 1881–1980; Popovi: 1922–1971)
Polychrome Olla, 1966. Native clays and paints, 8½ × 5⅛ × 10½ in.
Philbrook Museum of Art
A2007.7061

Plate 142 (above)
Blue Corn (Crucita Gonzales Calabaza) (U.S., San Ildefonso, 1921–1999)
Plate, Carved Avanyu, c. 1970
Native clays and paints, 2½ × 14¾ in.
Philbrook Museum of Art
A2007.7212

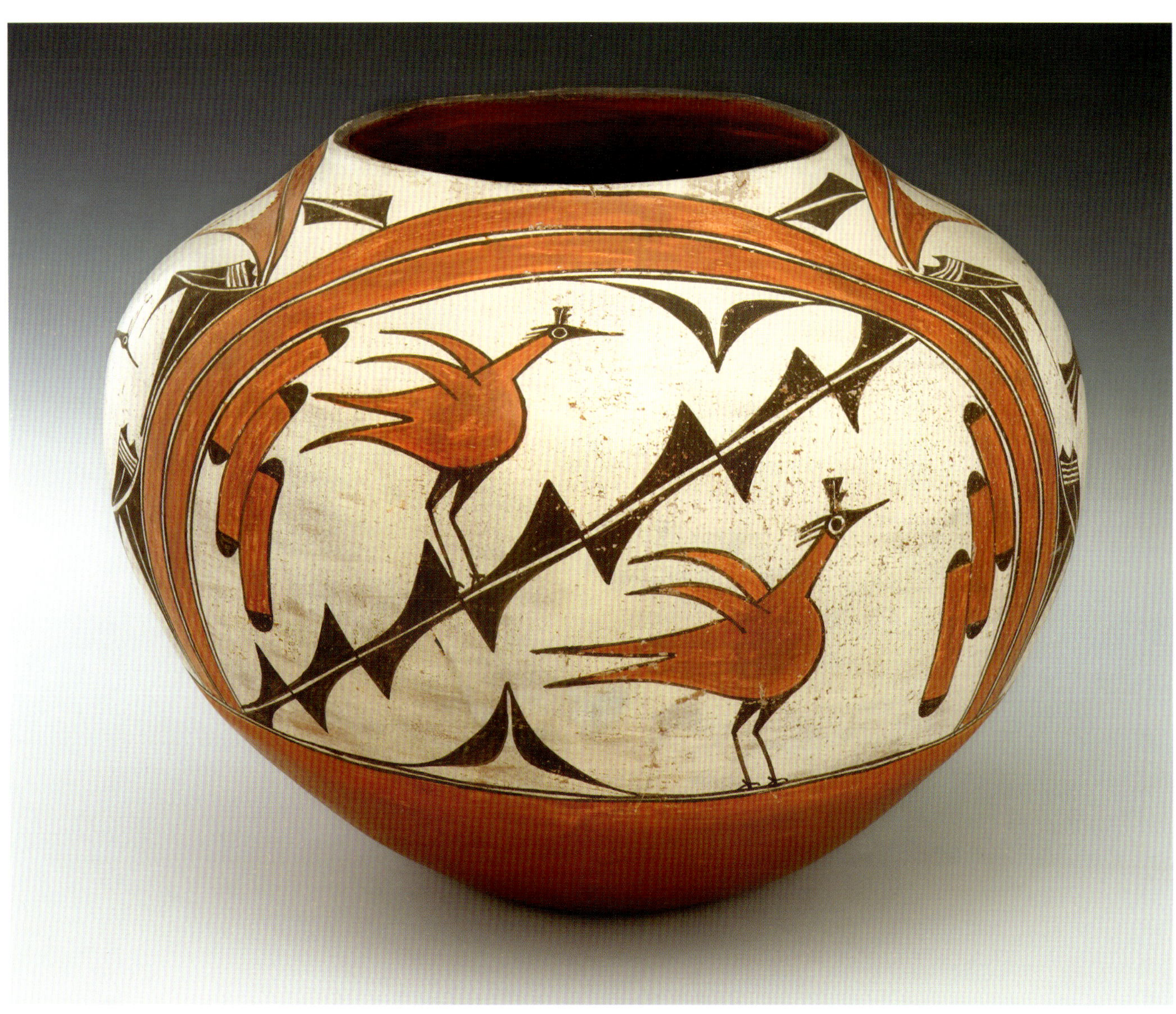

Plate 143 (above)
Unknown (U.S., Zia)
Storage Jar, c. 1940. Native clays and paints, 14¾ × 19^{15}/16 in.
Fred Jones Jr. Museum of Art
A2007.7055

Plate 144 (facing page)
Unknown (U.S., Zia)
Storage Jar, c. 1940. Native clays and paints, 15 × 16½ in.
Fred Jones Jr. Museum of Art
A2007.7011

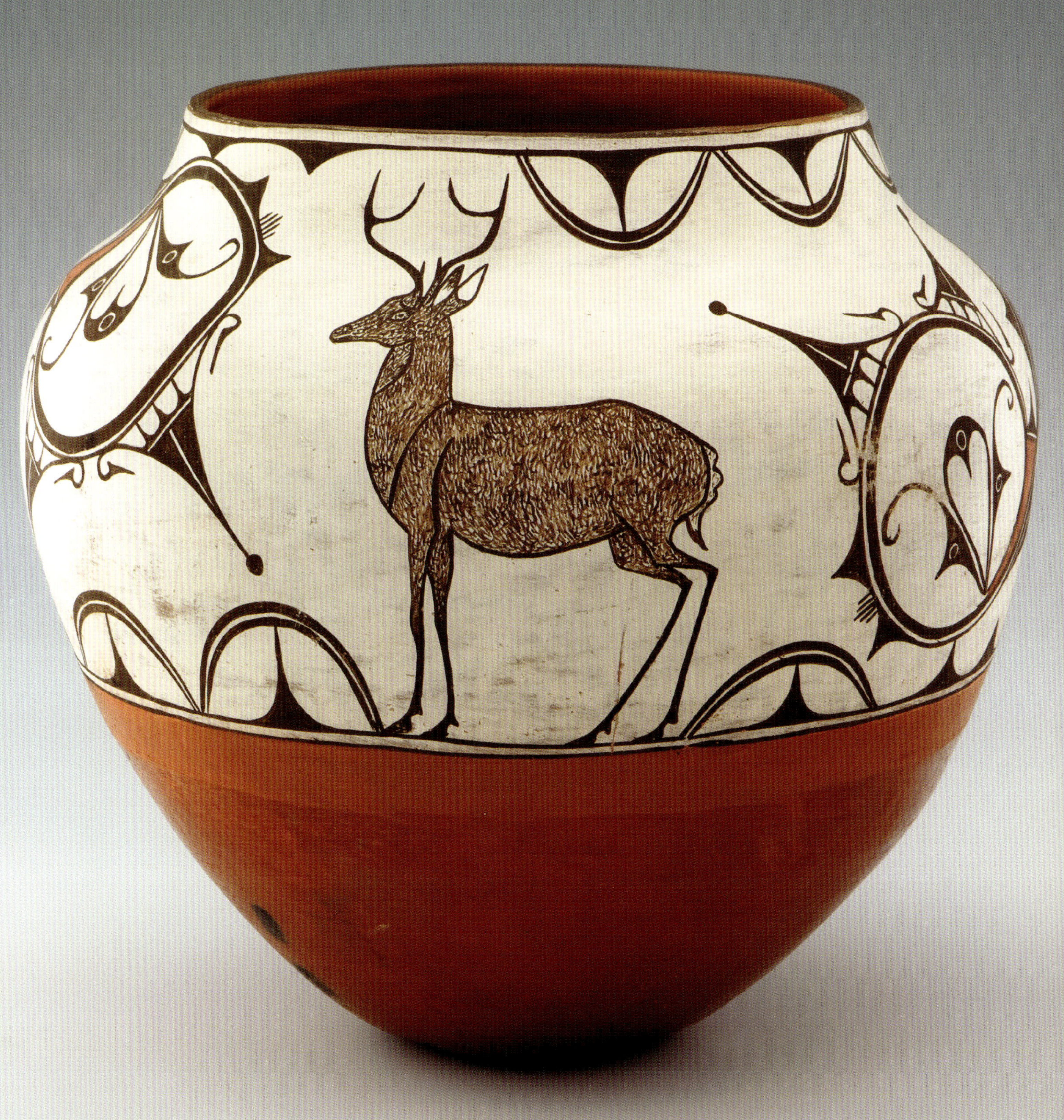

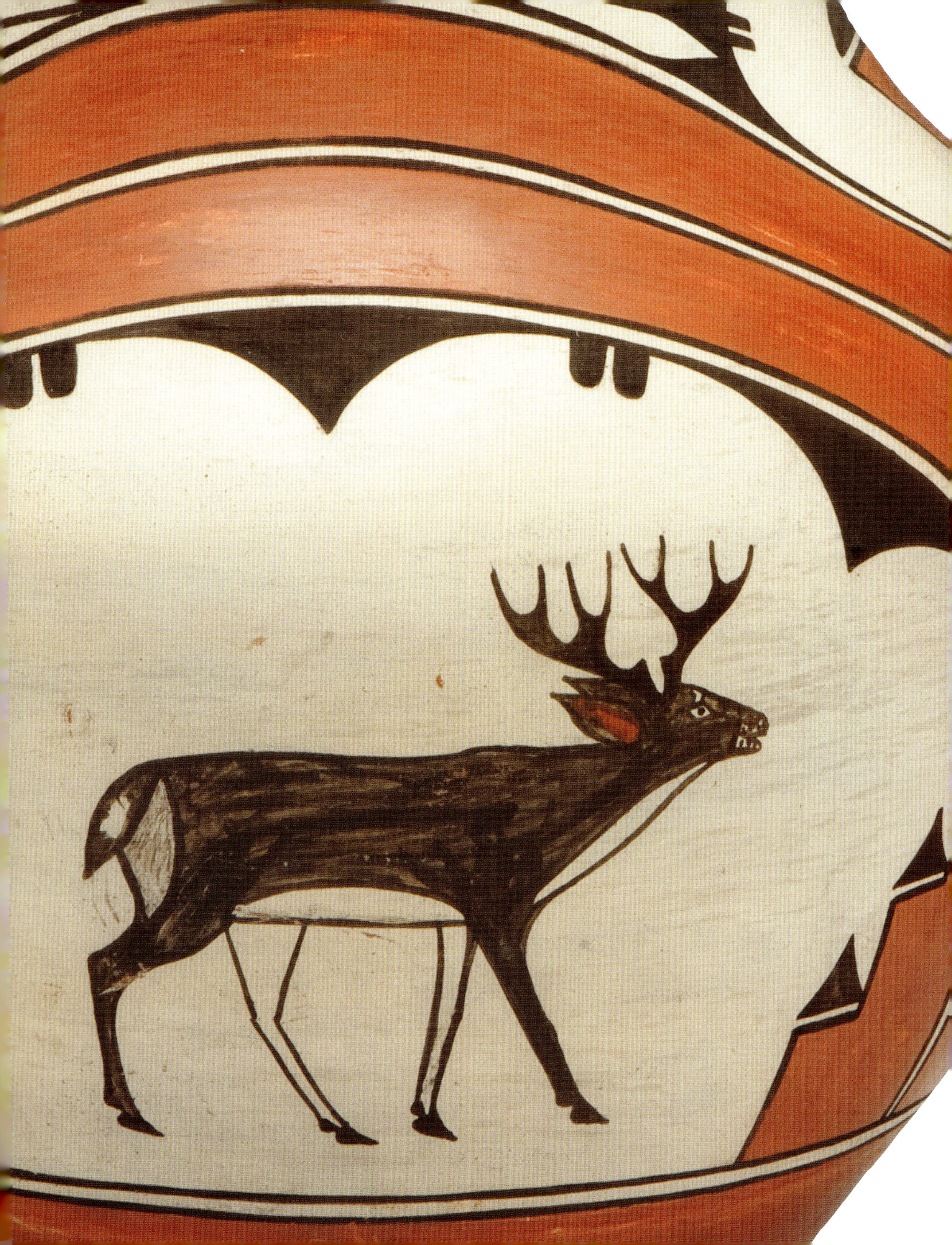

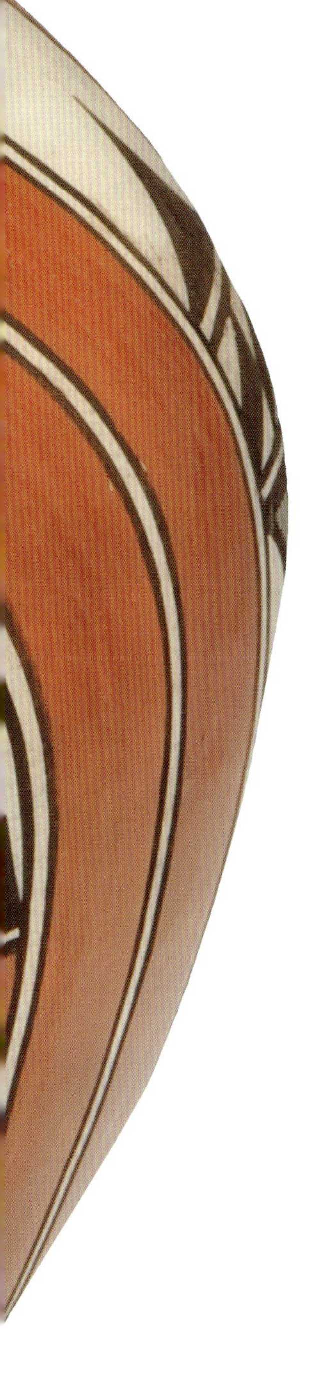

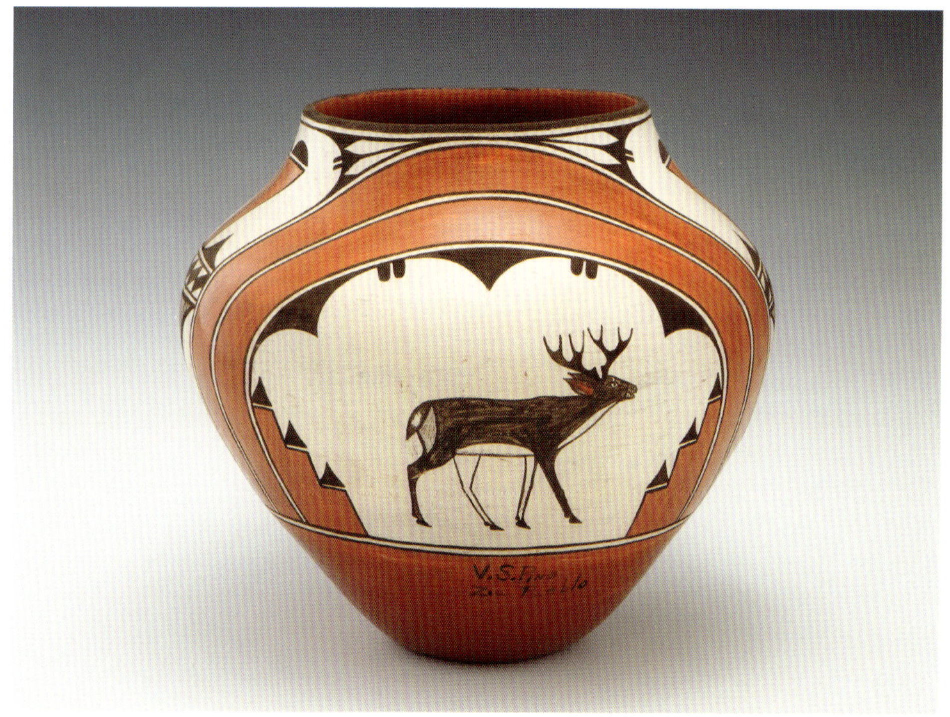

Plate 145 (detail, facing page)
Vicentitia S. Pino (U.S., Zia, 1917–2009)
Polychrome Jar with Deer, c. 1970
Native clays and paints, 9⅜ × 10½ in.
Fred Jones Jr. Museum of Art
a2007.7215

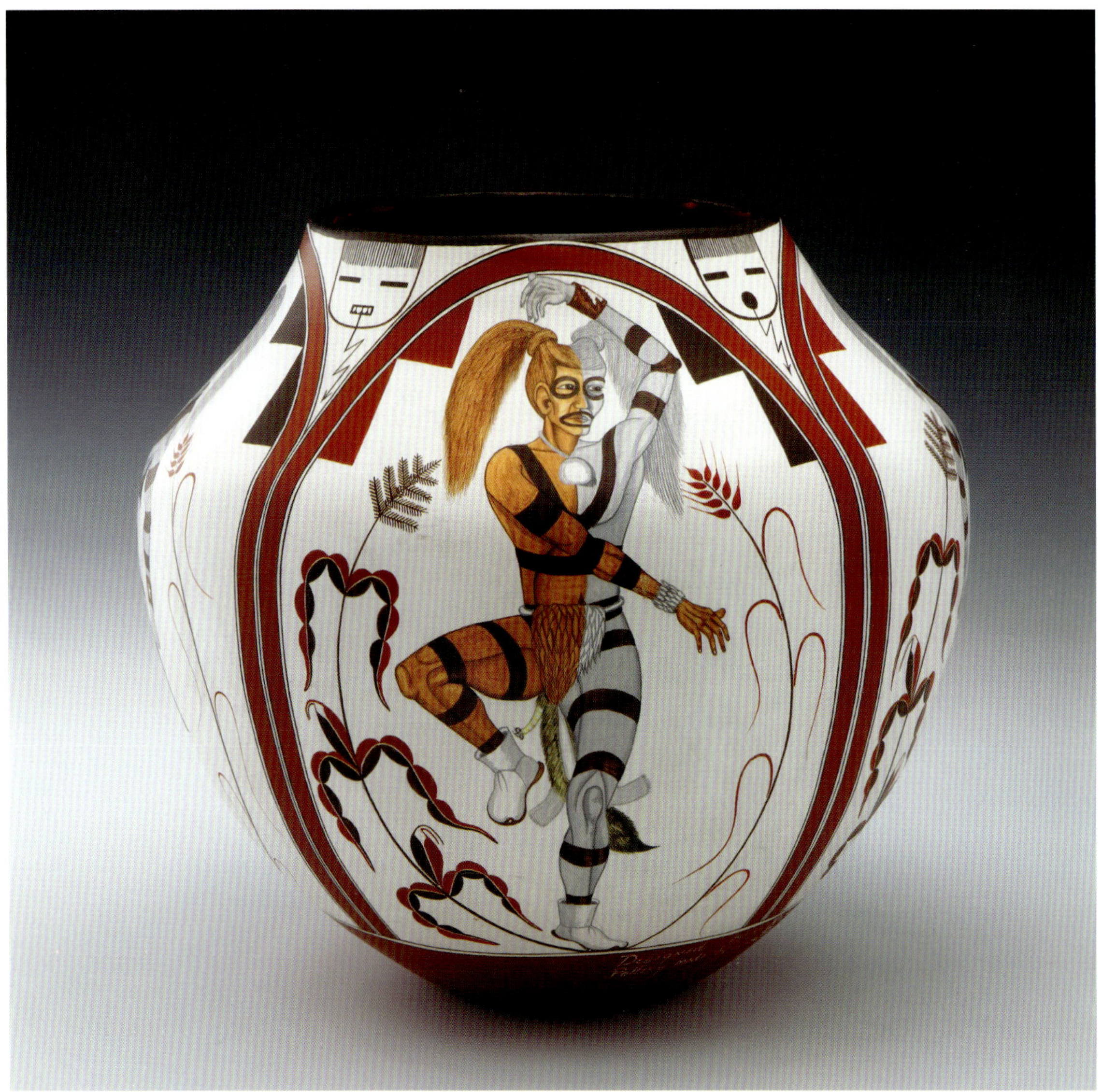

Plate 146 (detail, facing page)
Rafael Medina and Sofia Medina (U.S., Zia, Rafael b. 1929, Sofia b. 1932)
Jar, 1972. Native clay and acrylic paint, 13⅝ × 15 1/16 in.
Fred Jones Jr. Museum of Art
A2007.7218

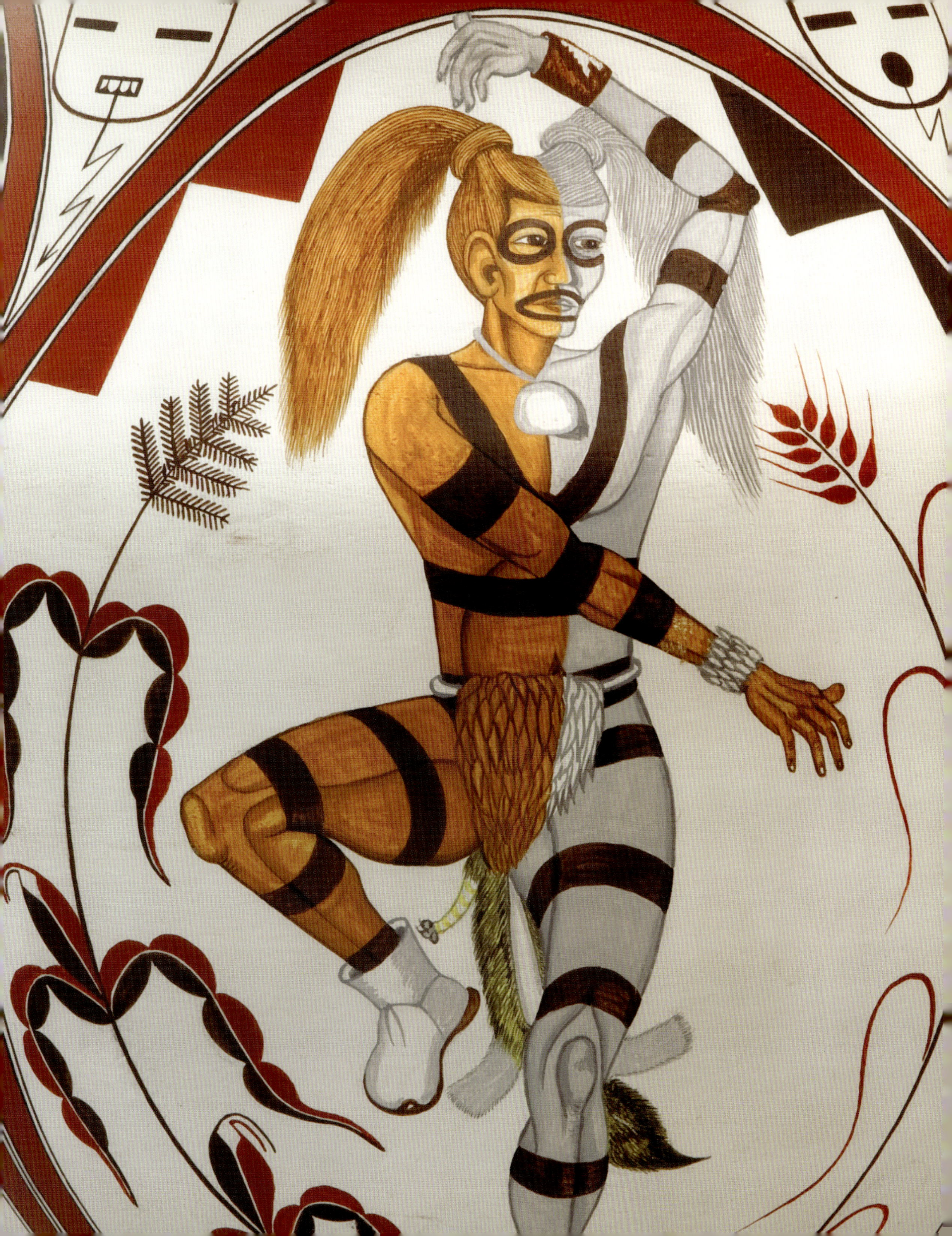

Hopi

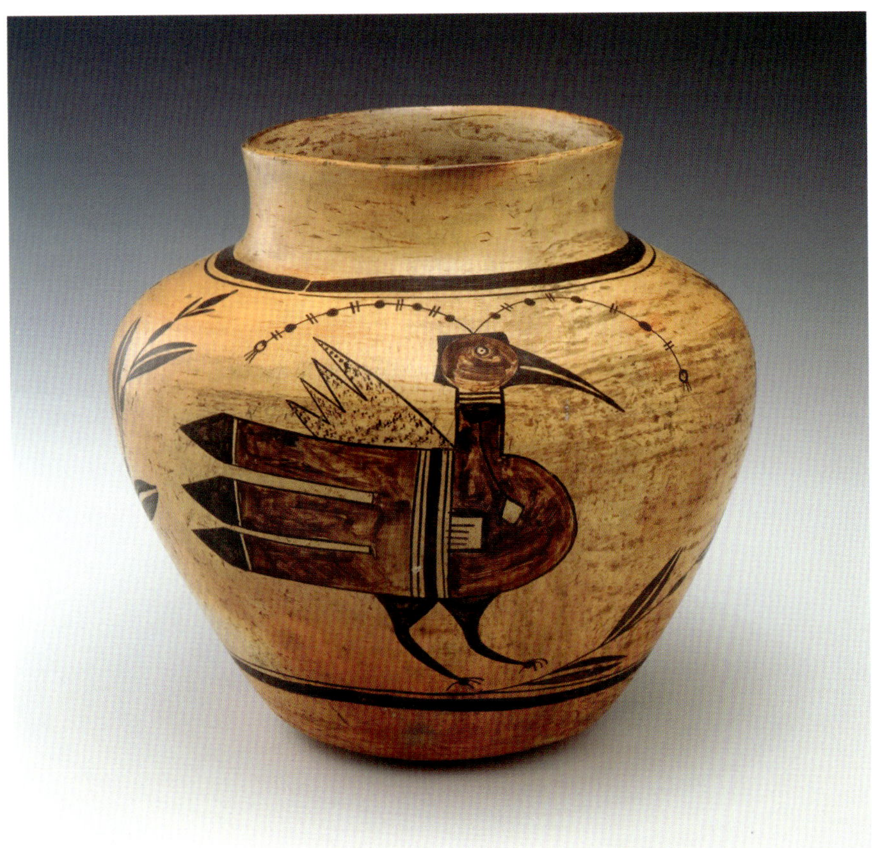

Plate 147
Nampeyo (attributed) (U.S., Hopi, c. 1859/1860–1942)
Polychrome Jar, c. 1900
Native clays and paints, 11½ × 13$^{3}/_{16}$ in.
Fred Jones Jr. Museum of Art
A2007.7234

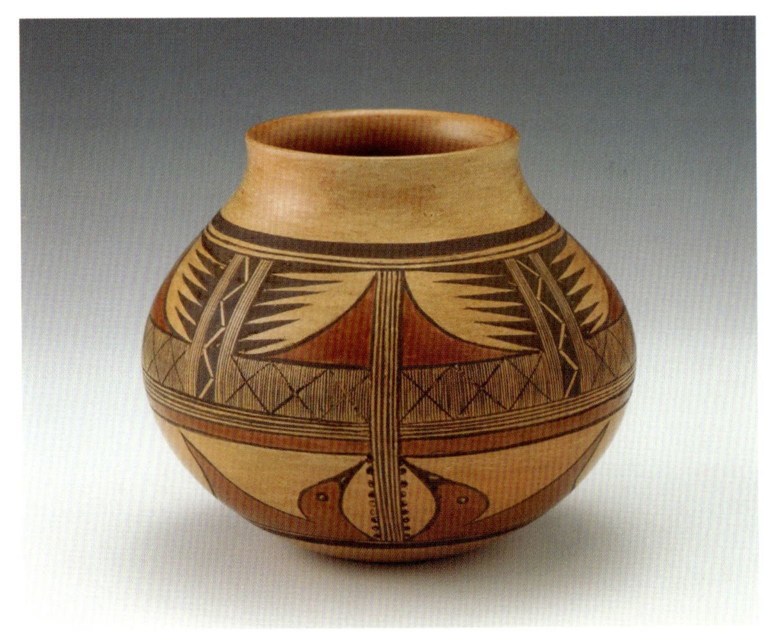

Plate 148
Dextra Quotskuyva Nampeyo
(U.S., Hopi, b. 1928)
Miniature Polychrome Jar, 1981. Native clays and paints, 3⅜ × 4$^{3}/_{16}$ in.
Fred Jones Jr. Museum of Art
A2007.7226

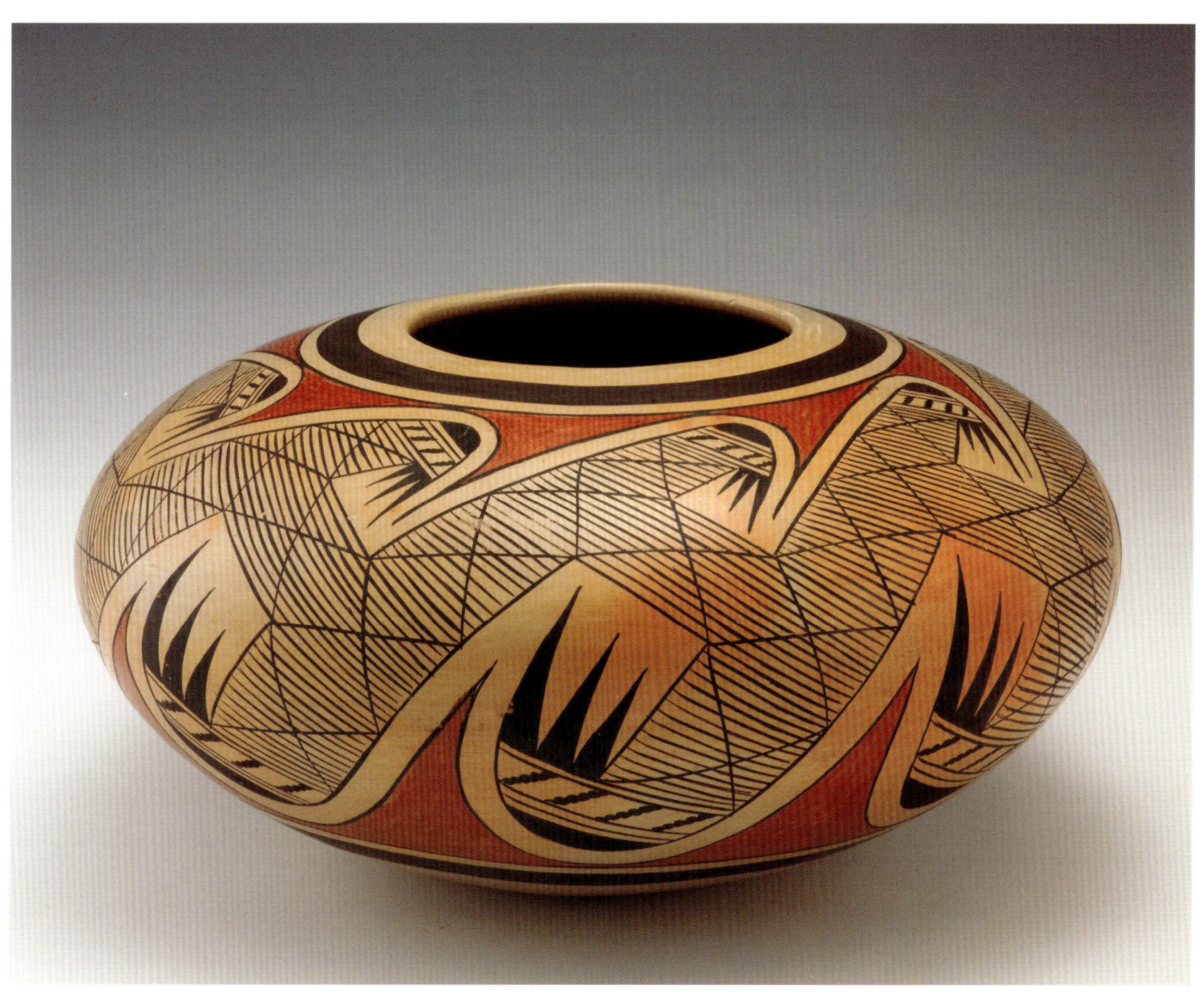

PLATE 149
Fannie Nampeyo (U.S., Hopi, 1900–1987)
Polychrome Jar, Migration Design, 1972
Native clays and paints, 6⅜ × 12⅞ in.
Fred Jones Jr. Museum of Art
A2007.7260

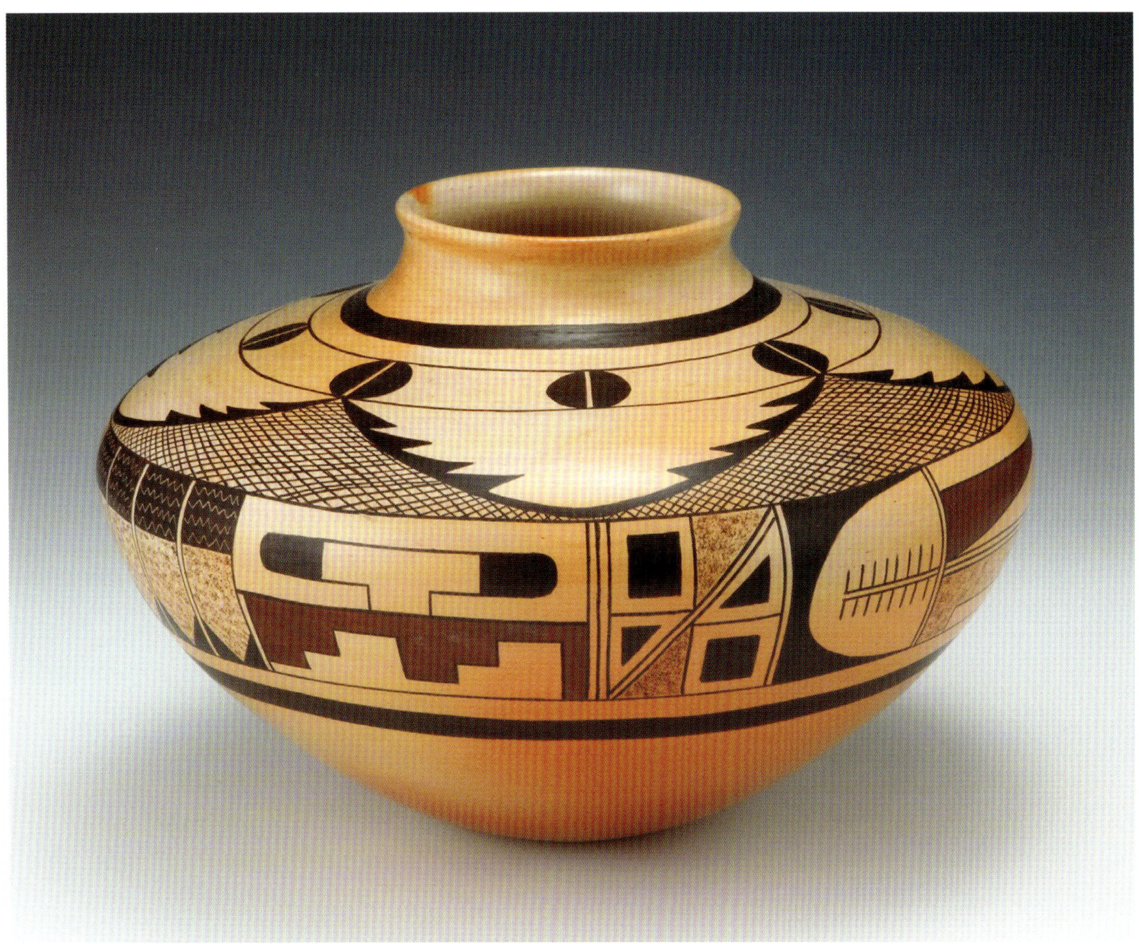

Plate 150 (above)
Mark Tahbo (U.S., Hopi, b. 1958)
Polychrome Jar, 1989. Native clays and paints, 5½ × 8⅝ in.
Fred Jones Jr. Museum of Art
a2007.7371

Plate 151 (facing page)
Grace Chapella (U.S., Hopi, 1874–1980)
Polychrome Jar, c. 1960. Native clays and paints, 10⅛ × 15½ in.
Fred Jones Jr. Museum of Art
a2007.7261

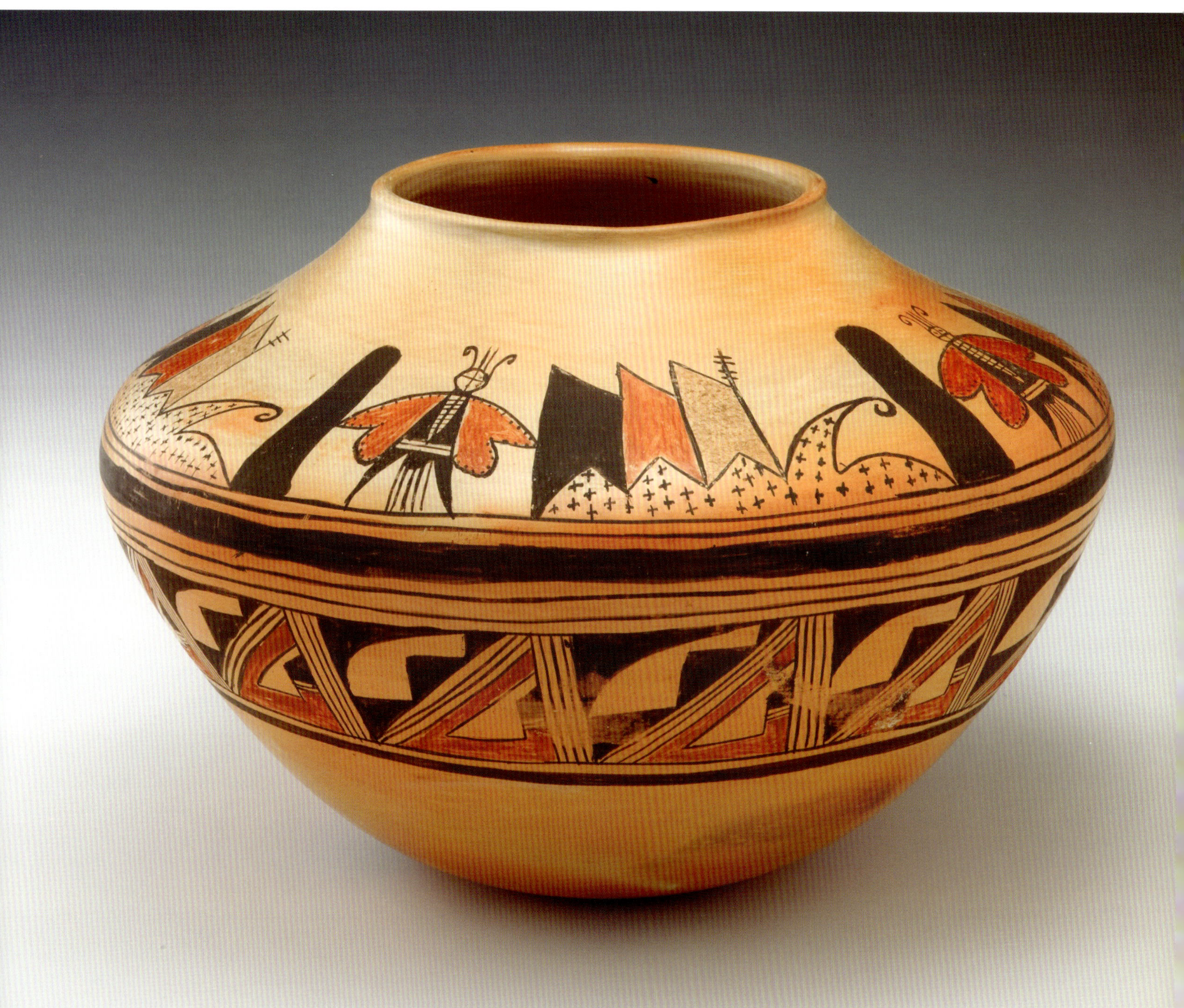

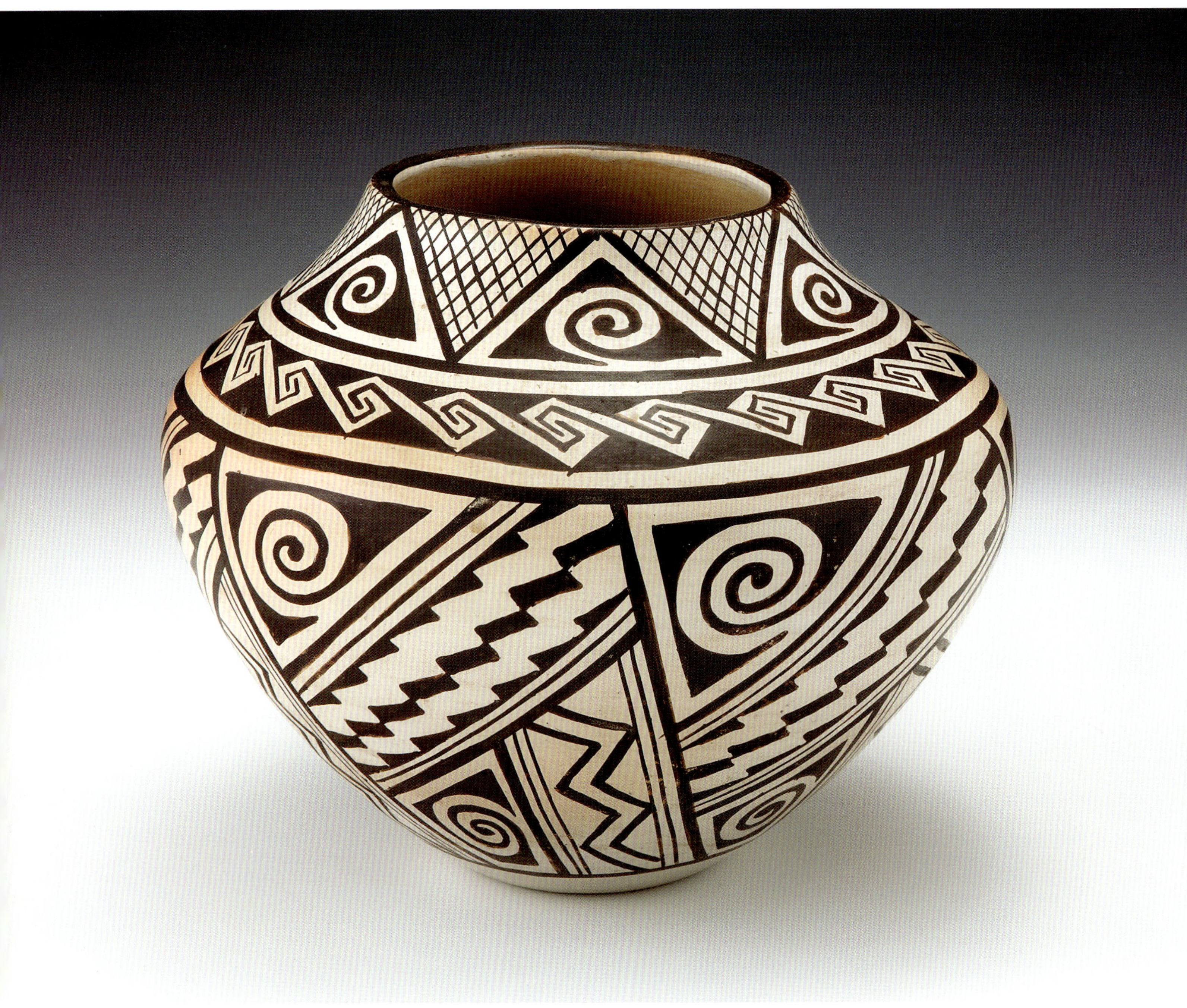

Plate 152
Helen Naha (Feather Woman) (U.S., Hopi, 1922–1993)
Black on White Olla, c. 1960. Native clays and paints, 6⅞ × 8⅝ in.
Fred Jones Jr. Museum of Art
a2007.7240

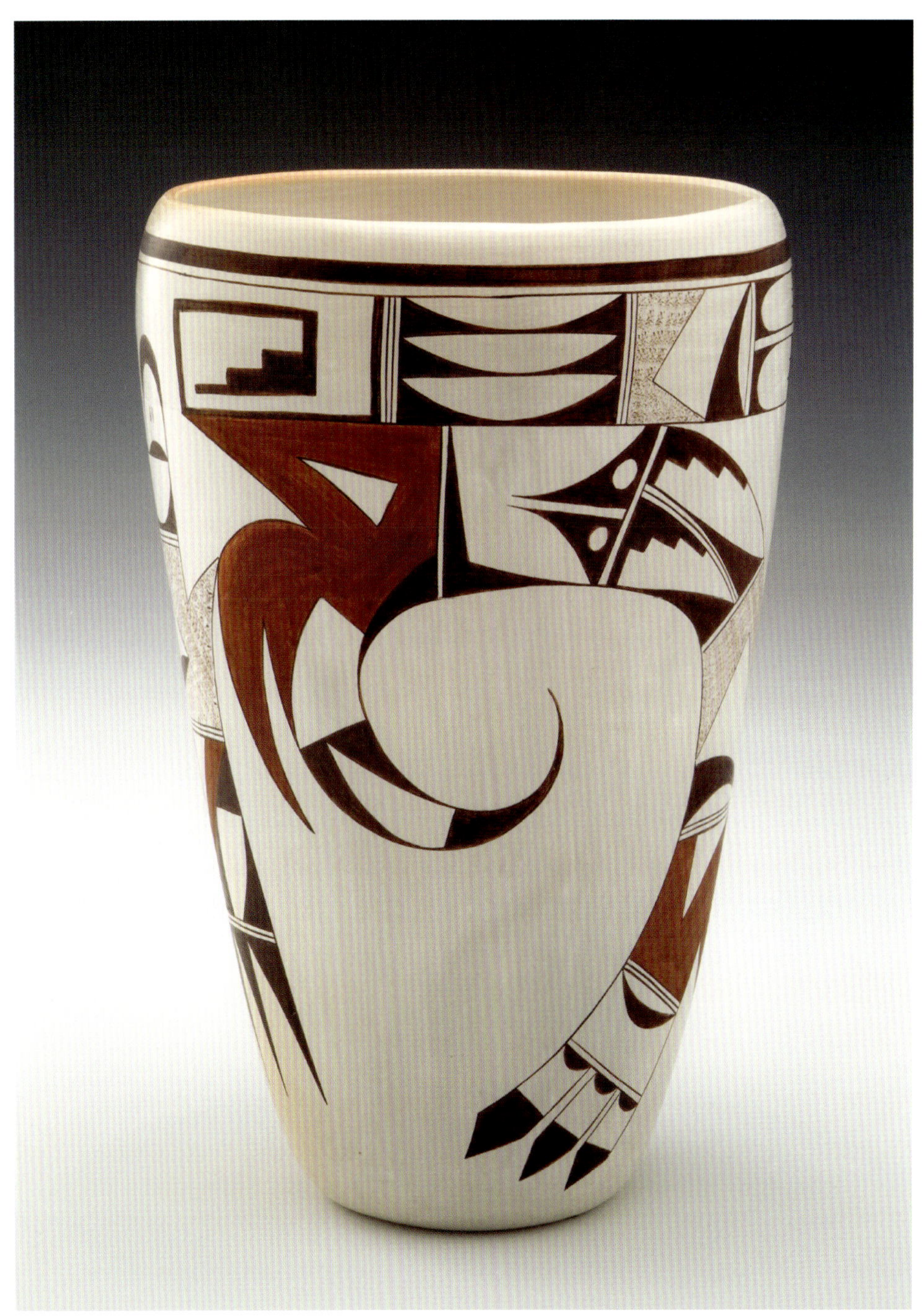

PLATE 153
Joy Navasie (Frog Woman) (U.S., Hopi, b. 1919)
Polychrome Vase, c. 1970. Native clays and paints, 13 × 8½ in.
Philbrook Museum of Art
A2007.7229

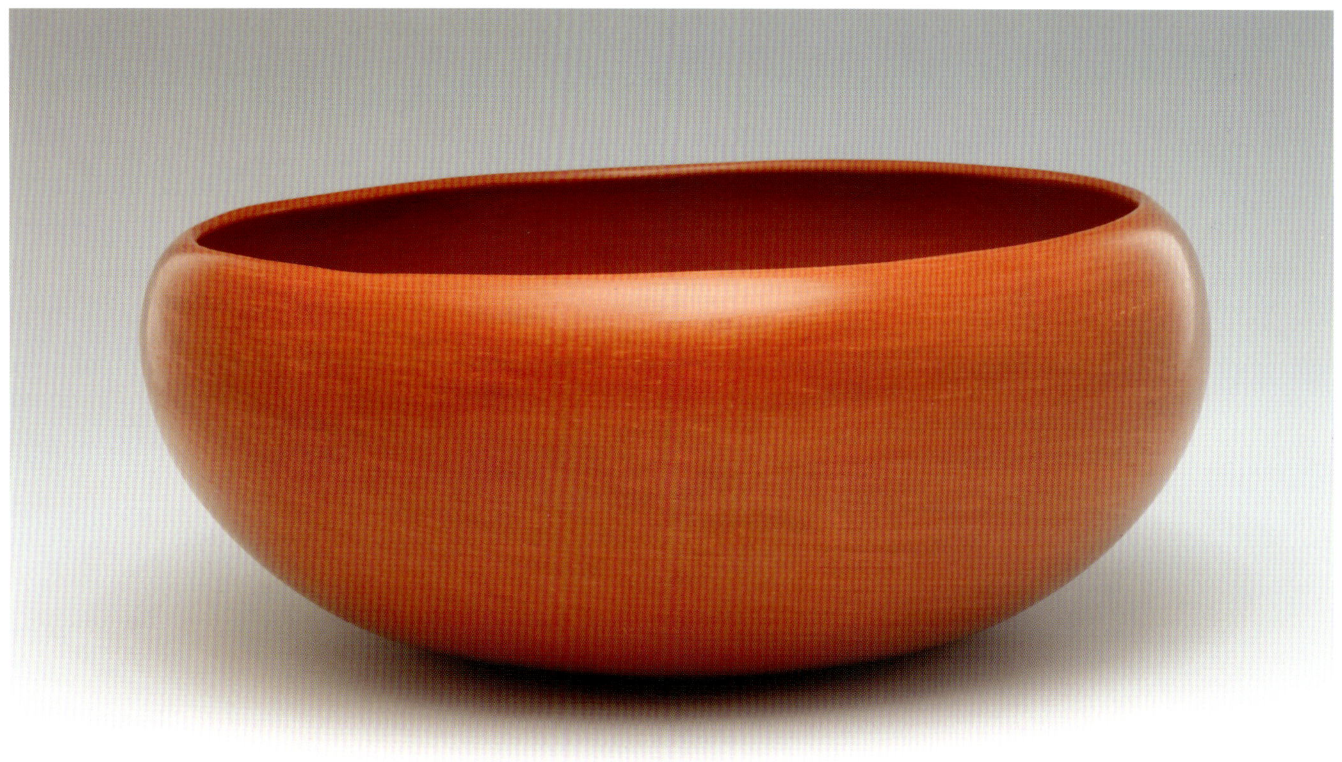

Plate 154 (above)
Garnet Pavatea (U.S., Hopi, 1915–1981)
Bowl, 1964. Native clays, 6¼ × 16¼ in.
Fred Jones Jr. Museum of Art
A2007.7018

Plate 155 (facing page)
Garnet Pavatea (U.S., Hopi, 1915–1981)
Canteen, c. 1960. Native clays and paints, 12¾ × 12 × 7¾ in.
Fred Jones Jr. Museum of Art
A2007.7231

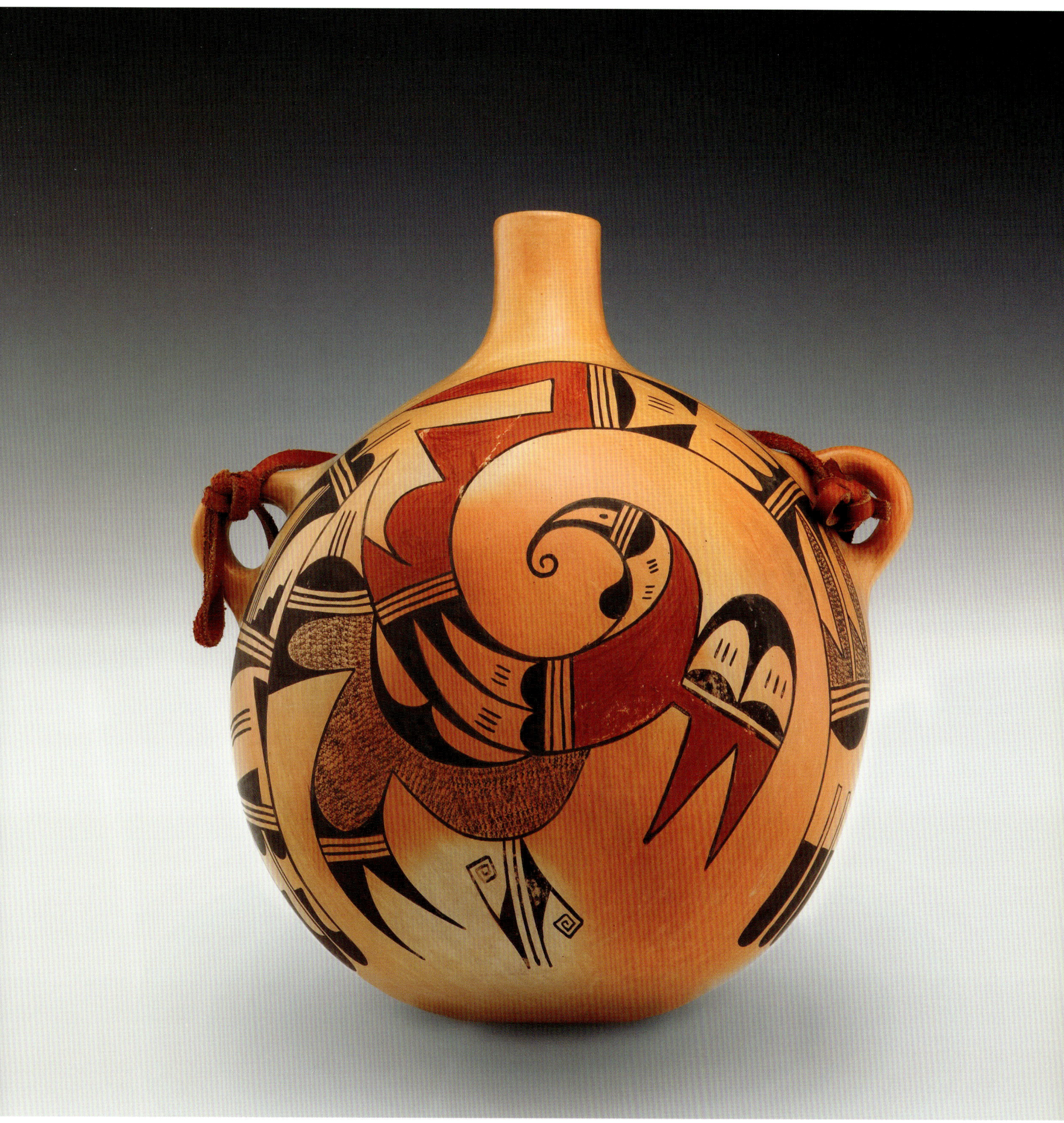

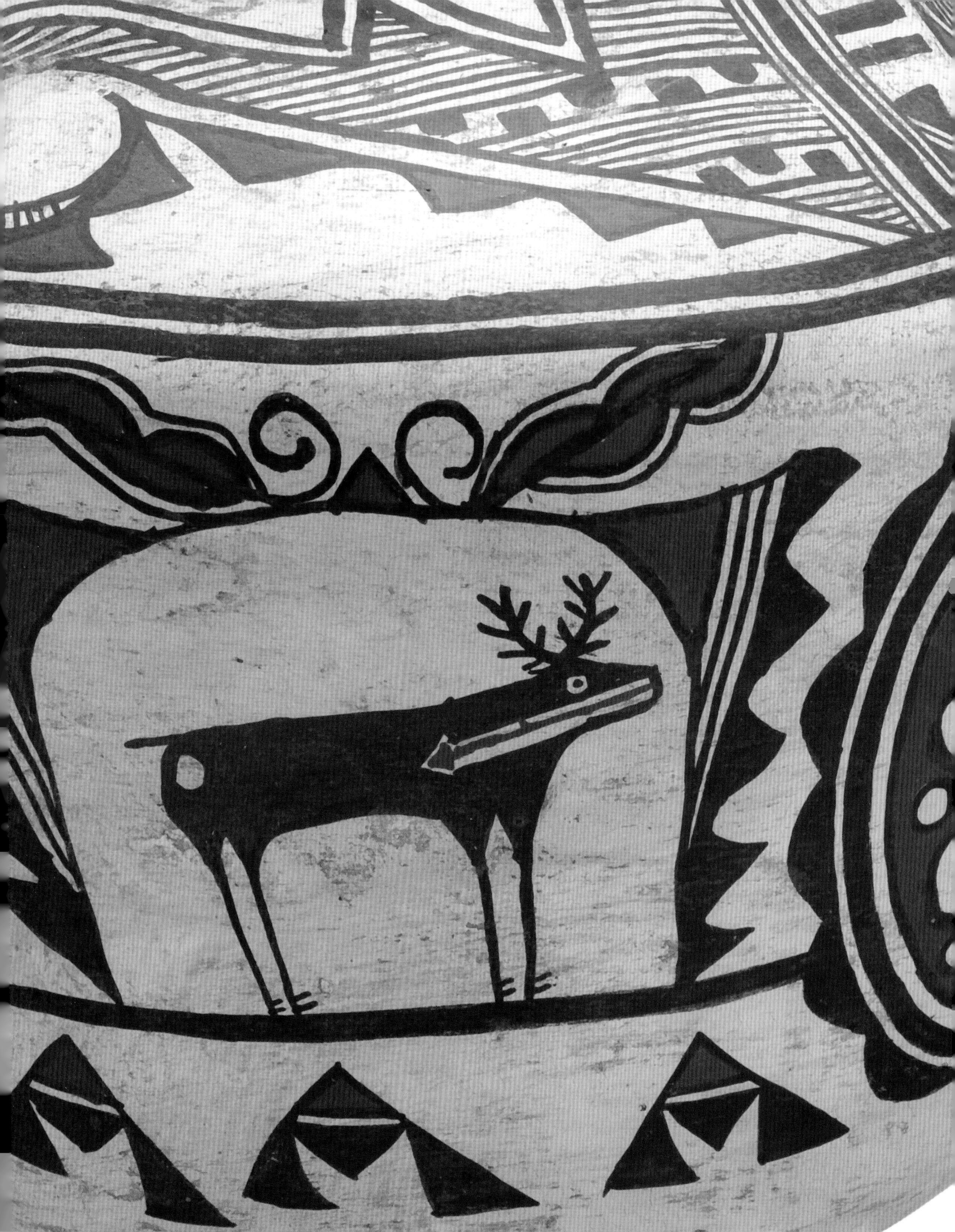

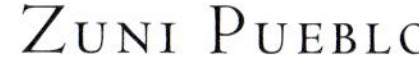

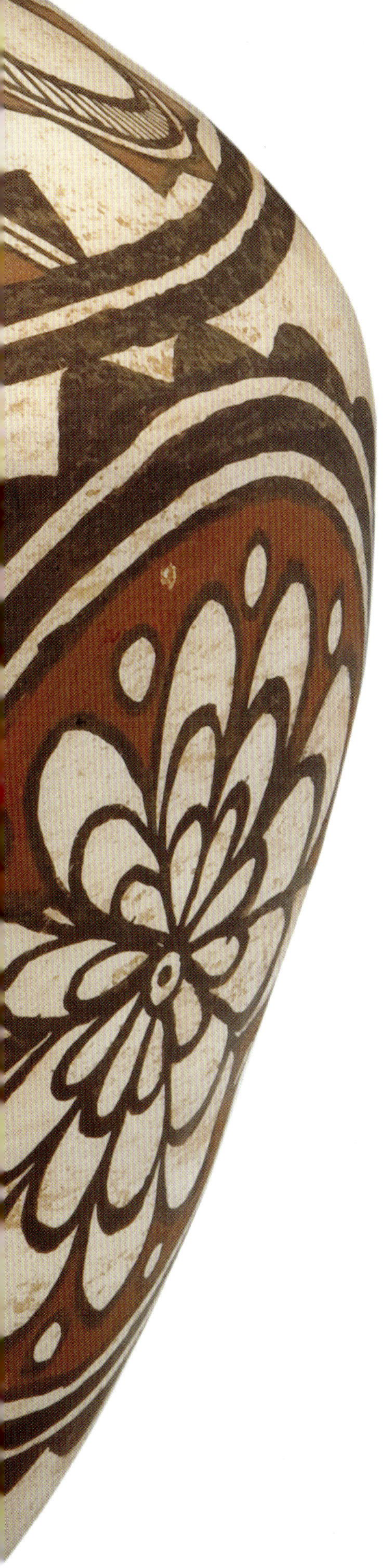

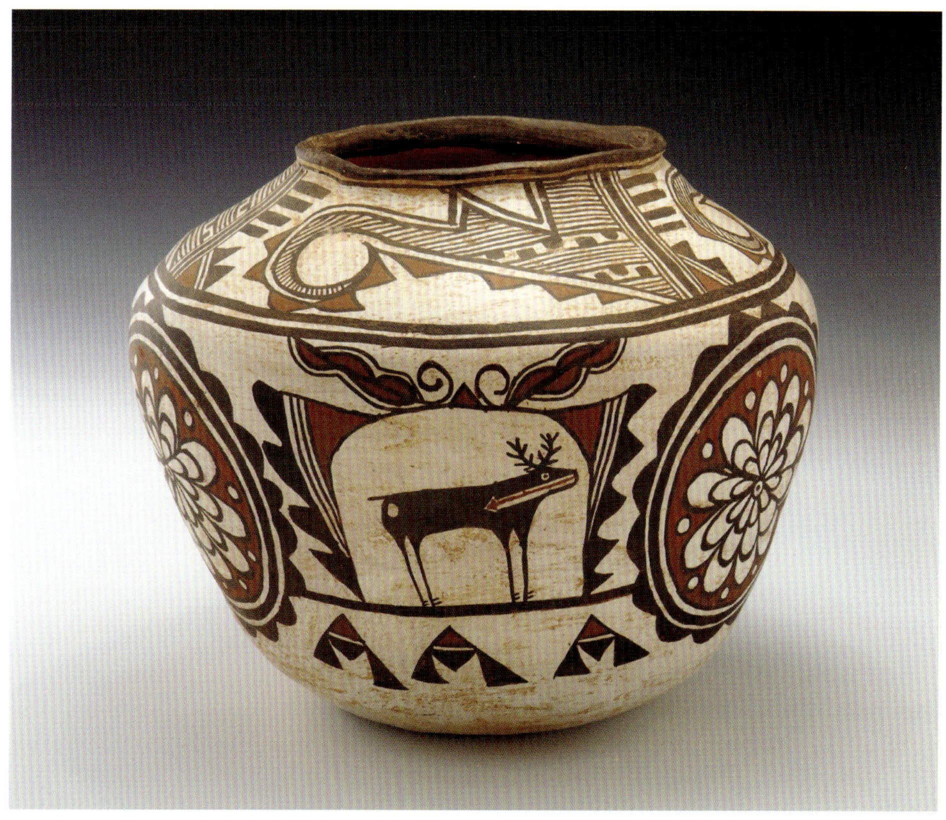

Plate 156 (detail, facing page)
Unknown (U.S., Zuni)
Storage Jar, c. 1950. Native clays and paints, 12¼ × 15½ in.
Fred Jones Jr. Museum of Art
A2007.7281

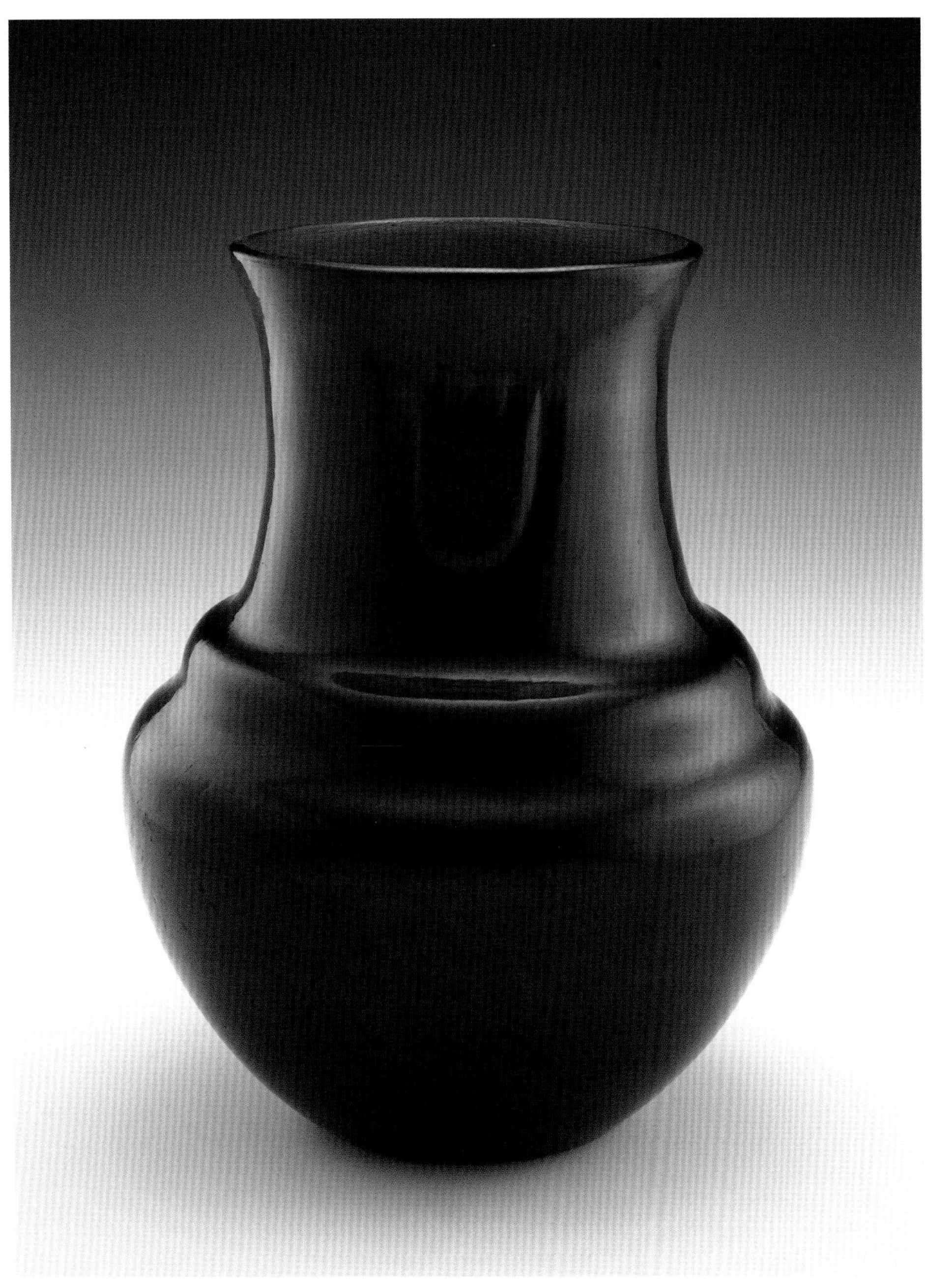

Plate 157 (above)
Margaret Tafoya (U.S., Santa Clara, 1904–2001)
Bear Paw Jar, 1960. Native clays, 13 × 11 in.
Fred Jones Jr. Museum of Art
A2007.7129

Plate 158 (facing page)
Margaret Tafoya (U.S., Santa Clara, 1904–2001)
Red Wedding Vase, Carved Avanyu, 1964. Native clays, 21 × 12¾ in.
Philbrook Museum of Art
A2007.7132

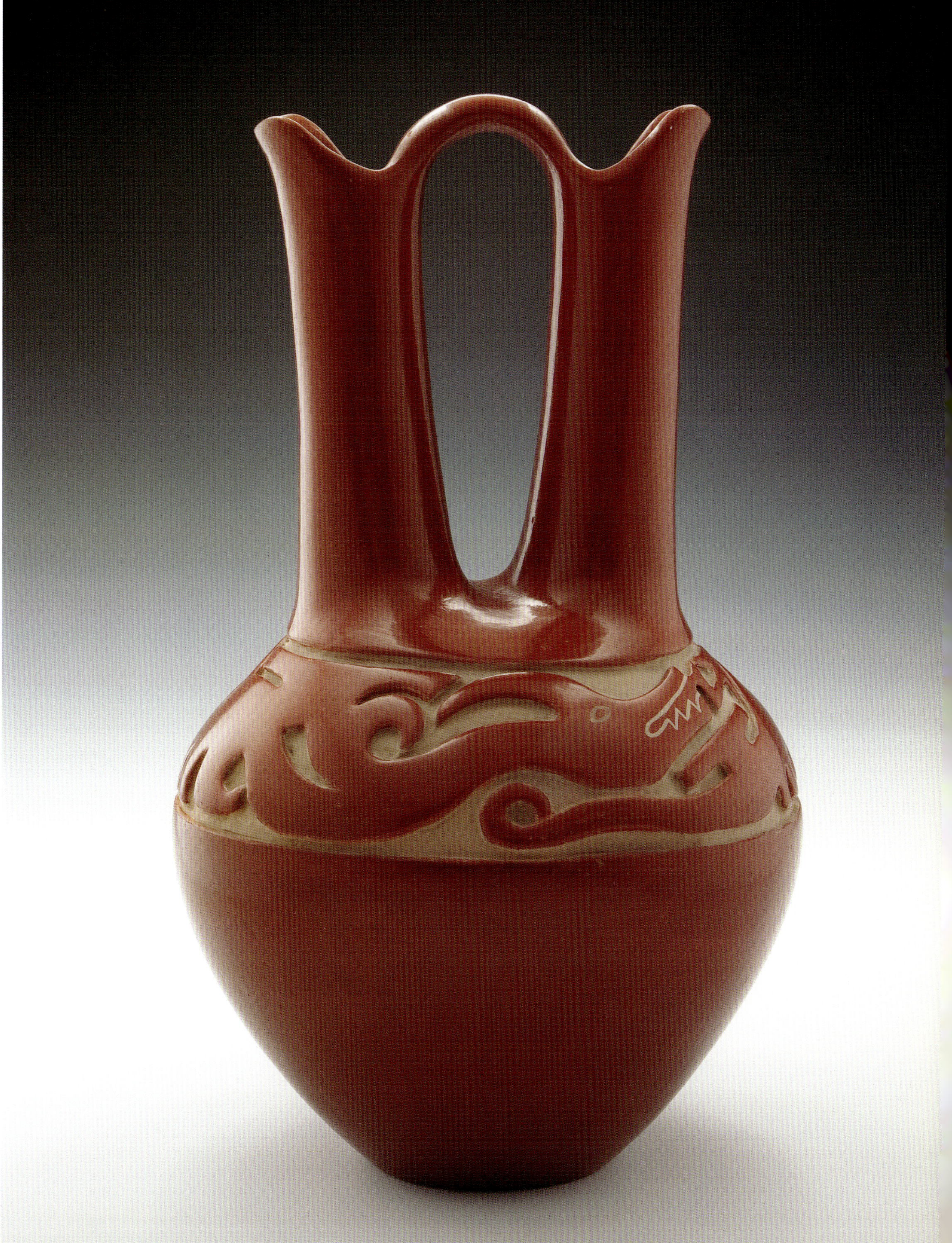

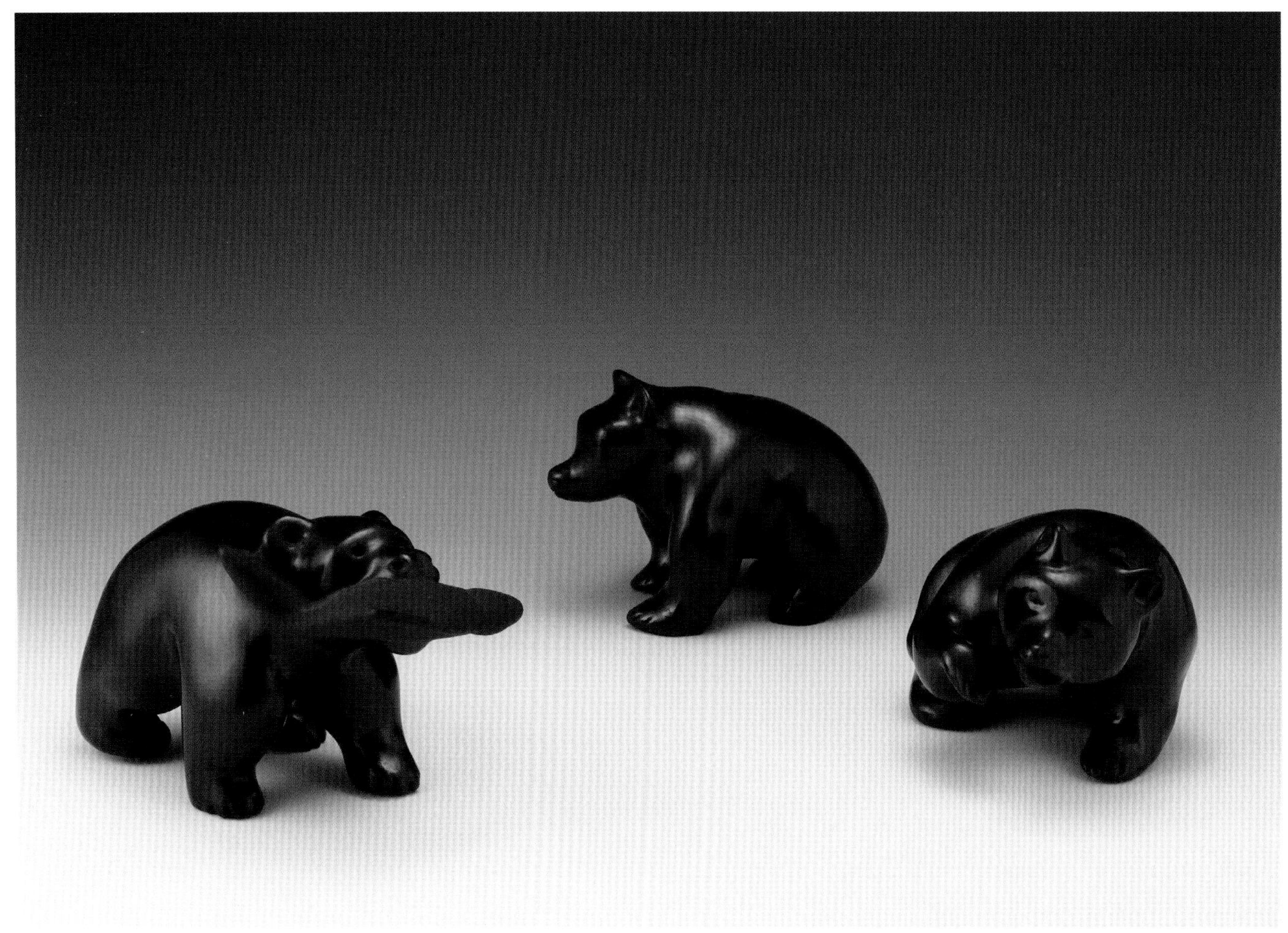

Plate 159 (above)
Pula Gutierrez (U.S., Santa Clara, 1925–1997)
Polished Black Bears, n.d. Native clays, 3½ in.
Fred Jones Jr. Museum of Art
A2007.7159

Plate 160 (facing page)
Virginia Ebelacker (U.S., Santa Clara, 1925–2001)
Black Bear Paw Jar, c. 1970. Native clays, 12⅝ × 16¾ in.
Fred Jones Jr. Museum of Art
A2007.7140

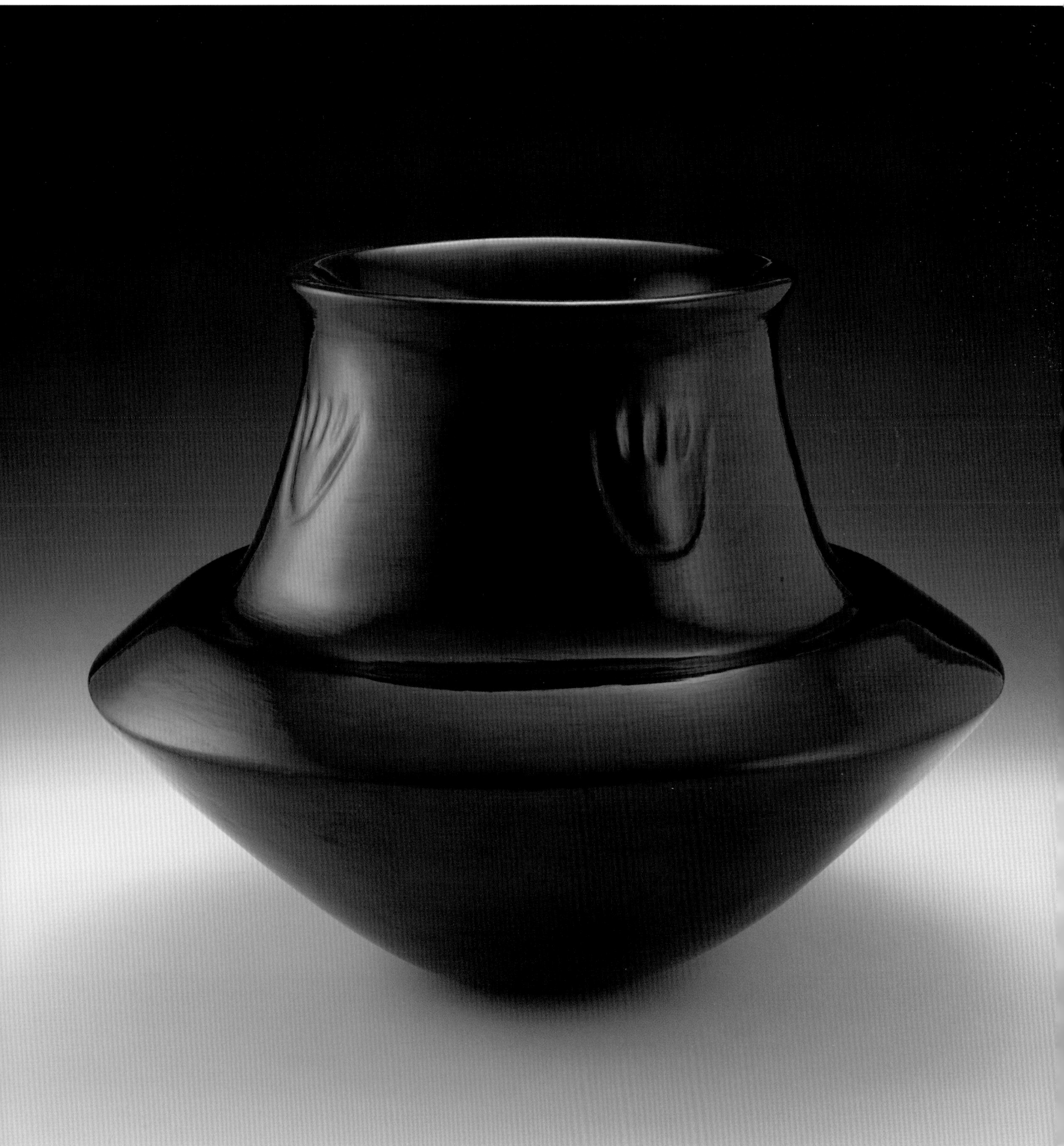

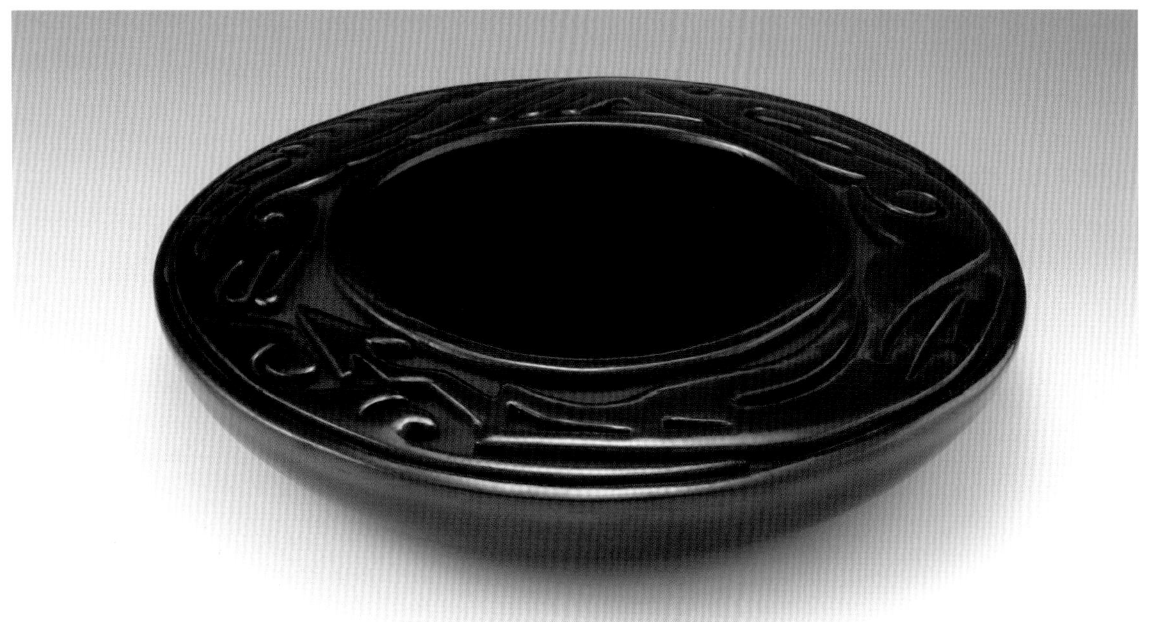

Plate 161 (above)
Teresita Naranjo (U.S., Santa Clara, 1919–1999)
Black Bowl, Carved Avanyu, 1964
Native clays, 2⅜ × 11¼ in.
Fred Jones Jr. Museum of Art
A2007.7137

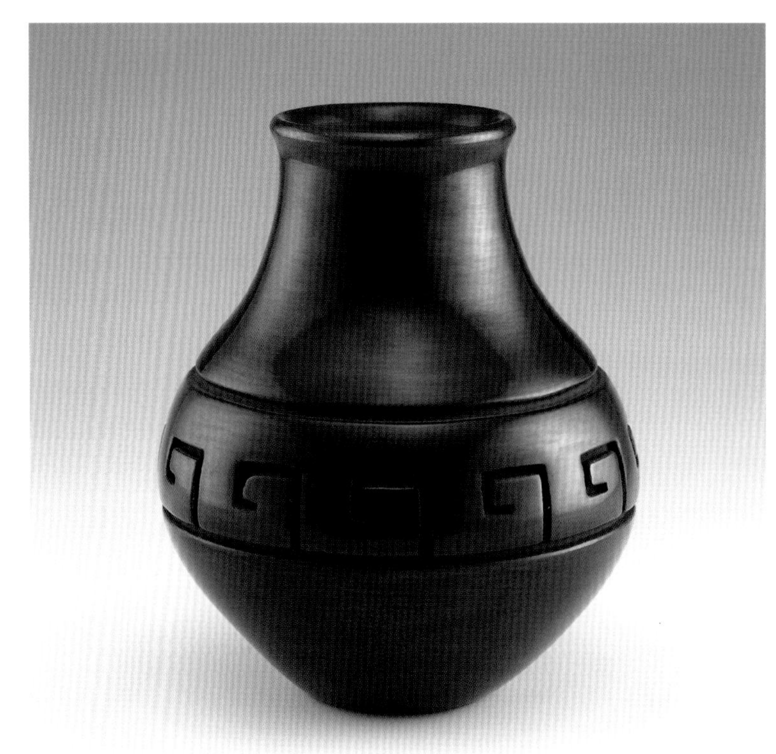

Plate 162 (right)
Nathan Youngblood (U.S., Santa Clara, b. 1954)
Jar, Incised, 1978. Native clays, 9¼ × 7 15/16 in.
Fred Jones Jr. Museum of Art
A2007.7141

Plate 163 (facing page)
Helen Shupla (U.S., Santa Clara, 1928–1985)
Melon Pot, 1978. Native clays, 8½ × 14 in.
Fred Jones Jr. Museum of Art
A2007.7146

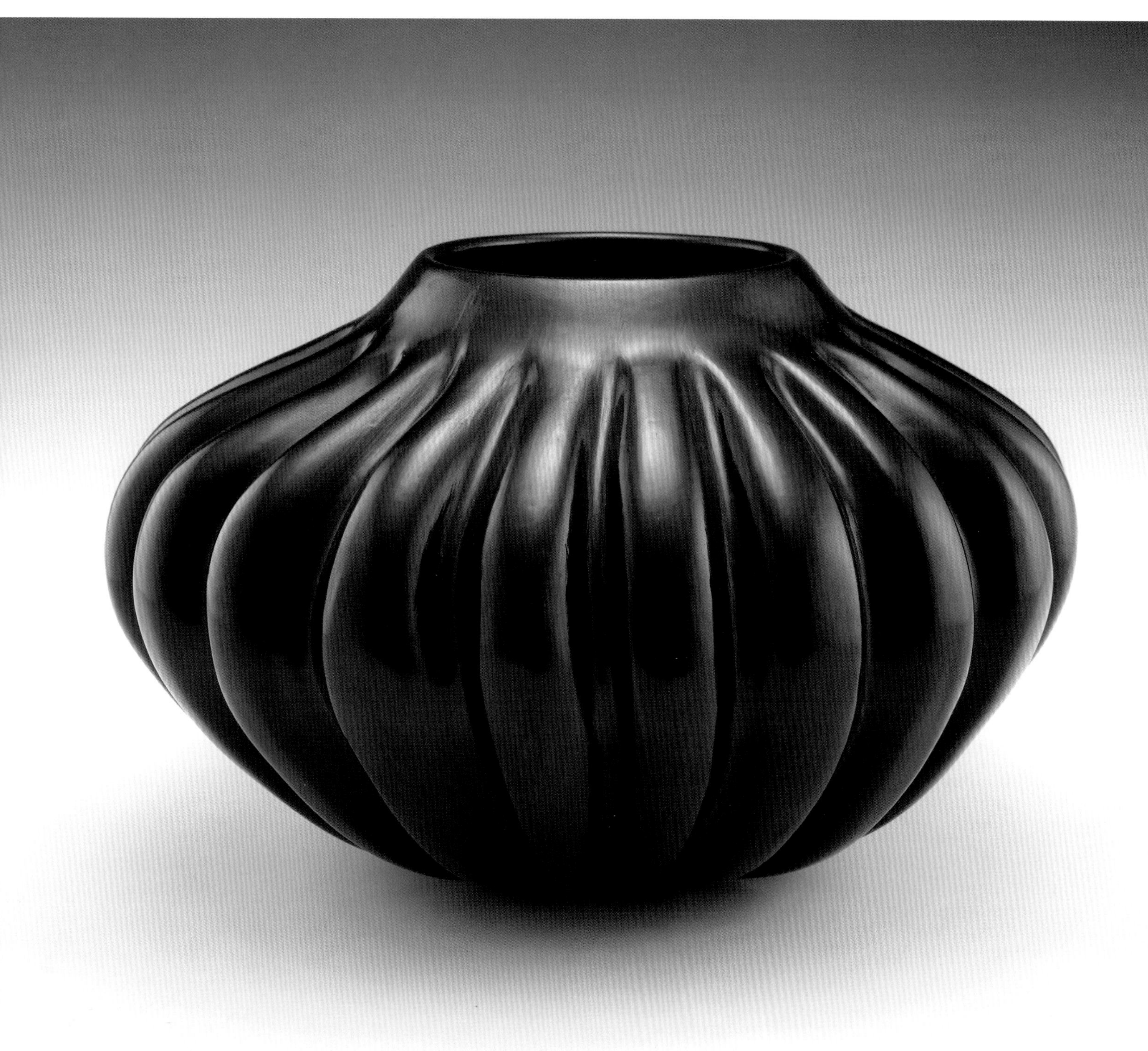

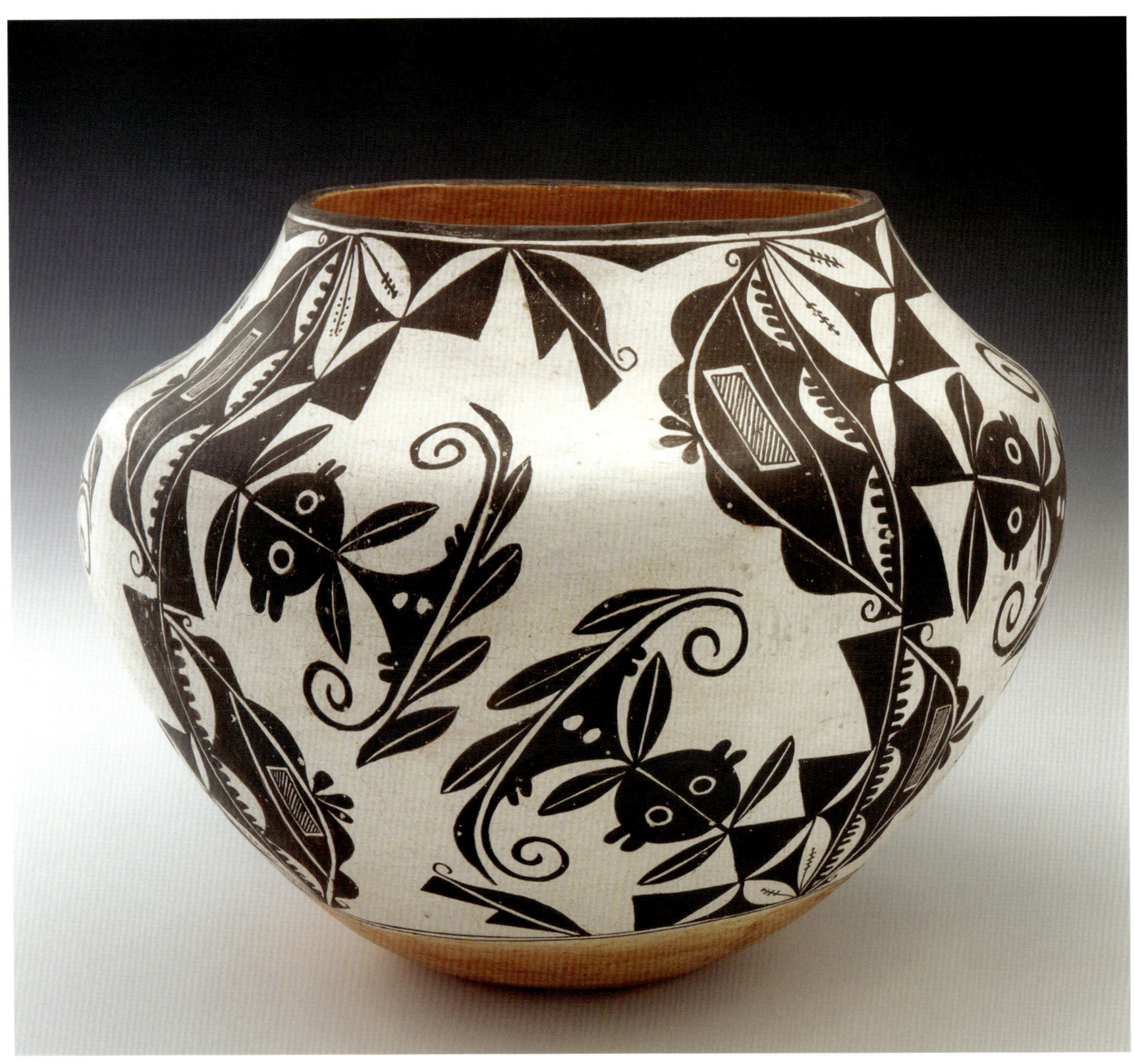

Plate 164 (above)
Marie Zieu Chino (U.S., Acoma, 1907–1982)
Black on White Jar, 1965
Native clays and paints, 15½ × 20⅛ in.
Fred Jones Jr. Museum of Art
A2007.7023

Plate 165 (facing page)
Rose Chino Garcia (U.S., Acoma, 1920–2000)
Polychrome Plate, 1982
Native clays and paints, 2⅛ × 13¼ in.
Fred Jones Jr. Museum of Art
A2007.7175

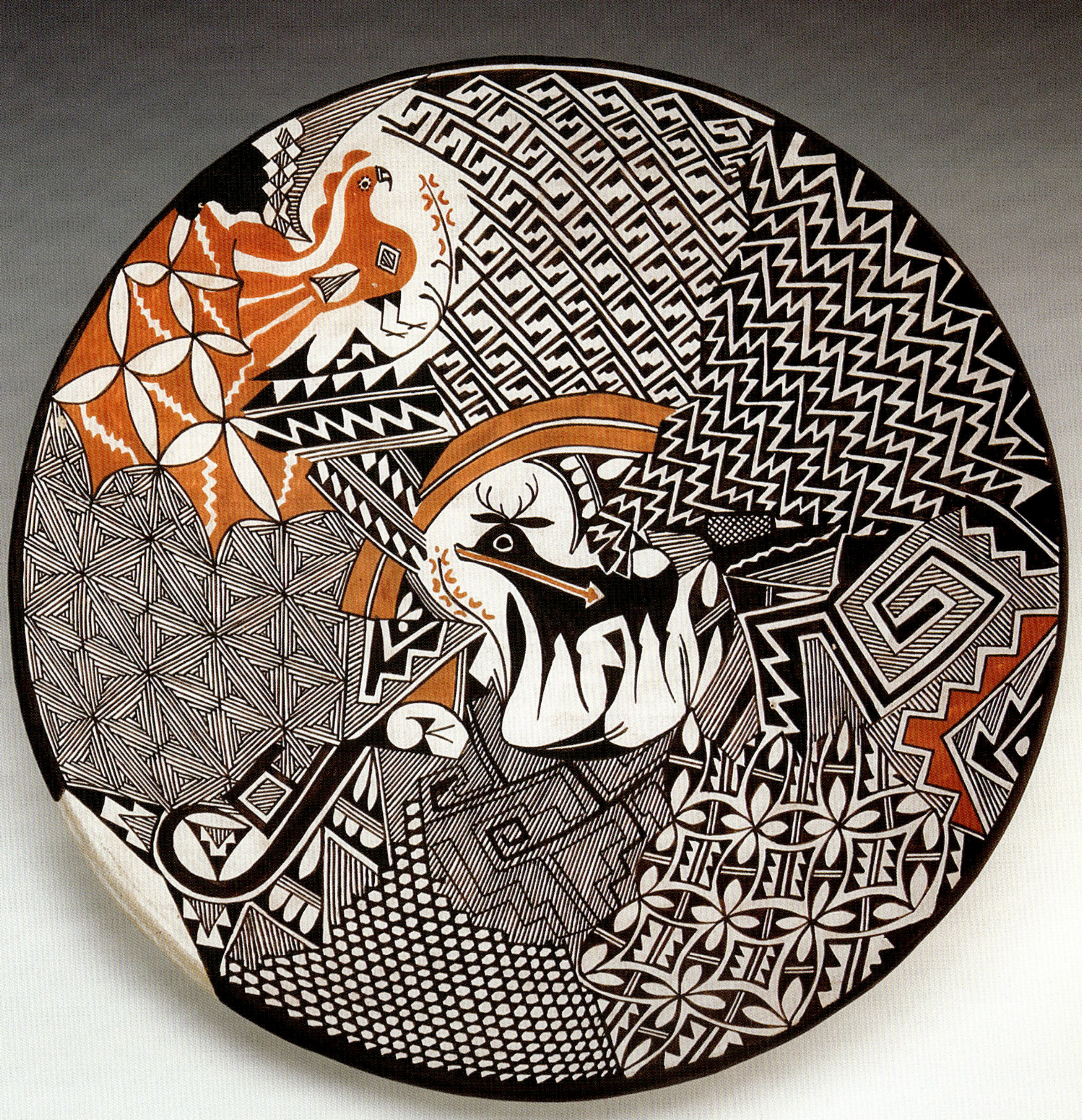

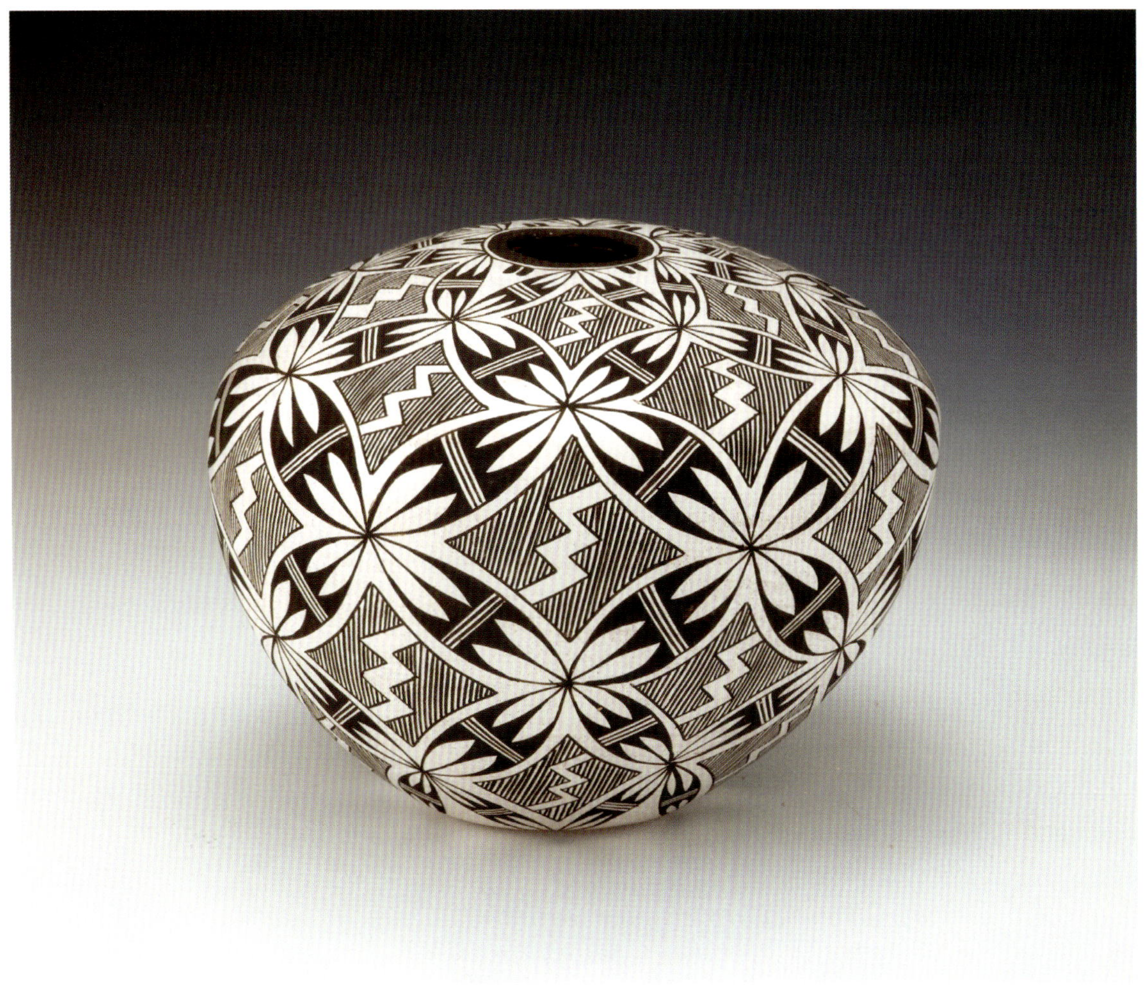

Plate 166 (detail, facing page)
Marie Zieu Chino (U.S., Acoma, 1907–1982)
Black on White Jar, 1978. Native clays and paints, 6¼ × 8½ in.
Philbrook Museum of Art
A2007.7178

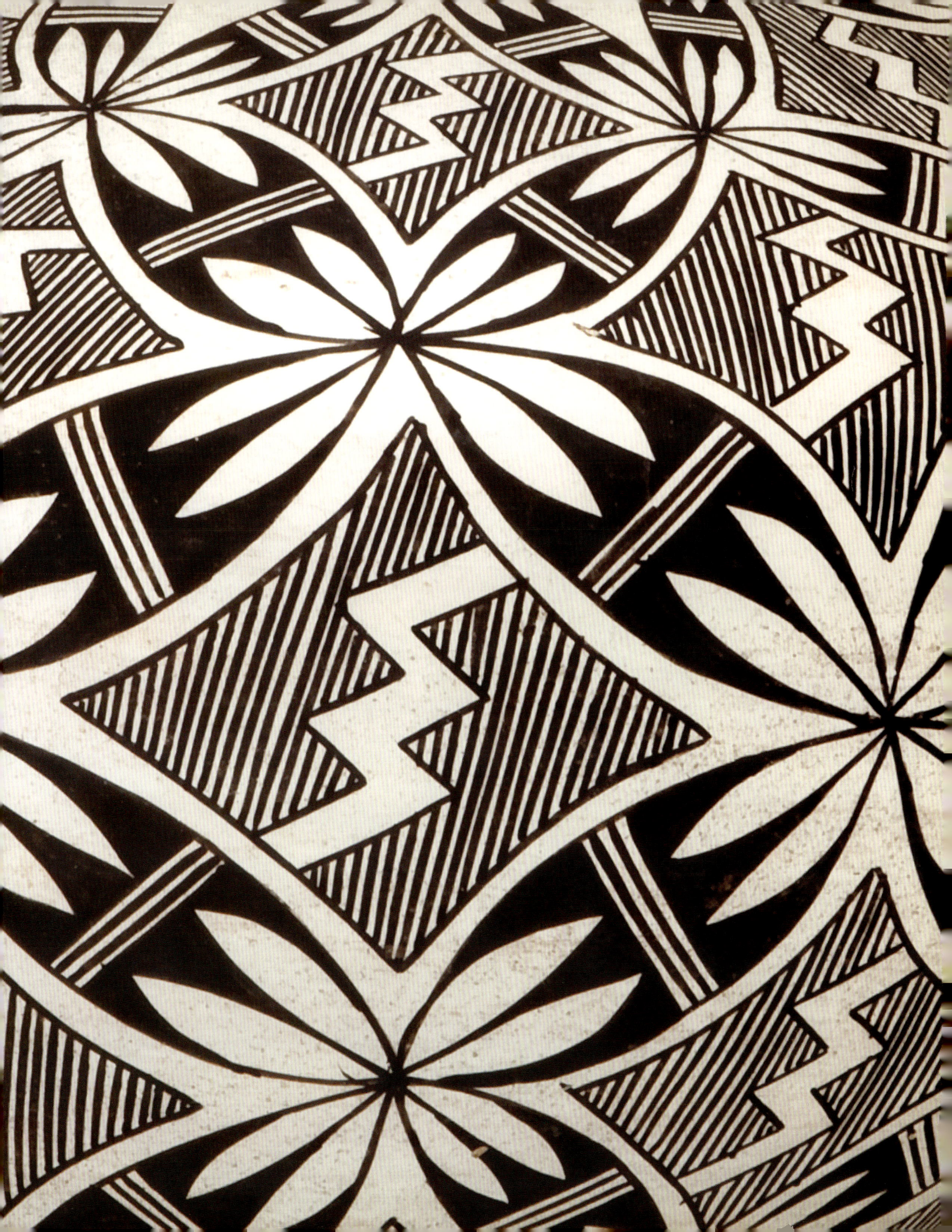

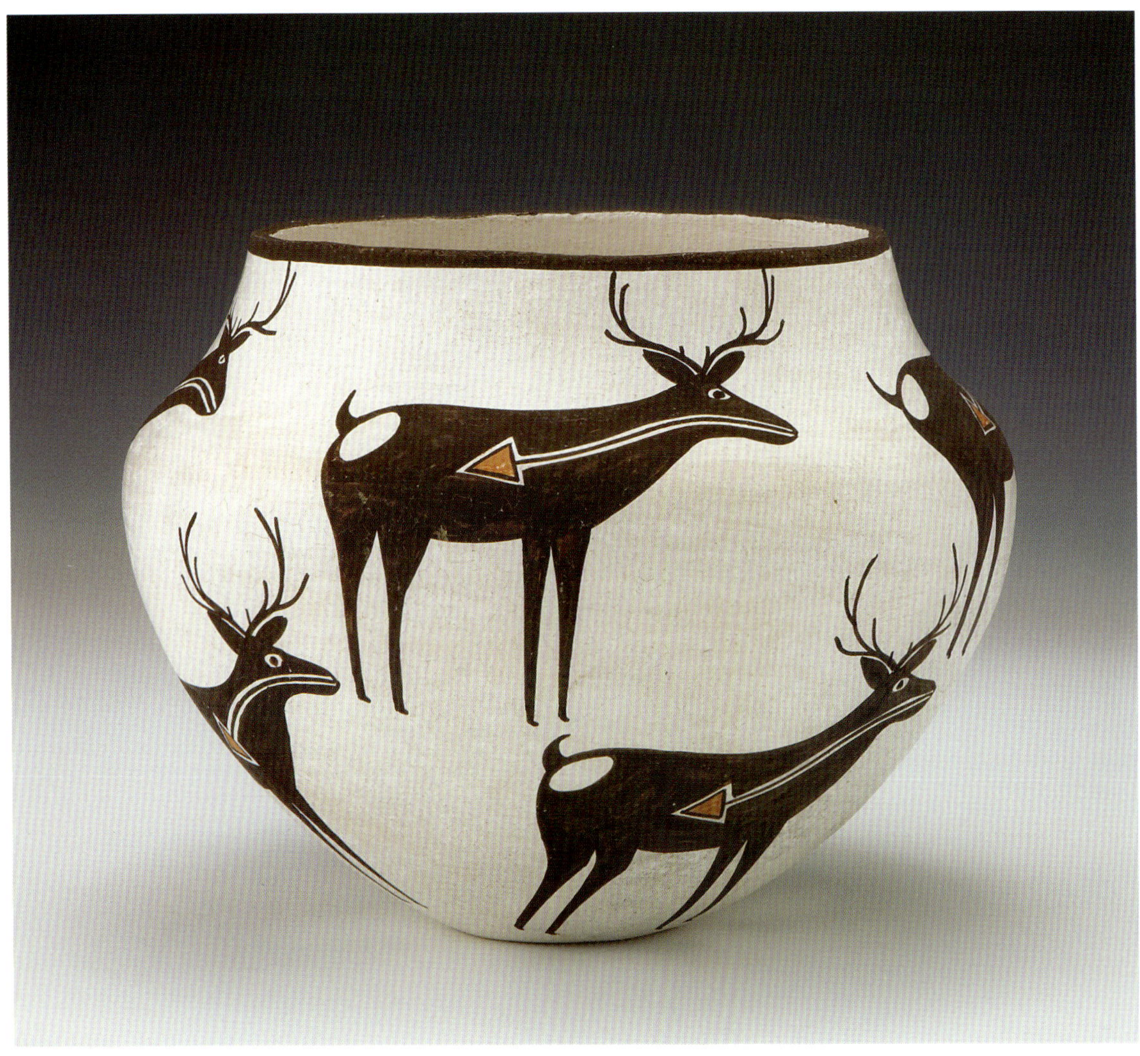

Plate 167 (above)
Lucy Martin Lewis (U.S., Acoma, c. 1898–1992)
Jar, Heartline Deer Design, c. 1960
Native clays and paints, 5⅝ × 7½ in.
Fred Jones Jr. Museum of Art
A2007.7189

Plate 168 (facing page)
Lucy Martin Lewis (U.S., Acoma, c. 1898–1992)
Wedding Vase with Parrot, 1963
Native clays and paints, 10¾ × 8¼ in.
Philbrook Museum of Art
A2007.7198

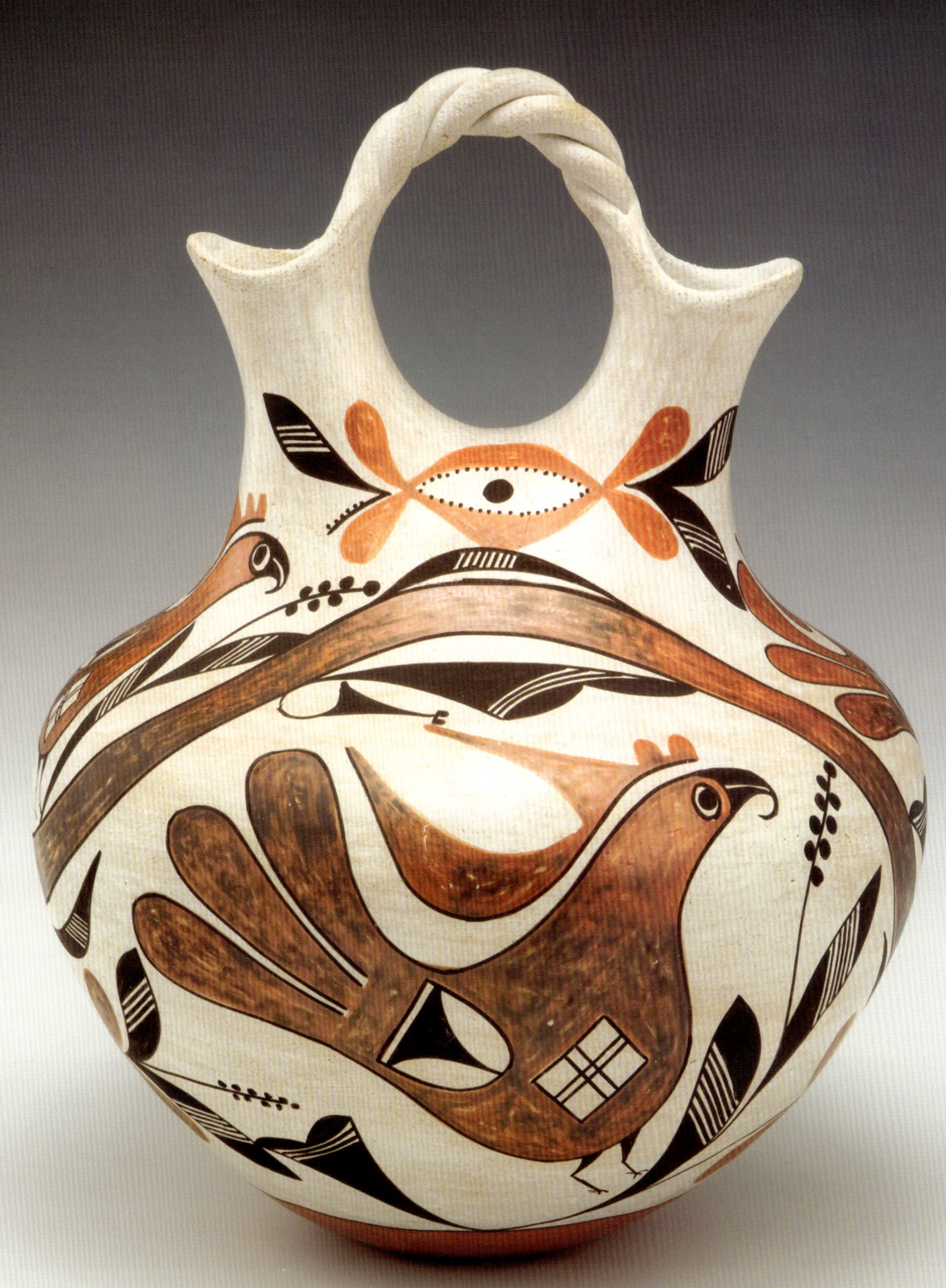

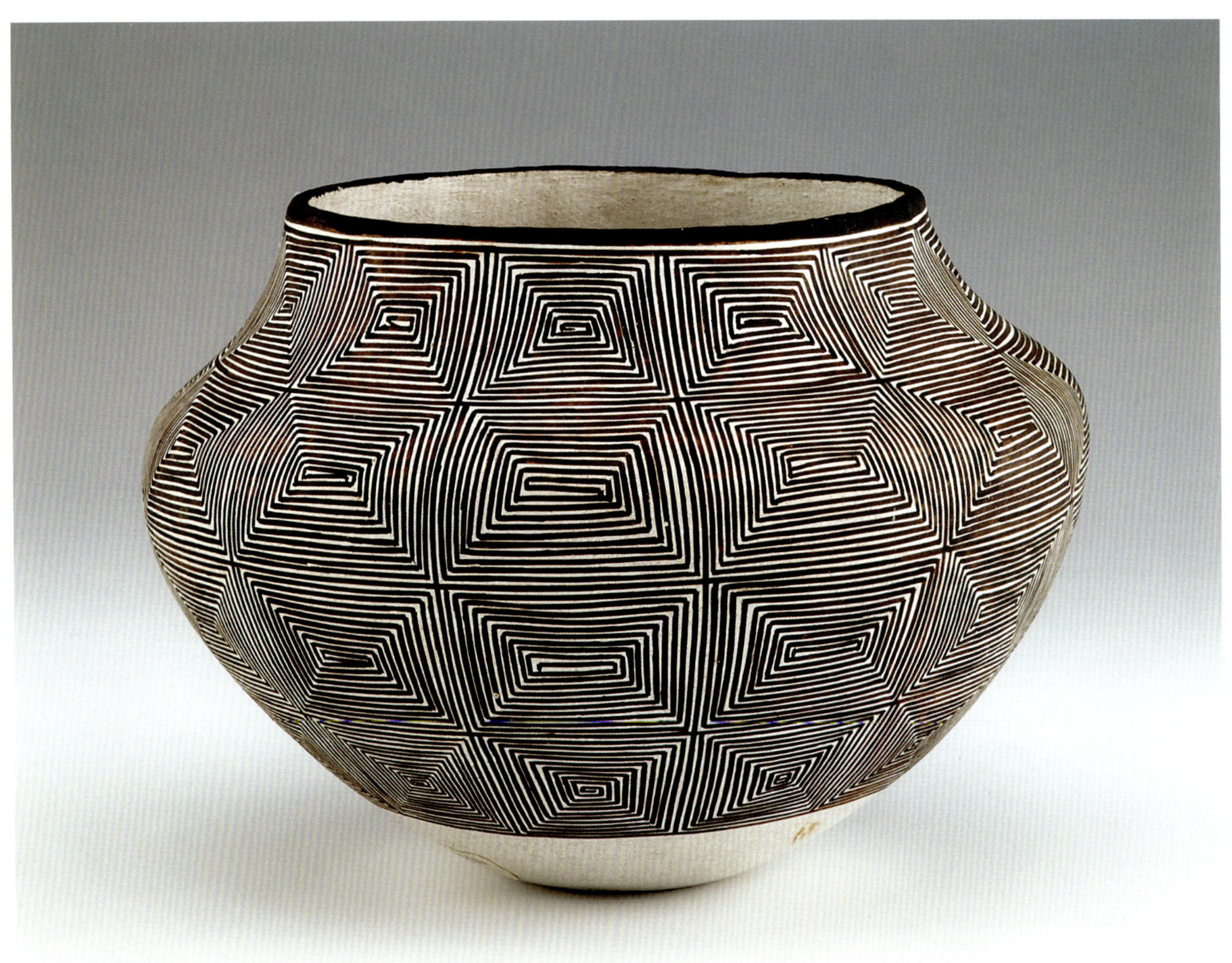

Plate 169 (above)
Lucy Martin Lewis (U.S., Acoma c. 1898–1992)
Black on White Fine Line Jar, 1963
Native clays and paints, 8 × 5¼ in.
Philbrook Museum of Art
A2007.7196

Plate 170 (facing page)
Emma Lewis Mitchell (U.S., Acoma, b. 1931)
Plate with Seven Figures, 1978
Native clays and paints, 1½ × 10¾ in.
Philbrook Museum of Art
A2007.7173

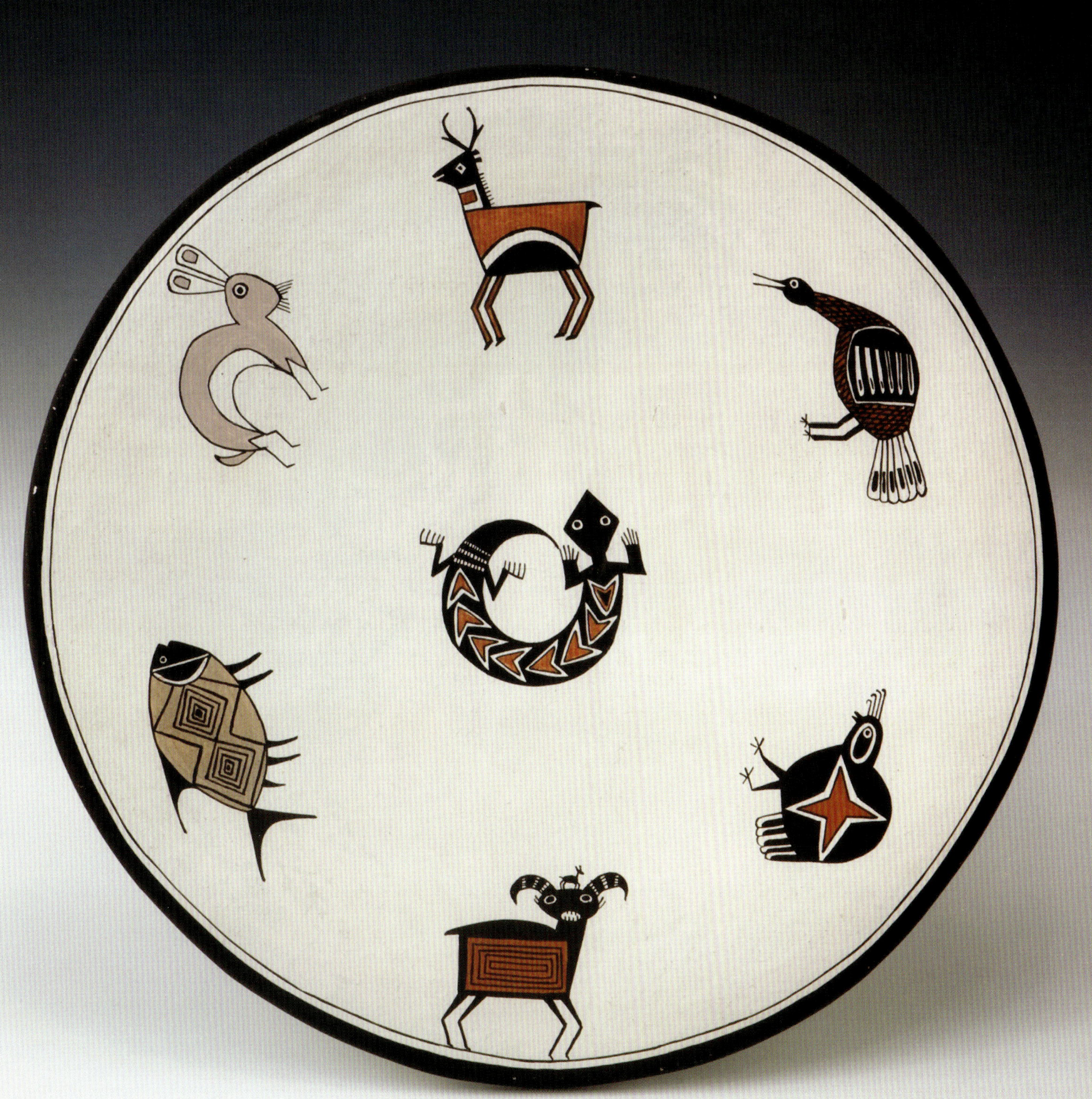

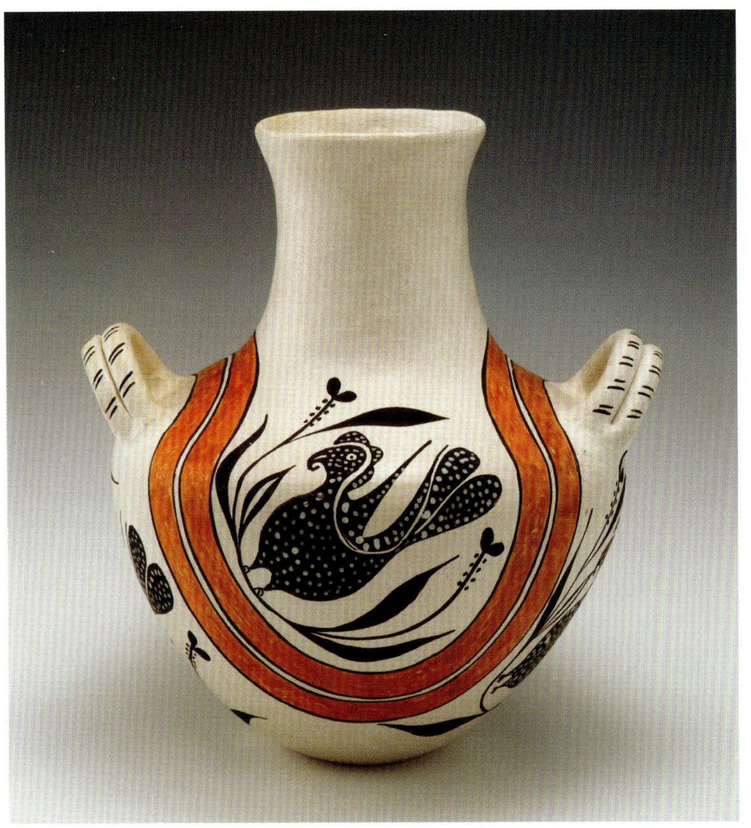

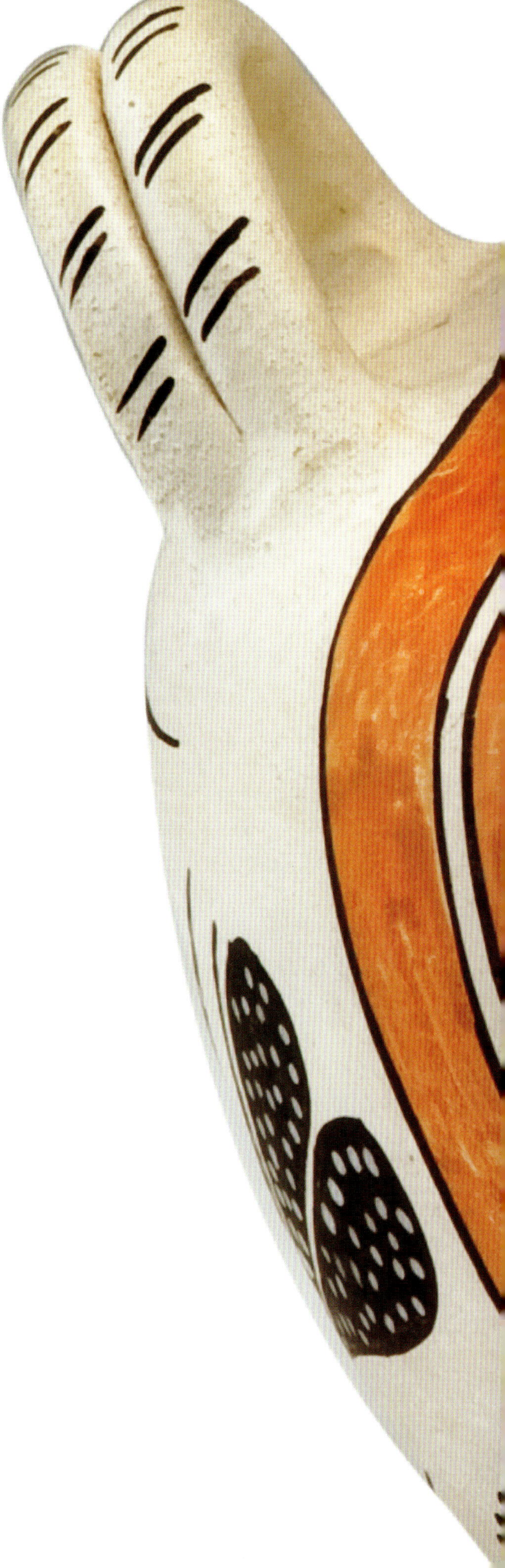

Plate 171 (detail, facing page)
Jessie Garcia (U.S., Acoma, c. 1920s–1990s)
Polychrome Jar with Handles, c. 1960
Native clays and paints, 10¼ × 8½ in.
Fred Jones Jr. Museum of Art
A2007.7046

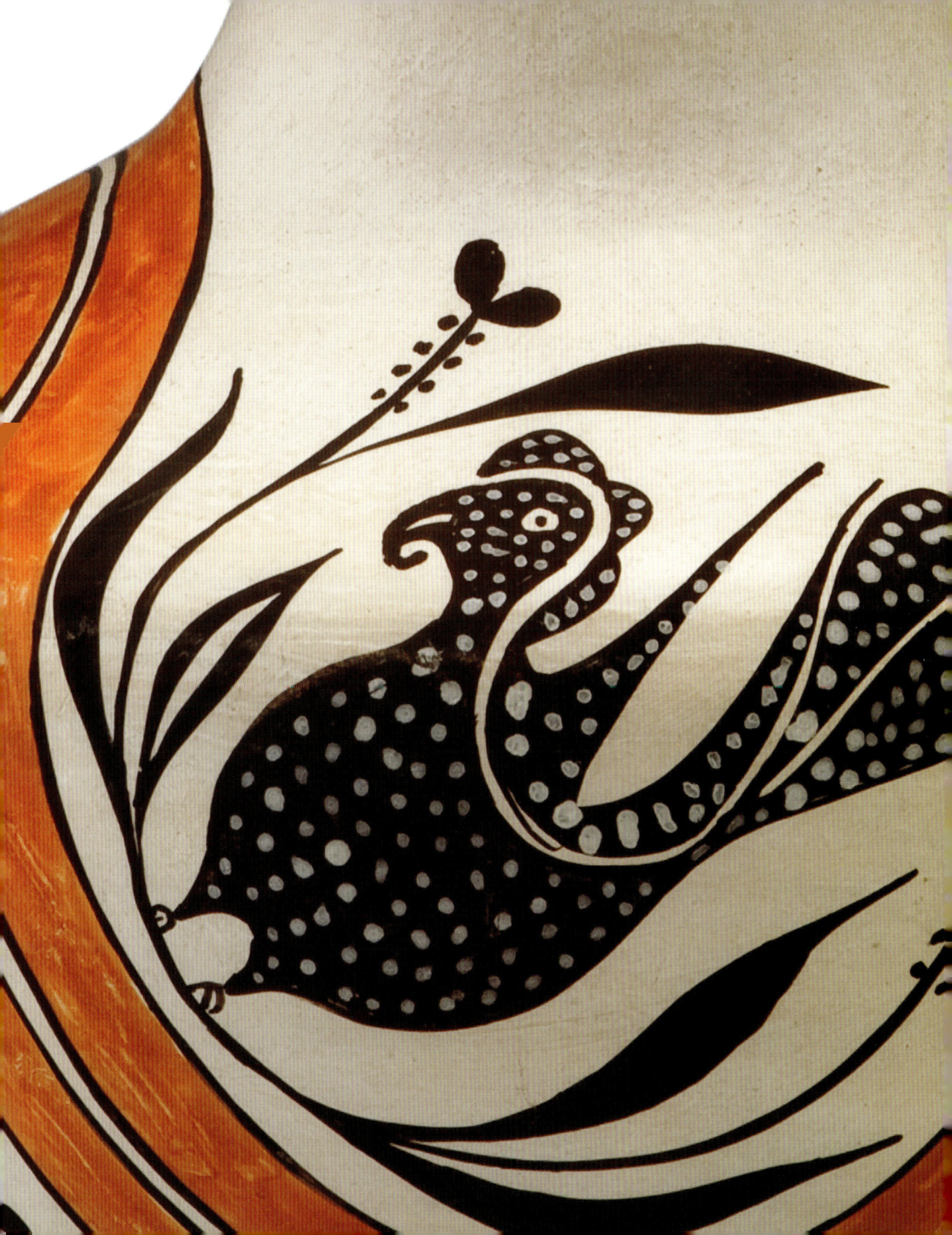

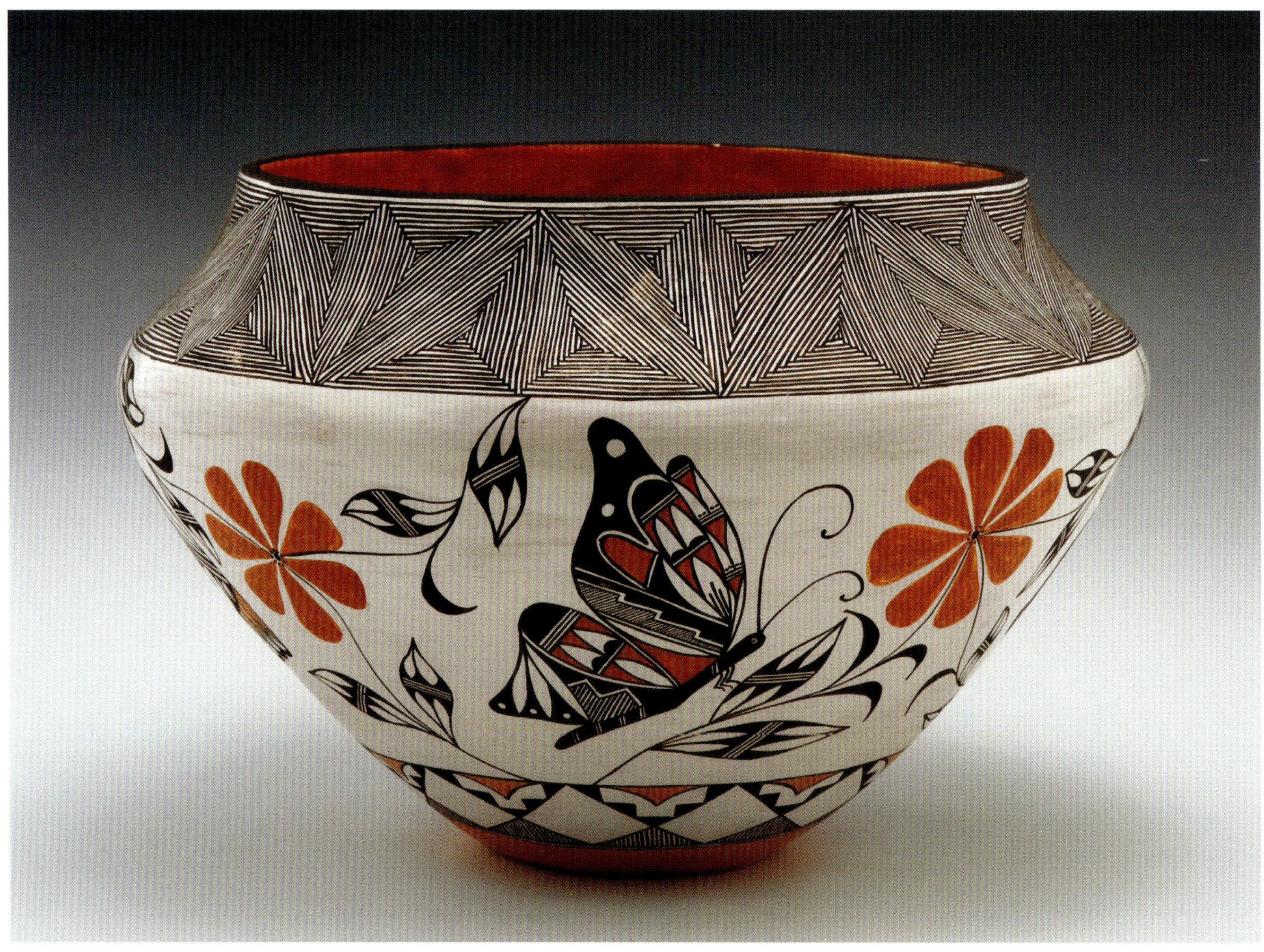

Plate 172
Rebecca Lucario (U.S., Acoma, b. 1951)
Polychrome Bowl, 1983. Native clays and paints, 8¼ × 12⅝ in.
Fred Jones Jr. Museum of Art
A2007.7181

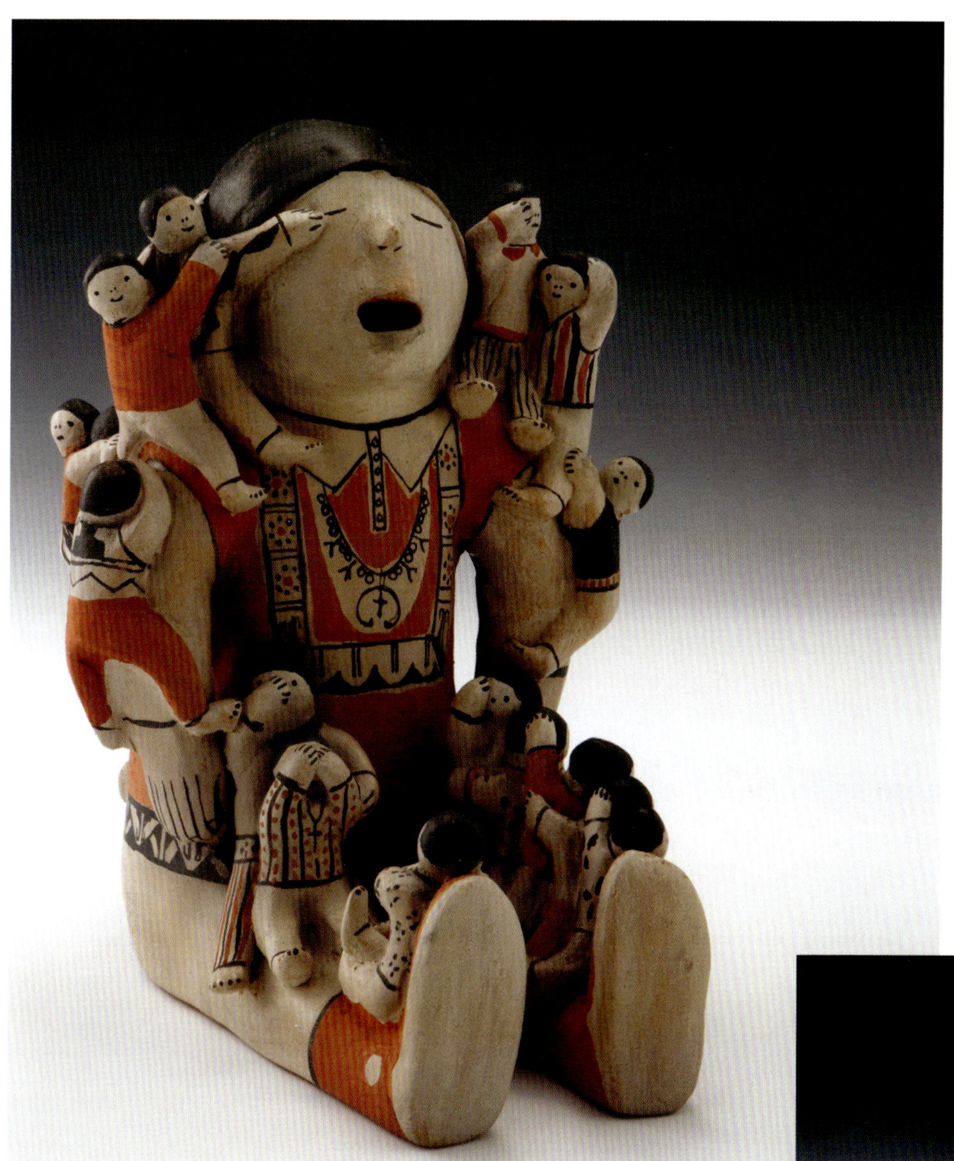

Plate 173
Helen Cordero (U.S., Cochiti, 1915–1994)
Storyteller, c. 1980. Native clays and paints, 9¼ × 7¼ × 9⅜ in.
Philbrook Museum of Art
A2007.7286

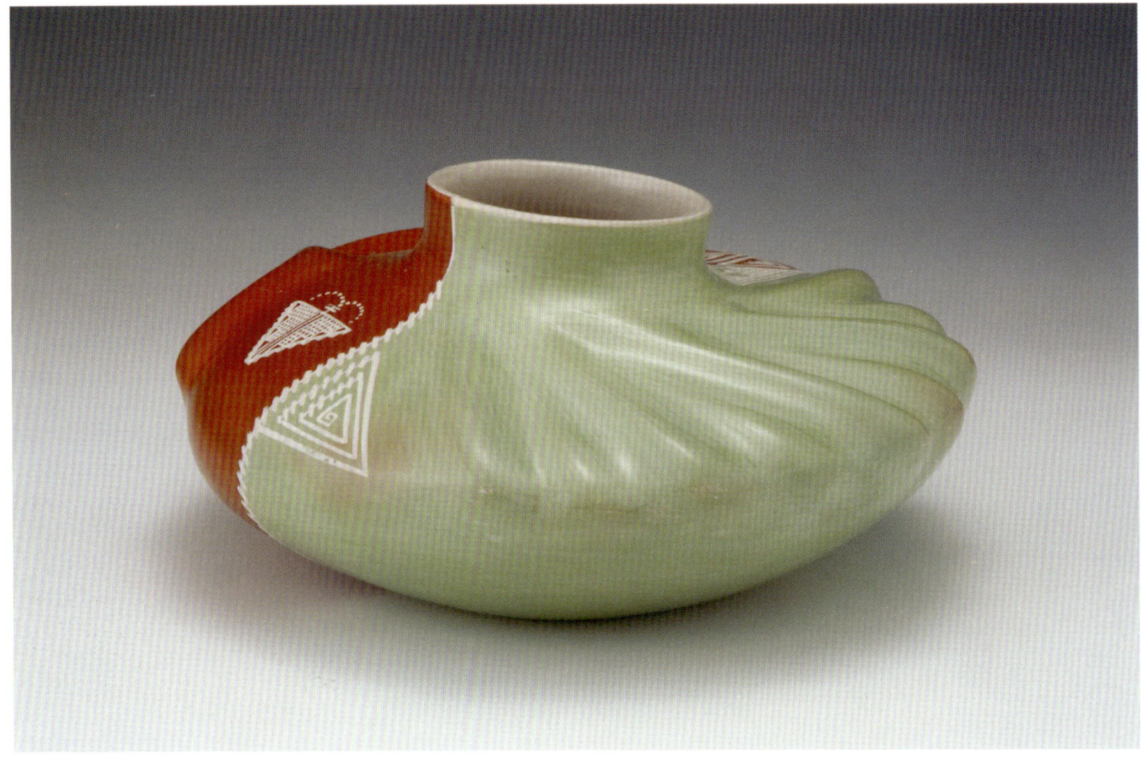

Plate 174 (above)
Nathan Begaye (U.S., Hopi/Navajo, 1959–2010)
Fluted Jar, c. 1980
Native clays, 3⅞ × 8⅛ in.
Fred Jones Jr. Museum of Art
A2007.7223

Plate 175 (facing page above)
Christine Nofchissey McHorse (U.S., Navajo, b. 1948)
Bowl, 1986. Native clay, 7 × 12⅝ in.
Fred Jones Jr. Museum of Art
A2007.7265

Plate 176 (facing page below)
Christine Nofchissey McHorse (U.S., Navajo, b. 1948)
Bowl, c. 1970. Native clay, 7½ × 14 in.
Philbrook Museum of Art
A2007.7329

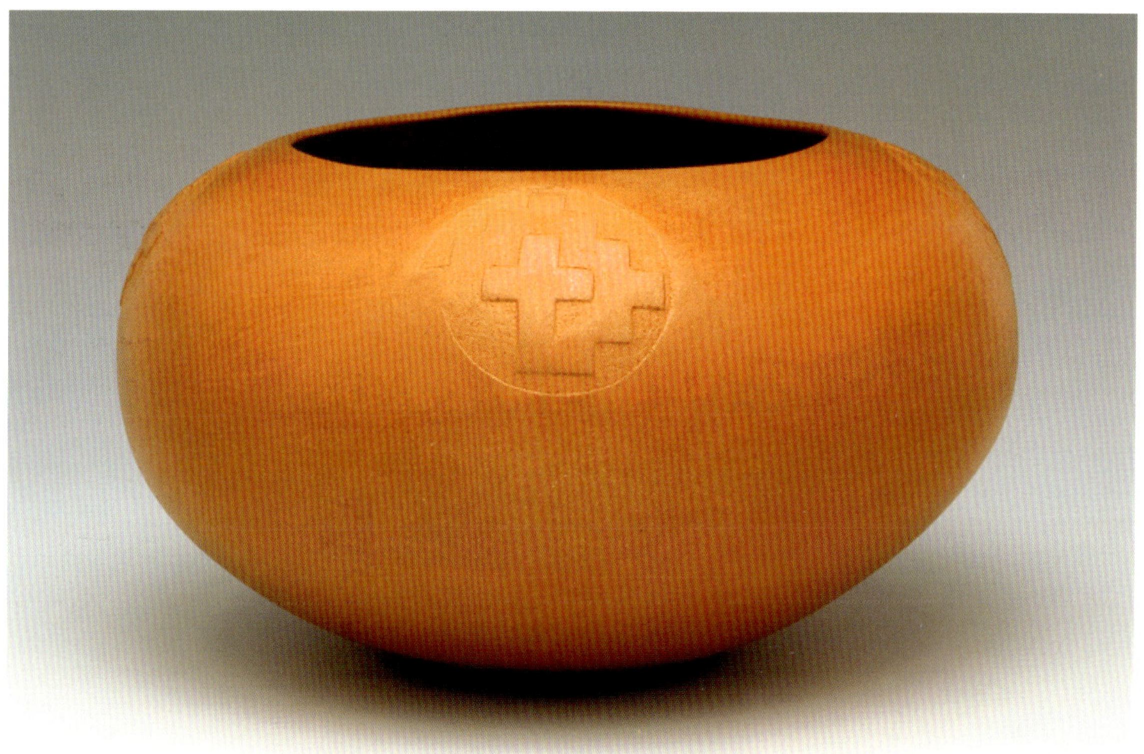

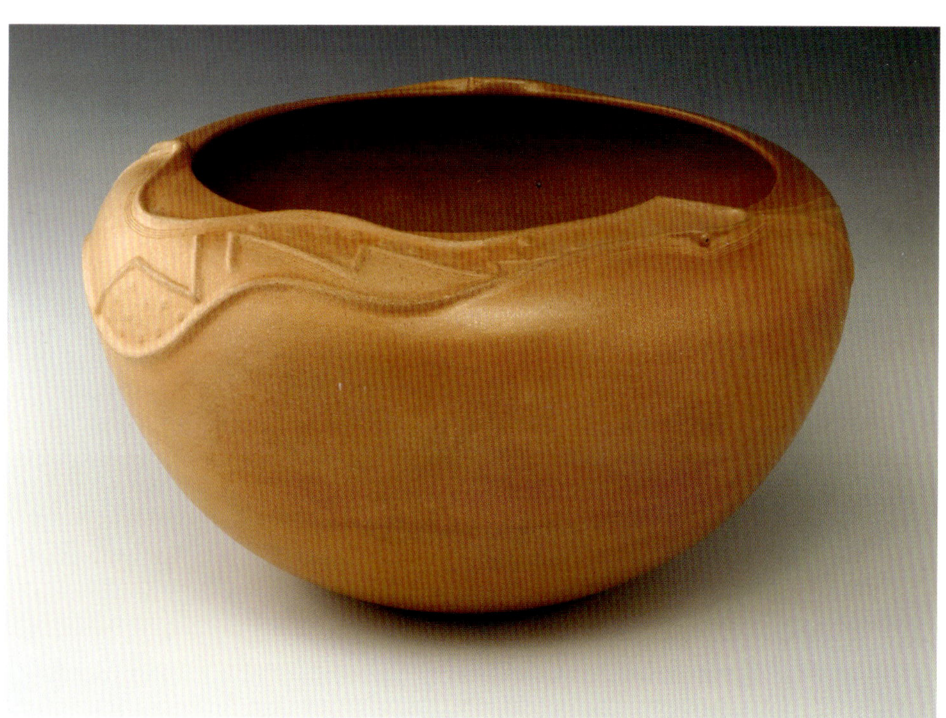

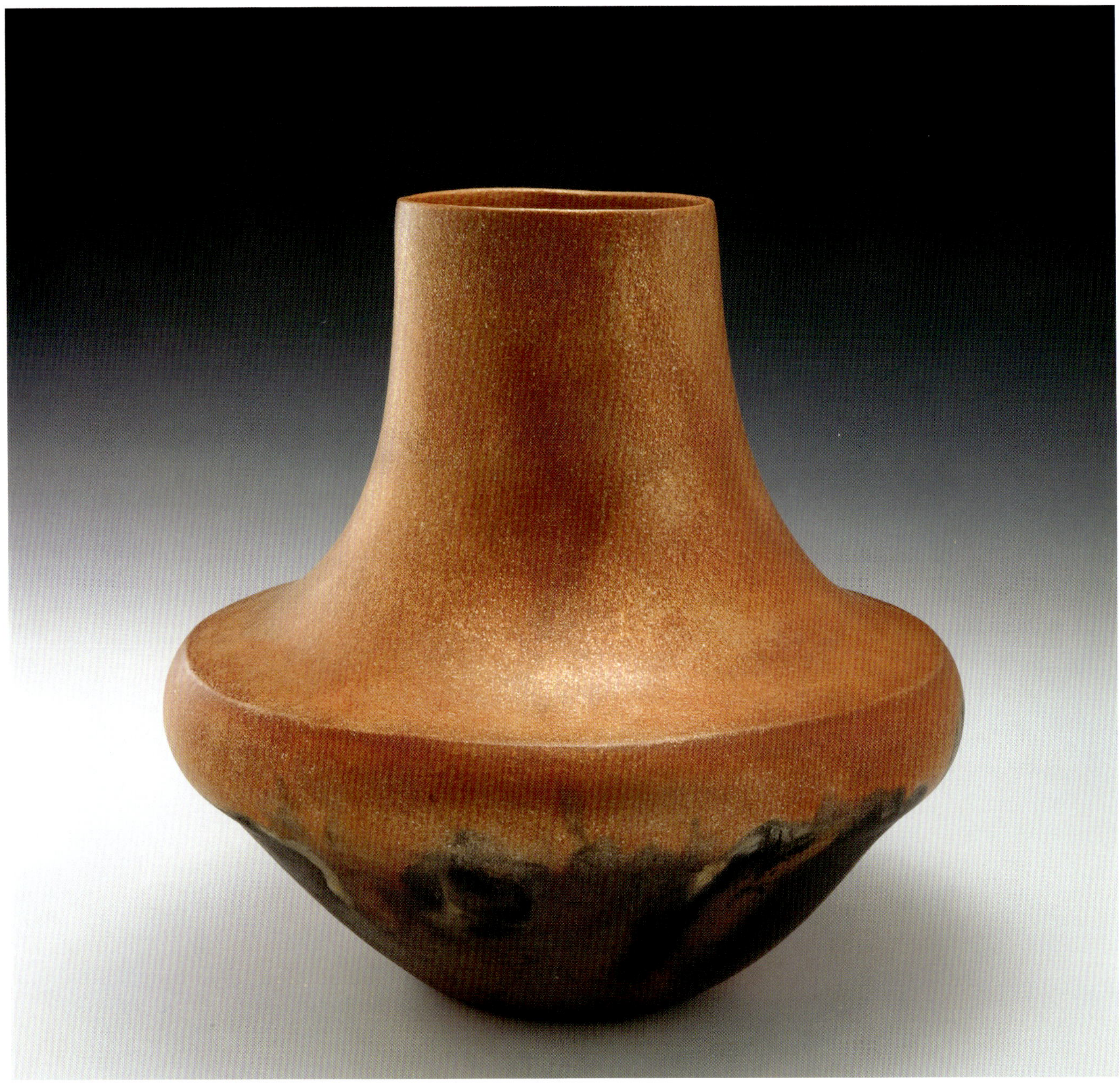

Plate 177
Lonnie Vigil (U.S., Nambe, b. 1949)
Micaceous Water Jar, 1990. Native clay, 16½ × 17⁵⁄₁₆ in.
Fred Jones Jr. Museum of Art
A2007.7000

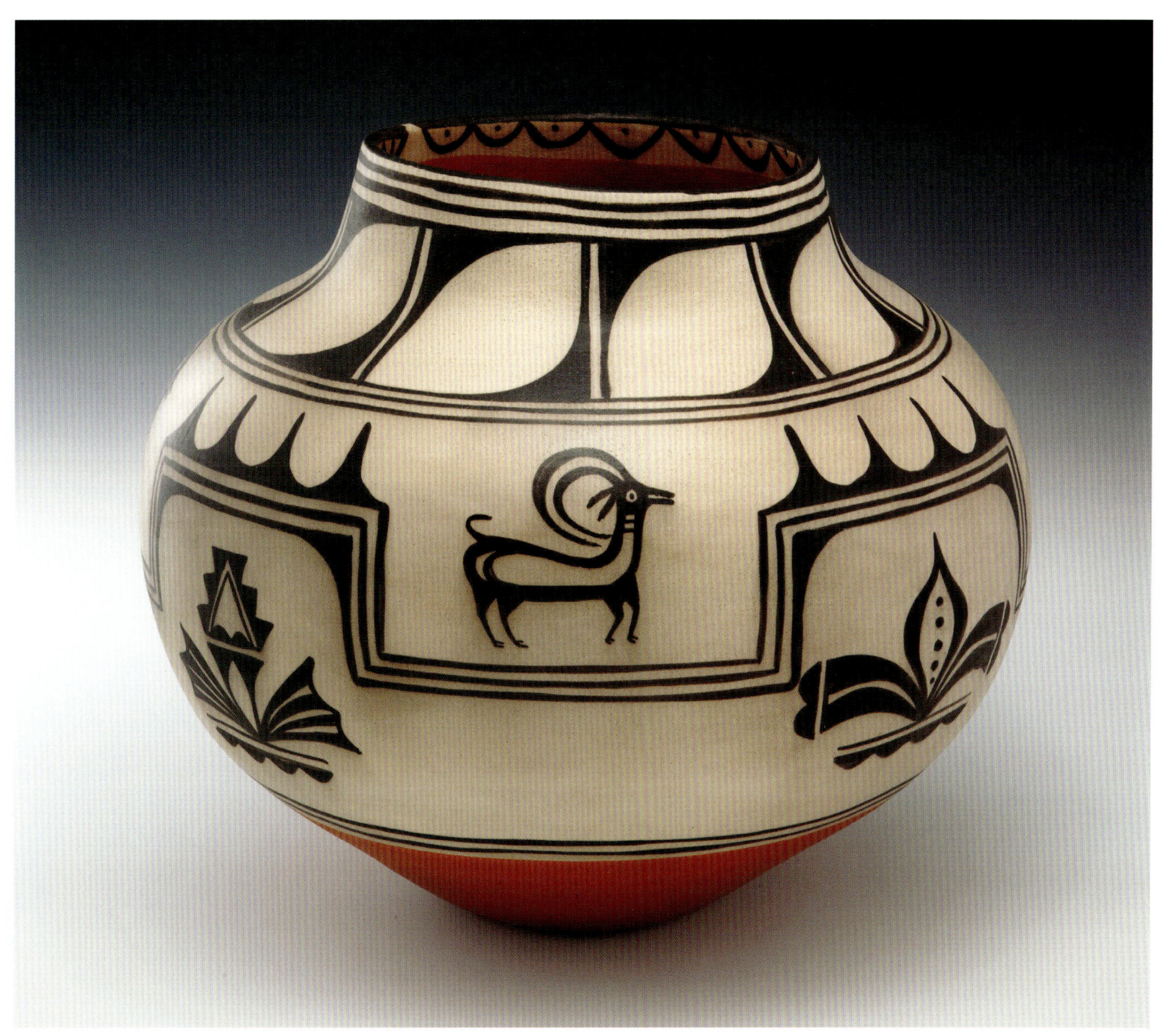

Plate 178
Robert Tenorio (U.S., Santo Domingo, b. 1950)
Storage Jar, 1980. Native clays and paints, 15 × 17¾ in.
Fred Jones Jr. Museum of Art
A2007.7014

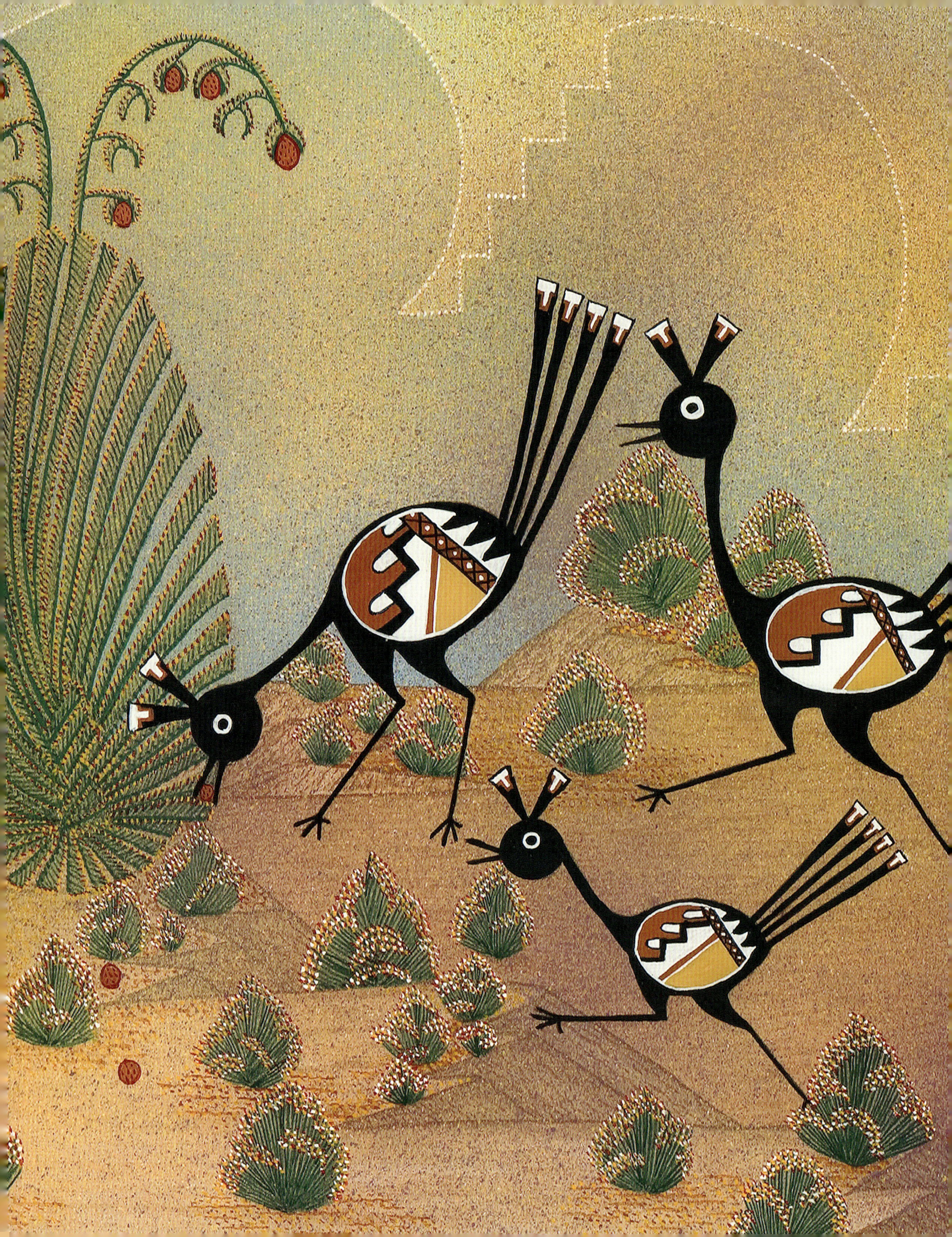

Notes

INTRODUCTION *The Collecting Odyssey of Eugene B. Adkins*

1. "Philbrook Museum and OU Receive Adkins Art Collection," www.artknowledgenews.com/Eugene_B_Adkins.html (accessed August 18, 2010).

2. Ibid.; Lynette Lobban, "Best of the West," *Sooner Magazine* (Spring 2008), www.oufoundation.org/sm/spring08/story.asp?ID=278 (accessed August 10, 2010); Joseph E. Howell, "Tate Brady: Tulsa's First Mr. Tulsa," *Tulsa Tribune*, undated clipping in Eugene Brady Adkins Library and Archives, Philbrook Museum of Art, Tulsa, Oklahoma [hereafter EBA Library and Archives]; Bessie LeClaire Brady Adkins, United Daughters of the Confederacy Certificate, April 192_, EBA Library and Archives.

3. James D. Watt, Jr., "Philbrook, OU to Share Art Collection," July 16, 2007, www.tulsaworld.com/news/article.aspx? articleID=070716_1_A1_ATTSJ31874 (accessed July 10, 2010); Old Man and Mama Thompson et al., postcard to EBA, postmarked February 5, 1943, EBA Library and Archives.

4. Barbara L. Eikner, "The Passion of the Collector," *Art Focus Oklahoma*, 23, no. 5, (September-October 2008): 12; St. John's College, Annapolis, Md., *Commencement Exercises Monday, June Fifteenth[,] Nineteen Hundred Fifty Three*, program in EBA Library and Archives; R.D.A. Puckle, "A Visit with Eugene Adkins," typed draft [1971], EBA Library and Archives.

5. Puckle, "A Visit with Eugene Adkins"; Thomas Goldthwaite, "Oklahoman Lends Collection of Western Art," *Arizona Republic*, November 14, 1971, 14–N.

6. Bess Brady Adkins married Sam Lacy of Tulsa after the death of Eugene Sloan Adkins in 1946. For examples of her collecting activities, see Philip Suval Antiques, New York, N.Y., bill of sale to Mrs. E. S. Adkins, February 17, 1943, and H. Peter Krause Antiques, Berlin, Germany, bill of sale to Mrs. Sam Lacy, Tulsa, Okla., March 31, 1960, EBA Library and Archives. For the gift to the Philbrook Art Center, see Philbrook Art Center, Tulsa, Okla., certificate for gifts, March 9, 1950, EBA Library and Archives; Christine Knop to Mrs. Sam W. Lacy, May 19 and July 12, 1983, EBA Library and Archives; Philbrook Art Center, Tulsa, Okla., loan form (return receipt), March 22, 1988, EBA Library and Archives.

7. For overviews of the collecting activities of Frank Phillips and Thomas Gilcrease, see Joe Williams, *Woolaroc* (Bartlesville, Okla.: Frank Phillips Foundation, 1991) and Duane King et al., *Thomas Gilcrease* (Tulsa, Okla.: Gilcrease Museum, 2009).

8. Eugene B. Adkins [hereafter EBA], copy of letter to [Dorothy] Brett, August 8, 1964, EBA Library and Archives.

9. Ibid.

10. For an overview of the era, see B. Byron Price, "Western Art Comes of Age," *Southwest Art* 25 (May 1996): 46, 48, 50, 52–56.

11. Puckle, "A Visit with Eugene Adkins"; Goldthwaite, "Oklahoman Lends Collection"; O'Brien's Art Emporium, Scottsdale, Ariz., invoice to EEBA, June 26, 1963, EBA Library and Archives; William V. O'Brien to Whom It May Concern, June 25, 1963, EBA Library and Archives.

12. Van Deren Coke, *Kenneth M. Adams: A Retrospective Exhibition* (Albuquerque: University of New Mexico Press, 1964); Ted Schuyler to EBA, May 13, 1964, EBA Library and Archives; Kenneth M. Adams to EBA, April 7, 1964, EBA Library and Archives.

13. Kenneth M. Adams to EBA, May 18, 1964, EBA Library and Archives.

14. Virginia Van Soelen to EBA, May 12 and June 4, 5, 1964, EBA Library and Archives; EBA, copy of letter to Virginia Van Soelen, June 7, 1964, EBA Library and Archives; Jane Hiatt, The Village Gallery, Taos, New Mexico, receipt to EBA, October 25, 1963, EBA Library and Archives.

15. Richard S. Morris, copy of letter to Paul Weaver, June 17, 1964, EBA Library and Archives; Frank Waters, *Of Time and Change: A Memoir* (Denver: McMurray and Beck, 1998), 116, 123–24; The Museum of New Mexico, Santa Fe, New Mexico, in loan agreement with EBA, September 9, 1965, EBA Library and Archives.

16. EBA, untitled handwritten notes [c. April 24, 1967], EBA Library and Archives; William M. Balfour to EBA, April 12 and May 3, 1967, EBA Library and Archives.

17. Goldthwaite, "Oklahoman Lends Collection."

18. R.D.A. Puckle to EBA, July 1, 23, and September 13, 1971, EBA Library and Archives. G. Clarke Bean to Member, December 1971, EBA Library and Archives.

DETAIL OF PLATE 67 (p. 115)
Pablita Velarde (U.S., Santa Clara, 1918–2006)
Mealtime on the Mesa, 1982

19. R.D.A. Puckle to EBA, September 21, 1971; Phoenix Art Museum, *Western Art from the Eugene B. Adkins Collection: Phoenix Art Museum, Western Art Associates, November 1971–January 1972* (Phoenix, Ariz.: Western Art Associates, 1971).

20. Phoenix Art Museum, *Western Art from the Eugene B. Adkins Collection*; "Along the Art Scene," *Scottsdale Daily Progress*, December 17, 1971, This Weekend sec.; Puckle, "A Visit with Eugene Adkins."

21. Mrs. John Porter Sands to EBA, November 2, 1971, EBA Library and Archives; "Western Art Opens at Phoenix Museum," *Courier* (Prescott, Ariz.), November 22, 1971, 5.

22. Marlan Miller, "Art Exhibits Picture the West," *Phoenix Gazette*, undated clipping, EBA Library and Archives.

23. "Along the Art Scene."

24. Ibid.

25. Quoted in Goldthwaite, "Oklahoman Lends Collection."

26. Ruth Koerner Oliver to EBA, January 10, 1972, EBA Library and Archives.

27. Ibid.

28. Adkins paid for his purchases in five installments, with the Oklahoma Museum of Art brokering the deal. See Oklahoma Museum of Art, Oklahoma City, invoice to EBA, January 31, 1969, EBA Library and Archives; Wolf Pogzeba to EBA, June 7, 1969, EBA Library and Archives; Pogzeba Art Studio, copy of payment to Oklahoma Museum of Art, May 31, 1969, EBA Library and Archives; EBA [collector's statement, 1972], EBA Library and Archives.

29. Barton A. Wright to EBA, November 15, 1971, and February 10, 1972, EBA Library and Archives; Museum of Northern Arizona, *The Art of Nicolai Fechin from the Collection of Eugene B. Adkins* (Flagstaff, Ariz.: Northland Press, 1972).

30. Fechin died in 1955. EBA, collector's statement.

31. Phoenix Art Museum, receipt to EBA, July 28, 1975, EBA Library and Archives; EBA to Ron Hickman, July 1, 1975, EBA Library and Archives; Phoenix Art Museum, *Nicolai Fechin 1881–1955, Phoenix Art Museum, March 26, 1976–May 9, 1976* (Phoenix: Museum, 1976). James K. Ballinger to EBA, January 28, 1976; Phoenix Art Museum, outgoing receipt to EAB, May 21, 1976; Phoenix Art Museum, deed of gift from EBA, December 13, 1999; James K. Ballinger to EBA, December 15, 1999; Phoenix Art Museum, deed of gift from EBA, December 30, 1999; James K. Ballinger to EBA, December 30, 1999, all in EBA Library and Archives.

32. National Collection of Fine Arts, Smithsonian Institution, loan agreement with EBA, December 24, 1971, EBA Library and Archives. Exhibit tour stops included Bucharest, Berlin, London, Zagreb, Madrid, and Istanbul. See National Collection of Fine Arts, Smithsonian Institution, loan agreement with EBA, March 31, 1972, EBA Library and Archives; Florine E. Lyons to EBA, August 24, 1972, EBA Library and Archives.

33. Gene [Adkins] postcard to EBA, August 17, 1994; Jerome Tiger to EBA, May 21, 1966; the Heard Museum, sales receipt to EBA, November 2, 1981; Jonathan Batkin to EBA, August 25, 2004, all in EBA Library and Archives. Ample evidence of Adkins's note-taking proclivities can be found throughout the EBA Library and Archives.

34. EBA [collector's statement].

35. Canyon Road Art Gallery, Santa Fe, NM [consignment agreements] with EBA, May 14 and December 14, 1971, January 12, August (n.d.), and October 16, 1972, and July 2, 10, 1974, EBA Library and Archives; O'Brien's Art Emporium, Scottsdale, Ariz., consignment receipt, November 14, 1972, EBA Library and Archives; Christie's, New York, N.Y., property receipt to EBA, September 25, 1992, and Christie's, New York, N.Y., consignment agreements with EBA, October 2, 1992, March 24, 1994, and April 6, 1995, EBA Library and Archives; Debra Force to EBA, April 17, 1991, and August 9, 1996, EBA Library and Archives.

36. I was among those present on the occasion described.

37. Eikner, "The Passion of the Collector," 12.

38. Quote from Margo Belden Todd to EBA, February 8, 1991, EBA Library and Archives.

39. Star and Paul Dyck to EBA, March 27, 1991, EBA Library and Archives; Vicente M. Martinez and Barbara Brenner to EBA, January 16, 1994, and Brenner appended note to EBA, dated January 14, 1994, EBA Library and Archives; Gene [Adkins] postcards to EBA, April 9 and October 8, 1991, and July 6, 1992, EBA Library and Archives.

40. See Gene [Adkins] postcards to EBA, March 3, April 9, and October 1, 5, and 8, 1991, EBA Library and Archives.

41. [Adkins] postcard to EBA, October 1, 1991.

42. [Adkins] postcard to EBA, October 5, 1991.

43. "Philbrook Museum and OU Receive Adkins Art Collection"; Lobban, "Best of the West."

Chapter 1. *Time and Modernity in the Art of the American Southwest*

1. Traditionally, the painting has been dated 1865, likely in part because Whittredge dated his trip as June 1865 to October 1866; however, he likely backdated the painting, since Pope did not leave on his inspection of the Department of the Missouri until

June 1, 1866. Since the tour lasted only four months and concluded by October, the painting should be dated 1866. For a discussion of Pope's assignment, see Peter Cozzens, *General John Pope: A Life for the Nation* (Urbana: University of Illinois Press, 2000), 272–75. For Whittredge's account of the trip, which does not mention the stop at Pecos, see John I. H. Baur, ed., *The Autobiography of Worthington Whittredge, 1820–1910* (New York: Arno Press, 1969), 45–53. On page 52, Baur notes that Pope inspected Fort Union; the party likely passed Pecos on the trip from Santa Fe to the fort.

2. For a history of Pecos Pueblo, see Frances Levine, *Our Prayers Are in This Place: Pecos Pueblo Identity over the Centuries* (Albuquerque: University of New Mexico Press, 1999).

3. Charles F. Lummis, "The Land of Poco Tiempo" *Scribner's Magazine* 10, no. 6 (December 1891): 760.

4. T. J. Jackson Lears has dubbed this cultural tendency antimodernism, or "the recoil from an 'overcivilized' modern existence to more intense forms of physical or spiritual experience." Although Lears observed that Americans tended to find escape in medieval and Oriental cultures, the American Southwest offered the key elements of antimodern desire: premodern cultures that had no connection to the dominant American faiths of Protestantism and positivism, and a less hospitable environment, whether mountains or desert, that demanded physical and mental vitality, resulting in an "authentic," or unmediated experience. *No Place of Grace: Antimodernism and the Transformation of American Culture, 1880–1920* (Chicago: University of Chicago Press, 1981), xv-xvi.

5. Walter Hough, *The Moki Snake Dance: A Popular Account of That Unparalleled Dramatic Pagan Ceremony of the Pueblo Indians of Tusayan, Arizona, with Incidental Mention of Their Life and Customs* (Chicago: Passenger Department, Santa Fe Route, 1898), 20–21.

6. John C. Van Dyke, *The Desert: Further Studies in Natural Appearances* (New York: Charles Scribner's Sons, 1901), x.

7. Martha Blue, *Indian Trader: The Life and Times of J. L. Hubbell* (Walnut, California: Kiva Publishing, 2000), 205.

8. Ibid., 37–41.

9. Borg quoted in Helen Laird, *Carl Oscar Borg and the Magic Region* (Layton, Utah: Gibbs M. Smith, 1986), 75.

10. Jessie A. Selkinghaus, "The Art of Carl Oscar Borg," *American Magazine of Art* 18, no. 3 (March 1927): 147.

11. Leigh, "My Life" (1952), an unpublished manuscript, quoted in June DuBois, *W. R. Leigh: The Definitive Illustrated Biography* (Kansas City, Mo.: Lowell Press, 1977), 63.

12. B. McArthur, "As the Artist Sees the World," in R. Brownell McGrew, *R. Brownell McGrew* (Kansas City, Mo.: Lowell Press, 1978), 4.

13. Maynard Dixon, "Navajo Land," *Arizona Highways* 34 (May 1942): 34.

14. For information on the Somaíkoli and Ya Ya Society, see Frank Waters, *Book of the Hopi* (New York: Ballantine Books, 1969), 300–302, and Elsie Worthington Clews Parsons, *Pueblo Indian Religion* (Chicago: University of Chicago Press, 1939), 920–21. Dixon may have been interested in the connection of Somaíkoli to witchcraft. Hagerty has noted that Dixon took special interest in the witchcraft legends of the Hopi. Donald Hagerty, *Desert Dreams: The Art and Life of Maynard Dixon* (Salt Lake City, Utah: Gibbs-Smith, 1998), 126.

15. Dixon to MacBeth, quoted in Hagerty, *Desert Dreams*, 119.

16. Sharyn R. Udall, "The Irresistible Other: Hopi Ritual Drama and Euro-American Audiences," in *Contested Terrain: Myth and Meaning in Southwest Art* (Albuquerque: University of New Mexico Press, 1996), 45.

17. Hough, *Moki Snake Dance*, 5. The snake dance is one part of an extensive ritual meant to create harmony between the Hopi and the cosmos, thus ensuring the necessary water for future harvests.

18. "Art Matters," *Chicago Daily Tribune*, November 1, 1897, 8.

19. "The Fiesta Art Exhibit," *El Palacio* 13, no. 8 (October 16, 1922): 99. Henderson exhibited *Walpi Snake Dance* at the 1922 Fiesta Exhibition at the Museum of New Mexico under the title *Snake Priests at Walpi.*

20. Carl Sandburg quoted in "Henderson's Pastels at Chicago," *El Palacio* 10, no. 8 (March 15, 1921): 2.

21. Mabel Dodge Luhan, *Taos and Its Artists* (New York: Duell, Sloan and Pearce, 1947), 16.

22. W. Herbert Dunton, "The Painters of Taos," *El Palacio* 13, no. 4 (15 August 1922): 45.

23. Julie Schimmel, *The Art and Life of W. Herbert Dunton, 1878–1936* (Austin: University of Texas Press, 1984), 60.

24. Dasburg quoted in Sheldon Reich, *Andrew Dasburg: His Life and Art* (Lewisburg, Pa.: Bucknell University Press, 1989), 104. The quote originated from an unedited transcript for Iris Jordan's 1976 film *Andrew Dasburg: Freedom from a Resisting World.*

25. Ward Lockwood asked Marin why his early watercolors in Taos were not very abstract, and Marin responded that "when the country is new I can't take any liberties with it at the start—so I look and search and paint what I see." Marin watercolors from later months are more typical to his oeuvre. Lockwood, "The Marin I Knew: A Personal Reminiscence," *Texas Quarterly* 10, no. 1 (Spring 1967): 109. Taos Mountain is the site of Blue Lake, the place of origin for the Taos people. President Theodore Roosevelt claimed the mountain and

surrounding forest in 1906 as part of the National Park Service, and the Pueblo fought to regain the territory until 1970, when President Richard Nixon returned it to them. For further information, see R. C. Gordon-McCutchan, *The Taos Indians and the Battle for Blue Lake* (Santa Fe, N.Mex.: Red Crane Books, 1991).

26. Vierra's obituary from the January 7, 1938, *Santa Fe New Mexican* is quoted in Arrell Morgan Gibson, *The Santa Fe and Taos Colonies: Age of the Muses, 1900–1942* (Norman: University of Oklahoma Press, 1983), 91.

27. Rose Henderson, "Architecture of the Southwest: New Type Evolved in New Mexico from Pueblos of the Indians and Missions of the Early Spanish Padres," *El Palacio* 16, no. 2 (15 January 1924): 19. Henderson reports that Oscar Berninghaus, Dunton, Bert Phillips, and Joseph Henry Sharp all built in the adobe style (20). For an insightful history of Santa Fe's architectural history, see Chris Wilson, *The Myth of Santa Fe: Creating a Modern Regional Tradition* (Albuquerque: University of New Mexico Press, 1997).

28. Van Deren Coke lists the date of *Interior of Church at Santa Cruz* as circa 1940. The photograph of the painting in *Taos and Santa Fe* indicates that Ellis may have retouched the floor in the painting sometime between the publication and Adkins's acquisition of the painting. Coke, *Taos and Santa Fe: The Artist's Environment, 1882–1942* (Albuquerque: University of New Mexico Press, 1963), 60.

29. Ibid., 22.

30. Dean Porter has dated *Ledoux Street* to circa 1918 in *Victor Higgins: An American Master* (Salt Lake City, Utah: Peregrine Smith Books, 1991), 69. Higgins lived on Ledoux for only a short time, and his exact residence there is unknown.

31. For more information, see Peter H. Hassrick, "Taos in the 1920s," in Peter Hassrick and Elizabeth J. Cunningham, , *In Contemporary Rhythm: The Art of Ernest L. Blumenschein* (Norman: University of Oklahoma Press, 2008), 192. In a 1929 meeting of the Taos Lion's Club, Blumenschein lamented what he considered a growing abandonment of traditional adobe building styles. *Village, Northern New Mexico* was a study for *Adobe Village—Winter* (1929).

32. William H. Truettner, "The Art of Pueblo Life," in Charles C. Eldredge, Julie Schimmel, and William H. Truettner, *Art in New Mexico, 1900–1945: Paths to Taos and Santa Fe* (New York: Abbeville Press, 1986), 59–60.

33. Dorothy Brett, "Painting Indians," *New Mexico Quarterly* 21, no. 2 (Summer 1951): 169.

34. "Gaspard Exhibit at Chicago," *El Palacio* 16, no. 11 (2 June 1924): 178.

35. According to Frank Waters, Gaspard and his guide, Stzanim Nagumba, were held for ransom by Yang San Hungstan, who threatened to behead them. Gaspard supposedly won his freedom by immortalizing the bandit in paint, thus impressing his captor. Gaspard made a small sketch from which he produced the later painting; Frank Waters, *Leon Gaspard* (Flagstaff, Arizona: Northland Press, 1981), 52–55. Waters admitted, however, that "Gaspard's stories cannot be substantiated by historical fact. Some of them are manifestly untrue" (6). Gaspard painted the image on silk as if to acknowledge the connection of his palette to textiles.

36. Mary N. Balcomb, *Nicolai Fechin* (Flagstaff, Ariz.: Northland Press, 1975), 47. Fechin painted *Negro Girl with Orange* while teaching at the New York Academy of Art at the Grand Central Gallery. The sitter's violet dress "inspired Fechin to place a peeled, ripe, succulent orange in her hand."

37. Van Deren Coke, *Taos and Santa Fe: The Artist's Environment, 1882–1942* (Albuquerque: University of New Mexico Press, 1963), 76–77.

38. Phillips's comment is posted on the back of the study for *Song to the Moonbow*. Julie Schimmel and Robert R. White, *Bert Geer Phillips and the Taos Art Colony* (Albuquerque: University of New Mexico, 1994), 256. Jacqueline Cochran, who owned the painting before Eugene Adkins, reported that Phillips had recounted his experience with the moonbow but was reticent to discuss it for fear no one would believe him. Jacqueline Cochran to Eugene B. Adkins, 17 July 1975, EBA Library and Archives.

39. Schimmel and White, *Bert Geer Phillips*, 162.

40. The Bursum Bill was introduced by New Mexican senator Holm Olaf Bursum to settle a land dispute between the Pueblo and non-Pueblo settlers. Many of the artists and writers responded to the Bursum Bill with the "Protest of Artists and Writers against the Bursum Bill." For more information, see Lynn Cline, *Literary Pilgrims: The Santa Fe and Taos Writers' Colonies, 1917–1950* (Albuquerque: University of New Mexico Press, 2007).

41. Virginia Couse Leavitt observed that her grandfather, who owned many of the pots in the painting, had enlarged most of the objects to stress their importance. Leavitt, *Eanger Irving Couse: Image Maker for America* (Albuquerque, N.Mex.: The Albuquerque Museum, 1991), 170. Leavitt also identifies the artifacts in the painting, which include an Apache water bottle and pottery from Acoma, Santa Clara, Santa Juan, San Ildefonso, and Taos.

42. Rose Henderson, "A Painter of Pueblo Indians," *American Magazine of Art* 11, no. 11 (September 1920): 400.

43. Dean Porter has dated *Indian Composition* to circa 1937 in *Victor Higgins*, 192.

44. Ibid., 190. Modernists sometimes connected feminine creativity to the body itself, and such connections were common for critics of Georgia O'Keeffe, although the artist often resisted such analogies. For more information, see Anna C. Chave, "O'Keeffe and the Masculine Gaze," *Art in America* 78, no. 1 (January 1990): 114–25, 177, 179.

45. Lula Merrick, "Walter Ufer, Painter of Indians," *International Studio* 77, no. 314 (July 1923): 299.

46. Dean Porter dates this work to circa 1935–1937 in *Victor Higgins*, 271.

47. Joseph Traugott, *The Art of New Mexico: How the West Is One* (Santa Fe: Museum of New Mexico Press, 2007), 150. Writer Richard Bradford referred to the atom bomb, and Los Alamos by implication, as a "watershed" in the history of Santa Fe. John Pen La Farge, ed., *Turn Left at the Sleeping Dog: Scripting the Santa Fe Legend, 1920–1955* (Albuquerque: University of New Mexico Press, 2001), 371.

48. Jerry West quoted in ibid., 372. The emphasis is West's.

Chapter 2. *The Character of a Collection*

1. Fred Maxwell to EBA, May 2, 1967, EBA Library and Archives.

2. Personal correspondence between author and Virginia Couse Leavitt, Kibby Couse's daughter and Eanger Irving Couse's granddaughter, March 19, 2009.

3. Barbara Mathes to EBA, June 1, 1984, EBA Library and Archives.

Chapter 3. *The Aesthetic and the Ethnographic*

1. While Lummis may have doubted photography's future in the Southwest, it is abundantly apparent that the landscape and its people offer unlimited artistic inspiration, and photography continues to play a dominant role in the arts of the Southwest. Charles F. Lummis, "The Land of Poco Tiempo," *Scribner's Magazine* 10, no. 6 (December 1891): 764.

2. Laura Gilpin, *The Enduring Navajo*, 3rd paperback ed. (Austin: University of Texas Press, 1994), 250.

3. William Clift quoted in Thomas F. Barrow, *Photography: New Mexico* (Albuquerque, N.Mex.: Fresco Fine Art Publications, 2008), 71.

Chapter 4. *Influence and Invention*

1. See Lowery Stokes Sims, ed., *Fritz Scholder: Indian Not Indian* (New York: Prestel for the National Museum of the American Indian, 2008).

2. See W. Jackson Rushing, *Native American Art and the New York Avant-Garde: A History of Cultural Primitivism* (Austin: University of Texas Press, 1995), 13–24.

3. David W. Penney and Lisa A. Roberts, "America's Pueblo Artists: Encounters on the Borderlands," in *Native American Art in the Twentieth Century*, ed. W. Jackson Rushing III (New York and London: Routledge, 1999), 25.

4. For the summer project and the IAIA, see Joy L. Gritton, *The Institute of American Indian Arts: Modernism and U.S. Indian Policy* (Albuquerque: University of New Mexico Press, 2000). On Joe Herrera and Pueblo modernism, see my essay, "Modern By Tradition," in Bruce Bernstein and W. Jackson Rushing, *Modern by Tradition: American Indian Painting in the Studio Style* (Santa Fe: Museum of New Mexico Press, 1995), 61–73.

5. Nancy J. Parezo, *Navajo Sandpainting: From Religious Act to Commercial Art* (Albuquerque: University of New Mexico Press, 1983), 89.

6. For Nampeyo, see Barbara Kramer, *Nampeyo and Her Pottery* (Albuquerque: University of New Mexico Press, 1996). For Dextra Quotskuyva, see Martha H. Struever, *Painted Perfection: The Pottery of Dextra Quotskuyva* (Santa Fe, N.Mex.: Wheelwright Museum of the American Indian, 2001). For Narciso Abeyta, see Dorothy Dunn, *American Indian Painting of the Southwest and Plains Area* (Albuquerque: University of New Mexico Press, 1968), 302–303, 319, 349.

7. See Jeanne Shutes and Jill Mellick, *The Worlds of P'otsúnú: Geronima Cruz Montoya of San Juan Pueblo* (Albuquerque: University of New Mexico Press, 1996).

8. See W. Jackson Rushing, *Allan Houser: An American Master* (New York: Harry N. Abrams, 2004), 132.

Chapter 5. *Tradition and Innovation*

1. Jewelry and fetishes are integrated into a single category for several reasons. One is that many of the same materials and techniques are used in both, specifically lapidary work on turquoise and other stones. Another is that fetishes are the primary component of some jewelry (see the necklace by Zuni carver David Tsikewa, plate 84). Sometimes artists might add a fetish to silver or other materials to create a ring, bracelet,

or buckle (see the piece by Zuni master carver Leekya Deyuse, plate 103). Christina E. Burke, "Jewelry and Silverwork in the Eugene B. Adkins Collection," *American Indian Art* 34, no. 3 (Autumn 2009): 40–49, 82.

2. Deborah C. Slaney, *Blue Gem, White Metal: Carvings and Jewelry from the C. G. Wallace Collection* (Phoenix, Ariz.: Heard Museum, 1998); Kathleen L. Howard and Diana F. Pardue, *Inventing the Southwest: The Fred Harvey Company and Native American Art* (Flagstaff, Ariz.: Northland Press, 1996); E. W. Jernigan, *White Metal Universe: Navajo Silver from the Fred Harvey Collection* (Phoenix, Ariz.: Heard Museum, 1981); Allison Bird, "Jewelry Collection at the School of American Research," *American Indian Art* 18, no. 4 (Autumn 1993): 56–63.

3. Diana F. Pardue, *Contemporary Southwestern Jewelry* (Layton, Utah: Gibbs Smith, 2007).

4. Kari Chalker, ed., *Totems to Turquoise: Native North American Jewelry Arts of the Northwest and Southwest* (New York: Harry N. Abrams, 2004); Dexter Cirillo, "Back to the Past: Tradition and Change in Contemporary Pueblo Jewelry," *American Indian Art* 13, no. 2 (Spring 1988): 46–55, 60, 63; Dexter Cirillo, *Southwestern Indian Jewelry: Crafting New Traditions* (New York: Rizzoli, 2008); Diana F. Pardue, *The Cutting Edge: Contemporary Southwestern Jewelry and Metalwork* (Phoenix, Ariz.: Heard Museum, 1996); Pardue, *Contemporary Southwestern Jewelry*.

5. In repoussé, the stamp is placed on the reverse or underside of the piece so that the design is raised or embossed on the front.

6. In channel inlay, shell and stone pieces are separated by a thin channel of silver.

7. Dexter Cirillo, "Back to the Past: Tradition and Change in Contemporary Pueblo Jewelry," *American Indian Art* 13, no. 2 (Spring 1988): 46–55, 60, 63; Dexter Cirillo, *Southwestern Indian Jewelry*; Slaney, *Blue Gem, White Metal*; Shelby Tisdale, *Fine Indian Jewelry of the Southwest: The Millicent Rogers Museum Collection* (Santa Fe, N.Mex.: Museum of New Mexico, 2006).

8. Jerry D. Jacka, "Innovations in Southwestern Indian Jewelry: Fine Art in the 1980s," *American Indian Art* 9, no. 1 (1984): 30.

9. Slaney, *Blue Gem, White Metal*.

10. Cirillo, "Back to the Past," 48; Chalker *Totems to Turquoise*; Slaney, *Blue Gem, White Metal*.

11. For a history of such pieces, see Allison Bird, *Heart of the Dragonfly: Historical Development of the Cross Necklaces of the Pueblo and Navajo Peoples* (Albuquerque: University of New Mexico, 1992).

12. Jacka, "Innovations," 33 (plate 101).

13. Cirillo "Back to the Past," 46–50.

14. Although this piece is not signed, it is attributed to Lambert Homer (Zuni), a master jeweler who was known to create such pieces, often in collaboration with Navajo jewelers such as Roger Skeet, Sr. who did the silversmithing. See Slaney, *Blue Gem, White Metal*, 46–47.

15. See Deborah C. Slaney, "Zuni Figurative Carving from the C. G. Wallace Collection," *American Indian Art* 19, no. 1 (Winter 1993): 69–75. and Jim Ostler, "Zuni Fetishes: Art and Change," *American Indian Art* 25, no. 4 (Autumn 2000): 38–45, 80.

16. This piece is illustrated in the auction catalogue, Lot #241, p. 46, Sotheby Parke Bernet Sale No. 3806, Sotheby Parke Bernet, 1975. See Slaney, *Blue Gem, White Metal*.

17. This was probably purchased at a one-man show the Heard Museum hosted for Loloma in December 1971; see Loloma show brochure, with notations and prices, EBA Library and Archives.

18. Begay was prolific at creating serviceware, much of which he sold through the White Hogan, a gallery owned by trader John Bonnell, which began in Flagstaff in 1950 and later moved to Scottsdale.

19. Streuver, Martha H. *Loloma: Beauty Is His Name* (Santa Fe, N.Mex.: Wheelwright Museum of the American Indian, 2005).

Chapter 6. *Materials of the Earth and Its People*

Epigraph: Clara Lee Tanner, *Prehistoric Southwestern Craft Arts* (Tucson: University of Arizona Press, 1976), 15.

1. Ibid., 16.

2. Sara Peabody Turnbaugh and William A. Turnbaugh, *Indian Baskets* (West Chester, Pa.: Schiffer Publishing, 1986), 233.

3. The 1967 award-winning basket of Chester Yellowhair (Navajo), a male weaver, is in the Adkins Collection. Numerous male weavers are currently in the Navajo tribe and among the Hopi.

4. J. Walter Fewkes, "Hopi Basket Dances," *Journal of American Folklore* 12, no. 45 (April-June 1899): 81–96. This article discusses the basket dances of the Hopi women at the end of a ceremony called the Lalakonti.

5. Bruce Bernstein, *The Language of Native American Baskets: From the Weavers' Point of View* (Washington D.C.: Smithsonian Institution, 2003), 10.

6. Susan Brown McCreevy, *Indian Basketry Artists of the Southwest* (Santa Fe, N.Mex.: School of American Research, 2001), 16–17.

7. Clara Lee Tanner, *Indian Baskets of the Southwest* (Tucson: University of Arizona, 1983), 41.

8. Tanner, *Indian Baskets of the Southwest,* 15.

9. Estelle Reel, U.S. Department of the Interior, *Course of Study for the Indian Schools of the United States—Industrial and Literary* (Washington , D.C.: Government Printing Office, 1901), 27.

10. Larry Dalrymple, *Indian Basketmakers of the American Southwest* (Santa Fe: Museum of New Mexico Press, 2000), 1.

11. Gregory Schaaf, *American Indian Baskets I* (Santa Fe, N.Mex.: CIAC Press, 2006), 165.

12. Lydia L. Wyckoff, ed., *Woven Worlds: Basketry from the Clark Field Collection at the Philbrook Museum of Art* (Tulsa, Okla.: Philbrook Museum of Art, 1996), 87.

13. Schaaf, *American Indian Baskets,* 165.

14. Ibid.

15. Jerold L. Collings, "Profile of a Chemehuevi Basket Weaver," *American Indian Art Magazine* 4, no. 4 (Autumn 1979): 63.

16. Wyckoff, *Woven Worlds,* 87–88.

17. Schaaf, *American Indian Baskets,* 165.

18. Ibid., 169.

19. Larry Dalrymple, *Indian Basketmakers of California and the Great Basin* (Santa Fe: Museum of New Mexico Press, 2000), 34–35.

20. Ibid., 48.

21. For an insightful look at this relationship, see Marvin Cohodas, "Louisa Keyser and the Cohns: Mythmaking and Basket Making in the American West," in *The Early Years of Native American Art History,* ed. Janet Catherine Berlo (Seattle: University of Washington Press, 1992), 88–133.

22. Dalrymple, *Indian Basketmakers of California,* 48.

23. Schaaf, *American Indian Baskets,* 189.

24. Dalrymple, *Indian Basketmakers of California,* 50.

25. Tanner: *Indian Baskets of the Southwest,* 49.

26. Helga Teiwes, *Hopi Basket Weaving: Artistry in Natural Fibers* (Tucson: University of Arizona Press, 1996), 51–59; McCreevy, *Indian Basketry Artists of the Southwest,* 72. Paybacks are plaques that are a means of returning favors for a woman's wedding robes or other work provided to families and clan relatives.

27. Schaaf, *American Indian Baskets,* 50.

28. McCreevy, *Indian Basketry Artists of the Southwest,* 72.

29. Teiwes, *Hopi Basket Weaving,* 32–49.

30. Andrew Hunter Whitford, "Pueblo and Athabascan Baskets in the Southwest," in *I Am Here: Two Thousand Years of Southwest Indian Art and Culture* (Santa Fe: Museum of New Mexico Press, 1989), 10–27.

31. Georgiana Kennedy Simpson, *Navajo Ceremonial Baskets* (Summertown, Tenn.: Native Voices, 2003), 34.

32. Simpson, *Navajo Ceremonial Baskets,* 42

33. Tanner, *Prehistoric Southwestern Craft Arts,* 49.

34. Ibid., 49, 56–57.

35. Marian Rodee, *Weaving of the Southwest* (West Chester, Pa.: Schiffer Publishing, 1987), vi.

36. Tanner, *Prehistoric Southwestern Craft Arts,* 50.

37. Ibid., 52.

38. Paul S. Martin, "Prehistory: Mogollon," in *Southwest,* vol. 9 of *Handbook of North American Indians* (Washington: Smithsonian Institution, 1979), 61–74 (see p. 65).

39. David W. Penney, *North American Indian Art* (New York: Thames and Hudson, 2004), 92.

40. Ibid. 87.

41. Tanner, *Prehistoric Southwestern Craft Arts,* 66–92.

42. Rodee, *Weaving of the Southwest,* 10.

43. Ibid.

44. Ibid.

45. Ibid., 39.

46. Teresa J. Wilkins, *Patterns of Exchange: Navajo Weavers and Traders* (Norman: University of Oklahoma Press, 2008). Wilkins presents an interesting view of the influence of traders among the Navajo and the respondent culture that ensued between these two entities.

47. Eulalie H. Bonar, ed, *Woven by the Grandmothers* (Washington, D.C.: National Museum of the American Indian, 1996), 75.

48. Gregory Schaaf, *American Indian Textiles* (Santa Fe, N.Mex.: CIAC Press, 2001), 7.

49. Bonar, *Woven by the Grandmothers,* 1.

50. Tyrone Campbell, Joel Kopp, and Kate Kopp, *Navajo Pictorial Weaving 1880–1950* (New York: Dutton Studio Books, 1991), 10. It is interesting to note that about the same time, potters at the various pueblos began making clay images of trains, whose presence changed the way Native peoples practiced the arts in much of the American Southwest.

51. Ibid., 1–84.

52. Rodee, *Weaving of the Southwest,* 14.

Select Bibliography

Archives

Adkins, Eugene Brady. Library and Archives, Philbrook Museum of Art, Tulsa, Oklahoma.

Books and Articles

Arizona Highways. *Turquoise Blue Book and Indian Jewelry Digest.* Arizona Highways Collectors Series. Phoenix: Arizona Highways, 1975.

Artists of Santa Fe: Their Works and Words. Santa Fe, N.Mex.: C. R. Wenzell, 1965.

Bahti, Mark. *Silver + Stone: Profiles of American Indian Jewelers,* Tucson, Ariz.: Rio Nuevo, 2007.

Balcomb, Mary N. *Nicolai Fechin.* Flagstaff, Ariz.: Northland Press, 1975.

Ballinger, James K., and Andrea D. Rubenstein. *Visitors to Arizona: 1846–1980.* Phoenix, Ariz.: Phoenix Art Museum, 1980.

Barrow, Thomas F. *Photography: New Mexico.* Albuquerque, N.Mex.: Fresco Fine Art Publications, 2008.

Barter, Judith. *Window on the West: Chicago and Art of the New Frontier, 1890–1940.* Chicago: Art Institute of Chicago, 2003.

Baur, John I. H., ed. *The Autobiography of Worthington Whittredge, 1820–1910.* New York: Arno Press, 1969.

Bell, David, and Daphne Anderson Deeds. *William Penhallow Henderson: Master Colorist of Santa Fe.* Phoenix: Phoenix Art Museum, 1984.

Berlo, Janet. *Early Years of Native American Art History: The Politics of Scholarship and Collecting.* Seattle: University of Washington Press, 1992.

Bernstein, Bruce. *The Language of Native American Baskets: From the Weavers' Point of View.* Washington D.C.: Smithsonian Institution, 2003.

Bernstein, Bruce, and W. Jackson Rushing. *Modern by Tradition: American Indian Painting in the Studio Style.* Santa Fe: Museum of New Mexico Press, 1995.

Bickerstaff, Laura M. *Pioneer Artists of Taos.* Denver: Sage Books, 1955.

Bird, Allison. *Heart of the Dragonfly: Historical Development of the Cross Necklaces of the Pueblo and Navajo Peoples.* Albuquerque: University of New Mexico, 1992.

DETAIL OF PLATE 164 (p. 230)
Marie Zieu Chino (U.S., Acoma, 1907–1982)
Black on White Jar, 1965

———. "Jewelry Collection at the School of American Research." *American Indian Art* 18, no. 4 (Autumn 1993): 56–63.

Bird, Gail, et al. *Be Dazzled! Masterworks of Jewelry and Beadwork from the Heard Museum,* Phoenix, Ariz.: Heard Museum, 2002.

Blue, Martha. *Indian Trader: The Life and Times of J. L. Hubbell.* Walnut, Calif.: Kiva Publishing, 2000.

Blumenschein, Ernest L., and Bert G. Phillips. "Appreciation of Indian Art." *El Palacio* 6, no. 12 (May 24, 1919): 178–79.

Bonar, Eulalie H., ed. *Woven by the Grandmothers.* Washington, D.C.: National Museum of the American Indian, 1996.

Brett, Dorothy. "Painting Indians." *New Mexico Quarterly* 21, no. 2 (Summer 1951): 167–73.

Broder, Patricia Janice. *Taos: A Painter's Dream.* Boston: New York Graphic Society, 1980.

Brody, J. J. *Indian Painters and White Patrons.* Albuquerque: University of New Mexico Press, 1971.

———. *Pueblo Indian Paintings: Tradition and Modernism in New Mexico, 1900–1930.* Santa Fe, N.Mex.: School for Advanced Research Press, 1997.

Burke, Christina E. "Jewelry and Silverwork in the Eugene B. Adkins Collection." *American Indian Art* 34, no. 3 (Autumn 2009): 40–49, 82.

Burke, Flannery. *From Greenwich Village to Taos: Primitivism and Place at Mabel Dodge Luhan's.* Lawrence: University of Kansas Press, 2008.

Cahill, E. H. "America Has Its Primitives." *International Studio* 75 (March 1920): 80–83.

Campbell, Tyrone, Joel Kopp, and Kate Kopp. *Navajo Pictorial Weaving.* New York: Dutton Studio Books, 1991.

Chalker, Kari, ed. *Totems to Turquoise: Native North American Jewelry Arts of the Northwest and Southwest.* New York: Harry N. Abrams, 2004.

Chave, Anna C. "O'Keeffe and the Masculine Gaze." *Art in America* 78, no. 1 (January 1990): 114–25, 177, 179.

Cirillo, Dexter. "Back to the Past: Tradition and Change in Contemporary Pueblo Jewelry." *American Indian Art* 13, no. 2 (Spring 1988): 46–55, 60, 63.

———. *Southwestern Indian Jewelry: Crafting New Traditions,* New York: Rizzoli, 2008.

Cline, Lynn. *Literary Pilgrims: The Santa Fe and Taos Writers' Colonies, 1917–1950.* Albuquerque: University of New Mexico Press, 2007.

Cohodas, Marvin. "Louisa Keyser and the Cohns: Mythmaking and Basket Making in the American West." In *The Early Years of Native American Art History*, edited by Janet Catherine Berlo, 88–133. Seattle: University of Washington Press, 1992.

Coke, Van Deren. *Andrew Dasburg*. Albuquerque: University of New Mexico Press, 1979.

———. *Kenneth M. Adams: A Retrospective Exhibition.* Albuquerque: University of New Mexico Press, 1964.

———. *Taos and Santa Fe: The Artist's Environment, 1882–1942.* Albuquerque: University of New Mexico Press, 1963.

Collings, Jerold L. "Profile of a Chemehuevi Basket Weaver." *American Indian Art Magazine* 4, no. 4 (Autumn 1979): 60–67.

Cosentino, Andrew J. *The Paintings of Charles Bird King (1785–1862).* Washington, D.C.: Smithsonian Institution, 1977.

Cozzens, Peter. *General John Pope: A Life for the Nation.* Urbana: University of Illinois Press, 2000.

Current, Karen. *Photography and the Old West.* New York: Harry N. Abrams, 1978.

Curtis, Natalie. "A New Art in the West." *International Studio* 63 (November 1917): xiv-xvii.

———. "The Perpetuating of Indian Art." *Outlook* 105 (November 22, 1913): 623–31.

Dalrymple, Larry. *Indian Basketmakers of the American Southwest.* Santa Fe: Museum of New Mexico Press, 2000.

———. *Indian Basketmakers of California and the Great Basin.* Santa Fe: Museum of New Mexico Press, 2000.

d'Harnoncourt, Rene, and Frederick Douglas. *Indian Art of the United States.* New York: Museum of Modern Art, 1941.

Dickey, Roland. "Theodore van Soelen." *New Mexico Quarterly* 30, no. 1 (Spring 1960): 60–62.

Dilworth, Leah. Imagining Indians in the Southwest: Persistent Visions of a Primitive Past. Washington, D.C.: Smithsonian Institution, 1997.

Dittert, Alfred E., and Fred Plog. *Generations in Clay: Pueblo Pottery in the American Southwest.* Flagstaff, Ariz.: Northland Press in cooperation with the American Federation of the Arts, 1980.

Dixon, Maynard. "Navajo Land." *Arizona Highways* 34 (May 1942): 34–37.

Dockstader, Frederick J. *Oscar Howe: A Retrospective Exhibition.* Tulsa: Thomas Gilcrease Museum Association, 1982.

DuBois, June. *W. R. Leigh: The Definitive Illustrated Biography.* Kansas City, Mo.: Lowell Press, 1977.

Dunn, Dorothy. *American Indian Painting of the Southwest and Plains Area.* Albuquerque: University of New Mexico Press, 1968.

W. Herbert Dunton, "The Painters of Taos," *El Palacio* 13, no. 4 (August 15, 1922): 45.

Eikner, Barbara L. "The Passion of the Collector." *Art Focus Oklahoma* 23, no. 5 (September-October 2008): 12–13.

Eldredge, Charles C., Julie Schimmel, and William H. Truettner. *Art in New Mexico, 1900–1945: Paths to Taos and Santa Fe.* New York: Abbeville Press, 1986.

Fair, Susan. "Charles Loloma." *American Indian Art* 1, no. 4 (Autumn 1975): 54–56.

Fewkes, J. Walter. "Hopi Basket Dances." *Journal of American Folk-Lore* 12, no. 45 (April-June 1899): 81–96.

Frost, Richard. "The Romantic Inflation of Pueblo Culture." *American West* 17 (January-February 1980): 5–9; 56–60.

Gibson, Arrell Morgan. *The Santa Fe and Taos Colonies: Age of the Muses, 1900–1942.* Norman: University of Oklahoma Press, 1983.

Gidley, Mick. *Edward S. Curtis and the North American Indian, Incorporated.* Cambridge and New York: Cambridge University Press, 1998.

Gilpin, Laura. *The Enduring Navajo.* 3rd paperback ed. Austin: University of Texas Press, 1994.

Gordon-McCutchan, R. C. *The Taos Indians and the Battle for Blue Lake.* Santa Fe, N.Mex.: Red Crane Books, 1991.

Graburn, Nelson H. H., ed. *Ethnic and Tourist Arts: Cultural Expressions for the Fourth World.* Berkeley: University of California Press, 1979.

Grant, Blanche C. *When Old Trails Were New: The Story of Taos.* New York: Press of the Pioneers, 1934.

Graybill, Florence Curtis. *Edward Sheriff Curtis: Visions of a Vanishing Race.* Albuquerque: University of New Mexico Press, 1986.

Gritton, Joy L. *The Institute of American Indian Arts: Modernism and U.S. Indian Policy.* Albuquerque: University of New Mexico Press, 2000.

Guthe, C. E. *Pueblo Pottery Making: A Study at the Village of San Ildefonso.* Papers of the Phillips Academy Southwest Expedition, No. 2. New Haven, Conn.: Yale University Press, 1925.

Hagerty, Donald. *Desert Dreams: The Art and Life of Maynard Dixon.* Rev. ed. Salt Lake City, Utah: Gibbs Smith, 1998.

Hait, Pam. "Gold, Silver and a Touch of Forever: Indian Jewelry Goes Contemporary." *Arizona Highways* 55, no. 4 (April 1979): 2–9.

Harlow, Francis H., and John V. Young. *Contemporary Pueblo Indian Pottery.* Santa Fe: Museum of New Mexico Press, 1972.

Hartley, Marsden. "Aesthetic Sincerity." *El Palacio* 5, no. 20 (December 9, 1918): 332–33.

———. "America as Landscape." *El Palacio* 5, no. 21 (December 21, 1918): 340–42.

———. "Red Man Ceremonials: An American Plea for American Esthetics." *Art and Archaeology* 9 (January 1920): 7–14.

———. "The Scientific Esthetic of the Redman." *Art and Archaeology* 13 (March 1922): 113–19.

———. "Tribal Esthetics." *The Dial* 65 (November 1918): 399–401.

Hassrick, Peter, and Elizabeth J. Cunningham. *In Contemporary Rhythm: The Art of Ernest L. Blumenschein*. Norman: University of Oklahoma Press, 2008.

Haury, Emil W. *Mogollon Culture in the Forestdale Valley*. Tucson: University of Arizona Press, 1985.

Henderson, Alice Corbin. "A Boy Painter Among the Pueblo Indians and Unspoiled Native Work." *New York Times Magazine* (September 6, 1925): 18–19.

Henderson, Rose. "Architecture of the Southwest: New Type Evolved in New Mexico from Pueblos of the Indians and Missions of the Early Spanish Padres." *El Palacio* 16, no. 2 (January 15, 1924): 19–22.

———. "A Painter of Pueblo Indians." *American Magazine of Art* 11, no. 11 (September 1920): 400–405.

Hewitt, Edgar L. "Crescencio Martinez—Artist." *El Palacio* 5, no. 5 (August 3, 1918): 67–69.

———. "Native American Artists." *Art and Archaeology* 13 (March 1922): 103–112.

Hough, Walter. *The Moki Snake Dance: A Popular Account of That Unparalleled Dramatic Pagan Ceremony of the Pueblo Indians of Tusayan, Arizona, with Incidental Mention of Their Life and Customs.* Chicago: Passenger Department, Santa Fe Route, 1898.

Howard, Kathleen L., and Diana F. Pardue. *Inventing the Southwest: The Fred Harvey Company and Native American Art*. Flagstaff, Ariz.: Northland Press, 1996.

Jacka, Jerry D. "Innovations in Southwestern Indian Jewelry: Fine Art in the 1980s." *American Indian Art* 9, no. 1 (1984): 28–37.

Jernigan, E. W. *White Metal Universe: Navajo Silver from the Fred Harvey Collection*. Phoenix, Ariz.: Heard Museum, 1981.

King, Duane, Randy Ramer, Kimberly Roblin, Anne Morand, April Miller, Gary Moore, Carole Klein, and Eric Singleton. *Thomas Gilcrease*. Tulsa, Okla.: Gilcrease Museum, 2009.

Kraft, James, and Helen Farr Sloan. *John Sloan in Santa Fe*. Washington, D.C.: Smithsonian Institution, 1981.

Kramer, Barbara. *Nampeyo and Her Pottery*. Albuquerque: University of New Mexico Press, 1996.

La Farge, John Pen, ed. *Turn Left at the Sleeping Dog: Scripting the Santa Fe Legend, 1920–1955*. Albuquerque: University of New Mexico Press, 2001.

Laird, Helen. *Carl Oscar Borg and the Magic Region*. Layton, Utah: Gibbs Smith, 1986.

Landis, Ellen, and Sharyn R. Udall. *John Marin in New Mexico*. Albuquerque, N.Mex.: Albuquerque Museum, 1999.

Lawrence, D. H. "America, Listen to Your Own." *New Republic* 25 (December 15, 1920): 69.

———. "Just Back from the Snake Dance—Tired Out." *Laughing Horse* no. 11 (September 1924): n.p.

Lears, T. J. Jackson. *No Place of Grace: Antimodernism and the Transformation of American Culture, 1880–1920*. Chicago: University of Chicago Press, 1981.

Leavitt, Virginia Couse. *Eanger Irving Couse: Image Maker for America*. Albuquerque, N.Mex.: The Albuquerque Museum, 1991.

Leeds, Valerie. *Robert Henri in Santa Fe: His Work and His Influence*. Santa Fe, N.Mex.: Gerald Peters Gallery, 1998.

Levine, Frances. *Our Prayers Are in This Place: Pecos Pueblo Identity over the Centuries*. Albuquerque: University of New Mexico Press, 1999.

Lobban, Lynette. "Best of the West." *Sooner Magazine* 28, no. 3 (Spring 2008), www.oufoundation.org/sm/spring08/story.asp?ID=278 (accessed August 10, 2010).

Lockwood, Ward. "The Marin I Knew: A Personal Reminiscence." *Texas Quarterly* 10, no. 1 (Spring 1967): 107–112.

Luhan, Mable Dodge. "Awa Tsireh." *Arts* 11 (June 1927): 298–300.

———. "A Bridge Between Cultures." *Theater Arts Monthly* 9 (May 1925): 297–301.

———. *Edge of Taos Desert—An Escape to Reality*. New York: Harcourt, Brace, 1937.

———. *Taos and Its Artists*. New York: Duell, Sloan and Pearce, 1947.

Lummis, Charles F. "The Land of Poco Tiempo." *Scribner's Magazine* 10, no. 6 (December 1891): 760–71.

Mahood, Ruth I., ed. *Photographer of the Southwest: Adam Clark Vroman, 1856–1916*. Ward Ritchie Press, 1961.

Marcus, George E., and Fred R. Myers. *The Traffic in Culture: Refiguring Art and Anthropology*. Berkley: University of California Press, 1995.

Marshall, Ann E. "A Small Building to Put Things In." *American Indian Art* 30, no. 3 (Summer 2005): 50–61.

Martin, Paul S. "Prehistory: Mogollon." In *Southwest*, vol. 9 of *Handbook of North American Indians*, 61–74. Washington: Smithsonian Institution, 1979.

Maxwell Museum of Anthropology. *Seven Families in Pueblo Pottery*. Albuquerque, N.Mex.: Maxwell Museum, 1974

McCreevy, Susan Brown. *Indian Basketry Artists of the Southwest*. Santa Fe, N.Mex.: School of American Research, 2001.

McGrew, R. Brownell. *R. Brownell McGrew*. Kansas City, Mo.: Lowell Press, 1978.

Melton, John R. *The American Indian Speaks*. Vermillion, S.Dak.: Dakota Press, 1969.

Merrick, Lula. "Walter Ufer, Painter of Indians." *International Studio* 77, no. 314 (July 1923): 299.

Monthan, Guy, and Doris Monthan. *Art and Indian Individualists: The Art of Seventeen Contemporary Artists and Craftsmen*. Flagstaff, Ariz.: Northland Press, 1975.

Museum of Northern Arizona. *The Art of Nicolai Fechin from the Collection of Eugene B. Adkins*. Flagstaff, Ariz.: Northland Press, 1972.

National Collection of Fine Arts. *Two American Painters: Fritz Scholder and T. C. Cannon*. Washington, D.C.: Smithsonian Institution, 1972.

Neff, Emily Ballew. *The Modern West: American Landscapes, 1890–1950*. New Haven, Conn.: Yale University Press, 2006.

Nelson, Mary Carroll. *The Legendary Artists of Taos*. New York: Watson-Guptill, 1980.

Ortiz, Alfonso, ed. *Southwest*. Vol. 9 of *Handbook of the North American Indians*. Washington D.C.: Smithsonian Institution, 1979.

Ostler, Jim. "Zuni Fetishes: Art and Change." *American Indian Art* 25, no. 4 (Autumn 2000): 38–45, 80.

Pardue, Diana F. *Contemporary Southwestern Jewelry*. Layton, Utah: Gibbs Smith, 2007.

———. *The Cutting Edge: Contemporary Southwestern Jewelry and Metalwork*. Phoenix, Ariz.: Heard Museum, 1996.

———. "Native American Silversmiths in the Southwest." *American Indian Art* 30, no. 3 (Summer 2005): 62–69.

———. *Shared Images: The Innovative Jewelry of Yazzie Johnson and Gail Bird*. Phoenix, Ariz.: Heard Museum, 2007.

Parezo, Nancy J. *Navajo Sandpainting: From Religious Act to Commercial Art*. Albuquerque: University of New Mexico Press, 1983.

Parsons, Elsie Worthington Clews. *Pueblo Indian Religion*. Chicago: University of Chicago Press, 1939.

Peixotto, Ernest. "The Taos Society of Artists." *Scribner's Magazine* 60 (August 1916): 257–260.

Penney, David W. *North American Indian Art*. New York: Thames and Hudson, 2004.

Penney, David W., and Lisa A. Roberts. "America's Pueblo Artists: Encounters on the Borderlands." In *Native American Art in the Twentieth Century*, edited by W. Jackson Rushing III, 21–38. New York and London: Routledge, 1999.

Peterson, Susan. *Maria Martinez: Five Generations of Potters*. Washington, D.C.: Smithsonian Institution, 1978.

Phillips, Ruth B., and Christopher C. Steiner. *Unpacking Culture: Art and Commodity in Colonial and Postcolonial Worlds*, Berkley: University of California Press, 1999.

Phoenix Art Museum. *Nicolai Fechin 1881–1955, Phoenix Art Museum, March 26, 1976–May 9, 1976*. Phoenix, Ariz.: Phoenix Art Museum, 1976.

———. *Western Art from the Eugene B. Adkins Collection: Phoenix Art Museum, Western Art Associates, November 1971–January 1972*. Phoenix, Ariz.: Western Art Associates, 1971.

Pinney, Christopher, and Nicolas Peterson, eds. *Photography's Other Histories*. Durham, N.C.: Duke University Press, 2003.

Porter, Dean. *Victor Higgins: An American Master*. Salt Lake City, Utah: Peregrine Smith Books, published in cooperation with the Snite Museum of Art, University of Notre Dame, Ind., 1991.

Porter, Dean, Teresa Hayes Ebie, and Suzan Campbell. *Taos Artists and Their Patrons, 1898–1950*. Notre Dame, Ind.: Snite Museum of Art, 1999.

Price, B. Byron. "Western Art Comes of Age." *Southwest Art* 25 (May 1996), 46, 48, 50, 52–56.

Reel, Estelle. U.S. Department of the Interior. *Course of Study for the Indian Schools of the United States—Industrial and Literary*. Washington D.C.: Government Printing Office, 1901.

Reich, Sheldon. *Andrew Dasburg: His Life and Art*. Lewisburg, Pa.: Bucknell University Press, 1989.

Robertson, Edna, and Sarah Nestor. *Artists of the Canyons and Caminos*. 2nd ed. Layton, Utah: Ancient City Press, 2006.

Rodee, Marian. *Weaving of the Southwest*. West Chester, Pa.: Schiffer, 1987.

Rudnick, Lois P. *Mabel Dodge Luhan: New Woman, New World*. Albuquerque: University of New Mexico Press, 1987.

———. *Utopian Vistas: The Mabel Dodge Luhan House and the American Counterculture*. Albuquerque: University of New Mexico Press, 1998.

Rushing III, W. Jackson. *Allan Houser: An American Master*. New York: Harry N. Abrams, 2004.

———. *Native American Art and the New York Avant-Garde: A History of Cultural Primitivism*. Austin: University of Texas Press, 1995.

———. ed. *Native American Art in the Twentieth Century*. New York and London: Routledge, 1999.

Sandweiss, Martha A. *Print the Legend: Photography and the American West*. New Haven, Conn.: Yale University Press, 2002.

Schaaf, Gregory. *American Indian Baskets I*. Santa Fe, N.Mex.: CIAC Press, 2006.

———. *American Indian Textiles*. Santa Fe, N.Mex.: CIAC Press, 2001.

Schimmel, Julie. *The Art and Life of W. Herbert Dunton, 1878–1936*. Austin: University of Texas Press, 1984.

Schimmel, Julie, and Robert R. White. *Bert Geer Phillips and the Taos Art Colony*. Albuquerque: University of New Mexico, 1994.

Selkinghaus, Jessie A. "The Art of Carl Oscar Borg." *American Magazine of Art* 18, no. 3 (March 1927): 144–47.

Shutes, Jeanne, and Jill Mellick. *The Worlds of P'otsúnú: Geronima Cruz Montoya of San Juan Pueblo.* Albuquerque: University of New Mexico Press, 1996.

Simpson, Georgiana Kennedy. *Navajo Ceremonial Blankets.* Summertown, Tenn.: Native Voices, 2003.

Sims, Lowery Stokes, ed. *Fritz Scholder: Indian Not Indian.* New York: Prestel for the National Museum of the American Indian, 2008.

Slaney, Deborah C. *Blue Gem, White Metal: Carvings and Jewelry from the C. G. Wallace Collection.* Phoenix, Ariz.: Heard Museum, 1998.

———. "Zuni Figurative Carving from the C. G. Wallace Collection." *American Indian Art* 19, no. 1 (Winter 1993): 69–75.

Sloan, John. "The Indian Dance from an Artist's Point of View." *Arts and Decoration* 20 (January 1924): 17, 56.

———. "Randall Davey." *New Mexico Quarterly* 21, no. 1 (Spring 1951): 19–25.

Smith, Thomas Brent, and Donald Hagerty. *A Place of Refuge: Maynard Dixon's Arizona.* Norman: University of Oklahoma Press, 2008.

Sotheby Parke Bernet. *The C. G. Wallace Collection of American Indian Art.* Auction catalogue, Sale No. 3806, 1975.

Struever, Martha H. *Loloma: Beauty Is His Name.* Santa Fe, N.Mex.: Wheelwright Museum of the American Indian, 2005.

———. *Painted Perfection: The Pottery of Dextra Quotskuyva.* Santa Fe, N.Mex.: Wheelwright Museum of the American Indian, 2001.

Tanner, Clara Lee. *Indian Baskets of the Southwest.* Tucson: University of Arizona Press, 1983.

———. "The Naja." *American Indian Art* 7, no. 2 (Spring 1982): 64–71.

———. *Prehistoric Southwestern Craft Arts.* Tucson: University of Arizona Press, 1976.

———. *Southwest Indian Painting: A Changing Art.* Tucson: University of Arizona Press, 1973.

Teiwes, Helga. *Hopi Basket Weaving: Artistry in Natural Fibers.* Tucson: University of Arizona Press, 1996.

Tisdale, Shelby. *Fine Indian Jewelry of the Southwest: The Millicent Rogers Museum Collection.* Santa Fe, N.Mex.: Museum of New Mexico, 2006.

Torres-Nez, John. *Beesh Ligaii in Balance: The Diane and Sandy Besser Collection of Navajo and Pueblo Silverwork.* Santa Fe, N.Mex.: Museum of Indian Arts and Culture, 2005.

Traugott, Joseph. *The Art of New Mexico: How the West Is One.* Santa Fe: Museum of New Mexico Press, 2007.

Turnbaugh, Sara Peabody, and William A. Turnbaugh. *Indian Baskets.* West Chester, Pa.: Schiffer Publishing, 1986.

Udall, Sharyn R. *Contested Terrain: Myth and Meaning in Southwest Art.* Albuquerque: University of New Mexico Press, 1996.

———. *Santa Fe Art Colony, 1900–1942: July 17–August 8, 1987.* Santa Fe, N.Mex.: Gerald Peters Gallery, 1987.

Van Dyke, John C. *The Desert: Further Studies in Natural Appearances.* New York: Charles Scribner's Sons, 1901.

Walter, Paul A. F. "The Santa Fe—Taos Art Movement." *Art and Archaeology* 4 (December 1916): 330–38.

Waters, Frank. *Book of the Hopi.* New York: Ballantine Books, 1969.

———. *Leon Gaspard.* Flagstaff, Ariz.: Northland Press, 1964.

———. *Of Time and Change: A Memoir.* Denver: McMurray and Beck, 1998.

Wells, Helen P. "The Fred Harvey Fine Arts Collection." *American Indian Art* 1, no. 2 (Spring 1976): 32–34.

Whitford, Andrew H. *I Am Here: Two Thousand Years of Southwest Indian Art and Culture.* Santa Fe: Museum of New Mexico Press, 1989.

Wilkins, Teresa J. *Patterns of Exchange: Navajo Weavers and Traders.* Norman: University of Oklahoma Press, 2008.

Wilkins, Thurman. *Thomas Moran, Artist of the Mountains.* Norman: University of Oklahoma Press, 1966.

Williams, Joe. *Woolaroc.* Bartlesville, Okla.: Frank Phillips Foundation, 1991.

Wilson, Chris. *The Myth of Santa Fe: Creating a Modern Regional Tradition.* Albuquerque: University of New Mexico Press, 1997.

Witt, David. *Modernists in Taos: From Dasburg to Martin.* Santa Fe, N.Mex.: Red Crane Books, 2002.

Wyckoff, Lydia L., ed. *Visions + Voices: Native American Painting from the Philbrook Museum of Art.* Tulsa, Okla.: Philbrook Museum of Art, 1996.

———. *Woven Worlds: Basketry from the Clark Field Collection at the Philbrook Museum of Art.* Tulsa, Okla.: Philbrook Museum of Art, 2001.

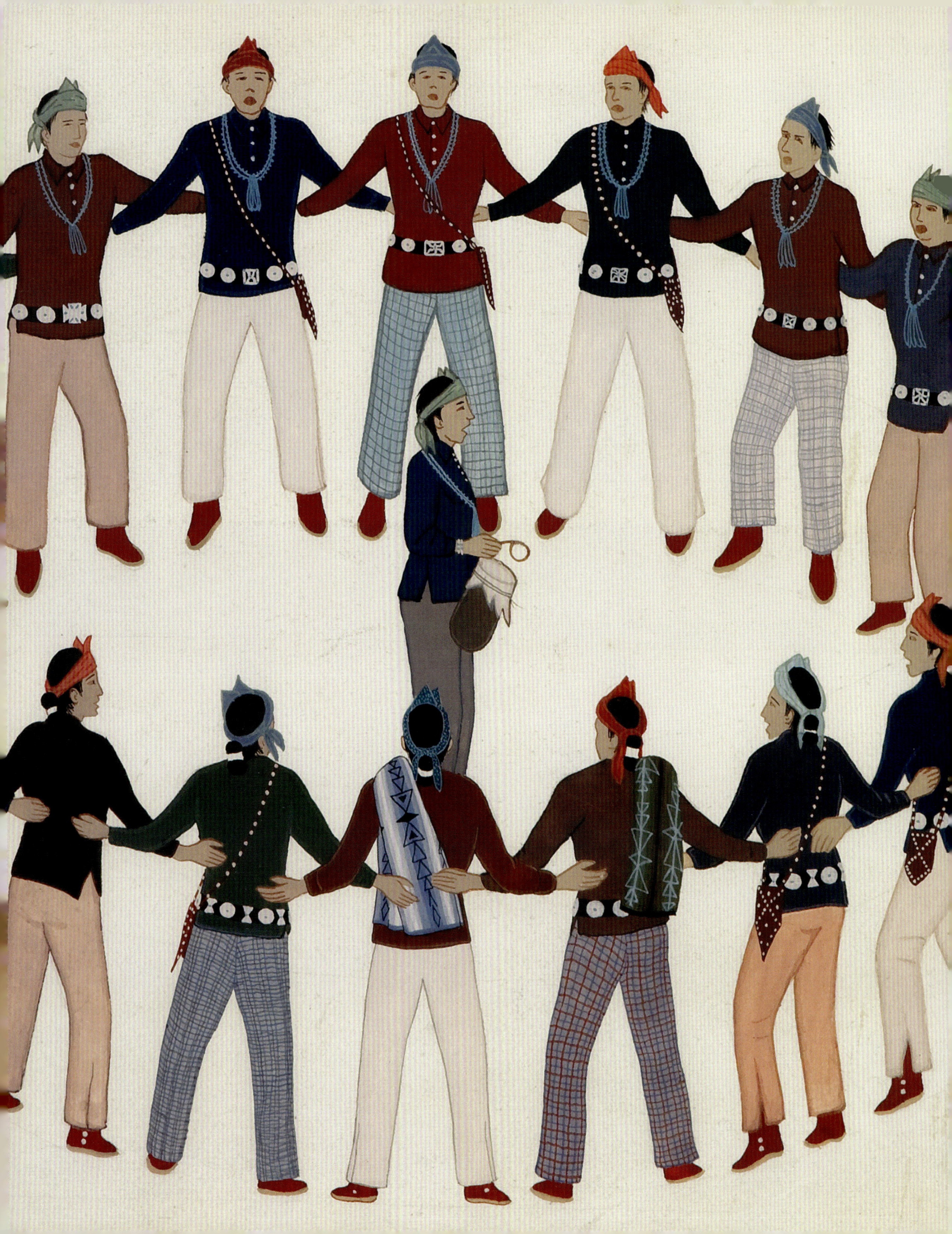

List of Contributors

Jane Ford Aebersold is Professor of Ceramics in the University of Oklahoma School of Art and Art History and Curator of Ceramics at the Fred Jones Jr. Museum of Art.

Christina E. Burke is Curator of Native American and Non-Western Art at the Philbrook Museum of Art.

James Peck is Curator of Collections at the Rockwell Museum of Western Art, Corning, New York.

B. Byron Price holds the Charles Marion Russell Memorial Chair in the University of Oklahoma School of Art and Art History. He is both Director of the Charles M. Russell Center for the Study of Art of the American West at the University of Oklahoma and Director of the University of Oklahoma Press.

W. Jackson Rushing III is Eugene B. Adkins Presidential Professor of Art History and Mary Lou Milner Carver Chair in Native American Art in the University of Oklahoma School of Art and Art History.

Mary Jo Watson is Director of the School of Art and Art History at the University of Oklahoma and Curator of Native American Art at the Fred Jones Jr. Museum of Art.

Mark A. White is the Eugene B. Adkins Curator at the Fred Jones Jr. Museum of Art.

DETAIL OF PLATE 64 (p. 112)
Harrison Begay (U.S., Navajo, b. 1917)
Untitled, n.d.

About the Venues

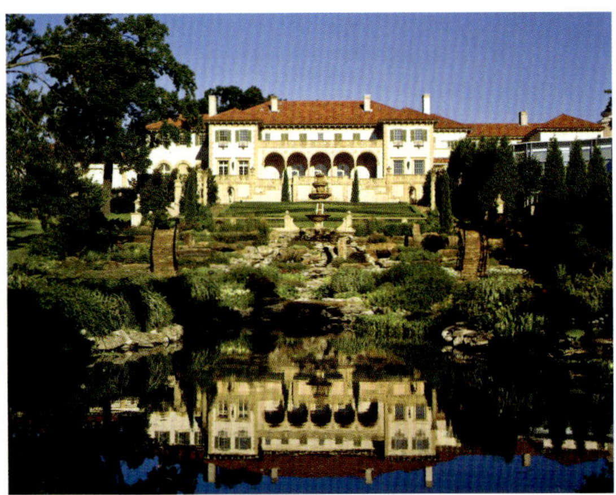

Philbrook Museum of Art
2727 South Rockford Road
Tulsa, Oklahoma 74114
www.philbrook.org

Philbrook Museum of Art

Philbrook Museum of Art is the premier cultural institution in the city of Tulsa and a statewide leader in the cultural life of Oklahoma. It is distinguished by nationally recognized collections, facilities, gardens, and innovative educational programming.

The museum was founded in 1938 when oil magnate Waite Phillips donated his 1927 residence to the Southwestern Art Association to create Tulsa's first art museum. Villa Philbrook, with its spacious rooms, wide corridors, and great halls, was a "natural" for the future museum. In 1939, the museum opened its doors to the public. In 1979, Villa Philbrook was listed on the National Register of Historic Places. In 1990, the museum opened the 75,000-square-foot Kravis Wing, transforming a historic house museum into a modern museum complex.

Philbrook's outstanding architecture and twenty-three acres of beautiful gardens make it unique. It is Oklahoma's only art museum with collections offering an overview of major art movements in Western civilization as well as excellent examples of non-Western artistic expression, including those of Asia and Africa. In addition, the permanent collection boasts particular strength in Renaissance and Baroque painting, art of the Southwest, modern and contemporary design, and twentieth-century Native American art.

Randall Suffolk

Following seven years as Director of The Hyde Collection in Glens Falls, New York, Randall Suffolk was named Director and President of Philbrook Museum of Art in June 2007. Suffolk earned a bachelor's degree from Connecticut College and advanced degrees in Higher Education Administration and the History of Art from Columbia University and Bryn Mawr College respectively.

Fred Jones Jr. Museum of Art • University of Oklahoma

Over the years, the permanent collection of the Fred Jones Jr. Museum of Art has grown exponentially through the generosity of donors such as Max Weitzenhoffer and Jerome M. Westheimer, Sr. In 1996, with an initial gift of $1 million from Mrs. Fred Jones, OU President David L. Boren and First Lady Molly Shi Boren spearheaded the successful fundraising campaign to acquire the important collection of the late Richard H. and Adeline J. Fleischaker, which is composed primarily of Native American and Southwestern art. Today, the Fred Jones Jr. Museum of Art is one of the finest university art museums in the United States. Strengths of the 8,000–object permanent collection are French Impressionism, twentieth-century American painting and sculpture, contemporary art, traditional and contemporary Native American art, art of the Southwest, ceramics, Asian art, photography, and graphics from the sixteenth century to the present. Temporary exhibitions are mounted throughout the year that explore the art of various periods and cultures.

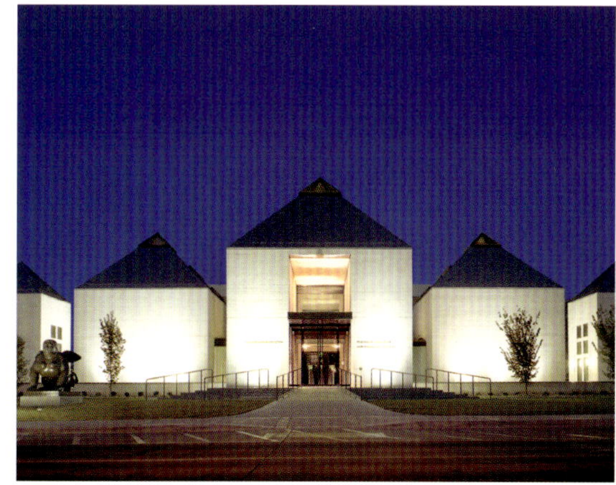

The Fred Jones Jr. Museum of Art
The University of Oklahoma
555 Elm Street, Norman, Oklahoma 73019
www.ou.edu/fjjma

Ghislain d'Humières

After studying history and art history at the Sorbonne in Paris, Ghislain d'Humières became a specialist in eighteenth-century furniture for Sotheby's London, and then transferred to New York. He became the director of the jewelry department at Christie's of Los Angeles and then transferred to Christie's in Geneva, where he was in charge of international clients from Europe and South America. In 2004, the Fine Arts Museum of San Francisco hired him as assistant director in charge of the opening of the new de Young Museum. Following that appointment, d'Humières joined the University of Oklahoma as the Bill and Wylodean Saxon Director of the Fred Jones Jr. Museum of Art.

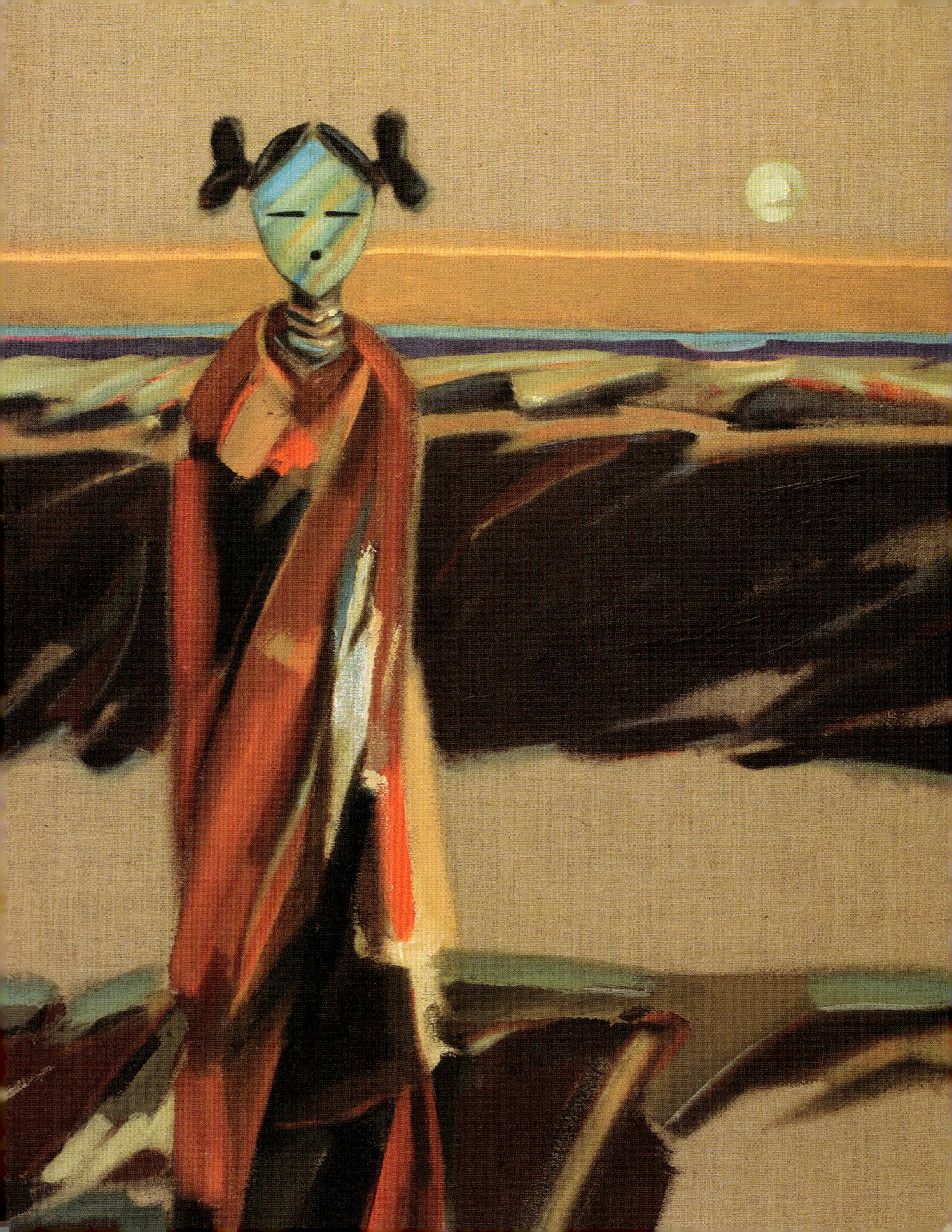

Index

References to illustrations are in italic type.

DETAIL OF PLATE 74 (p. 122)
Dan Namingha (U.S., Tewa-Hopi, b. 1950)
Night Singer, n.d.

Copyedited by Melanie Mallon
Indexed by Heather Laskey

Book design by Eric Anderson
Set in Centaur, with Centaur display and Minion ornaments
Image prepress by University of Oklahoma Printing Services

Printed by Everbest Printing, China, through FourColour Imports, Louisville, Kentucky
Printed on 157 gsm Gold East Matte